Android™ User Interface Design

Turning Ideas and Sketches into Beautifully Designed Apps

Ian G. Clifton

Addison-Wesley

Upper Saddle River, NJ • Boston • Indianapolis • San Francisco
New York • Toronto • Montreal • London • Munich • Paris • Madrid
Capetown • Sydney • Tokyo • Singapore • Mexico City

The publisher offers excellent discounts on this book when ordered in quantity for bulk purchases or special sales, which may include electronic versions and/or custom covers and content particular to your business, training goals, marketing focus, and branding interests. For more information, please contact:

U.S. Corporate and Government Sales
(800) 382-3419
corpsales@pearsontechgroup.com

For sales outside the United States, please contact:

International Sales
international@pearsoned.com

Visit us on the Web: informit.com/aw

Library of Congress Cataloging-in-Publication Data is on file.

ISBN-13: 978-0-321-88673-6
ISBN-10: 0-321-88673-9

Text printed in the United States on recycled paper at R.R. Donnelley in Crawfordsville, Indiana.

First printing: May 2013

Editor-in-Chief
Mark Taub

Acquisitions Editor
Laura Lewin

Development Editor
Songlin Qiu

Managing Editor
Kristy Hart

Project Editor
Betsy Gratner

Copy Editor
Bart Reed

Indexer
Lisa Stumpf

Proofreader
Jess DeGabriele

Technical Reviewers
Joseph Annuzzi
Cameron Banga
Joshua Jamison

Editorial Assistant
Olivia Basegio

Cover Designer
Chuti Prasertsith

Compositor
Nonie Ratcliff

Praise for *Android User Interface Design*

"*Android User Interface Design* is a truly excellent book, written by one of the most experienced and knowledgeable Android developers. This is a very practical, highly readable guide and a great how-to resource for every Android developer. Each chapter reveals a clear and deep understanding of UI design. I highly recommend this book to anyone wishing to develop Android apps with superior UI."

—Kyungil Kim

Software Engineer, Facebook

"I recommend this book for all Android developers who work alone and want to give a professional look to their apps. The content of the book is excellent and covers all aspects needed to understand how to design Android apps that stand out."

—Gonzalo Benoffi

CEO, Coffee and Cookies, Android Development

"Design was never part of a developer's job until mobile app development started; now it's a must. This book gives a simple yet effective way to design your apps. It's easy for beginners and informative for experienced developers as well. This is the best book I could ever refer to anyone who is in Android development. A one-time read of this book covers the experience you might gain from three years of learning development. I am amazed to see instructions on how to design starting from wireframes, which is something no other book has provided clear enough explanation of. (Some don't even cover it.) I really love it. Thanks to Ian for this wonderful contribution to the Android developer community. Best, simple, and effective!"

—Chakradhar Gavirineni

Android Application Developer, Adeptpros IT Solutions Pvt Ltd.

"Ian's book is an invaluable resource for everything there is to know about designing, creating layouts, and rendering Android applications. The 'Common Task Reference' appendix is an excellent addition that makes this book a must-have. Make sure to keep this one within arm's reach of your desk."

—Josh Schumacher

Software Engineer, HasOffers

"From the first few pages, this book provides a wealth of tips, tricks, and techniques for developing Android user interfaces. If you are grappling with all the various view types, then read this book—it really helps cement when and why you should include the various UI components to great effect (with worked examples!). Well worth a read by anyone looking for inspiration to improve their user interface into a great user experience."

—Richard Sey

PassBx Developers

Dedicated to my family

Contents

PREFACE

Whether you have been working with the Android SDK since before the first device was released in September of 2008 or you just finished your first "Hello, World" app, you are likely aware of the incredible pace at which Android has been developed. The operating system itself has changed and matured, and the apps have followed suit. That means it is more challenging than ever to stand out. It's no longer enough to create a functional user interface that's "good enough." Now there is enough competition that apps with poor UI and apps that are half-hearted ports from other operating systems are outright rejected by users. Google has shown their commitment to design with the major UI and usability fixes in Android 4.0, Ice Cream Sandwich, and users have learned to expect more from their devices and the apps they download. With the additional work of "Project Butter" in Android 4.1 and continued improvements in Android 4.2, it has become more important than ever to ensure your app is smooth and efficient.

Design has many purposes, but two of the most important are usability and visual appeal. You want brand-new users to be able to jump into your app and get started without any effort because mobile users are more impatient than users of nearly any other platform. Users need to know exactly what they can interact with, and they need to be able to do so in a hurry while distracted. That also means you have to be mindful of what platform conventions are in order to take advantage of learned behavior.

You also want your app to stand out because visual appeal can get users excited about your app and can strengthen your brand. It gives a sense of quality when done right and can immediately lead to a larger user base when your users show the app off to their friends. Comparing your app to a car, you can think of design as the visual appearance and usability as the controls. There is a good bit of flexibility with the appearance of a car, limited only by practicality and the need for it to be usable to the potential owner. If you were to get into a car and not have a steering wheel, you would immediately start looking around and wonder, "How do I control this thing?" The same is true of your app. If the user opens it up and is immediately confused by the controls, your app has failed the most basic usability test.

If you have picked up this book, I probably do not need to go on and on about how important design is. You get it. You want to make the commitment of making beautiful apps.

This book primarily focuses on Android from a developer's perspective, but it also has a large amount of design sensibility built in. This is an attempt to both bridge the gap between designer and developer and to teach you how to implement great designs. We are not here to focus extensively on color theory or Photoshop techniques; we are here to understand what goes into designing an app and how to actually make that app come alive. When you are done with this book, you will be able to communicate your needs and feedback with designers and even do some design on your own.

This book will serve as a tutorial for the entire design and implementation process as well as a handy reference that you can keep using again and again. You will understand how to talk with designers and developers alike in order to make the best applications possible. You will be able to make apps that are visually appealing while still easy to change when those last-minute design requests inevitably come in.

Ultimately, designers and developers both want their apps to be amazing, and I am excited to teach you how to make that happen.

—Ian G. Clifton

ACKNOWLEDGMENTS

Despite having been writing fervently since I was barely old enough to hold a pencil, this book would not have been possible without the help of many individuals. I'd like to thank Executive Editor, Laura Lewin, who kept me on track despite the fact that I am perhaps the worst author to ever estimate chapter sizes and level of effort. Olivia Basegio, the Editorial Assistant, kept track of all the moving pieces despite that some days they moved slowly and others they moved at lightning speed. Songlin Qiu was the Development Editor for this book and managed to make sense out of my 4 a.m. draft chapter postings so that the final chapters could be much improved. I am very appreciative of all the work by the technical reviewers; having done that job myself in the past, I know how much work it can be, so thanks go out to Joseph Annuzzi, Cameron Banga, and Joshua Jamison.

Writing is certainly a full-time job, so balancing it among a full-time job at A.R.O., family (especially during the holidays), and several other projects was quite the challenge. Special thanks goes out to Andy Hickl at A.R.O. for his flexibility and support of my book, along with all my other friends and coworkers for not raising pitchforks when I had to work from home to cut out commute time for this book or even take time off to get chapters done on schedule.

Of course, I have to thank my family for their support. My parents told me I could do anything while growing up, and apparently I misunderstood that to mean I had to do everything. I have never stopped pushing myself to learn more and accomplish more than I ever thought I would, and I am grateful for their ability to believe in me.

ABOUT THE AUTHOR

Ian G. Clifton is the Director of User Experience and lead Android developer at A.R.O. in Seattle, where he develops Saga, an Android and iOS app that learns about you in order to let you live a better life with minimal interaction. He has worked with many designers in the course of his career and has developed several well-known Android apps, such as CNET News, CBS News, Survivor, Big Brother, and Rick Steves' Audio Europe.

Ian's love of technology, art, and user experience has led him along a variety of paths. Besides Android development, he has done platform, web, and desktop development. He served in the United States Air Force as a Satellite, Wideband, and Telemetry Systems Journeyman and has also created quite a bit of art with pencil, brush, and camera.

You can follow Ian G. Clifton on Twitter at http://twitter.com/IanGClifton and see his thoughts about mobile development on his blog at http://blog.iangclifton.com. He also published a video series called "The Essentials of Android Application Development," available at http://my.safaribooksonline.com/video/programming/android/9780132996594.

INTRODUCTION

Audience of This Book

This book is intended primarily for Android developers who want to better understand user interfaces in Android, but it also has a strong design focus, so designers can benefit from it as well. In order to focus on the important topics of Android user interface design, this book makes the assumption that you already have a basic understanding of Android. For example, if you're looking to learn about the development side, this book makes the assumption that you've at least made a "Hello, World" Android app and don't need help setting up your computer for development (if that's not the case, the Android developer site is a good place to start: http://developer.android.com/training/basics/firstapp/index.html). If you're a designer, you may find some of the code examples intimidating, but the book is written to give enough information to be useful for designers as well. For example, Chapter 13, "Working with the Canvas and Advanced Drawing," covers detailed examples of concepts such as PorterDuff compositing. Although most designers haven't heard of these concepts and don't care about the mathematical implementations, they have usually encountered them in other software such as Photoshop, where they are more simply referred to as blending modes (for example, "multiply" and "lighten"). By looking at the sample images and the intro details, designers can understand the capabilities of Android and point developers to the specific details.

Organization of This Book

This book is organized into four parts. Part I, "The Basics of Android User Interface," provides an overview of the Android UI and trends before diving into the specific classes used to create an interface in Android. It also covers the use of graphics and resources. Part II, "The Full Design and Development Process," mirrors the stages of app development, starting with just ideas and goals, working through wireframes and prototypes, and developing complete apps that include efficient layouts, animations, and more. Part III, "Advanced Topics for Android User Interfaces," explores making apps more useful by creating automatically updating ListViews, custom components that combine views, fully custom views, and even advanced techniques such as image compositing. Finally, Part IV, "Helpful Guides and Reference," consists of three appendixes: one that covers Google Play assets, one that covers Amazon Appstore assets, and one that covers a variety of common UI-related tasks that are good to know but don't necessarily fit elsewhere (such as how to dim the onscreen navigation elements).

The emphasis throughout is on implementation in simple and clear ways. You do not have to worry about pounding your head against complex topics such as 3D matrix transformations in OpenGL; instead, you will learn how to create smooth animations, add PorterDuff compositing into your custom views, and efficiently work with touch events. The little math involved will be broken down, making it so simple that you barely realize any math is involved. In addition, illustrations will make even the most complex examples clear, and every example will be practical.

How to Use This Book

This book starts with a very broad overview before going into more specific and more advanced topics. As such, it is intended to be read in order, but it is also organized to make reference as easy as possible. Even if you're an advanced developer, it is a good idea to read through all the chapters because of the wide range of material covered; however, you can also jump directly to the topics that most interest you. For example, if you really want to focus on creating your own custom views, you can jump right to Chapter 12, "Developing Fully Custom Views."

This Book's Website

You can find the source code for the examples used throughout this book at http://auidbook.com and the publisher's website at www.informit.com/title/9780321886736. From there, you can clone the entire repository, download a full ZIP file, and browse through individual files.

Conventions Used in This Book

This book uses typical conventions found in most programming-related books. Code terms such as class names or keywords appear in `monospace font`. When a class is being referred to specifically (for example, "Your class should extend the `View` class"), then it will be in monospace font. If it's used more generally (for example, "When developing a view, don't forget to test on a real device"), then it will not be in a special font.

Occasionally when a line of code is too long to fit on a printed line in the book, a code-continuation arrow (➥) is used to mark the continuation.

> **note**
>
> Notes look like this and are intended to supplement the material in the book with other information you may find useful.

tip

Tips look like this and give you advice on specific topics.

warning

Warnings look like this and are meant to bring to your attention potential issues you may run into or things you should look out for.

CHAPTER 1

ANDROID UI OVERVIEW

It is a good idea to have an overview of the UI as it pertains to Android, so that's the starting point here. You will learn a brief history of Android design before diving into some core design principles. You will also learn some of the high-level components of Android design and some of the changes that have come about to Android design as the world's most popular mobile operating system has evolved.

A Brief History of Android Design

Android had a very technical start with a lot of amazing work going on to make it a platform that could run on a variety of devices without most apps having to care too much about the details. That base allowed Android to handle many types of hardware input (trackballs, hardware directional pads, sliding keyboards, touch interface, and so on). It also kept Android largely focused on scalable design, much more closely related to fluid web design than typical mobile design. Unfortunately, that also meant that early design for Android was blasé. Colors were bland and often inconsistent, and most input and visual organization was based on what had been done in the past rather than pushing things forward.

In 2010, Google hired Matias Duarte (most known for his excellent work with WebOS) as the Senior Director of Android User Experience, which made it clear that Google had become serious about the user experience for Android and its related visual design. The Android beta was released way back in 2007, so Matias and his colleagues had a lot of work in front of them. How do you go from a very functional but visually bland UI to one that enhances that functionality by improving the entire design and user experience?

About a year later, the first Android tablets running Honeycomb (Android 3.x) were revealed. These tablets gave Google the opportunity to really experiment with the UI because there was no prior version of Android that had been designed for tablets and therefore users did not have as strong of expectations. With the radical new Holo theme, these tablets were a significant departure from the previous Android styles.

By the end of 2011, Google revealed Android 4.0, Ice Cream Sandwich, which showed how they were able to improve the tablet-only Honeycomb styling in order to tone down some of the "techie-ness" and smooth out the user experience. The tablet/phone divide was eliminated and the platform was brought together in a much more cohesive manner, emphasizing interaction, visuals, and simplicity. Even the font changed to the newly created Roboto, significantly improving upon the previous Droid fonts. Even if you are not the kind of person who gets giddy over straight-sided Grotesk sans-serif fonts, you will appreciate the attention to detail this font signifies. You can see the change from early versions of Android to Gingerbread (2.3.x) to Jelly Bean (4.2) in Figure 1.1.

Android 4.1, Jelly Bean, was revealed at Google I/O in 2012. A release focused primarily on usability, Jelly Bean gave Android a much better sense of polish. "Project Butter" brought about a much more fluid user experience with graphics improvements such as triple buffering. Even components of Android that hadn't been touched in years, such as notifications, were updated to improve the user experience. Android 4.2 came just a few months later, with support for multiple users, the "Daydream" feature (essentially, application-provided screensavers with the ability to be interactive), support for photo spheres (panoramas that can cover 360 degrees), and wireless mirroring. It's clear that Android is getting better with every release, and it's an exciting time to be working on amazing apps!

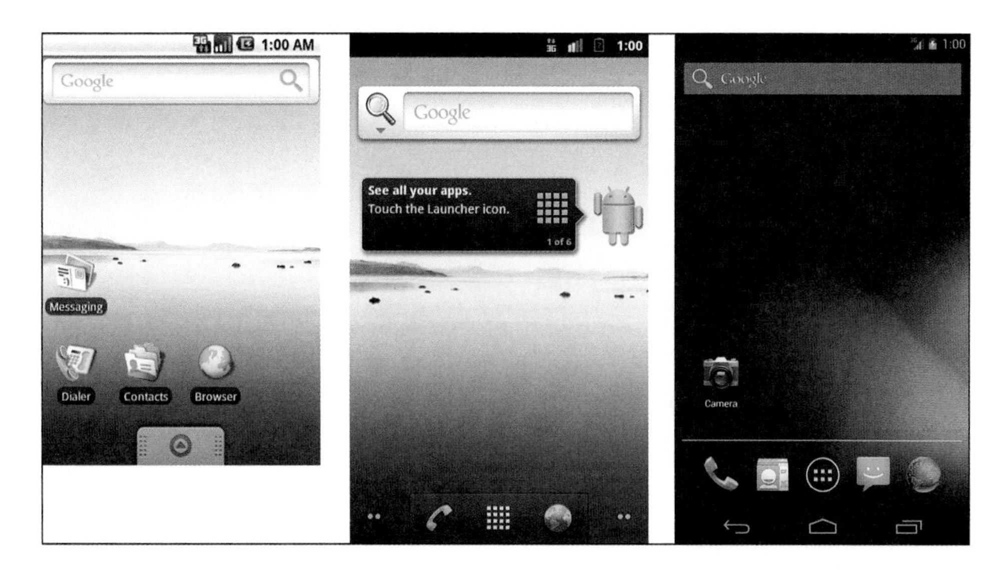

Figure 1.1 The home screen for Android 1.6 (left), 2.3 (middle), and 4.2 (right)

The Android Design Website

Enough with story time already! If you want to dive right into a rich resource for Android design and UI elements that will give you a lot of detail about the current state of Android design, take a look at the Android design website (http://developer.android.com/design/).

Before even beginning to sketch out a specific UI, take a thorough look at that site. You will see a lot of general feel information, such as "Delight me in surprising ways," that might not give you a concrete indication of what to do. However, there are also some very specific guidelines. If you are developing an app that is on another platform or is being developed for another platform simultaneously, you will find the section Pure Android especially helpful (http://developer.android.com/design/patterns/pure-android.html).

Although the design website will tell you about a lot of the pieces that go into a well-designed Android app, it will not give you many details about specific techniques or code samples. That's where this book comes in.

Core Principles

It is impossible to come up with a perfect checklist that lets you know your app is exactly right when everything is checked, but guiding principles can make a big difference. Start with your users' goals to define exactly what your app should do. You might be surprised how many apps do not have a clear user goal in mind before launching, and it is reflected in their design. User goals and product goals are explained in detail in Chapter 5, "Starting a New App," but it's important to look at the core principles first.

Do One Thing and Do It Well

If you ever want to build a mediocre app, a sure way to do so is by trying to make it do everything. The more narrowly focused your app is, the easier it is to make sure that it does what it is supposed to and that it does so well. When you're starting on a new app, list everything you want it to do. Next, start crossing off the least important things in that list until you have narrowed it down to just the absolute essentials. You can always add functionality later, but you can't add a clear focus halfway through making a jack-of-all-trades app.

You are probably ready when you can answer the question, "Why would someone use this app?" without including conjunctions (such as "and" and "or") and without using a second sentence. Here are two examples:

> **Good:** "Users will use this app to write quick notes to themselves."
>
> **Bad:** "Users will use this app to write notes to themselves and browse past notes and share notes with other users on Twitter."

Yes, being able to browse notes can be an important part of the app, but writing the notes is the most important part. Deciding that makes it clear that you should be able to begin a new note in a single touch from the starting screen. In fact, it might even start in a new note screen when it is opened. Of course, you could be building an app where organizing those notes is the most important part; in that case, you will emphasize browsing, sorting, and searching.

Consider the People app as an example (see Figure 1.2). It's really just a list of people who can have pictures and various data associated with them. From that app, you can call someone or email someone, but those actions happen outside of the People app.

As tempting as it can be to make an app that does many things, such as an email app that can modify photos before adding them as attachments, you need to start with a single focus and make that part of the app excellent before moving on. If the email portion is terrible, no one will download the app just to use the photo manipulation aspects of it.

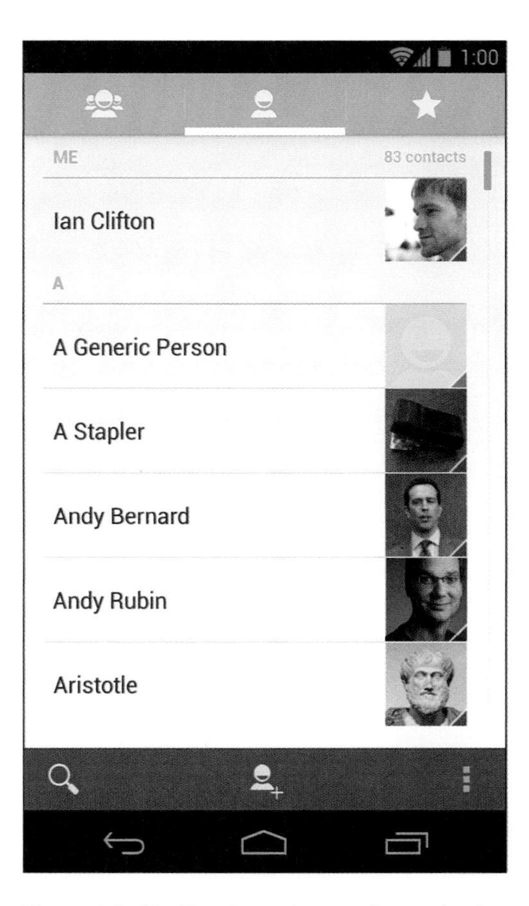

Figure 1.2 The People app is a good example of an app with a singular and obvious focus.

There are times when your app does have multiple purposes because these features are too intertwined to separate or the requirements are outside of your control. In those cases, you should split the functionality in a clear and meaningful way for the user. For instance, consider the Gallery in Android (shown in Figure 1.3). It allows users to look at their photos and manipulate them in simple ways. It doesn't allow users to draw images or manage the file system, so it has a clear and obvious focus. The Gallery has a quick link to jump to the Camera app, but it also has its own icon that the user can go to from the launcher. Conceptually, the Camera app just takes photos and videos (see how much the interface emphasizes this in Figure 1.4). As complex as the code is to do that well, users don't have to think about it. In fact, users do not need to know that the Camera app and the Gallery app are part of the same app in stock Android (some manufacturers do create separate, custom apps for these features). If users want to look at photos, they will go to the Gallery. If users want to take photos, they will go to the Camera app.

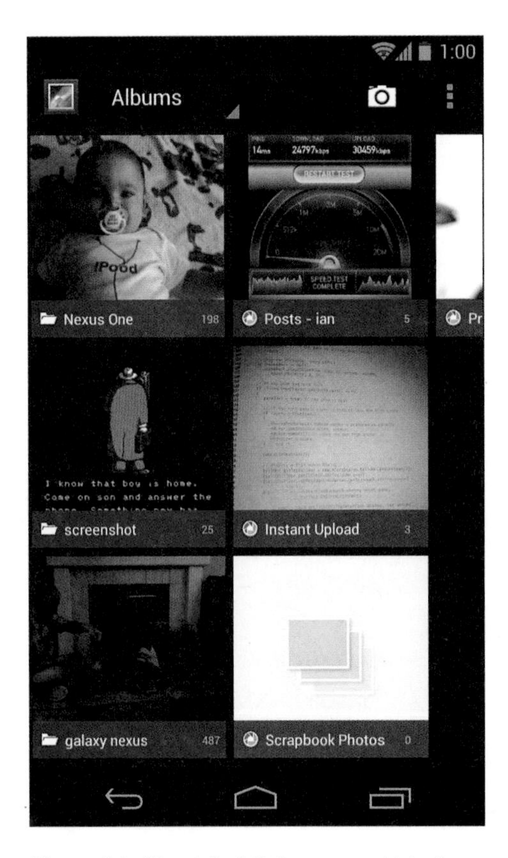

Figure 1.3 The default Gallery app, which allows users to view and update images

Figure 1.4 The Camera app. Notice that the primary action, taking a picture, has a large dedicated button.

Play Nicely with Others

Just because your app does only one thing extremely well doesn't mean it needs to limit the user's experience. One of the best parts about Android is that apps are really just components in the overall user experience. Your app should handle reasonable `Intents`, which is the class Android uses to indicate what the user is trying to do and to find an appropriate app to accomplish that objective. Is it an app for a particular site? Have it handle links for that site. Does it let the user modify images? Handle any `Intent` for working with an image.

Do not waste development time adding in sharing for specific sharing mechanisms such as Twitter and Facebook. If you do, you will have to decide on each and every other service, such as Google Plus. Do your users care about Google Plus? Why bother finding out when you can just let the user pick whichever apps he wants to share with? If Google Plus is important to a user, that user will have the app installed. With just a couple lines of work, you can present a dialog to the user (Figure 1.5), and you can also customize that dialog to better fit your app (Figure 1.6; notice that the app I most commonly share with, Gmail, is directly placed in the action bar). By creating specific code for sharing with a given service, you're actually removing support for sharing with every other service the user may want to use.

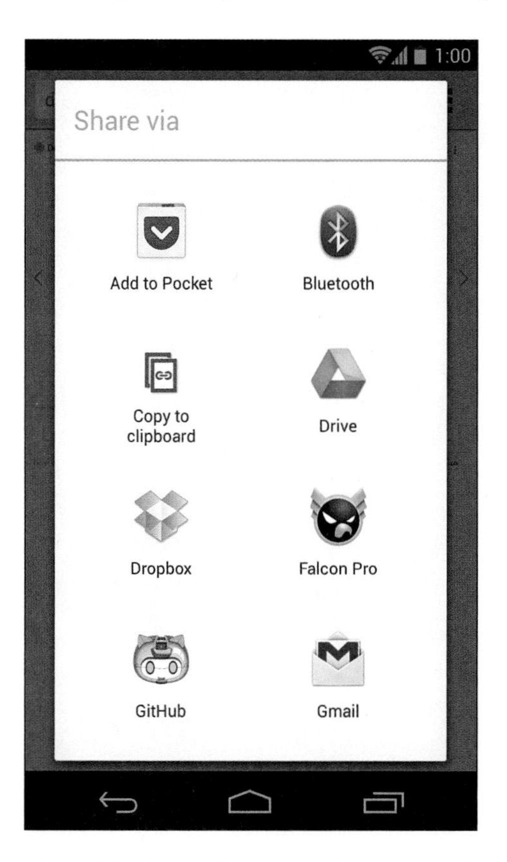

Figure 1.5 Standard example of letting a user share with whichever app he or she chooses

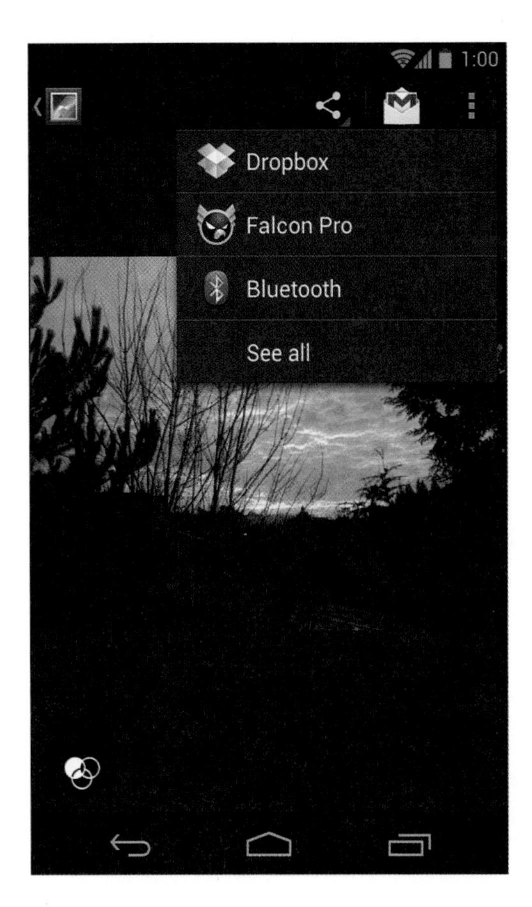

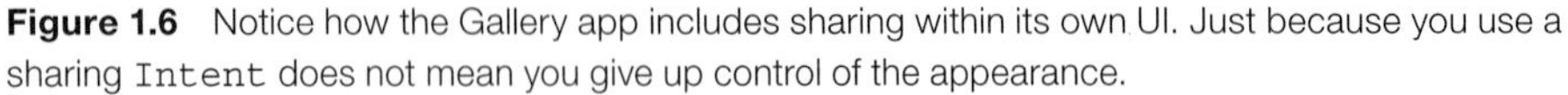

Figure 1.6 Notice how the Gallery app includes sharing within its own UI. Just because you use a sharing `Intent` does not mean you give up control of the appearance.

The time you spend implementing sharing for third-party services in your own app is just time that could be spent elsewhere. Why would you spend a week developing some tolerable sharing tools when you can pass that work off to the user's favorite apps? You can bet that regardless of whichever Twitter client the user is going to share with, the developer of that app spent more time on it than you can afford to for a single feature. You use existing Java classes, so why not use existing Android apps?

This does not just go for sharing either. You can build an amazing alarm app that, from the user perspective, just triggers other apps. That sounds simple, but once you combine it with the system to allow that app to start playing a music app or pre-load a weather or news app, your clear, easy functionality becomes extremely valuable.

Visuals, Visuals, Visuals

One of the major challenges of mobile applications is that you often have a lot of information to convey, but you have very little screen real estate to do so. Even worse, the user is frequently only taking a quick look at the app. That means it needs to be easy to scan for the exact information desired. Use short text for headers, directions, and dialogs. Make sure that buttons state a real action, such as "Save File" instead of "Okay," so that a button's function is immediately obvious.

Use images to convey meaning quickly. Use consistent visuals to anchor the user. Use animations to tell the user something is happening (for example, "You moved to a new part of the app, and pressing the back button will go to the previous part" or "Some content is still loading"). In fact, animations can be so important to the user experience that a big portion of Chapter 9, "Further Improving the App," covers how you should and should not use animations.

Always include all applicable touch states. At a minimum, anything the user can interact with should have a normal state, a pressed state, and a focused state. The pressed state is shown when the user is actively touching the view, so excluding it means the user is unsure what views can be interacted with and whether the app is even responding. The focused state is shown when a view is selected by means of the directional pad or other method so that the user knows what view will be pressed. It can also be used in touch mode, such as how an `EditText` will highlight to show users where they are entering text. Without a focused state, users cannot effectively use alternate means of navigation. See Figure 1.7 for an example of how to easily convert the standard Holo-style touch states to a version applicable to an app with a green theme.

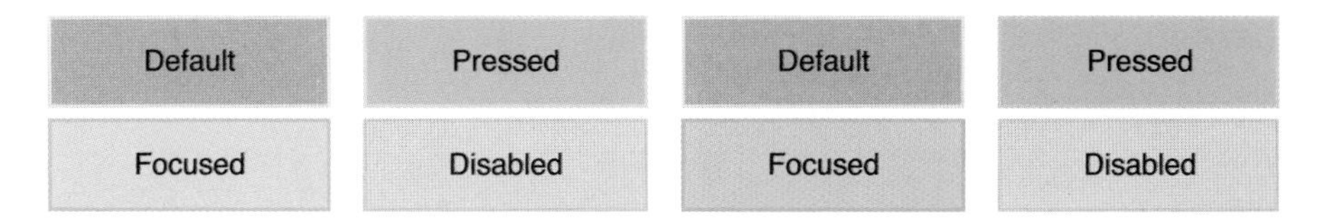

Figure 1.7 The standard Holo buttons are displayed on the left; on the right, they're shown with a simple hue shift.

Visuals are not just limited to images either. Users of your app will quickly learn to recognize repeated words such as headers. If a portion of your app always says "Related Images" in the same font and style, users will learn to recognize the shape of that text without even needing to read it.

Easy but Powerful

People are judgmental. People using an app for the first time are hyper-judgmental, and that means it is critical that your app is easy to use. The primary functions should be clear and obvious. This need ties in with visuals and a clear focus. If you jump into that note-taking app and see a big plus icon, you can guess right away that the plus button starts a new note. The powerful side of it comes when pressing that plus button also populates meta-data that the user does not have to care about (at that moment), such as the date the note was started or the user's location at that time. When the note is saved, the app can scan it for important words or names that match the user's contacts. Suddenly the app is able to do useful things such as finding all notes mentioning Albert in the past month without the user having to consider that ability when creating the note.

If your app provides photo filters, do not just say "stretch contrast" or "remove red channel." Instead, show a preview thumbnail so the user can see and understand the effect of the button (see Figure 1.8). When the user scrolls to the bottom of your list of news articles, automatically fetch the next group of articles to add to the list (an example of how to implement this specifically is given in Chapter 10, "How to Handle Common Components"). Simple features like these are intuitive and make the user feel empowered.

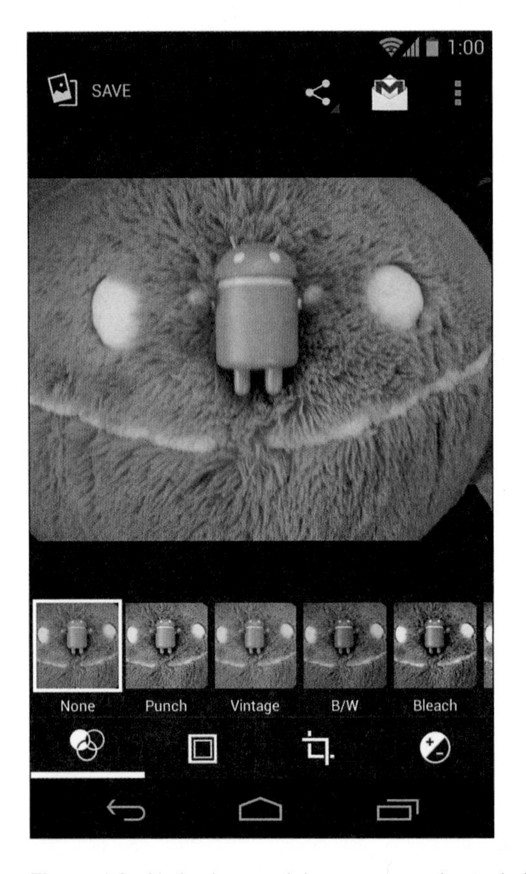

Figure 1.8 Notice how each image-processing technique along the bottom has both a text description and a simple thumbnail illustrating the effect.

One last thing to remember about making your app easy but powerful is that the user is always right, even when making a mistake. When the user presses a "delete" button, in 99% of cases, the user meant to press that button. Instead of asking the user every single time, "Did you really mean to do that thing you just did?", assume the user meant to, but make it easy to undo the action. Don't make features difficult to access in order to keep the user from making a mistake. Make features easy to use, including Undo, to encourage the user to explore your app. An app that does this extremely well is Gmail. When you delete an email, you have the option to undo it. The app doesn't ask you whether you meant to delete it because that gets in the way of a good user experience.

Platform Consistency

When in doubt, follow the user experience expectations of the platform. Even when you're not in doubt, you should follow the user experience expectations of the platform. In other words, unless you have an extremely good reason, you should not do things differently from how they are done in the built-in apps. "We want our iOS app and Android app to look/behave similarly" is *not* a good excuse. Your Android users use their Android devices on a daily basis; they rarely (if ever) use iOS devices (or other mobile platforms). These platforms have very different user expectations, and using something from one platform that is a foreign user experience would be like putting a steering wheel in a fighter jet. Sure, a steering wheel works well for a car, but it does not make sense in a fighter jet.

Other platforms can require navigational buttons such as a back button or an exit button; these do *not* belong in an Android app. The actual Android back button should have an obvious and intuitive function in your app, and adding another element to the UI that does the same thing creates user confusion. There is no need to exit your app, because the user can either back out of it or simply press the home button. Your button is either going to artificially replicate one of these scenarios or, worse, it will truly exit the app and slow down its next startup time. That does not just slow down the user experience; it wastes power rereading assets from disk that might have been able to stay in memory.

Using styling from another platform not only looks out of place, it is awkward for the user. For example, Android has a specific sharing icon that looks quite distinct from other platforms such as iOS and Windows Phone. Users are likely to be confused if an icon from another platform is used.

Bend to the User

One of the great things about Android is that users have a lot of choice right from the beginning. A construction worker might choose a rigid device with a physical keyboard over a more powerful, thin device. Someone with larger hands has the option to pick a device with a five-inch screen over a much smaller screen. Android makes it extremely easy to support these different scenarios. Just because it can be difficult to support landscape and portrait on other platforms does not mean the support should be dropped for Android as well.

Bending to the user does not just mean adjusting your app to give the best experience on a given device; it also means picking up on user habits. How much you pick up their habits is up to you. The simplest method is just giving preferences that the user can set. Is your app a reading app? It might make sense to offer an option to force a particular orientation for reading while lying down. If your app switches to white on black at night, but the user always switches it back to black on white, your app can learn that preference.

Standard Components

Regardless of whether you meticulously sketch your design concepts, quickly rough them out to refine later, or dip your pet's feet in ink and have him walk around on a large piece of paper hoping for something magical to appear, it is important to know the standard components of Android.

System Bars

Android has two system bars: the status bar and the navigation bar. The status bar (shown in Figure 1.9) is at the top of the screen and displays icons for notifications on the left and standard phone status info on the right, such as battery and signal levels. The navigation bar (shown in Figure 1.10) is at the bottom of the screen and consists of back, home, and recent apps software buttons when hardware buttons are not present. Apps that were designed against older versions of Android will also cause a menu button to appear in the navigation bar. Tablet devices had a combined bar that displayed both status and navigation controls for Android 3.x (Honeycomb), but the UI was updated for Android 4.2 to mirror phones, with the status bar on top and the navigation bar on the bottom.

Figure 1.9 The standard Android status bar

Figure 1.10 The standard Android navigation bar

For the most part, these do not need to be considered much during design. You can hide the status bar, but you almost never should. It's acceptable to hide the system bars during video playback and it's fine to hide the status bar when it might interfere with the user experience (for example, if you are making a game that involves frantic swiping, chances are accidentally swiping the status bar down will be problematic, so it is okay to hide the bar in that case). Casual games should typically still show the status bar (no reason for the user to have to leave a game of solitaire to check who that most recent email was from). Nearly all apps should show the status bar. How do you know if yours is an exception? Try your app with the status bar being displayed and see if it interferes with the user experience. If it does not, you should display the status bar. Code examples demonstrating how to show and hide these bars are available in Appendix C, "Common Task Reference."

Notifications

Right from the start, Android was designed with multitasking in mind. A user shouldn't have to stare at a progress bar in an app that is downloading resources, nor should a user have to exit an app to have access to the most important information on his or her device. Notifications are a great feature that many apps do not take advantage of. If your app does something in the background, such as syncing a playlist, it should show a notification while that is happening. If your app has important information the user should be aware of, such as a stock alert that the user has set, it should be displayed as a notification. Android 4.1 brought about richer notifications (see Figure 1.11) that allow notifications to have actions as well as larger displays. For example, an email notification might show just the subject and sender, but the expanded notification could show part of the actual message as well as buttons to reply or archive the email.

Action Bar

The action bar is fast becoming a design expectation of the Android platform. By using an action bar in your app, you not only take advantage of an excellent navigation and action component, you gain app usability simply from the muscle memory users have developed when interacting with the action bar in other apps. See Figure 1.12 for an example of the action bar in the Gallery app. The icon indicates the app, and the "Albums" text with the triangle indicator shows the current location and functions as a navigational element. The camera icon is an action item, and the three dots signify the overflow menu, where all the less frequently used action items go (as well as any that don't fit on a given device). Items not commonly used, such as settings and help, should always go in the overflow menu.

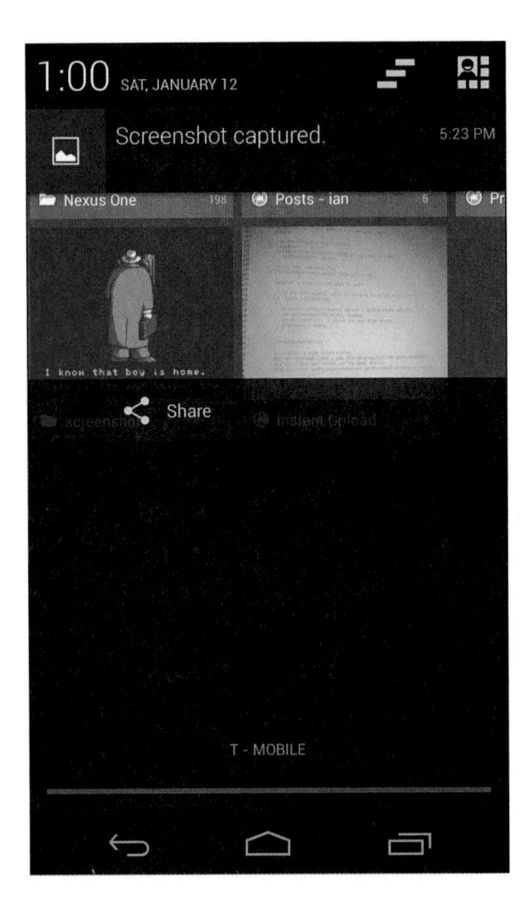

Figure 1.11 Notice the larger notification shows more of the screenshot and can be immediately shared.

Figure 1.12 An example of the action bar in the Gallery app

Split Action Bar

At times when your action bar cannot contain all the actions that it should, you can choose to use a split action bar. With a split action bar, additional actions are contained in a bar directly below the main action bar or in a bar at the bottom of the content area. See Figure 1.13 for an example of the Gmail app (with private info removed), which uses a split action bar to put all of the action items at the bottom.

Figure 1.13 The Gmail app shows an excellent use of the split action bar, where the primary actions are along the bottom of the app instead of the top.

Supporting Multiple Devices

Although already briefly touched on in the "Bend to the User" section, the importance of supporting multiple devices cannot be overstated. If you're not doing anything with the NDK (and if you don't know what that is, you're not using it, so wipe that sweat off your forehead), it's typically very easy to support a range of devices wider than you even know to exist. In fact, most work that you do to support a variety of devices will be done simply by providing alternate layouts for different devices. You will group UI components into fragments (more on those in Chapter 3, "Creating Full Layouts with View Groups and Fragments") and combine fragments as necessary to provide an ideal experience on each different device. The fragments will typically contain all the logic necessary to load data, handle interactions, and so on, so they can be easily used across different device types. Because your views will use identifiers, your code can say something like "Change the additional info `TextView` to say 'Bacon'" and it does not have to worry about whether that `TextView` is at the top of the screen, the bottom, or is currently invisible.

> **note**
>
> If your curiosity gets the better of you and you want to know what the NDK is, it's the native development kit that allows you to develop Android apps in C/C++. You can read more about it here: http://developer.android.com/tools/sdk/ndk/index.html.

Throughout this book, you will see many different techniques for supporting multiple devices. At this point, it is just important for you to keep in mind the devices that are out there. Best practices go a long way toward making your app usable on devices that you might not have even considered. For example, including a focused state for all of your UI elements allows you to remove the dependency on having a touch screen. That means your app will be usable on Google TV (though you will want to provide a specific set of layouts for that platform), and it will also be more usable for people with impairments who find that a means of navigation other than the touchscreen works better.

Notable Changes

Although Android's standardization of design is a relatively recent process, some design patterns came about previously. It is particularly important to call out two of these that are now considered outdated: the menu key and the context menu.

Goodbye Menu Key

Prior to Android 3.x, devices were expected to have a menu key. Unfortunately, this actually led to several problems. For one, the user had no way of knowing if the menu key did anything in a given app. He or she had to press it to see what happened. The menu key was also meant to be contextual to the current screen contents (it was essentially the precursor to the action bar and the overflow menu), but many developers and designers used the menu key in inconsistent ways, even abusing it as a full navigational menu. Fortunately, all you have to know now is that you should not use the menu key. Your apps should target the newest version of Android so that a software menu key does not appear.

Long Press

The long press gesture was used to bring up a context menu, similar to right-clicking on a desktop application. This use of the long press has gone away and should instead be replaced with selection. Long pressing on a given item should select it and then enable a contextual action bar. Selecting one or more items might give you the options to delete, archive, or flag them. If your app does not have the ability to select items, then long press should not do anything.

The long press is also used to display the title of an action bar item. Thus, you can long press on an unclear icon and have it display the title so that you know what it does. Fortunately, Android will handle this for you as long as you declare titles for your menu items (and you always should since they're also used for accessibility).

Summary

Now that you have finished this chapter, you should have a good idea about what a modern Android app looks like. You now know the standard components (such as the action bar) and the outdated ones that should be avoided (such as the menu button). You understand some high-level goals from the "Core Principles" section that you can apply to future apps, and you may find it useful to come back to this chapter later on once your app has started being designed.

Before continuing on to the next chapter, be sure to look at the Android design website (at http://developer.android.com/design/), if you haven't already. You might also find it beneficial to pick a few apps that work really well and see how they fit in with what you have learned in this chapter. Paying attention to what current apps on the platform do is a great way to ensure that your app behaves in a way that the user expects and is at least as good as what's already available. You might even notice a way that you can improve an app that you previously thought was perfect.

CHAPTER 2

UNDERSTANDING VIEWS—THE UI BUILDING BLOCKS

Sometimes it is best to start with the building blocks before diving into much more complex topics, and that is the goal here. This chapter is all about views, which allow your apps to display their content to your users. You will learn all the major view subclasses and gain a fundamental understanding of key attributes such as view IDs, padding, and margins. If you have already built any apps, most of this will be review for you, so feel free to skim through the chapter as you move toward the heart of the book.

What Is a View?

Views are the most basic component of the user interface, and they extend the `View` class. They always occupy a rectangular area (although they can display content of any shape) and can handle both drawing to the screen and events such as being touched. Everything that is displayed on the screen utilizes a view.

There are two primary types of views: those that stand alone, such as for displaying some text or a picture, and those that are meant to group other views. This chapter focuses on those that stand alone, with the exception of some specialized views. Chapter 3, "Creating Full Layouts with View Groups and Fragments," covers `ViewGroup` and its subclasses (that is, views that group together one or more other views).

Android gives you the flexibility of defining how you use your views using Java within the application code and with XML in external files, typically referred to as "layouts." In most cases, you should define your layouts with XML rather than creating them programmatically because it keeps your application logic separate from the visual appearance, thus keeping your code cleaner and easier to maintain. You also get the advantage of resource qualifiers, which are explained in Chapter 4, "Adding App Graphics and Resources."

Views are highly customizable, and the easiest way to make changes to views is by changing XML attributes in your layout files. Fortunately, most XML attributes also have Java methods that can accomplish the same thing at runtime. And, if nothing else, you can always extend an existing view to modify it in some way or extend the view class itself to create something completely custom.

See Table 2.1 for a list of the most commonly used attributes for the `View` class. Remember that all other views extend the `View` class, so these attributes apply to all views (though child classes can handle the attributes differently or even ignore them). The API levels refer to the version of the Android SDK where the attributes were introduced. API level 4 was Android 1.6, called "Donut." API level 11 was Android 3.0, or "Honeycomb." API level 16 was Android 4.1, the first version of "Jelly Bean." For a complete list of the API levels, you can see the table at http://developer.android.com/guide/topics/manifest/uses-sdk-element.html#ApiLevels.

Table 2.1 `View`'s Most Commonly Used Attributes

Attribute	Method	API	Description
`alpha`	`setAlpha(float)`	11	Defines the alpha level of the view as a floating point from 0 (fully transparent) to 1 (fully opaque).
`background`	`setBackground` ➥`Resource(int)`	1	Sets the `Drawable` to use for the background (drawables are covered in Chapter 4).

Attribute	Method	API	Description
`clickable`	`setClickable` `➥(boolean)`	1	Defines whether this view will react to click events; generally, you won't need to set this because setting an `OnClickListener` will set this to true for you.
`content` `➥Description`	`setContent` `➥Description` `➥(CharSequence)`	4	Sets text to be used to briefly describe this view for accessibility (for example, an `ImageButton` is not descriptive to someone with a visual impairment, so you can describe it to be the "cancel button" or similar). When defining a view in XML and you know the view provides no content (for example, a shadow that's only there for aesthetics), use `"@null"` as the value for `contentDescription`.
`duplicate` `➥ParentState`	N/A	1	Setting this to true in XML means that the view will get its current state (for example, pressed or focused) from its parent. This is most commonly used when a `ViewGroup` is acting as a button.
`focusable`	`setFocusable` `➥(boolean)`	1	Sets whether the view can take focus; this is false by default.
`focusable` `➥InTouchMode`	`setFocusableIn` `➥TouchMode(boolean)`	1	Sets whether the view can take focus while the app is in "touch mode." If it is set to true, then touching the view will cause it to gain focus.
`id`	`setId(int)`	1	Defines an ID for the view so that you can find it in code. More on this shortly.
`importantFor` `➥Accessibility`	`setImportantFor` `➥Accessibility` `➥(boolean)`	16	Defines whether this view is important to accessibility. If it is, the view will trigger accessibility events and can be queried by accessibility services. Although this was not defined until Jelly Bean, you can still use the XML attribute in apps with a `minSdk` prior to Jelly Bean, as long as your target is at least 16.
`longClickable`	`setLongClickable` `➥(boolean)`	1	Defines whether this view will react to long click events; generally, you won't need to set this because setting an `OnLongClickListener` will set this to true for you.

Attribute	Method	API	Description
`minHeight`	`setMinimumHeight` ➥`(int)`	1	Defines a minimum height that the view will take up. Explained shortly.
`minWidth`	`setMinimum` ➥`Width(int)`	1	Defines a minimum width that the view will take up. Explained shortly.
`padding`	`setPadding` ➥`(int, int,` ➥`int, int)`	1	There are five variants to this attribute: `padding`, `paddingLeft`, `padding-Top`, `paddingRight`, and `padding-Bottom`, which are all used to specify padding.
`visibility`	`setVisibility` ➥`(int)`	1	Sets whether the view is visible (normal case), invisible (not drawn but still takes up space), or gone (neither measured nor drawn).

View IDs

As you might suspect, view IDs are used to identify views. They allow you to define your layouts in XML and then modify them at runtime by easily getting a reference to the view. Defining a view in XML is done with `android:id="@+id/example"`. The at symbol (@) signifies that you're referring to a resource rather than providing a literal value. The plus (+) indicates that you are creating a new resource reference; without it, you're referring to an existing resource reference. Then comes `id`, defining what type of resource it is (more on this in Chapter 4). Finally, you have the name of the resource, `example`. These are most commonly defined using lowercase text and underscores (for example, `title_text`) but some people use title case (for example, `TitleText`). It's really up to you. The most important thing is that you're consistent. In Java, you can refer to this value with `R.id.example`, where `R` represents the resources class generated for you, `id` represents the resource type, and `example` is the resource name. Ultimately, this is just a reference to an int, which makes resource identifiers very efficient.

> **note**
>
> The `R` class is generated for you by the Android Development Tools, or ADT. By default, this is built for you whenever it needs to be updated. If you're using Eclipse as your IDE, you can make sure this is the case by expanding the Project menu and verifying that Build Automatically is checked.

> **warning**
>
> Although your `R` class will be generated for you, there is also an `android.R` class. Unfortunately, IDEs will sometimes import this class when you really mean the `R` class that's specific to your app. If you see your resource references not resolving, verify that you have not imported `android.R`.

Understanding View Dimensions

One of the challenges designers and developers alike often have when first starting to think about layouts in Android is the numerous possible screen sizes and densities. Many design specialties (for example, print and iOS) are based on exact dimensions, but approaching Android from that perspective will lead to frustration and apps that do not look good on specific resolutions or densities.

Instead, Android apps are better approached from a more fluid perspective in which views expand and shrink in order to accommodate a given device. The two primary means of doing so are `match_parent` (formerly `fill_parent`) and `wrap_content`. When you tell a view to use `match_parent` (by specifying that as a dimension in either the XML layout or by programmatically creating a `LayoutParams` class to assign to a view), you are saying it should have the same dimensions as the parent view. When you tell a view to use `wrap_content`, you are saying it should only be as big as it needs to be in order to display its content.

When you do want to use an exact size, you should specify it in density independent pixels (abbreviated as either dip or dp). Because screens have different densities, specifying your layouts in pixels will cause screen elements to appear to shrink the higher the density of the device (for example, specifying a line to be 100px long would be one inch on a device that displays one hundred pixels per inch, but it'd only be half an inch on a display that is 200 pixels per inch). Instead, you can use dp in order to have dimensions automatically scale for you based on the device's density. Android currently specifies five different densities based on dots per inch (DPI): LDPI (low dots per inch), MDPI (medium dots per inch), HDPI (high dots per inch), XHDPI (extra high dots per inch), and XXHDPI (extra, extra high dots per inch). The original Android devices were MDPI devices with an approximate density of 160 dots per inch. There were a few low-end devices that came shortly thereafter that were LDPI (about 120 dots per inch), but the main push was toward HDPI (about 240 dots per inch). These higher-density devices produced better images and sharper text. In 2011, XHDPI devices started to show up, with around 320 dots per inch. XXHDPI devices (about 480 dots per inch) are the next step up and are not common now; however, large tablets use launcher icons from one density bucket above their display's actual density in order to create a larger touch target. That means XHDPI tablets such as the Nexus 10 display XXHDPI icons on the home screen.

Fortunately, you don't have to create specific layouts for each density. The main consideration with so many densities is the graphical assets. A line that is four pixels thick on an XHDPI screen will be three pixels thick on an HDPI screen, two pixels thick on an MDPI screen, and just one pixel thick on the rare LDPI screens. Keep in mind that a touch target should generally be at least 48dp for its smallest dimension (roughly nine millimeters). For specific information about using grids and the minimum touchable size, see http://developer.android.com/design/style/metrics-grids.html.

There are also times when you want a view to be at least a certain size but bigger if needed. In these cases, you can use the `minHeight` and `minWidth` properties. For example, you might have a view that is meant to be touched, so you define a `minHeight` of 48dp but the `layout_height` as `wrap_content`. That guarantees the view will be at least large enough to touch, but it can be larger to accommodate more content.

Two other parts of layouts are important to understand: padding and margins. If you were to set your phone next to another phone and think of each device as a view, you could think of the screens as the actual content, the bevel around the screens as the padding, and the space between the devices as the margins. Visually, it's not always obvious whether spacing is from padding or margins, but conceptually padding is part of the width of a layout and margins are not. See Figure 2.1 for a visual depiction of margins and padding.

Figure 2.1 A visual demonstration of layouts with margins and padding

Displaying Text

One of the most fundamental ways in which you will communicate with your users is through text. Android gives you tools both to make displaying text easy and to make handling localization almost no work at all. Resources, covered in depth in Chapter 4, allow you to specify the displayed strings (among other types of content) outside of your layouts, letting the system automatically select the correct strings for a given user's language.

`TextView`

`TextView` is one of the most common views in Android. As its name suggests, it displays text. What its name does not tell you is that it actually supports a wide variety of appearances and content. In fact, you can even specify a `Drawable` (such as an image) to appear to the left, top, right, and/or bottom of the `TextView`. You can add text shadows, change colors, and have portions of text bold and others italicized. You can even have metadata associated with specific portions of text within the `TextView`, allowing for click events on specific words or phrases, for example. Figure 2.2 shows a single `TextView` that has a variety of styles applied to it and even displays an inline image. Examples of `TextView` are shown throughout the book, but Chapter 10, "How to Handle Common Components," shows the specifics about how to accomplish what is shown in Figure 2.2.

Figure 2.2 A single `TextView` showing a variety of styles

`TextView` is robust but very easy to use. In fact, the majority of views that display text extend `TextView` precisely for those reasons. In addition, utilities are available that make some of the more difficult processes easy to do, such as converting portions of the text to links with `Linkify` (you can specify whether you want phone numbers to go to the dialer, links to go to a browser, or even custom patterns to do what you'd like) and converting most basic HTML (with the aptly named `HTML` class) into styled text that uses the `Spanned` interface.

A wide variety of attributes can be used to make `TextView` work and look exactly how you want. See Table 2.2 for the most commonly used attributes.

Table 2.2 `TextView`'s Most Commonly Used Attributes

Attribute	Method	API	Description
`drawable`	`setCompound ➥Drawables ➥WithIntrinsic ➥Bounds ➥(int, int, ➥int, int)`	1	There are six XML variants of this attribute: `drawableLeft`, `drawableTop`, `drawableRight`, and `drawableBottom` as well as both `drawableStart` and `drawableEnd`. These attributes allow you to specify a resource-based `Drawable` to be displayed along with the text without requiring an additional `View`.
`drawable ➥Padding`	`setCompound ➥Drawable ➥Padding(int)`	1	Specifies the padding between the text and the drawable(s) defined with any of the drawable attributes.
`ellipsize`	`setEllipsize ➥(TextUtils. ➥TruncateAt)`	1	Setting the `ellipsize` location for a `TextView` lets it end the text with an ellipsis when it won't all fit within the bounds.
`fontFamily`	`setTypeface ➥(Typeface)`	1	Sets the font family to be used, defined as a string. The method `setTypeface(Typeface)` can be used with custom fonts.
`gravity`	`setGravity ➥(int)`	1	Specifies the alignment of text along the X and/or Y axis. For XML you will primarily use `left`, `top`, `right`, `bottom`, `center`, `center_vertical`, and `center_horizontal`, though there are others. You can also combine values with a pipe (for example, `left|bottom`). For the method, see the `Gravity` class for the constants you can use. Keep in mind this is the gravity within the dimensions of the `TextView`.

Attribute	Method	API	Description
hint	setHint(int)	1	Mostly used for EditText; this defines the text to show when it is empty.
inputType	setRawInputType ➥(int)	1	Mostly used for EditText; this defines the type of data being put into the view, allowing the system to better select an input method (such as a keyboard that includes the at sign if it's for an email address).
lineSpacing ➥Extra	setLineSpacing ➥(float, float)	1	Sets extra spacing to include between lines of text, commonly used with custom fonts to give a little more breathing room.
lineSpacing ➥Multiplier	setLineSpacing ➥(float, float)	1	Sets the line spacing multiplier (for example, 2 is double-spaced).
lines	setLines(int)	1	Sets the exact number of lines of text for this view. If this is 1, it will cut off text that is longer (see ellipsize). If this is 2, the spacing will be reserved for the second line, even if the text is not two lines long.
maxLines	setMaxLines(int)	1	Sets the maximum number of lines that this view can grow to display.
minLines	setMinLines(int)	1	Sets the minimum number of lines worth of spacing that this view reserves.
shadowColor	setShadowLayer ➥(float, float, ➥float, int)	1	Defines the text shadow's color.
shadowDx shadowDy	setShadowLayer ➥(float, float, ➥float, int)	1	Defines the x/y offset of the shadow.
shadowRadius	setShadowLayer ➥(float, float, ➥float, int)	1	Sets how much blur the shadow has; must be defined for the text shadow to appear. Because this is a float, fractional values are allowed (for example, .01) but mostly appear as no blur.
text	setText ➥(CharSequence)	1	Sets the actual text to display. There are several methods for doing this via code.
textColor	setTextColor(int)	1	Sets the color of the text.

Attribute	Method	API	Description
textIs ➥Selectable	N/A	11	If true, allows the view's text to be selected (for example, for copying). You should usually set this to true because you never know what content from your app a user might want to share.
textSize	setTextSize ➥(int, float)	1	Sets the size of the text.
textStyle	setTypeface ➥(Typeface)	1	Sets the style (for example, bold or italic) of the text.
typeface	setTypeface ➥(Typeface)	1	Sets the Typeface of the text.

EditText

EditText is the primary means for allowing the user to input text such as a username or password. Because it extends TextView, the attributes in Table 2.2 are applicable. With EditText, you can specify the type of text the user will input via the inputType attribute or setRawInputType(int) method. For example, saying that the user will input numbers allows the keyboard to display numbers rather than all the letters with numbers on a second screen. You can also provide a hint, which is displayed before the user has entered any text and is a good way of providing context. When a user has entered text that is invalid such as an incorrect username, EditText can easily display error messages as well. See Figure 2.3 for examples of EditText.

Button

Like EditText, Button extends TextView. The primary difference is that a button is simply meant to be pressed, but the displayed text lets the user understand what the button will do. In most cases, the fact that Button extends TextView will be mostly irrelevant. Rarely should you use a mixture of styles in a button or ellipsize it. A button should be obvious with a short string explaining its purpose. Additional styling such as bolding a particular word in the button creates a distraction and confuses users. See Figure 2.4 for examples of Button.

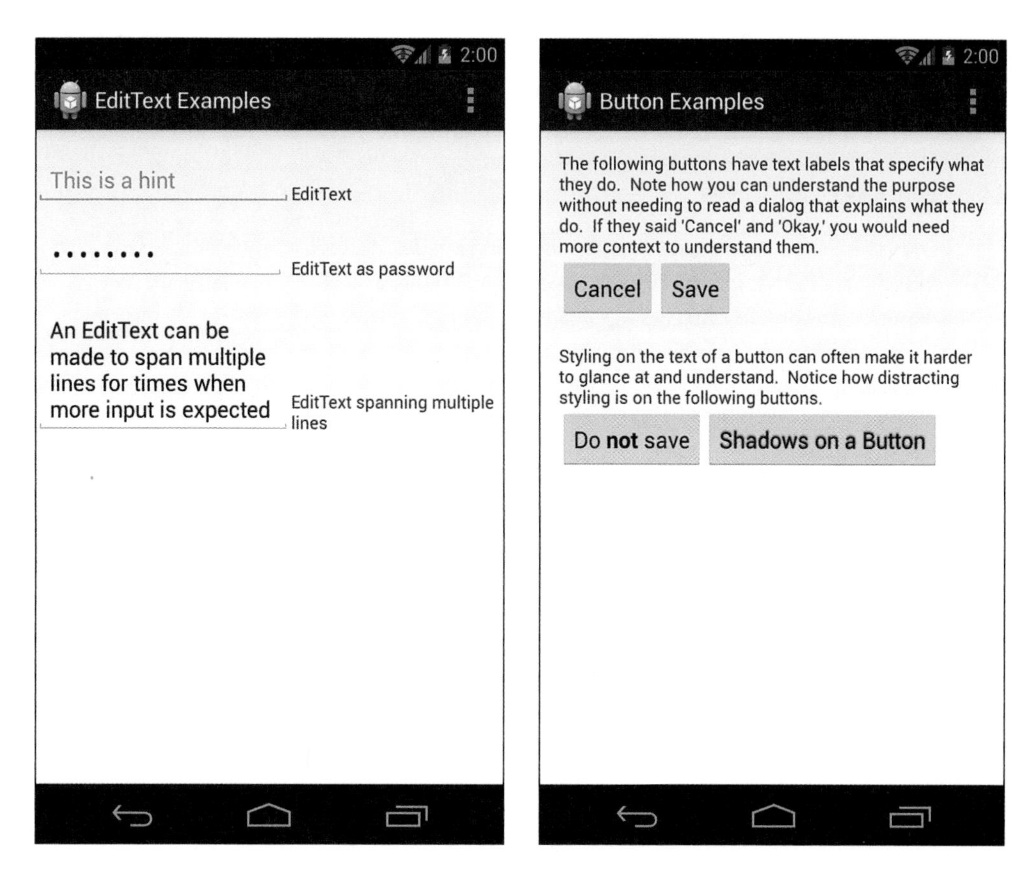

Figure 2.3 Examples of using `EditText` for different types of input

Figure 2.4 Examples of `Button` with different text and styling

Displaying Images

Although displaying text is vital for nearly any application, an app with text alone is not likely to get everyone screaming with excitement. Fortunately, there are many ways for displaying images and other graphical elements in your apps.

Backgrounds

In many cases, you will be able to apply an image to the background of the view and it will work as expected. One great benefit of doing this is that you do not have to create an extra view, so you save the system a little bit of processing and memory. Unfortunately, you do not have as much control over the backgrounds of views as you do over views that are designed to display images specifically.

In Chapter 4, the various `Drawable` subclasses supported by Android are covered in depth. All of these drawables can be used as the background for views, so they give you a fair amount of control over the display of graphical content for your apps.

ImageView

`ImageView` is the primary class used for displaying images. It supports automatic scaling and even setting custom tinting, for instance. Keep in mind that an `ImageView` can also have a background, so you can actually stack images with this one view type. Fortunately, this class has far fewer attributes to consider than `TextView`.

The most obvious attribute of `ImageView` is `src`, which defines the source of the image to display. You can also set the image via `setImageBitmap(Bitmap)`, `setImageDrawable(Drawable)`, and `setImageResource(int)` in order to dynamically set or change the image displayed by this view.

Although later chapters will discuss working with images and `ImageView` in much more depth, one more extremely common `ImageView` attribute that you should know is `scaleType`, which defines how the view handles displaying an image that is larger or smaller than the view's area. See Table 2.3 for details and Figure 2.5 for a visual example that shows each of the different ways of scaling an image as well as the full-sized image.

Table 2.3 `ScaleType` Values for `ImageView`

XML Attribute Value	ScaleType Enum	Description
`matrix`	`MATRIX`	Scales using an image matrix that is set via `setImageMatrix(Matrix)`.
`fitXY`	`FIT_XY`	Sets the image's width and height to match those of the view, ignoring aspect ratio.
`fitStart`	`FIT_START`	Scales the image down or up, maintaining aspect ratio, and aligns the top left of the image to the top left of the view.
`fitCenter`	`FIT_CENTER`	Scales the image down or up, maintaining aspect ratio, so that at least one dimension will be equal to that dimension of the view.
`fitEnd`	`FIT_END`	Like `fitStart` but aligns the bottom-right corner.
`center`	`CENTER`	Centers the image in the view without scaling.

XML Attribute Value	ScaleType Enum	Description
centerCrop	CENTER_CROP	Scales the image down if needed, maintaining aspect ratio, so that both width and height will be equal to or greater than the size of the view.
centerInside	CENTER_INSIDE	Scales the image down if needed, maintaining aspect ratio, so that both the width and height will be equal to or less than the size of the view.

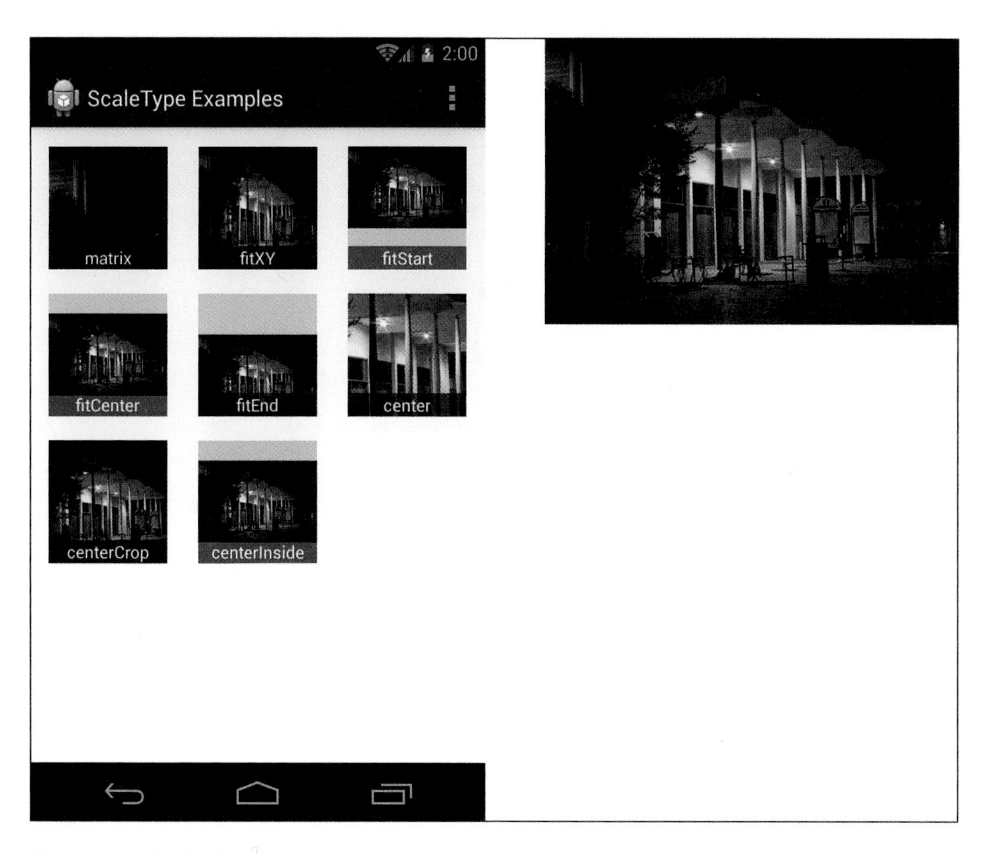

Figure 2.5 Each of the ScaleTypes are shown on the left, and the image that is being scaled is shown on the right.

ImageButton

An ImageButton is a class that extends ImageView to display an image on top of a standard button. You set the image the same way as with ImageView (typically using the src attribute or any of the setImageBitmap(Bitmap), setImageDrawable(Drawable), or `setImageResource(int)` methods), and you can change the button by setting the background to something other than the default.

Views for Gathering User Input

You already know about `EditText`, which you can get user input from, as well as both `Button` and `ImageButton` for handling simple touch events, but many more views can be used for collecting user input. Although any view can actually handle user feedback, the following views are specifically designed to do so:

`AutoCompleteTextView`—This is essentially an `EditText` that has an adapter to supply suggestions as the user is typing.

`CalendarView`—This view lets you easily display dates to users and allow them to select dates. See Figure 2.6 for an example.

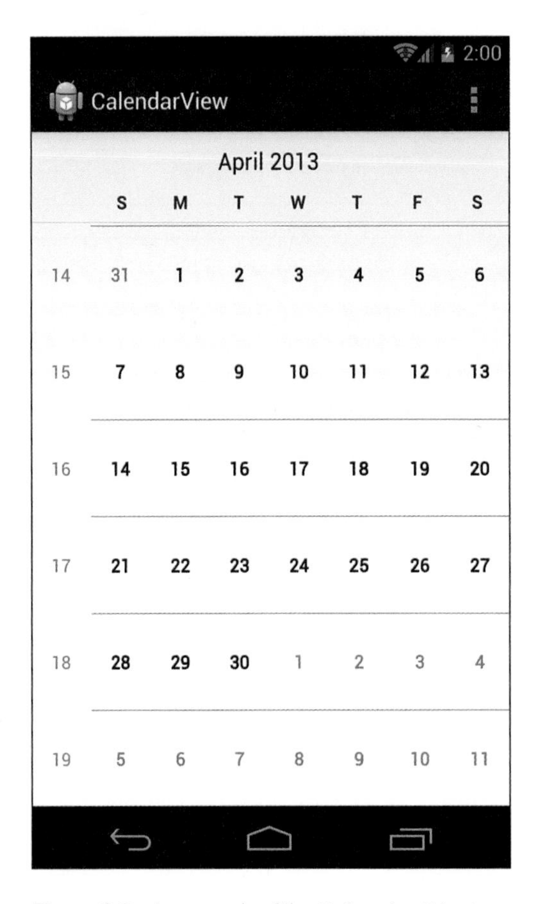

Figure 2.6 An example of the `CalenderView`

CheckBox—This is your typical check box that has a checked and unchecked state for binary choices. Note that the *B* is capitalized. See Figure 2.7 for an example.

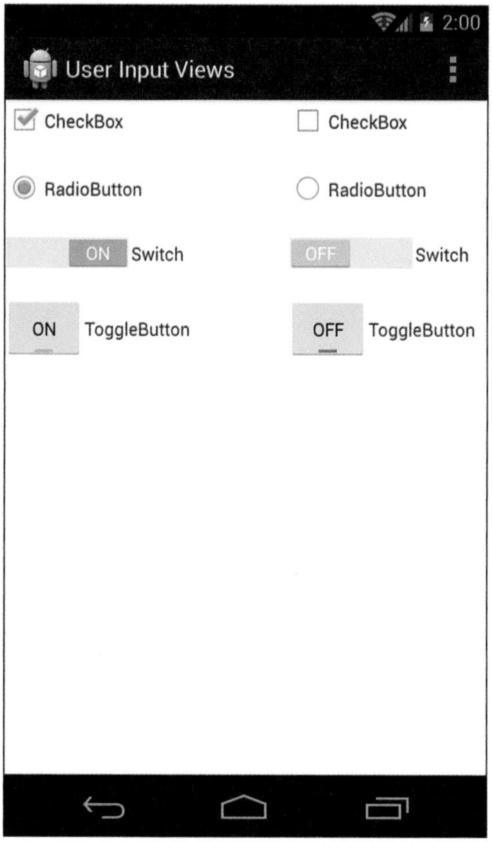

Figure 2.7 An example of CheckBox, RadioButton, Switch, and ToggleButton with on (left) and off (right) states

CheckedTextView—This is basically a TextView that can be checked and is sometimes used in a ListView (discussed in the next chapter).

CompoundButton—This is an abstract class that is used to implements views that have two states, such as the CheckBox class mentioned earlier.

DatePicker—This class is used for selecting a date and is often combined with CalendarView. See Figure 2.8 for an example.

MultiAutoCompleteTextView—This class is similar to AutoCompleteTextView, except that it can work on a subset of the text.

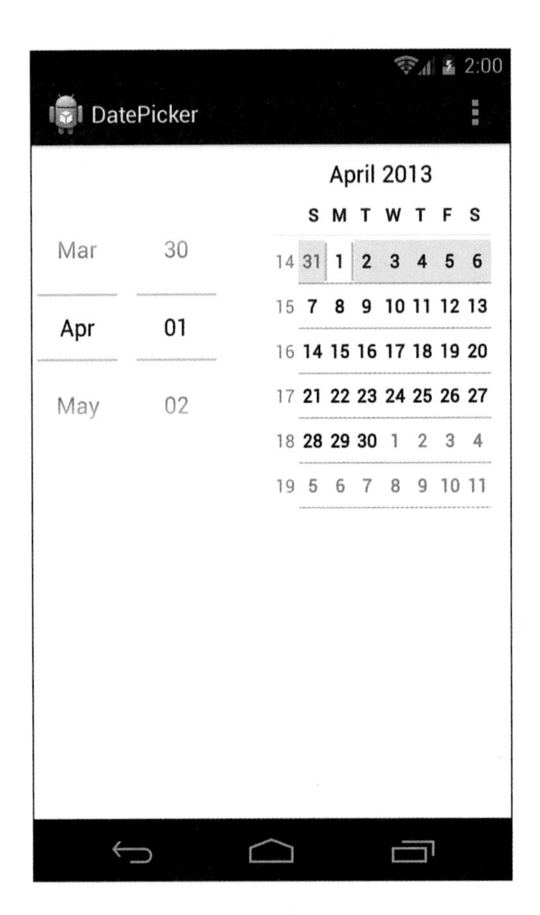

Figure 2.8 An example of the `DatePicker`

`NumberPicker`—This class lets users pick a number, but you probably figured that out already.

`RadioButton`—This view is used with a `RadioGroup`. Typically, you have several `RadioButton`s within a `RadioGroup`, allowing only one to be selected at a time. See Figure 2.7 for an example.

`RadioGroup`—This is actually a `ViewGroup` that contains `RadioButton`s that it watches. When one is selected, the previously selected option is deselected.

`RatingBar`—This view represents your typical "four out of five stars" visual rating indicator, but it is configurable to allow for fractions, different images, and more.

`SeekBar`—This view is your typical seek bar that has a "thumb" the user can drag to select a value along the bar.

`Spinner`—This view is commonly called a drop-down or drop-down menu (it's also referred to as a combo box or a picker view). It shows the current option but, when selected, shows the other available options.

`Switch`—This view is basically a toggle switch, but the user can tap it or drag the thumb. Keep in mind this was not introduced until API level 14. See Figure 2.7 for an example.

`TimePicker`—This view lets users pick a time, but that was pretty obvious, wasn't it? See Figure 2.9 for an example.

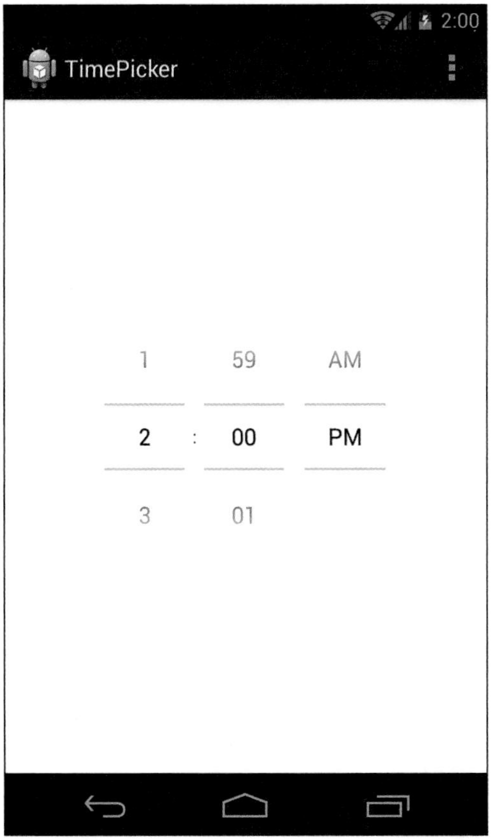

Figure 2.9 An example of the `TimePicker`

`ToggleButton`—This view is conceptually quite similar to a `CheckBox` or a `Switch`, but it is usually displayed as a button with a light that indicates whether or not it is on, and it can have different text to display depending on whether it is on or off. See Figure 2.7 for an example.

Other Notable Views

Whew, you've made it through the bulk of the chapter, but there are dozens of other views and far more to the views we've discussed so far. Fortunately, there is no need for you to use all of them, and you'll see much more in-depth usage in later chapters. For now, it's sufficient to have just a quick explanation of some of the remaining views:

> **`AnalogClock`**—As you can probably guess, this view displays an analog clock. You are likely to never use it, though it can be a good starting place for a custom analog clock. See Figure 2.10 for an example.

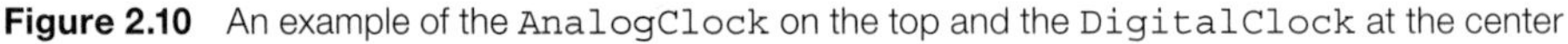

Figure 2.10 An example of the `AnalogClock` on the top and the `DigitalClock` at the center

> **`Chronometer`**—This view is basically a simple timer, like on a stopwatch.

> **`DigitalClock`**—A simple extension of `TextView`, this class displays a digital clock that just triggers a `Runnable` every second to update the display. See Figure 2.10 for an example.

`ExtractEditText`—This is a child class of `EditText` for handling the extracted text. You probably won't directly use this class.

`GLSurfaceView`—This `SurfaceView` class is for displaying OpenGL ES renders.

`KeyboardView`—Another well-named class, this view is for displaying a virtual keyboard.

`MediaRouteButton`—This is a new view to Jelly Bean that can be used to control the routing of media (such as outputting it to external speakers or another device). See Figure 2.11 for an example.

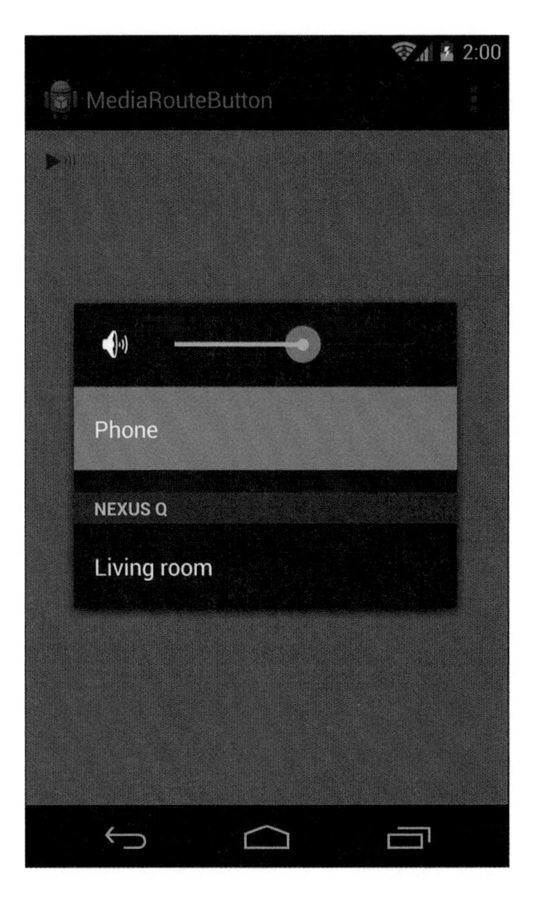

Figure 2.11 An example of the dialog shown when the user presses the `MediaRouteButton` at the top left

`QuickContactBadge`—Added in Android 2.0, this class allows you to easily display a contact that can handle various actions when tapped (such as email, text, call, and so on).

ProgressBar—This class can be used for showing progress, including indeterminate progress (that is, progress for which you don't have a clear sense of where you are in the process, just whether you have started or finished).

RSSurfaceView—When using RenderScript for graphics, you will render to an `RSSurfaceView`.

RSTextureView—Another RenderScript class; this one was added in API level 14 only to be dropped in API level 16 in favor of `TextureView`.

Space—This is a simple subclass of `View` that is intended only for spacing and does not draw anything. Since it was added in API level 14, you can use `View` directly to accomplish something similar or simply copy the source into your own project (although you should rarely need to use a view just for spacing because there are many ways of moving around content).

SurfaceView—This view is intended for custom drawing, primarily for content that is frequently changing. Games that are relatively simple can use this view to display the graphics with reasonable efficiency.

TextureView—Introduced in Ice Cream Sandwich (API level 14), this view is used for displaying hardware-accelerated content streams such as video or OpenGL.

VideoView—This view is a `SurfaceView` that simplifies displaying video content.

WebView—When you want to display web content (whether remote or local), `WebView` is the class to use.

ZoomButton—This is another class you probably won't use, but it essentially allows the triggering of on-click events in rapid succession, as long as the user is holding down the button (as opposed to just triggering a long press event).

Listening to Events

You can listen for a number of events simply by registering the appropriate listener. Unlike some frameworks, Android's methods for settings listeners take the form of `setOnEventListener` (where "Event" is the event to listen for), meaning that only one of a given listener is registered at a time. Setting a new listener of a given type will replace the old one. This may seem like a limitation, but in practice it rarely is and it helps simplify your code. When you really do need more than one class to listen to a particular event, you can always have one listener act as a relay to trigger other listeners.

One point worth noting is that listeners will return a reference to the view that triggered the event. That means you can have one class handle the events for multiple views, such as having your fragment handle clicks for three different buttons. Most commonly you will determine how to react by switching on the ID of the view with `getId()`, but you can also compare view references or even types.

`OnClickListener`

This is the single most common listener you will use. A "click" event is the default event triggered when a view is tapped or when it has focus and the select key is pressed (such as the d-pad center key or a trackball).

`OnLongClickListener`

A long click event is when a click (typically a touch) lasts longer than the value returned by `ViewConfiguration.getLongPressTimeout()`, which is currently 500ms. This action is now most commonly used for enabling multiselect mode.

`OnTouchListener`

Although "touch" is a bit misleading, this listener allows you to react to `MotionEvent`s, potentially consuming them so that they are not passed on to be handled elsewhere. `OnTouchListener` implementations often make use of helper classes such as `GestureDetector` to make it easier to track touches over time. This technique is discussed in later chapters.

Other Listeners

A few other listeners are much less commonly used but are good to know about in case they come in handy. They are as listed here:

`OnDragListener`—This listener lets you intercept drag events to override a view's default behavior, but it is only available in Honeycomb (API level 11) and newer.

`OnFocusChangeListener`—This listener is triggered when focus changes for a view so that you can handle when a view gains or loses focus.

`OnHoverListener`—New in Ice Cream Sandwich (API level 14), this listener allows you to intercept hover events.

`OnGenericMotionListener`—This listener allows you to intercept generic `MotionEvent`s as of API level 12.

`OnKeyListener`—This listener is triggered on hardware key presses.

Summary

Whether you wanted to or not, you now know of the large number of views Android offers you. You also know the most commonly used attributes for the main views, so you can get them to look and behave how you want. At the end of the chapter, you concluded by learning how to handle events for views such as click events. Although not entirely exciting, the details of this chapter are key in breaking down UI concepts into concrete views in later chapters. Much more advanced techniques of using many of these views will also come later on, helping to solidify your knowledge of the Android UI.

CHAPTER 3

CREATING FULL LAYOUTS WITH VIEW GROUPS AND FRAGMENTS

The previous chapter focused on the various views available for you to use. In this chapter you will learn how to bring those views together into one layout and how to use the `Fragment` class to inflate and interact with those layouts. You will also learn about the variety of view groups available for you to combine views as needed.

ViewGroup

As mentioned in Chapter 2, "Understanding Views—The UI Building Blocks," the `ViewGroup` class is for views that can contain one or more child views. `ViewGroup` provides the standardized methods for these classes to use so that they can perform tasks such as adding, removing, getting, and counting child views. The primary method you will use to find a child is `findViewById(int)`, which is actually defined in the `View` class.

Each child class of `ViewGroup` has a different means of positioning the views it contains, as detailed shortly, but (with very few exceptions) views are drawn in the order they are added to a `ViewGroup`. For example, if you have an XML layout that defines a `TextView`, an `ImageView`, and a `Button`, those views will be drawn in that exact order regardless of their position on the screen. If they are placed at the exact same position, first the `TextView` will be drawn, then the `ImageView` will be drawn on top of it, and finally the `Button` will be drawn on the very top, likely obscuring the lower views.

One more useful thing to know is how to iterate through all the views belonging to a given `ViewGroup`. To do so, you will use `getChildCount()` and then a traditional `for` loop with `getChildAt(int)`. See Listing 3.1 for an example.

Listing 3.1 Iterating through a `ViewGroup`'s Children

```
final int childCount = myViewGroup.getChildCount();
for (int i = 0; i < childCount; i++) {
    View v = myViewGroup.getChildAt(i);
    // Do something with the View
}
```

FrameLayout

If you wanted to start off with something easy, this is the view to do it. The `FrameLayout` class just aligns each child view to the top left, drawing each view on top of any previous views. This might seem a bit silly as a way of grouping views, but this class is most commonly used as a placeholder, especially for fragments, which are covered later in the chapter. Instead of trying to figure out where to place a fragment within a view group that has several other views in it already, you can create a `FrameLayout` where you want that fragment to go, set its visibility to `View.GONE`, and you will be able to easily find it again by its ID. This technique is very common, and you will see it in future chapters.

LinearLayout

A `LinearLayout` aligns its children one after another, either horizontally or vertically (depending on its `orientation` attribute). You can specify `gravity`, which controls how the layouts are aligned within this view group (for example, you could have a vertical series of views aligned to the horizontal center of the view group). You can also specify `weight`, a very useful technique for controlling the way views in a `LinearLayout` grow to use the available space. This technique is demonstrated in Listing 3.2, which shows an XML layout that explicitly defines a weight of 0 for each of the views inside the `LinearLayout`. By changing the middle view (the second `TextView`) to have a weight of 1, it is given all the extra vertical space that was not used. See Figure 3.1 for a visual of what this layout looks like.

Listing 3.2 Utilizing `weight` within a `LinearLayout`

```
<?xml version="1.0" encoding="utf-8"?>
<LinearLayout xmlns:android="http://schemas.android.com/apk/res/
➥android"
    android:layout_width="match_parent"
    android:layout_height="match_parent"
    android:orientation="vertical" >

    <TextView
        android:id="@+id/textView1"
        android:layout_width="wrap_content"
        android:layout_height="wrap_content"
        android:layout_margin="5dp"
        android:layout_weight="0"
        android:background="@drawable/padding_bg"
        android:text="TextView 1" />

    <TextView
        android:id="@+id/textView2"
        android:layout_width="wrap_content"
        android:layout_height="wrap_content"
        android:layout_margin="5dp"
        android:layout_weight="0"
        android:background="@drawable/padding_bg"
        android:text="TextView 2" />

    <Button
        android:id="@+id/button"
        android:layout_width="wrap_content"
        android:layout_height="wrap_content"
        android:layout_gravity="right"
        android:layout_margin="5dp"
        android:layout_weight="0"
        android:text="Button" />

</LinearLayout>
```

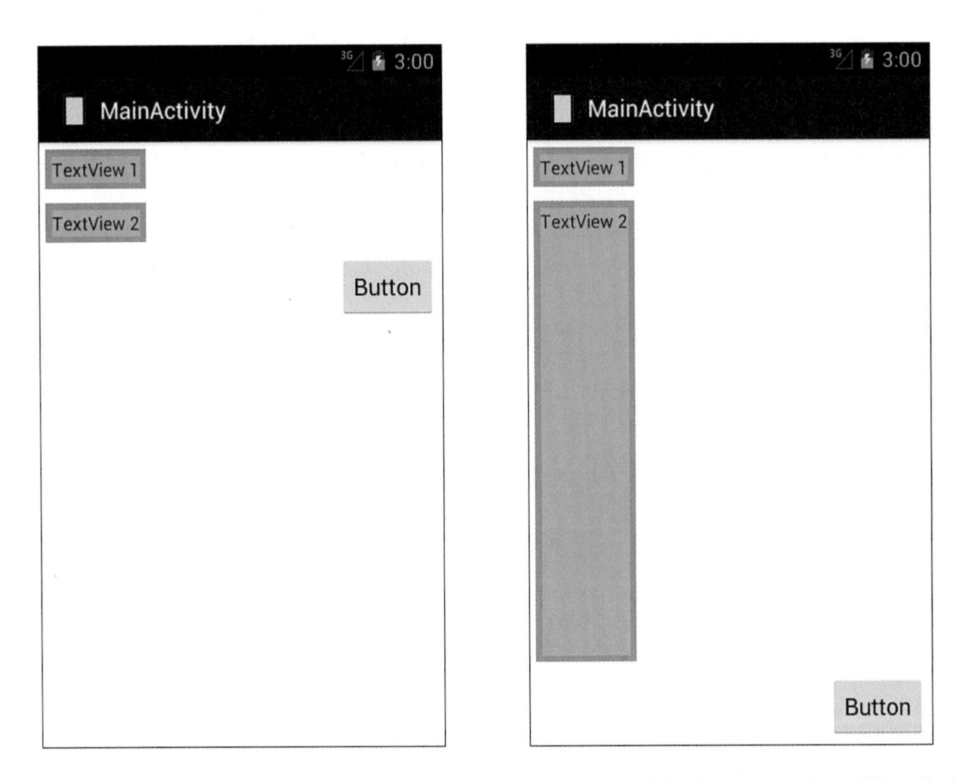

Figure 3.1 The left shows the layouts without weight applied; the right shows a weight of "1" applied to the second `TextView`.

Notice that the width of the weighted `TextView` does not change, only the height grows. That is because the `LinearLayout` has a vertical `orientation`. One more thing to note is that weight is taken into account *after* all the views are measured. That means you can usually optimize cases such as the second example by supplying a height of 0dp for the view(s) that have a weight specified. Because the weight of the view is going to cause it to take up the remaining space anyway, there is no need to measure it.

If you apply weight to more than one view, each view will grow in proportion to its weight. To calculate the ratio that it grows, you divide the weight of the view by the weight of all children in that `LinearLayout`. For example, if you have a view with a weight of 1 and a second view with a weight of 2 (total weight between the two views is 3), the first view will take up one-third of the available space and the second view will take up two-thirds.

warning

When you do not specify an orientation, `LinearLayout` defaults to being horizontally oriented. Because views often have a width of `match_parent`, it's easy to include several views within a `LinearLayout` without specifying an orientation and have all but the first view appear to be missing in your resulting layout. Because the first child view is set to `match_parent` for the width, it takes the full width of the `LinearLayout`. The next child would line up to the right of that, but that's outside of the viewable area. For this reason, you should always explicitly set the orientation of a `LinearLayout`.

`RelativeLayout`

Learning to use a `RelativeLayout` effectively is a little tricky at first, but once you are accustomed to using it, you will find it your go-to view group for a large portion of layouts. As the name indicates, you specify its children relative to each other or to the `RelativeLayout` itself. Not only is this an extremely efficient way to create semi-complex layouts that adapt to a variety of screens, it also allows you to create overlapping views and views that appear to float on top of others. See Table 3.1 for the `LayoutParams` that can be used with views within a `RelativeLayout`. Figure3.2 demonstrates a simple use of a `RelativeLayout` that contains four `TextViews`. And don't worry; this view will come up again in future chapters where real use cases make it more understandable.

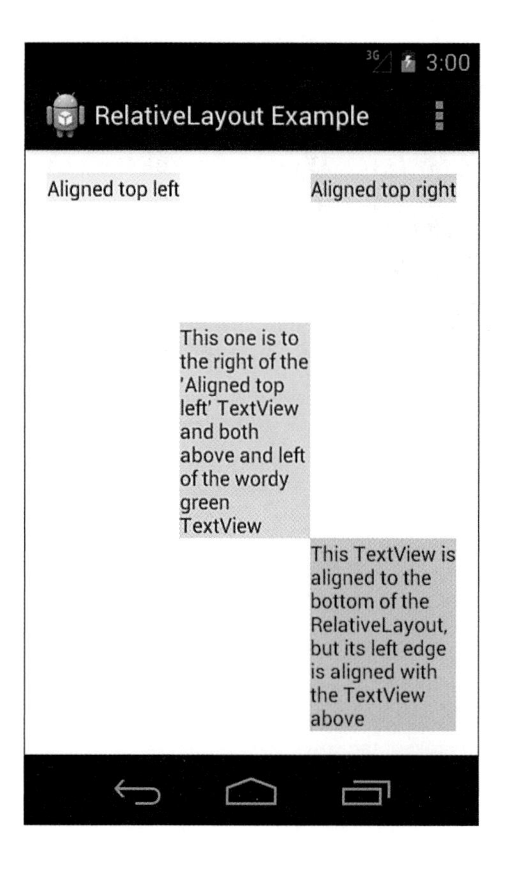

Figure 3.2 An example of positioning four `TextViews` within a `RelativeLayout`

Table 3.1 `RelativeLayout`'s `LayoutParams` Used for Aligning Views

Attribute	Description
`layout_above`	Aligns the bottom of this view to the top of the specified view (including spacing for the bottom margin of this view and the top margin of the specified view).
`layout_alignBaseline`	Aligns the baseline of this view to the baseline of the specified view. You can think of the baseline as the invisible line that text is written on, so this can be used to make two `TextViews` appear to be written on the same line or make another view appear inline with the text.
`layout_alignBottom`	Aligns the bottom of this view with the bottom of the specified view, accounting for a bottom margin.
`layout_alignLeft`	Aligns the left of this view with the left of the specified view, accounting for a left margin.
`layout_alignParentBottom`	Aligns the bottom of this view to the bottom of the `RelativeLayout`.
`layout_alignParentLeft`	Aligns the left of this view to the left of the `RelativeLayout`.
`layout_alignParentRight`	Aligns the right of this view to the right of the `RelativeLayout`.
`layout_alignParentTop`	Aligns the top of this view to the top of the `RelativeLayout`.
`layout_alignRight`	Aligns the right of this view with the right of the specified view, accounting for a right margin.
`layout_alignTop`	Aligns the top of this view with the top of the specified view, accounting for a top margin.
`layout_alignWith` `➥ParentIfMissing`	If the layout specified by other attributes (for example, `layout_alignBottom`) is missing, it will align to the `RelativeLayout`.
`layout_below`	Aligns the top of this view below the bottom of the specified view (including spacing for the top margin of this view and the bottom margin of the specified view).
`layout_centerHorizontal`	Horizontally centers the view within the `RelativeLayout`.
`layout_centerInParent`	Vertically and horizontally centers the view within the `RelativeLayout`.
`layout_centerVertical`	Vertically centers the view within the `RelativeLayout`.
`layout_toLeftOf`	Aligns the right of this view to the left of the specified view's left edge (including spacing for the right margin of this view and the left margin of the specified view).

Attribute	Description
layout_toRightOf	Aligns the left of this view to the right of the specified view's right edge (including spacing for the left margin of this view and the right margin of the specified view).

AdapterView

Sometimes you have a large data set to work with and creating views for every piece of data is impractical. Other times you simply want an easy and efficient way of creating views for some collection of data. Fortunately, AdapterView was created for these types of scenarios. AdapterView itself is abstract, so you will use one of its subclasses such as ListView, but the overall idea is the same. You have a data set, you throw it at an Adapter, and you end up with views in your layout (see Figure 3.3 for a simple conceptual illustration). Simple, right?

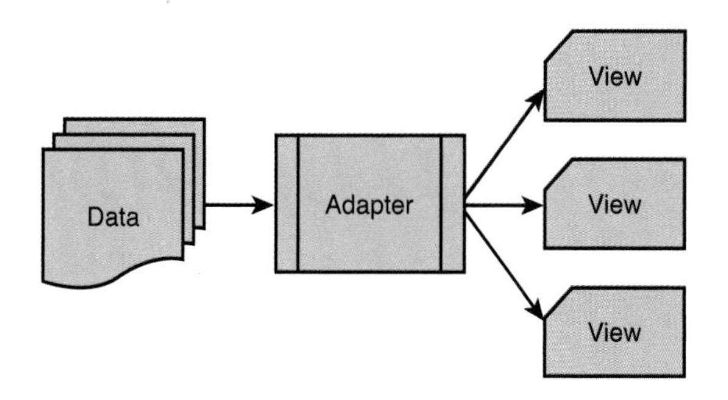

Figure 3.3 Converting a set of data to a usable set of views is what Adapters are made for.

ListView

Sometimes concepts are easier to understand with concrete examples, and ListView is a great example of AdapterView. It presents a vertically scrolling list of views that can be reused. As one view scrolls outside of the layout, it is added back to the other end of the ListView and your ListAdapter updates the view with a new set of data. This process is called "recycling" (as in avoiding garbage collection) and is extremely efficient because it means you do not have to keep inflating layouts; you simply update text and/or images. See Figure 3.4 for a visual example. Notice how the top rows are being added to the bottom of the view just as they pop off the top of the list. In a normal use case, you would change the text and/or images being displayed to give the illusion that these are completely new views.

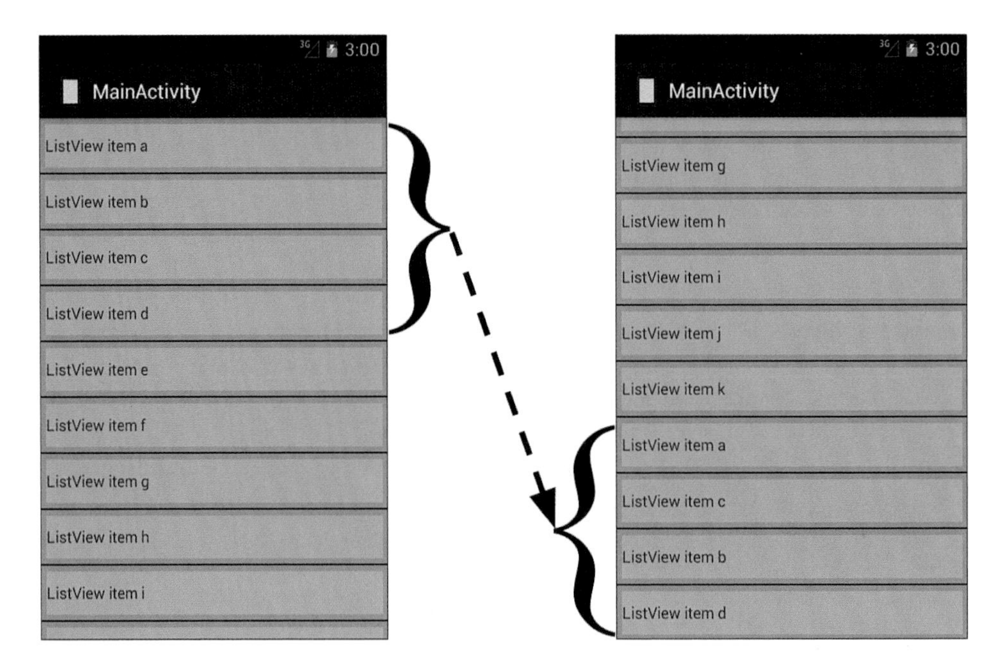

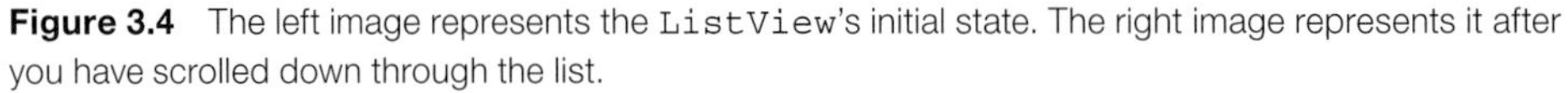

Figure 3.4 The left image represents the `ListView`'s initial state. The right image represents it after you have scrolled down through the list.

There is also a special version of `ListView` called `ExpandableListView`, which is used when you have two levels of content. For example, you might list all the countries of the world and then you could expand each country to show its states or provinces. `ExpandableListView` requires an `ExpandableListAdapter`.

`GridView`

A `GridView` is a two-dimensional grid of views populated by the associated `ListAdapter`. One nice feature is that you can let the number of columns be automatically determined based on size, which makes this view group easy to use. Most commonly, you will see this used for a series of icons or images, although it is not limited to that functionality. See Figure 3.5 for an example.

`Spinner`

When you need to give the user an easy way to select from multiple choices, a `Spinner` is often a good solution. This class shows the currently selected choice and, when tapped, presents a drop-down menu of all the choices. A `Spinner` requires a `SpinnerAdapter`, which determines what the drop-down choices look like. See Figure 3.6 for an example.

Figure 3.5 This is a simple example of a `GridView`.

`Gallery`

The `Gallery` class provides a way to show horizontally scrolling views backed by an `Adapter`. The original purpose was for, as its name states, displaying a gallery of (center-locked) photos. Each view was an `ImageView`. Because of this, `Gallery` does not recycle any of its views and is extremely inefficient. It also has some problems with scrolling, particularly on tablets where several views might be showing at once. `Gallery` has been deprecated, and you should not use it. It is mentioned here specifically because it comes up frequently as a solution to horizontally scrolling views, so you should be aware of it, but you should avoid using `Gallery` in your own apps. Instead, consider `ViewPager` (discussed shortly) or a custom solution.

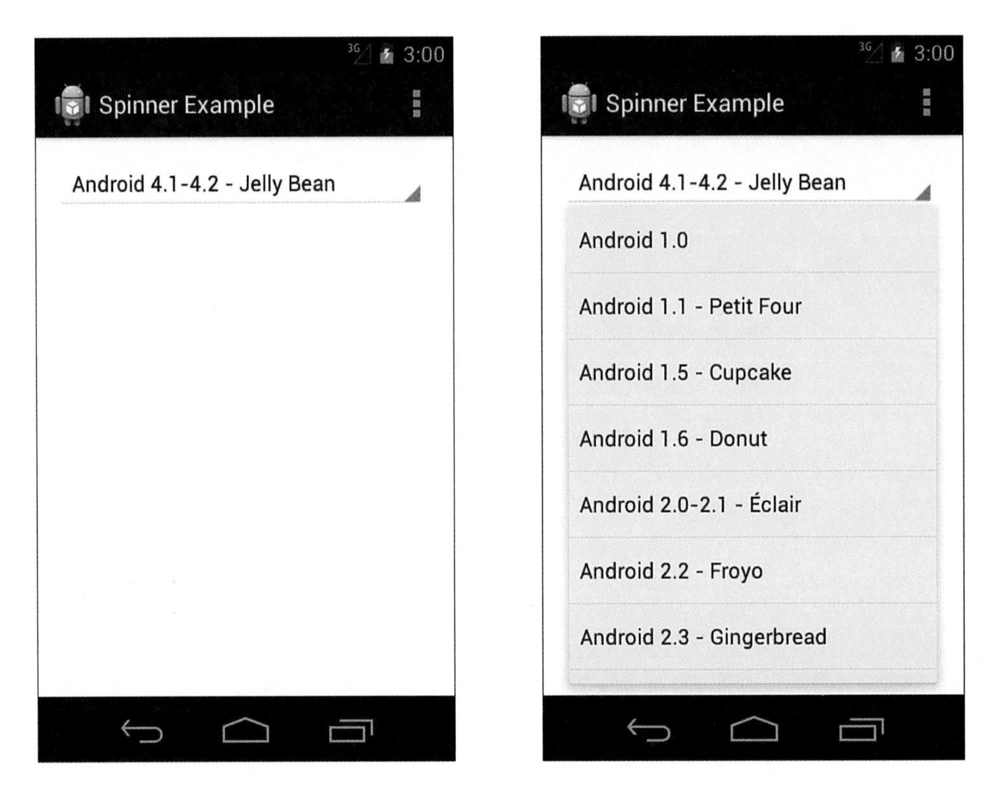

Figure 3.6 The `Spinner` on the left is in the default state; the right image shows the drop-down that appears after the `Spinner` is touched.

`Adapter`

`Adapter` is the interface that takes a data set and returns views representing that data. The adapter is able to say how many items there are, return an item for a specific position, and return the view associated with a position, among other things. For a `ListView`, you will use the `ListAdapter` interface that extends `Adapter` to add a couple of list-specific methods. Similarly, you will use the `SpinnerAdapter` interface for use in a `Spinner`.

Fortunately, you do not need to implement these from scratch every time. For many cases, you will be using an array of data, so you can use `ArrayAdapter` directly or extend it to meet your needs. If your data is backed by a `Cursor` (a sort of pointer to a result set from a database query), `CursorAdapter` is the class to use. In some cases, you need a bit more control but don't want to implement `ListAdapter` or `SpinnerAdapter` from scratch; fortunately, `BaseAdapter` gives a great starting place to extend.

The most important method of `Adapter` is `getView(int position, View convertView, ViewGroup parent)`. This is where the adapter provides the actual view that represents a given position. The `convertView` parameter is for passing in any existing view of the same type that can be reused, but you *must* handle the case of this being null because the first calls to this method will not have an existing view to reuse and `AdapterView` does not require recycling views when it is extended. The third parameter, `parent`, is the `ViewGroup` that the view you're building will be attached to. You should *not* attach the view yourself.

Interfaces for **`AdapterView`**

You will commonly use one of these `AdapterView` subclasses in order to allow each item to be interacted with. Instead of manually assigning event listeners to each view you generate, you can instead set a listener on the `AdapterView`. For example, to listen to clicks, you can create an implementation of the `OnItemClickListener` interface. There are also `OnItemLongClickListener` and `OnItemSelectedListener` interfaces. Each of these interfaces defines a single method that is passed the `AdapterView` itself, the view that the event was triggered on, the position of that view, and the ID for that position. Remember that you can use your `Adapter`'s `getItem(int position)` method within any of those methods when you need the object the view actually represents.

`ViewPager`

Being able to swipe horizontally through full pages of content has been common behavior since before Android, but its prevalence (for example, the default launcher in each Android version) did not mean that it was supported by a native component. Instead, this pattern, which was originally referred to as "workspaces," was implemented directly without abstraction.

Fortunately, the `ViewPager` is now available, and it provides this behavior in a standardized way that's easy to use and populate. It is a part of the v4 support library (http://developer.android.com/tools/extras/support-library.html), so you can add it to any project that runs Android 1.6 or newer. A `ViewPager` takes a `PageAdapter` that supplies the views, and one of the most common uses is to actually provide fragments via the `FragmentPagerAdapter`. Fragments are covered later in this chapter and throughout the book.

Other Notable ViewGroups

You would be bored out of your mind if you had to read paragraphs about every single view group available. The fact is, there are many available, and those that were covered previously in the chapter are the main ones you will use. However, it's worth knowing of these others to avoid spending the time coding them yourself when they already exist:

`AbsoluteLayout`—Deprecated layout that was used in order to position views based on exact pixels. Do not use this layout, but be aware that it exists so that you can shame developers who do use it.

`AdapterViewAnimator`—Switches among views that are supplied by an `Adapter`, using an animation for the transition. Introduced in API level 11.

AdapterViewFlipper—Similar to `AdapterViewAnimator` but supports automatically changing the view based on a time interval (for example, for a slideshow). Introduced in API level 11.

AppWidgetHostView—Hosts app widgets, so you will probably only use this if you create a custom launcher.

DialerFilter—Hosts an `EditText` with an ID of `android.R.id.primary` and an `EditText` with an ID of `android.R.id.hint` as well as an optional `ImageView` with an ID of `android.R.id.icon` in order to provide an easy means of entering phone numbers (including letters that can be converted to numbers). You will probably never use this.

FragmentBreadCrumbs—Simplifies adding "breadcrumbs" (like displaying "Settings > Audio" as the user navigates deeper into content) to the UI. Introduced in API level 11.

GestureOverlayView—Exists on top of one or more other views in order to catch gestures on those views.

GridLayout—Organizes its children into a rectangular grid to easily align multiple views. Introduced in API level 14 but exists in the support library.

HorizontalScrollView—Wraps a single child view (usually a `ViewGroup`) in order to allow it to scroll horizontally when the content is larger than the view's visible dimensions.

ImageSwitcher—Switches between images with an animation (see `ViewSwitcher`).

MediaController—Contains views to control media such as play, pause, fast forward, and so on.

PagerTabStrip—Provides interactivity to a `PagerTitleStrip`. Included in the support library.

PagerTitleStrip—Indicates the current, previous, and next pages for a `ViewPager` but cannot be directly interacted with. Included in the support library.

ScrollView—Wraps a single child view (usually a `ViewGroup`) in order to allow it to scroll vertically when the content is larger than the view's visible dimensions.

SearchView—Provides a UI for allowing the user to search with the results coming from a `SearchProvider`. Introduced in API level 11.

SlidingDrawer—Holds two views: One is a handle and the other is the content. The handle can be tapped to show or hide the content, and it can also be dragged. This is the original app drawer in Android 1.x.

StackView—Stacks multiple views that can be swiped through. The views are provided by an `Adapter` and are offset to show when more are below the top view. This is most commonly used as an app widget, and it was introduced in API level 11.

TabHost—Hosts tabs and a single FrameLayout for the content of the currently active tab.

TabWidget—Lives within a TabHost and provides the tab event triggers.

TableLayout—Allows you to organize content in a tabular fashion, although you should generally use a GridLayout because it is more efficient.

TableRow—Represents a row in a TableLayout, although it is essentially just a LinearLayout.

TextSwitcher—Animates between two TextViews. This is really just a ViewSwitcher with a few helper methods.

ViewAnimator—Switches among views, using an animation.

ViewFlipper—Similar to ViewAnimator but supports automatically changing the view based on a time interval (for example, for a slideshow).

ViewSwitcher—Animates between two views, where one is shown at a time.

ZoomControls—Controls zoom. No, really. It provides zoom buttons with callbacks for handling the zoom events.

Fragments

One problem that plagued Android a bit early on was that there was no standardized way to encapsulate view logic for use across activities. This was not a major issue because one screen was typically represented by one activity and one layout; however, it started to become a problem when tablets became popular. Where you might display a list of news articles on the phone that you can tap to go to a full detail page, you would probably show that list on the left side of the tablet and the details on the right, so they're always both visible. That presented a challenge because your code to populate the list was likely to be living in one activity and the detail page code was in another, but the tablet was only ever showing one activity and needed the logic from both. Enter the Fragment.

Like Activity, Context, and Intent, Fragment is another one of those classes that is a bit tough to describe up front but quickly makes sense as you use it. Think of a fragment as a *chunk* of your UI, containing the code necessary to inflate or construct a layout as well as handle user interaction with it. The fragment might even load content from the web or other source. A fragment can be simple, such as a full-screen ImageView, perhaps with a caption, or it can be complex, such as a series of form elements containing all the logic to validate and submit form responses. In fact, a fragment does not even have to be used for UI; it can be used to encapsulate application behavior needed for activities. But don't worry, this is a book about design, so there's no need to boggle your mind on why you'd do that!

The Fragment Lifecycle

Like activities, fragments have a lifecycle. In fact, activities are closely tied to fragments, and the activity lifecycle influences the lifecycle of the fragment associated with it. First, the fragment runs through this series of lifecycle events in the order they are presented here:

`onAttach(Activity)`—Indicates the fragment is associated with an activity

`onCreate(Bundle)`—Initializes the fragment

`onCreateView(LayoutInflater, ViewGroup, Bundle)`—Returns the view associated with the fragment

`onActivityCreated(Bundle)`—Triggered to coincide with the activity's `onCreate()` method

`onStart()`—Triggered to coincide with the activity's `onStart()` method and displays the fragment

`onResume()`—Triggered to coincide with the activity's `onResume()` method and indicates the fragment can handle interaction

After the fragment has "resumed," it will stay in that state until a fragment operation modifies that fragment (such as if you are removing the fragment from the screen) or its activity is paused. At that point, it will run through this series of lifecycle events in the order presented:

`onPause()`—Triggered to coincide with the activity's `onPause()` method or when a fragment operation is modifying it

`onStop()`—Triggered to coincide with the activity's `onStop()` method or when a fragment operation is modifying it

`onDestroyView()`—Allows the fragment to release any resources associated with its view

`onDestroy()`—Allows the fragment to release any final resources

`onDetach()`—Gives the fragment one last chance to do something before it is disassociated from its activity

Giving Fragments Data

One of the great things about fragments is that the system manages them very well for you. Things like configuration changes (for example, orientation changes) are easily handled because fragments can save state and restore state. In order to do so, they must have a default constructor (that is, a constructor that has no parameters). So, how do you pass data to them if they require a default constructor? The standard way is via a static `newInstance()` method that sets up the fragment's arguments before it is attached to an activity. See Listing 3.3 for a simple example.

Listing 3.3 Passing Arguments to a Fragment and Using Them When Creating the View

```
public class TextViewFragment extends Fragment {

    /**
     * String to use as the key for the "text" argument
     */
    private static final String KEY_TEXT = "text";

    /**
     * Constructs a new TextViewFragment with the specified String
     *
     * @param text String to associated with this TextViewFragment
     * @return TextViewFragment with set arguments
     */
    public static TextViewFragment newInstance(String text) {
        TextViewFragment f = new TextViewFragment();

        Bundle args = new Bundle();
        args.putString(KEY_TEXT, text);
        f.setArguments(args);

        return f;
    }

    /**
     * Returns the String set in {@link #newInstance(String)}
     *
     * @return the String set in {@link #newInstance(String)}
     */
    public String getText() {
        return getArguments().getString(KEY_TEXT);
    }

    @Override
    public View onCreateView(LayoutInflater inflater, ViewGroup
➥container, Bundle savedInstanceState) {
        TextView tv = new TextView(getActivity());
        tv.setText(getText());
        return tv;
    }
}
```

You can see that the static `newInstance(String)` method creates the fragment using the default constructor and then it creates a new `Bundle` object, puts the text into that bundle, and assigns that bundle as the fragment's arguments. The bundle is maintained when the fragment is destroyed and will be automatically set for you if it's created again (for example, when a rotation triggers a configuration change, your fragment is destroyed, but a new one is created and the bundle is assigned to its arguments).

Obviously, using a fragment just for a `TextView` is contrived, but it illustrates how you can set data on a fragment that is retained across configuration changes. In doing this, you can easily separate your data from its presentation. Ideally, `onCreateView(LayoutInflater, ViewGroup, Bundle)` would inflate an XML layout, which might be different for landscape versus portrait. With your code designed in this way, the orientation change will just work with no extra effort on your part.

Summary

You've survived another dry chapter! Give yourself a pat on the back; you've almost made it to the good stuff. You should now have a solid understanding of how the `ViewGroup` class and its subclasses work as well as how to use fragments to create reusable layouts with display and handling logic contained within. Combining that with the knowledge from Chapter 2 and you know the most important aspects of getting your layouts on the screen exactly where you want them.

Next up, Chapter 4, "Adding App Graphics and Resources," will explain how to add graphics to these views and how to utilize resources in an efficient, reusable manner. That is the last chapter before diving into the real-life process of designing an app.

CHAPTER 4

ADDING APP GRAPHICS AND RESOURCES

As the final chapter of the first part of this book, this chapter teaches you how the resource system works in Android, including the use of graphics. One of the considerations when developing for Android is that there are so many different devices out there. You have to consider displays of various densities, screens of all sizes, whether a device has a hardware keyboard, what orientation it is held in, and even what language should be displayed. Fortunately, Android's resource system makes all this easy.

Introduction to Resources in Android

A solid understanding of Android's resource system is not only essential to developing good apps, it's vital to saving your sanity. If you had to programmatically check every feature of the device every time you did anything, your code would be a mess and you would lose sleep at night (assuming you get any now). To ensure a good user experience, you should generally make adjustments for things such as the size of the screen and the orientation of the device. By using resource "qualifiers," you can let Android take care of this for you.

A qualifier is a portion of a directory's name that marks its contents as being used for a specific situation; this is best illustrated with an example. Your Android project contains a `res` directory (resources) that can contain several other directories for each of the resource types. Your layouts go in a directory called `layout`. If you have a layout specifically for landscape orientation, you can create a directory in `res` called `layout-land`, where "land" designates it as being used for landscape orientations. If you have a layout called `main.xml` in either directory, Android automatically uses the version appropriate to the given device orientation.

Resource Qualifiers

Okay, so you can have a different layout for landscape and portrait orientations, but what else? Actually, there are a *lot* of qualifiers, and they can be applied to any resource directory. That means you can have the images or even strings change based on orientation. It's important to know what folders go in the `res` directory and what content they contain before diving into how that content can differ based on qualifiers. Here's a list of the folder names:

`animator`—Property animations defined in XML.

`anim`—View animations defined in XML.

`color`—State lists of colors defined in XML. State lists are covered later in this chapter.

`drawable`—Drawable assets that can be defined in XML or image files (PNG, GIF, or JPG).

`layout`—Layouts defined in XML.

`menu`—Menus such as the action bar menu defined in XML.

`raw`—Any raw files such as audio files and custom bytecode.

`values`—Various simple values defined in XML, such as strings, floats, and integer colors.

`xml`—Any XML files you wish to read at runtime.

By no means are all of these required in any given app. In fact, it is not uncommon to only have `drawable`, `layout`, and `values` directories in an app, although you will nearly always have multiple `drawable` folders to accommodate different densities. These folders are generated for you when needed (for example, creating an XML menu in ADT creates the `menu` folder), but you can also create them yourself. For every file in these directories, Android's build tools will automatically create a reference in the `R` class (short for references) that is an `int` identifier, which can be used by a variety of methods. Chances are you have seen and used this class.

Take a look at Table 4.1 to see the resource qualifiers you can use. These are listed in the order that Android requires, meaning that if you use more than one, you must list them in the same order they appear in this table.

Table 4.1 A Complete List Of Resource Qualifiers

Qualifier Type	Examples	Description

Mobile country code
Mobile network code
	`mcc310`
	`mcc440`
	`mcc310-`
	➥`mnc800`
		The MCC (Mobile Country Code) can be used with or without an accompanying MNC (Mobile Network Code). Typically, you will not use these qualifiers, but they are occasionally used to provide country-specific legal information or carrier-specific data.
		For a list of mobile country codes and mobile network codes, see http://www.itu.int/dms_pub/itu-t/opb/sp/T-SP-E.212B-2011-PDF-E.pdf.

Language
Region
	`en`
	`en-rUS`
	`es`
	`es-rMX`
		The language is specified by two digits and is most commonly used for strings in order to easily support localization. You might also use the language qualifier for drawables where the text is part of the image. You can specify the region along with the language (but not separately) by using a lowercase *r* and the two-letter code.
		For a list of country codes, see this page: http://www.loc.gov/standards/iso639-2/php/code_list.php.
		For a list of regions, see this page: http://www.iso.org/iso/iso-3166-1_decoding_table.

Qualifier Type	Examples	Description
Smallest width	sw320dp sw480dp	This qualifier was added in API level 13. The smallest width is actually the smallest available dimension, regardless of orientation. For example, a device that is medium density and 320px by 480px has a smallest width of 320dp (density and the difference between px and dp is explained later in this chapter), regardless of whether it is in portrait or landscape orientation. It is also important to note that the system-level UI adjusts this amount. For example, some devices use part of their screen for the system buttons (back, home, and recent apps). The remaining portion of the screen not used for that UI is what determines the smallest width. In other words, the smallest width is the smallest dimension of the screen space available for your app to use.
Available width	w480dp w720dp	This qualifier was added in API level 13. Available width specifies the minimum available width in the current orientation at which the resource should be used. That means the resources in a given directory might be used while in landscape mode but not portrait mode.
Available height	h720dp h1024dp	This qualifier was added in API level 13. Available height works the same as available width, but is specific to the height.
Screen size	small normal large xlarge	The screen size qualifier allows you to specify "buckets" for different sizes and has been available since API level 4 (although xlarge was added in API level 9). To simplify these sizes, you can think of small as being smaller than a normal phone, normal as being a typical phone-sized device, large as being a 7" tablet, and xlarge as being a 10" tablet. More specifically: small—Typically low-density QVGA screens with a minimum size of roughly 320×426dp. normal—Nearly all phone-sized devices; these are usually at least 320×470dp. large—Screens with a minimum size of about 480×640dp. xlarge—Screens with a minimum size of about 720×960dp. Note that the system will look for resources that have a smaller qualifier but never a larger qualifier. In other words, a device that is large will first look for large, then normal, then small, but it will never look at the xlarge resources.

Qualifier Type	Examples	Description
Screen aspect	long notlong	Screen aspect is independent of the device's orientation and specifies whether the device is more square (notlong) or rectangular (long). For example, a 3:2 or 4:3 device is notlong but a 16:9 device is long.
Orientation	port land	Specifies resources for portrait or landscape orientation.
UI mode	car desk appliance television	This qualifier was added in API level 8. car—The device is in a car dock (commonly for navigation). desk—The device is in a desk dock. appliance—The device is being used as an appliance without a display. television—The device is displaying on a television (added in API level 13).
Night mode	night notnight	This qualifier was added in API level 8. Specifies whether the device is in nighttime mode or daytime (notnight) mode.
Density	ldpi mdpi hdpi xhdpi nodpi tvdpi	Specifies the density of the screen (covered in depth later in the chapter). ldpi—Low density (120dpi) mdpi—Medium density (160dpi) hdpi—High density (240dpi) xhdpi—Extra-high density (320dpi) nodpi—Not density-specific tvdpi—TV-specific density (roughly 213dpi) These qualifiers are nearly always used with drawables in order to provide differently sized assets for different densities.
Touchscreen type	finger notouch	Specifies whether or not the device has a touchscreen (finger).
Keyboard availability	keysexposed keyshidden keyssoft	Specifies the status of the keyboard: keysexposed—The device has a keyboard available (that is, the keys are exposed to the user) whether the keyboard is software or hardware. keyshidden—The device has a hidden hardware keyboard and the software keyboard is not enabled. keyssoft—The device has a software keyboard enabled (regardless of visibility).

Qualifier Type	Examples	Description

Hardware keyboard type	`nokeys`
	`qwerty`
	`12key`
		Specifies the type of hardware keyboard on the device (whether it is extended or not):
		`nokeys`—No hardware keyboard.
		`qwerty`—A qwerty keyboard exists.
		`12key`—A 12-key keyboard exists.

Navigation key availability	`navexposed` `navhidden`	Specifies whether the navigation keys are available (exposed) or hidden.

Primary non-touch navigation method	`nonav`
	`dpad`
	`trackball`
	`wheel`
		Specifies the type of navigation, other than the touch screen, that the device has:
		`nonav`—The device has only the touch screen for navigation.
		`dpad`—The device has a directional-pad (D-pad) available.
		`trackball`—The device has a trackball available.
		`wheel`—The device has one or more directional wheels available.

Platform version	`v4`
	`v8`
	`v11`
		Specifies the minimum platform version of the device. This is most commonly used to have assets blend better with a given platform version (for example, the notification icons have changed over time, so many apps provide version-specific images). This can also be used to provide strings based on the version such as an explanation of how to add a widget. The device will look for the highest version qualifier that is equal to or less than its version, falling back on qualifiers that aren't version specific.

Regardless of how many or how few qualifiers you use, the `R` class will only have one reference to a given set of resources. For example, you might have a file at the path `res/drawable-xhdpi/header.png` and the reference would be `R.drawable.header`. As you can probably see, the format is `R.[resource type without qualifiers].[file name without extension]`. Perhaps this header file also contains text, so you have language-specific versions such as `res/drawable-es-xhdpi/header.png`. Within the Java portion of your app, you will always refer to the resource as `R.drawable.header`. If the device's language is set to Spanish, the reference automatically points to the Spanish version, so you do not have to change anything in your code. If the device is an HDPI device, it would first look in the `drawable-hdpi` directory before the `drawable-xhdpi` directory. When you refer to a resource like `R.drawable.header`, you're asking the system to use whichever header drawable most fits the current device configuration.

warning

ALWAYS SPECIFY DEFAULTS One extremely important thing to note is that you need to specify defaults. With the exception of density qualifiers, all qualifiers are exclusive. For example, you can create a "hello" string. Within `res/values-es/strings.xml`, you define "hello" to be "hola" and within `res/values-en/strings.xml` you define "hello" as "hello." Everything seems good, and you can use that reference in your code as `R.string.hello`.

You test it on your English device, and it works correctly. You test it on your Spanish device, and it works correctly as well. However, when you test it on your Russian device, it crashes. That's because both of those qualifiers exclude Russian. Because you have not defined a Russian-specific values directory with that string in it, the system falls back on the values directory with no qualifier. Nothing is there, so the reference is invalid.

To avoid this situation, make sure your default directory (that is, the one without qualifiers) contains all references. The one exception is with density-specific assets, which Android is able to scale for you.

Understanding Density

Density is one of the most important aspects of an Android device to understand when it comes to design. Early Android devices had approximately 160 dots per inch (dpi)—and that is considered medium density (MDPI) now. Android 1.6 added support for both low density (LDPI or 120dpi) and high density (HDPI or 240dpi). Android 2.2 added extra high density (XHDPI or 320dpi) to the mix. Continuing the march toward higher and higher densities, Android 4.1 introduced extra, extra high density (XXHDPI or 480dpi).

What do all these letters and numbers mean to you? A given image will appear larger with a lower density and smaller with a higher density. If you take a piece of paper and draw a vertical line and a horizontal line, splitting it into four pieces, a single piece (pixel) will take up a quarter of the paper. If you divide each of those quarters into four pieces, then a single piece (pixel) is one fourth of the size that it was. It appears physically smaller even though the total size of the paper (the screen) has not changed.

Fortunately, Android makes handling this easy for you. Instead of specifying dimensions in raw pixels, you will use either density independent pixels (referred to as dip or dp) or scale independent pixels (sip or sp). Density independent pixels are based on MDPI, so one dp is one px at medium density. The difference between one sp and one dp is that sp takes into account the user's preferred font size. Therefore, all font sizes should be specified in sp and all other dimensions should be in dp.

There are a lot of numbers and terms to remember, so it can be helpful to break this down more. If you design for XHDPI first using units divisible by four, your design will easily translate to HDPI and MDPI. For example, you might decide that your default padding is going to be 16px for XHDPI. That means it will be 12px for HDPI and 8px for MDPI (which is also 8dp). Approach your design with the 2:3:4 ratio in mind; that's the ratio of MDPI pixels to HDPI pixels to XHDPI pixels. You will see this more in the coming chapters.

Supported Image Files

Android supports JPEGs, PNGs, and GIFs natively. Typically you should use JPEGs for photos that have already been compressed as JPEGs and PNGs for everything else. See Figure 4.1 for an example of heavy JPEG compression compared to no compression. Most of your UI should be done with PNGs because they are lossless (although they are compressed), so they don't suffer from the compression artifacts that JPEGs suffer from and they will give you the sharpest possible results. The PNG format also supports alpha transparency, so that means you can have pixels that are partially transparent, which is helpful for softening the edges of images. Although GIF is supported, PNG is a better file format and should be used instead.

Figure 4.1 Heavy JPEG compression on the left; no compression on the right

> note
>
> **PNG COMPRESSION** The Android build tools will automatically compress the PNGs by stripping them of all metadata and reducing the bit depth where possible. For example, an image might be converted to an 8-bit PNG with a custom color palette in order to reduce its file size. This reduces the overall size of your APK, but it does not affect the size of the image once it has been decoded.

Nine-Patch Images

Oftentimes, you do not know ahead of time how large an image should be. For example, a button will need the ability to be different sizes to accommodate different languages and text labels. Even if you tell it to be as wide as the screen, there are still many possible widths. It would be a huge amount of work to create an image for every possible width, and your app will look terrible if you hard-code the button to a specific size in pixels. The nine-patch image solves this problem.

If you think of a typical button, there are nine pieces to it: the four corners, the four sides (left, right, top, and bottom), and the center area where the text typically goes. To support a wider button, the top, center, and bottom portions have to be duplicated. For a taller button, the left, center, and right portions would be duplicated. This allows you to preserve the corners and edges while expanding the content area. See Figure 4.2 for an example of how a nine-patch can be resized.

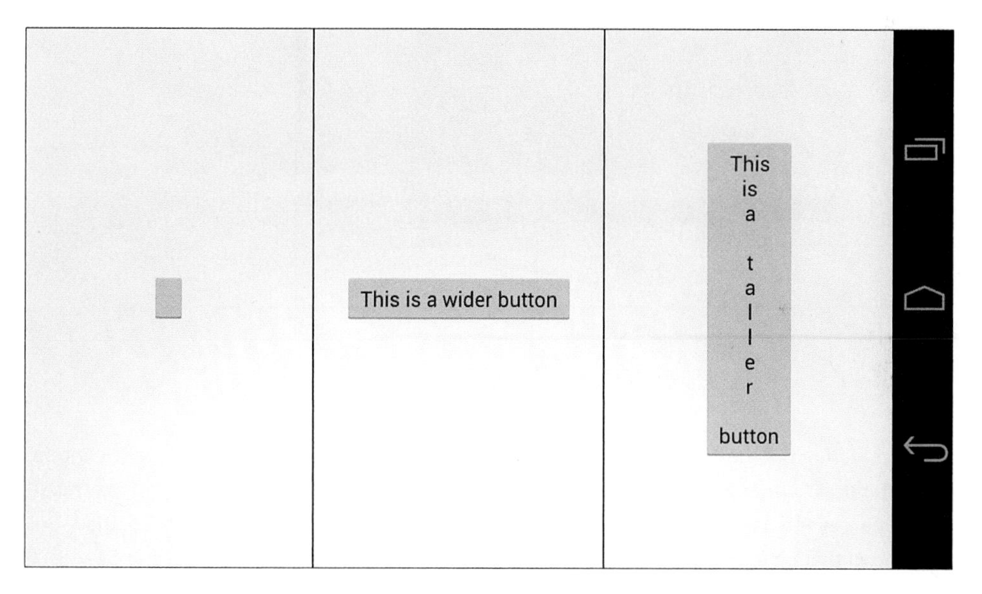

Figure 4.2 An example of a nine-patch accommodating different sizes

A nine-patch is actually just a PNG where the outside pixels are either fully transparent or fully black. The left and top of the image can contain black pixels to describe how to enlarge the image. Figure 4.3 highlights the "stretchable" area in green.

Figure 4.3 A nine-patch image with the stretchable area in green.

Another feature of nine-patch images is that the right and bottom of the image specify content areas. In the simplest case, you can think of the black part as where content goes and the transparent part as the padding. When you set a view's background to a nine-patch image, the padding of that image will be applied automatically; however, you can still override it. See Figure 4.4's purple area to understand where content can go. When the content is larger than this area, the image stretches along the parts that were highlighted green in Figure 4.3.

One last thing to note is that you can specify nine-patch images in XML. The image itself is still a standard nine-patch PNG, but the XML file allows you to specifically enable or disable dithering, which is a way of adding "noise" to an image in order to reduce artifacts such as banding, which is caused by low bitrate displays. See Listing 4.1 for an example of this.

Figure 4.4 The purple areas are where content can go, as defined by the right and bottom black pixels.

Listing 4.1 Specifying a Nine-Patch with XML

```
<?xml version="1.0" encoding="utf-8"?>
<nine-patch xmlns:android="http://schemas.android.com/apk/res/android"
    android:dither="true"
    android:src="@drawable/your_ninepatch" />
```

XML Drawables

In addition to standard image files, Android supports a variety of XML drawables (the term "drawable" refers simply to something that can be drawn to the screen). Some of these drawables are ways of using multiple image files for one resource; others allow you to actually specify colors within XML. A few you may never need, but some will prove extremely valuable, so it is worth knowing what is available to you.

Each type of drawable that can be defined in XML uses a different root node (which tells Android which class's `inflate` method to call). They are all inflated to specific drawables, but you can interact with them via the abstract `Drawable` class. Drawables that display more than one drawable define each one with the `item` tag. The `item` tag can typically take offsets (`android:left`, `android:top`, `android:right`, and `android:bottom`), which is useful for specific visual effects and for supporting images of different sizes.

Layer List

A layer list is an array of drawables defined in XML that creates a `LayerDrawable` instance when used. Each drawable can be offset on the left, top, right, and/or bottom by a different amount. The drawables are drawn in the order they are declared (just like views) and will be scaled to fit the available space. See Listing 4.2 for a sample layer list.

Listing 4.2 Example of a Simple Layer List

```
<?xml version="1.0" encoding="utf-8"?>
<layer-list xmlns:android="http://schemas.android.com/apk/res/android" >

    <item android:drawable="@drawable/example_green_screen"/>
    <item
        android:drawable="@drawable/example_red_screen"
        android:left="50dp"
        android:top="50dp">
    </item>

</layer-list>
```

If you do not want the drawables to be scaled, you can use gravity, like in Listing 4.3. Using gravity allows you to define the anchor point of the drawable. For example, you might be using a drawable as the background of a full screen view. The default behavior is to scale to the size of the view, but you can instead specify a gravity to align the image to a specific location such as the right side of the view. Notice that this requires a separate bitmap node that contains the gravity; the gravity does not go within the `item` tag itself.

Listing 4.3 Example of a Layer List Using Gravity

```
<?xml version="1.0" encoding="utf-8"?>
<layer-list xmlns:android="http://schemas.android.com/apk/res/android" >

    <item>
        <bitmap
            android:gravity="center"
```

```
            android:src="@drawable/example_green_screen" />
    </item>
    <item
        android:left="50dp"
        android:top="50dp">
        <bitmap
            android:gravity="center"
            android:src="@drawable/example_red_screen" />
    </item>

</layer-list>
```

For a comparison of the difference between letting the `LayerListDrawable` scale and keeping its size by the use of gravity, see Figure 4.5. Notice that the device with the green screen on the left is significantly larger than the others due to no offset and no gravity.

Figure 4.5 The left image is from Listing 4.2; the right is from Listing 4.3.

State List

A `StateListDrawable`, defined by the selector XML node, allows you to specify different drawables for different states. For example, a standard button will have different appearances based on whether it is enabled, focused, pressed, and so on. You can specify as few or as many drawables as you like, and you can also combine states (for example, show a particular drawable only if it is both focused and checked). See Figure 4.6 for an example of different images based on different states. You can use colors in a selector as well. You might decide that your button's text should normally be white but it should be gray when it is being pressed.

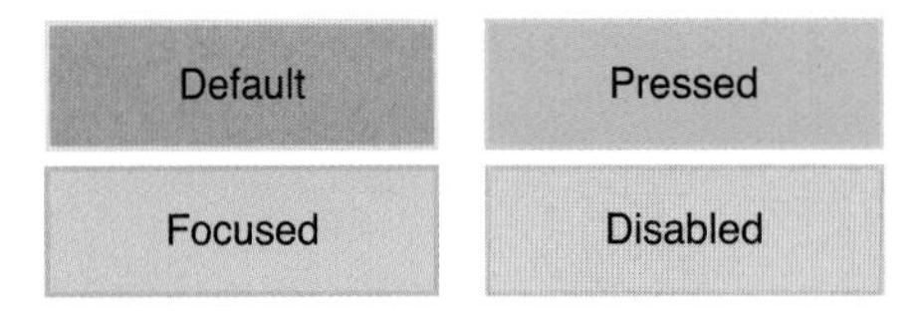

Figure 4.6 Examples of different appearances a drawable might have for each state

It is important to note that the drawable used will be the first that matches, which might not be the best match. For example, if the first item requires a state of pressed and the second item requires both pressed and enabled, the second item will never be used because any image that matches pressed, whether enabled or not, would match the first item immediately. Therefore, you should put the most specific states first and your last state should contain no state requirements.

Here is the list of states:

> **`android:state_activated`**—Added in API 11, this indicates the item is the activated selection. For example, on a tablet where you have a list of articles on the left and the full article on the right, the list item on the left that represents the article being displayed on the right would be activated. All other items in that list would be false for being activated.
>
> **`android:state_checkable`**—Indicates whether the item can be checked. This is really only useful when a view can change between being checkable and not checkable.
>
> **`android:state_checked`**—Indicates whether the item is currently checked.
>
> **`android:state_enabled`**—Indicates whether the item is enabled or disabled. This is commonly combined with other states.
>
> **`android:state_focused`**—Indicates whether the item is focused. Focus usually happens after an input has been tapped, such as an `EditText`, or after navigating to a given view by means other than touch (for example, a directional pad or trackball). Drawables that represent a focused state usually have a glow or generally highlighted appearance.
>
> **`android:state_hovered`**—Added in API 14, this indicates whether the item is currently being hovered over by the cursor. Typically, this is visually indicated in the same way as focus.
>
> **`android:state_pressed`**—Indicates whether the item is being pressed. This state happens when the item is clicked or touched and is usually shown by a visually depressed state (like a button being pushed in) or a brightened/colored appearance.

android:state_selected—Indicates that the item is currently selected. This is very similar to focus but slightly more specific. A particular view group (for example, ListView) can have focus while a specific child is selected.

android:state_window_focused—Indicates whether the app's window is focused. This is generally true unless it is obstructed, like when the notification drawer has been pulled down.

See Listing 4.4 for a simple example of how to use a StateListDrawable by defining a selector in XML.

Listing 4.4 Example of a Selector (StateListDrawable)

```
<?xml version="1.0" encoding="utf-8"?>
<selector xmlns:android="http://schemas.android.com/apk/res/android">

    <!-- Shown when the button is enabled but the window is not
➥focused -->
    <item android:drawable="@drawable/btn_default_normal_holo_light"
        android:state_enabled="true"
        android:state_window_focused="false"
    />

    <!-- Shown when the button is disabled and the window is not
➥focused -->
    <item android:drawable="@drawable/btn_default_disabled_holo_light"
        android:state_enabled="false"
        android:state_window_focused="false"
    />

    <!-- Shown when the button is pressed -->
    <item android:drawable="@drawable/btn_default_pressed_holo_light"
        android:state_pressed="true"
    />

    <!-- Shown when the button is enabled and focused -->
    <item android:drawable="@drawable/btn_default_focused_holo_light"
        android:state_enabled="true"
        android:state_focused="true"
    />

    <!-- Shown when the button is enabled but not focused -->
    <item android:drawable="@drawable/btn_default_normal_holo_light"
        android:state_enabled="true"
    />
```

```
    <!-- Shown when the button is focused but not enabled -->
    <item android:drawable="@drawable/
➥btn_default_disabled_focused_holo_light"
        android:state_focused="true"
    />

    <!-- Shown for all other cases -->
    <item android:drawable="@drawable/
➥btn_default_disabled_holo_light"/>

</selector>
```

Level List

A `LevelListDrawable` manages any number of drawables, assigning each one to a range of values. You can set the current level of the `LevelListDrawable` with `Drawable`'s `setLevel(int)` method. Whichever drawable fits in that range will then be used. This is particularly useful for visual indicators where you want to show some difference based on a value but do not want to worry about the exact image to display in your code. The battery indicator is a good example of this. You know that the range is from 0 to 100 percent, but your code does not need to know whether there is a different image for 38 percent versus 39 percent. Instead, you just set the level of the `LevelListDrawable` and the correct drawable will automatically be used. See Listing 4.5 for an example of re-creating the typical battery indicator.

Listing 4.5 A Level List for Indicating Battery Level

```
<?xml version="1.0" encoding="utf-8"?>
<level-list xmlns:android="http://schemas.android.com/apk/res/android">
    <item android:maxLevel="4" android:drawable="@drawable/
➥stat_sys_battery_0" />
    <item android:maxLevel="15" android:drawable="@drawable/
➥stat_sys_battery_15" />
    <item android:maxLevel="35" android:drawable="@drawable/
➥stat_sys_battery_28" />
    <item android:maxLevel="49" android:drawable="@drawable/
➥stat_sys_battery_43" />
    <item android:maxLevel="60" android:drawable="@drawable/stat_sys_
➥battery_57" />
    <item android:maxLevel="75" android:drawable="@drawable/stat_sys_
➥battery_71" />
    <item android:maxLevel="90" android:drawable="@drawable/stat_sys_
➥battery_85" />
    <item android:maxLevel="100" android:drawable="@drawable/stat_sys_
➥battery_100" />
</level-list>
```

TransitionDrawable

A `TransitionDrawable` allows you to specify two drawables that you can then crossfade between. Two methods `startTransition(int)` and `reverseTransition(int)` allow you to control the transition between the two drawables. Both methods take an `int`, which defines the duration in milliseconds.

This is not a particularly common drawable because crossfading is often done with views, but it is a fast and efficient way to transition between two drawables and has the advantage of only requiring one view. See Listing 4.6 for an example.

Listing 4.6 An Example of a Simple `TransitionDrawable`

```
<?xml version="1.0" encoding="utf-8"?>
<transition xmlns:android="http://schemas.android.com/apk/res/android" >

    <item android:drawable="@drawable/first_drawable"/>
    <item android:drawable="@drawable/second_drawable"/>

</transition>
```

InsetDrawable

An `InsetDrawable` allows you to inset, or push in, another drawable. It is useful when you have a drawable that you would like to appear smaller than a view or to appear padded. This might seem useless because you could just add transparent pixels to an image to accomplish the same thing, but what if you want to use that same image in one place without that extra spacing and in another with it? See Listing 4.7 for a simple example that insets a drawable by 10dp on all sides.

Listing 4.7 An Example of a Simple `InsetDrawable`

```
<?xml version="1.0" encoding="utf-8"?>
<inset
    xmlns:android="http://schemas.android.com/apk/res/android"
    android:drawable="@drawable/padding_bg"
    android:insetTop="10dp"
    android:insetRight="10dp"
    android:insetBottom="10dp"
    android:insetLeft="10dp" />
```

ClipDrawable

A ClipDrawable takes a single drawable and clips, or cuts off, that drawable at a point determined by the level. This is most frequently used for progress bars. The drawable that this ClipDrawable wraps would be the full progress bar (what the user would see at 100 percent). By using setLevel(int), your code can reveal more and more of the bar until it is complete. The level is from 0 to 10,000, where 0 does not show the image at all and 10,000 shows it completely without clipping.

You can specify whether the clipping is vertical or horizontal as well as the gravity. For example, a ClipDrawable with gravity set to left, clipOrientation set to horizontal, and its level set to 5,000 will draw the left half of the image. See Listing 4.8 for an example.

Listing 4.8 An Example of a Simple ClipDrawable

```
<?xml version="1.0" encoding="utf-8"?>
<clip xmlns:android="http://schemas.android.com/apk/res/android"
    android:drawable="@drawable/drawable_to_clip"
    android:clipOrientation="horizontal"
    android:gravity="left" />
```

ScaleDrawable

A ScaleDrawable allows you to use setLevel(int) to scale the drawable at runtime. This is sometimes also used for progress bars as well as general cases in which you want to scale a drawable based on some other value.

You specify a scaleWidth and a scaleHeight, which is the size of the drawable when the level is 10,000. For example, you can specify those both as 100 percent and set the level to 5,000 and you will have a drawable displayed at 50-percent width and 50-percent height. See Listing 4.9 for an example of a ScaleDrawable.

Listing 4.9 An Example of a Simple ScaleDrawable

```
<?xml version="1.0" encoding="utf-8"?>
<scale xmlns:android="http://schemas.android.com/apk/res/android"
    android:drawable="@drawable/drawable_to_scale"
    android:scaleGravity="center"
    android:scaleHeight="50%"
    android:scaleWidth="50%"
    android:useIntrinsicSizeAsMinimum="false" />
```

ShapeDrawable

A ShapeDrawable is a rectangle, oval, line, or ring that is defined in XML. If it is a rectangle, you can define rounded corners. If it is a ring, you can specify the innerRadius (that is, the radius of the hole) or innerRadiusRatio (the ratio of the shape's width to the inner radius) and the thickness or thicknessRatio. For all shapes, you can specify a stroke (that is, the line around the shape), solid fill color, or gradient fill colors, size, and padding.

You can use a variety of attributes to create your ShapeDrawable. See Table 4.2 for a complete list of the root node types and the corresponding attributes available.

Table 4.2 Attributes for ShapeDrawables

Root Node	Attribute	Description
shape	shape	Specifies the shape of the drawable—one of rectangle, oval, line, or ring.
shape	innerRadius	The radius of the center hole in a ring; ignored for other shape types.
shape	innerRadiusRatio	The radius of the center hole in a ring as a ratio of the shapes width to the inner radius; ignored for other shape types.
shape	thickness	The thickness of the ring; ignored for other shape types.
shape	thicknessRatio	The thickness of the ring as a ratio of the ring's width; ignored for other shape types.
shape	useLevel	When set to true, this shape can be used as a level list; you should generally set this to false because the level defaults to 0 (meaning the shape will not be shown).
corners	radius	Radius of all the corners of the drawable. This is often specified and then overridden by each of the corner-specific attributes; applicable to rectangles only.
corners	topLeftRadius	Radius of the top-left corner; applicable to rectangles only.
corners	topRightRadius	Radius of the top-right corner; applicable to rectangles only.
corners	bottomLeftRadius	Radius of the bottom-left corner; applicable to rectangles only.
corners	bottomRightRadius	Radius of the bottom-right corner; applicable to rectangles only.

Root Node	Attribute	Description
`gradient`	`angle`	The angle of the gradient in degrees, where 0 is from left to right and 90 is from bottom to top. Must be a multiple of 45.
`gradient`	`centerX`	The relative position for the center of the gradient along the x axis from 0.0 to 1.0. For example, 0.4 represents 40 percent from the left.
`gradient`	`centerY`	The relative position for the center of the gradient along the y axis, from 0.0 to 1.0. For example, 0.4 represents 40 percent from the top.
`gradient`	`centerColor`	The optional center color of the gradient.
`gradient`	`endColor`	The color that the gradient ends with.
`gradient`	`gradientRadius`	The radius of the gradient when using a radial gradient. Note that radial gradients often suffer from significant artifacting on low-quality devices, especially if the display has a low bit depth.
`gradient`	`startColor`	The color that the gradient starts with.
`gradient`	`type`	Type of gradient—one of linear, radial, and sweep.
`padding`	`left`	Left padding. Padding allows you to inset the `ShapeDrawable`.
`padding`	`top`	Top padding.
`padding`	`right`	Right padding.
`padding`	`bottom`	Bottom padding.
`size`	`height`	Height of the shape. Note that when a `ShapeDrawable` is used as the background of a view, it will scale to fill the view. If you wish it to be exactly the height and width specified, put it in an `ImageView` with `scaleType` set to `center`.
`size`	`width`	Width of the shape.
`solid`	`color`	Color to completely fill the shape with.
`stroke`	`dashGap`	Spacing between each dash (requires `dashWidth` to be set).
`stroke`	`dashWidth`	Width of each dash (requires `dashGap` to be set).
`stroke`	`color`	Color of the stroke line.
`stroke`	`width`	Thickness of the stroke line.

note

SPECIFYING ROUNDED CORNERS If you do specify rounded corners for your rectangle, you must specify all of them as rounded initially. In cases where you only want some of the corners rounded, your code should look like this (assuming you want the bottom corners to not be rounded and the top to have a radius of 8dp):

```
<corners
    android:radius="1dp"
    android:bottomLeftRadius="0dp"
    android:bottomRightRadius="0dp"
    android:topLeftRadius="8dp"
    android:topRightRadius="8dp" />
```

Notice that all corners are initially set to 1dp before being set to 0dp or another value.

As you can see, `ShapeDrawable` has a large number of attributes, which makes it very versatile. It is often a better option than providing multiple density-specific nine-patches, with the possible exception of gradients, where a graphics program will give you far more control.

Other Resources

In addition to visual resources, you can also specify many other resources in XML. You will see these throughout rest of the book, but it's a good idea to overview them now.

Strings

You should specify all user-facing strings in XML. Typically, you put these all in a file called `strings.xml` in `res/values`, although you can call it something else. Putting your strings into an XML file will allow you to easily localize your app at any point, even if you do not intend to in the first version. In addition, it will allow you to limit your vocabulary by reusing strings, which will make your app more accessible to everyone, especially those with a limited understanding of the language that it is in. See Listing 4.10 for a sample `strings` file containing a "hello" string and an "intro_paragraph" string.

Listing 4.10 An Example of a `strings` File

```
<?xml version="1.0" encoding="utf-8"?>
<resources>
    <string name="hello">Hello</string>
    <string name="intro_paragraph">Welcome to the greatest
➥application in the world!</string>
</resources>
```

At some point, you might decide to support Spanish, so you add a `strings.xml` file in `res/values-es` that looks like Listing 4.11.

Listing 4.11 A Spanish Version of the `strings` File

```
<?xml version="1.0" encoding="utf-8"?>
<resources>
    <string name="hello">Hola</string>
    <string name="intro_paragraph">Bienvenidos a la mejor
➥aplicación en el mundo!</string>
</resources>
```

In most cases, you will refer to strings in your layouts, setting the text for a `TextView` in XML, but you can also set it in code. Further, the `Context` class (which `Activity` extends) has a `getString(int)` method, where passing it the resource identifier for the string you desire (for example, `R.string.hello`) will return the applicable string ("Hello" or "Hola," depending on the device's language). The `getString(int)` method in `Context` is actually just a convenience method for calling `getResources().getString(int)`.

These strings also support substitutions. By including `%s` in the string, you can then call the `getString(int, Object...)` method to substitute values. For example, if the "hello" string was actually "Hello, %s" then you could call `getString(int, "Andy")`, which would give you either "Hello, Andy" or "Hola, Andy" (depending on device's language). You can include multiple substitutions, and they do not need to be at the end of the string.

You can also specify plural versions of strings. For example, English treats the number one specially (for example, you would say "word" when referring to a single word but for all other amounts, including zero, you say "words"). There are other languages that treat other numbers in different ways. Using the `plurals` tag, you can easily support these. The supported quantities are `zero`, `one`, `two`, `few`, `many`, and `other`. These quantities are based on grammar requirements. Because English only has a special requirement for single numbers, a case for `zero` or `few` would never be used. See Listing 4.12 for a simple example.

Listing 4.12 A `strings` File Containing a Plural String

```
<?xml version="1.0" encoding="utf-8"?>
<resources>
    <plurals name="child_count">
        <item quantity="one">One child</item>
        <item quantity="other">%s children</item>
    </plurals>
</resources>
```

In order to use the "child_count" string, you would call one of getQuantityString(int, int) (for retrieving a string with no substitution), getQuantityString(int, int, Object...) (for retrieving a string with substitution), or getQuantityText(int, int) (for retrieving a CharSequence). For example, you might call getQuantityString(R.plurals.child_count, 7) to get "7 children" back. Notice that it is R.plurals not R.string because of the XML node name.

Arrays

You can define arrays in XML, which is most often helpful for defining sets of data, such as for populating a Spinner or a ListView. When defining a string array, you use the string-array XML node with item child nodes. See Listing 4.13 for an example.

Listing 4.13 A Resources File Containing a String Array

```
<?xml version="1.0" encoding="utf-8"?>
<resources>
    <string-array name="sample_array">
        <item>First</item>
        <item>Second</item>
        <item>Third</item>
    </string-array>
</resources>
```

If you want to access the string array in code, you can use the getStringArray(int) method of Resources. The resource identifier in this case would be R.array.sample_array. Android also supports integer arrays (using the integer-array node) as well as TypedArrays (using the array node).

Colors

All of your colors should be specified in XML to ensure consistency and make design changes easy to propagate throughout the app. Colors are specified as alpha, red, green, and blue components in hex with two digits each. Although you can specify your colors as AARRGGBB, RRGGBB, ARGB, or RGB, it is best to be consistent, usually sticking with AARRGGBB. You can also use the Color class to use predefined colors and create colors from individual components. To use colors in code, you will typically use the getColor(int) method of Resources. Usually, you will specify your colors in res/values/colors.xml, but the name is a convention. Listing 4.14 shows an example of a simple resource file containing two colors: One refers to a system color and the other is specified in hex. When possible, it's a good idea to use names that are reflective of the intent of the colors. For example, calling a color "primary_accent_color" rather than "bright_blue" means that you can continue to use that name even if the design changes from blue to green.

Listing 4.14 A `colors.xml` File Containing Two Colors

```
<?xml version="1.0" encoding="utf-8"?>
<resources>
    <color name="black">@android:color/black</color>
    <color name="painfully_bright_red">#FFFF0000</color>
</resources>
```

Dimensions

Dimensions are yet another value you can define in XML, and they are far more valuable than they would appear at first glance. For example, you could define three primary font sizes in a `dimens.xml` file that you store in `res/values`. When you test the app on a 10" tablet, you would likely find those font sizes a little small. Instead of having to redefine all the `TextViews`, you could easily just add a new configuration-specific `dimens.xml` file. You can also use these values when using custom views to work with precise dimensions without having to worry about calculating pixels based on density yourself. See Listing 4.15 for a sample `dimens.xml` file.

Listing 4.15 A Simple dimens.xml File

```
<?xml version="1.0" encoding="utf-8"?>
<resources>
    <dimen name="default_padding">10dp</dimen>
    <dimen name="text_size_large">22sp</dimen>
    <dimen name="text_size_medium">18sp</dimen>
    <dimen name="text_size_small">14sp</dimen>
    <dimen name="text_size_tiny">12sp</dimen>
</resources>
```

Animations

Animations can be specified in XML as well as the resources that have been discussed so far; however, they are not covered here because they will be covered in depth in Chapter 9, "Further Improving the App."

Summary

The value of understanding Android's resource system cannot be overstated. You should never hard-code any user-facing strings, dimensions, or any other value that can be specified in resources. Even if you never expect to support a language other than your native language or a device other than what you have in your pocket, you should follow the best practices of properly using the resource system; your code will be cleaner for it. What's more, should you decide to support other device configurations, you'll be quite glad you did.

This marks the end of the first part of the book. You now have a strong foundational knowledge of Android's overall design, views, view groups, and the resource system. Next up, it's time to get started on a real-world app with brainstorms, wireframes, and flowcharts.

CHAPTER 5

STARTING A NEW APP

This chapter marks the start of the real process behind designing and developing an app. Here, you will take a goal-driven approach, defining exactly what you are trying to accomplish to make sure each subsequent decision enforces your goals. This chapter is focused on the user experience (or UX) and information hierarchy to provide a solid foundation for the app.

Defining Goals

The most important part of creating a new app is deciding on goals. What are the goals of the users who actually use the app and what are the goals of the app from a product perspective? A surprising number of apps are designed without strongly defined goals. Typically, this process starts out okay but becomes challenging as specific design decisions are being made. What buttons should be included on a given screen if you do not know the actual goal of the app? Once you have defined the goals, you can much more easily ensure that each decision along the way, especially UX decisions, will cater to those goals. It does not matter how beautifully you have designed and developed an app if it has a lack of focus, leading to user frustration.

User Goals

Starting out with user goals is a great way to get in the mindset of a user and decide what is really important in the app. The challenge is making sure you are defining goals and not tasks. For example, a task for a new Twitter app might be to be able to "read tweets in my timeline" (note that putting goals in first person helps you see them from the user's perspective), whereas a goal might be to be able to "read all the tweets that I find important." These two sound similar, but the first makes assumptions that the second does not. Consider the following:

- Does the user's timeline contain all the tweets the user cares about?
- Does the user's timeline consist only of tweets the user cares about?
- Is a chronological order the best for tweets?

By making these goals broad, you keep them separate from the means by which the user accomplishes them. It might just be that a simple, chronological timeline is the best way to read through tweets, but there is a chance that it's not. What if you were to categorize tweets by content or the type of user who is posting them? What if you included tweets from people who might be interesting to the user but aren't being followed? What if the user can give feedback about which tweets are valuable and that can be used to push those types of tweets to the top of the list?

Sometimes it can seem a bit challenging to create meaningful user goals. Maybe you're creating an image manipulation app and all you can come up with is "I want to be able to easily manipulate photos." That is not a very helpful goal, so you can break it down further. First, think of basic navigation requirements: How will users get to the photos? Next, why are they manipulating the photos? Finally, after they've manipulated the photos, what can they do with them? With a bit of brainstorming, your list might look more like this:

- I want to browse all images on my device.
- I want to improve the visual quality of my photos.
- I want to make people in my photos look better.
- I want to share the modified photos.

You can certainly come up with a more exhaustive list than this, but this is a good start. Notice that the two photo manipulation goals do not define specific ways they are accomplished. Later, you can define features that allow the user to accomplish these goals. You might decide that the app needs to support easy fixing of blemishes such as pimples and also needs to correct red-eye; both of those features are ways to accomplish the third goal: "I want to make people in my photos look better."

User Personas

An extremely helpful tool in analyzing what your goals mean to your app is the creation of user personas. Personas are represented as individual users, but they are reflective of a group of users with specific behavior and motivations. For example, you might define Susan, an excellent photographer with an eye for perfection. When she is not using her $8,000 digital SLR for photography, she's trying to squeeze every bit of photo quality out of her top-of-the-line phone. She likes to share a few of her photos to Google Plus, but she is very picky about what she shares since her clients might see them. She also mentally organizes her photos by events, such as all the photos from a birthday party or all the photos from a wedding. You could also define Jim, a guy who couldn't care less what SLR stands for and just wants to share good photos with his friends. His phone is fairly average and does not take great photos, but he loves being able to immediately share whatever he is doing with all his social networks. You could explain to him that red-eye happens in photos when the flash is too close to the photo sensor, but he doesn't care. Obviously eyes shouldn't be red, so the device should be able to fix that automatically.

Consider the previously defined photo manipulation app and how these two users would use the app to accomplish their goals. Susan wants the photos organized by events, whereas Jim wants the newest photos to be first in the list because they are most likely what he wants to share. Susan cares about manually tweaking the white balance, contrast of shadows, and other features Jim could not care less about; he just wants to easily make the photo look good. Their requirements around making people in photos look good are similarly different. Susan wants to select a precise skin tone, whereas Jim just wants to be able to tap on that one horrible Friday night pimple and have it disappear. Finally, they both use sharing but in different ways. Fortunately, sharing content in Android is extremely easy.

Product Goals

Sadly, the reality of app design and development has to hit you at some point and you realize it can't just be all about the users. We would all love for all apps to be free and work on every device, but creating great apps costs money, and supporting all devices takes time. Product goals are the goals that cover monetization, branding, and other considerations that stakeholders in the app have. A list of product goals might look like this:

- Reach 50,000 app downloads in three months.
- Earn $5,000 gross in three months.
- Reflect company XYZ's branding.
- Release beta version to board members in six weeks.
- Release 1.0 to Google Play in eight weeks.

Notice that these goals are not direct considerations of the users, but they do affect the users. The intent to monetize means the app may cost money, it might have ads, it could have in-app purchases, or some other means of making money such as premium account support. The length of time allowed for development controls which features can be included. These are requirements, but to the best of your ability you should not let them define the app.

Device and Configuration Support

Those who are inexperienced with Android find the question of device support intimidating, often relying on a "wait and see" approach that means the app works well on a typical phone and poorly on everything else. Even if your intent is only to focus on phones early on, it is worth spending some time figuring out how your app would support other devices and other configurations such as landscape. In most cases, a little bit of thinking up front can make support for a variety of devices and configurations relatively easy, especially because best practices in Android development solve many of the challenges. In short, unless you have an extremely good reason, both the design and development processes should consider the wide variety of Android devices out there.

The other part of device support is determining the minimum version of Android you will support. Fortunately, this decision is rarely driven by design, instead depending on technical considerations and sometimes product goals. In most cases, even design that comes from newer versions of Android such as Ice Cream Sandwich can be applied to older versions of Android through the use of the support library, third-party libraries, and even custom solutions. Most apps developed now support version 2.2 (Froyo) and above or 2.3 (Gingerbread) and above. If your app does not require any newer features to work, then consider targeting one of these versions.

> **tip**
>
> The Android landscape is always changing and it's important to keep up with the trends to understand what devices and device types are most common to make decisions about what you should support. The Android developer dashboard (http://developer.android.com/about/dashboards/index.html) gives you what percentage of devices run a particular version of Android or have a specific density, which can help make the decision.

When it comes to configurations, Android does not have a distinct concept of a "tablet app." Instead, apps can run on any device, unless you specifically set them not to. It is up to you to decide whether you want to provide an experience optimized for a tablet, television, or any other device. It is fine to release an app that does not have a tablet-specific experience in version one, but users appreciate knowing that up front, so be sure to let them know in your app description.

note

EXTERNAL LIBRARIES Although Android is frequently criticized for "fragmentation," the majority of features you will want to use are available in external libraries. For instance, fragments were not available until Android 3.0 (Honeycomb), but they are available through the support library (http://developer.android.com/tools/extras/support-library.html) provided by Google. That library requires version 1.6 of Android and above—that's the version that the original Android phone, the G1 on T-Mobile, can currently run.

Even when features aren't in the official support library, they are usually available through third-party libraries. For instance, the `ActionBar` is extremely well supported by Jake Wharton's ActionBarSherlock library (http://actionbarsherlock.com/); he has also written the ViewPagerIndicator library (http://viewpagerindicator.com/) for use with a `ViewPager` to indicate the current position.

The lesson is that you can support almost any version of Android as long as you're willing to put in the effort. In most cases, the effort is minimal because external libraries are already available for you.

High-Level Flow

The first graphical step to designing a new app is working on the high-level flow and grouping of actions based around meeting the previously established user goals. This is where you decide on the overall structure of the app. Which screen is the main screen? What are the secondary screens? How do you navigate between them? What actions can you take on a given screen?

The high-level flow is very directly tied to the goals you have established for your users. If your primary user goal is "read all the tweets that I find important," then the main screen should facilitate accomplishing that goal. One consideration to keep in mind is that you do not want to overwhelm the user with too many options on any given screen. It's ideal to have a primary action for a screen and possibly secondary actions.

For a brief time, apps were using the "dashboard" pattern. That meant that they would open to a screen that would feature several icons or buttons to accomplish each of the main tasks. In general, that pattern has faded out of practice because it always places a barrier in the way of the user. Sure, your Twitter app can show a page with an icon to start a tweet, an icon to view the timelines, and icon to go to settings, and so on, but why not dive right into the screen for viewing the tweets? From there, the user should be able to accomplish the other popular tasks, such as tweeting, with just a click or two.

The main way that people choose to work on high-level flow is with flowcharts. Typically, you represent screens with shapes that have lines or arrows connecting to other screens. This lets you quickly see how easy or difficult it is to navigate through the app. In some cases, people like to create very crude drawings of screens to more easily understand what goes in them. Do whichever works best for you. Plenty of software options are available, such as full desktop solutions like Visio (http://visio.microsoft.com/en-us/pages/default.aspx) and web-based options such as Google Drawings (http://www.google.com/drive/start/apps.html#drawings). Whether you're creating the flowchart digitally, on a whiteboard, on paper, or even on a random chunk of Styrofoam, this early planning is exceedingly valuable.

Take a look at two different examples. Figure 5.1 shows a crude flowchart of a game drawn out on Styrofoam. Here, the purpose was to consider all the screens that would be in the app. Notice that the screens have some detail to give a hint of what they should show, but they are not styled. They are, however, numbered, which is helpful when dealing with a large number of screens; your later wireframes can then be numbered to match the corresponding screens in the flowchart. A second set of wireframes would typically be done after something like this to detail the individual screens.

Figure 5.2, on the other hand, is an example of a more methodical approach of an app done digitally. Digital wireframes tend to be cleaner, better organized, and easier to share, but sometimes it is easier to start freehand with a simple drawn flowchart and then refine it. In this case, the app is a real estate app that allows the user to find properties on a map or a list. The user can also star/save properties as well as see sold properties. The user can also search, which would filter the properties shown on the map and in the list. From any of the main screens, the user can get to settings or get to a detailed property page. That property page also leads to a page about the real estate agent's details.

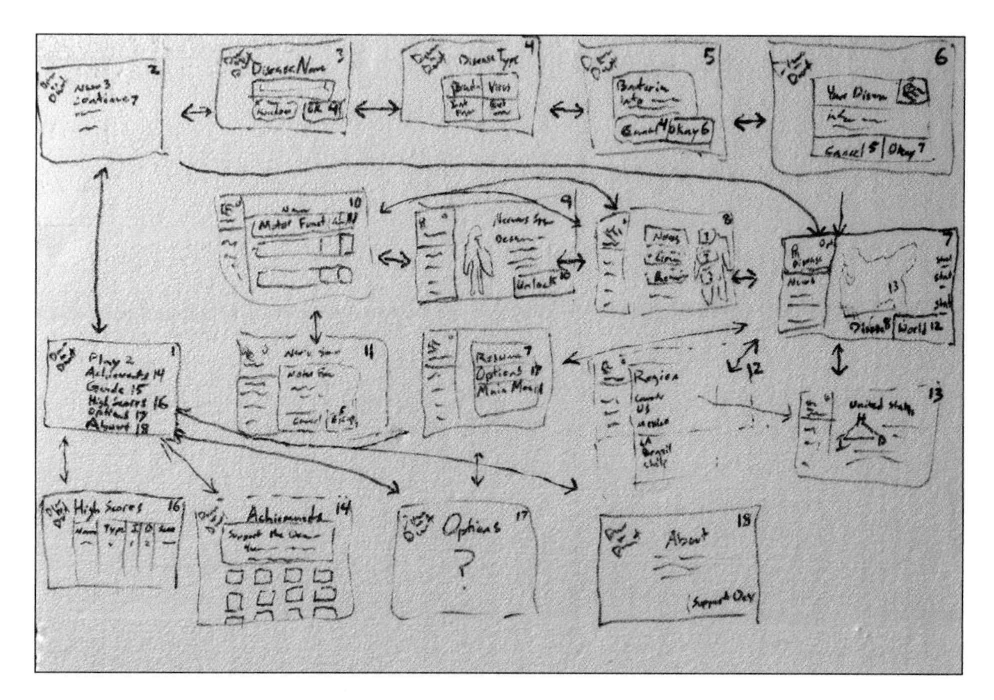

Figure 5.1 A crude game flowchart drawn on Styrofoam

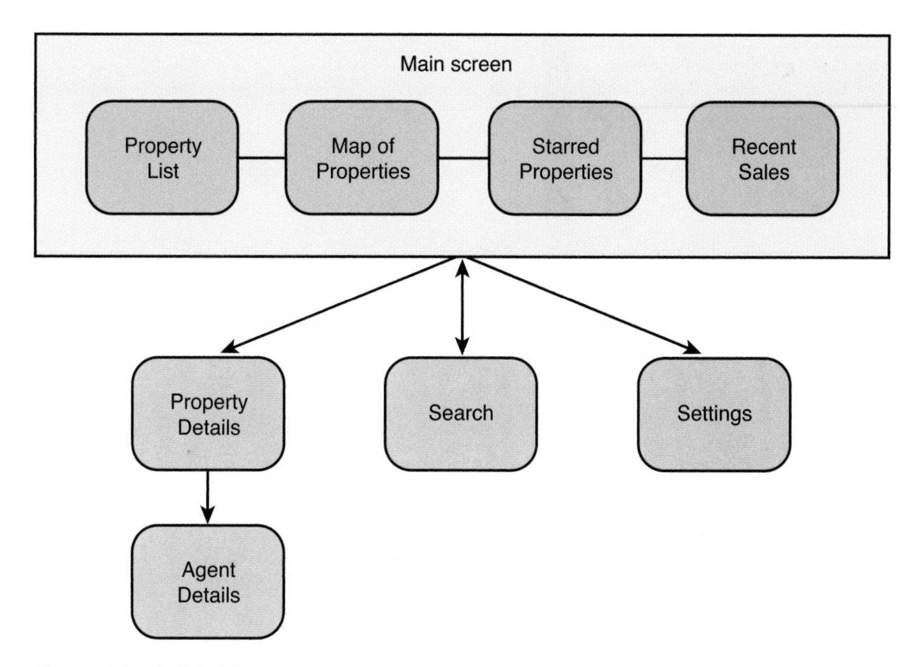

Figure 5.2 A digital flowchart of a real estate app

Wireframes

Wireframes represent the skeleton of your app. They attempt to explain the layout without any visual treatment to focus on functionality and usability. Wireframes ensure that data is grouped logically, touch targets are reasonably placed, the information hierarchy makes sense, and the data to be displayed on a given screen makes sense.

There are many different tools for wireframing. Starting out with a simple sheet of paper and a pen or pencil is a great way to quickly try out a few different ideas. If you want your wireframe sketches to be more professional or at least more consistent, consider using stencils such as the Android UI Stencil Kit (http://www.uistencils.com/products/android-stencil-kit). Figure 5.3 shows a simple example of a wireframe that was drawn. Wireframes like this are excellent as a first draft, but you will often want to revise them with digital tools afterward.

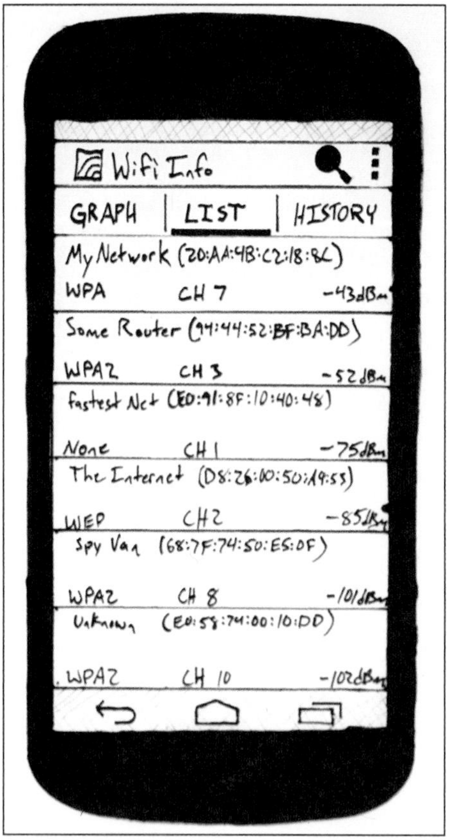

Figure 5.3 An example of a wireframe of a Wi-Fi app

When you're ready to work with software to create more polished wireframes, a lot of different tools are available to you. Many designers are already familiar with vector-based programs such as Adobe Illustrator and prefer to stick with those. Others prefer programs designed more specifically for creating wireframes such as the freely available Pencil (http://pencil.evolus.vn), which can run as a standalone app or a Firefox plug-in. Figure 5.4 demonstrates a simple wireframe created with Pencil using the Android 4.0 stencils (http://pencil.evolus.vn/en-US/Downloads/Stencils.aspx). Wireframe Sketcher can be used as a standalone app or as part of an IDE such as Eclipse (http://wireframesketcher.com/) and has Android stencils (http://wireframesketcher.com/mockups/android-ice-cream-sandwich.html). Another great app for wireframing is Omnigraffle for Macs (http://www.omnigroup.com/products/omnigraffle/), which can use the officially provided stencils (http://developer.android.com/design/downloads/index.html). If you are looking for a web app for creating wireframes, there are many of those available as well, such as Balsalmiq (http://www.balsamiq.com/), which also has Android-specific stencils (https://mockupstogo.mybalsamiq.com/projects/android/grid), and Fluid ID (http://www.fluidui.com/). Clearly, there are a lot of tools out there, and the sheer number of options can be a bit overwhelming at first, but it's a good idea to give a few of them a try. See what works best for you. You might even find that you like to mix and match tools because one works better for some things.

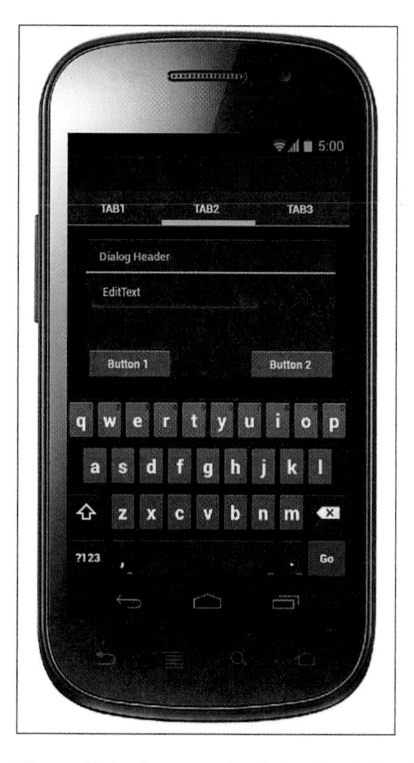

Figure 5.4 An example of simple wireframing done with Pencil

It is important to remember that the purpose of wireframing is not graphical design. Your wireframes should generally not use custom colors unless they are for defining content groups, showing interaction (for example, a touch or swipe), or showing alignment. In fact, many wireframing tools use very sketch-like graphics to help keep the focus on the content and its positioning rather than its appearance. It is fine to use native components (such as a standard Holo-style button), but avoid adding in your own custom controls with any more detail than necessary. You can show a custom chart, but you should not add gradients or other visual treatments. Ultimately, the purpose is to put the emphasis on the content positioning and its hierarchy and not on the visual design. This is your opportunity to determine positioning and sizing of elements on the screen relative to the other elements.

Starting with Navigation

The beginning of any project can be intimidating, as you stare at a blank paper waiting for inspiration. Some people are able to just dive right in; others need to be more methodical. If you fall into the latter group, sometimes it helps to start with the pieces. After having created a flowchart, determining navigation should be relatively easy.

Take a look back at Figure 5.2, which showed a sample real estate app. The four main screens are grouped together because they are very closely related. This is a great opportunity to use horizontal tabs. There are two primary ways to handle horizontal tabs: scrolling and not scrolling. The general guideline is that if you have more than three tabs, you should use scrolling tabs; otherwise, use stationary tabs. In this case, there are four choices: property list, map of properties, starred properties, and recent sales. However, you might make the case that a list and map are two different presentations of the same information. For example, you could have a toggle to go between list and map mode for the properties, starred properties, and recent sales. Doing that eliminates a separate tab, which allows all three tabs to be on the screen at once. That sounds like a good approach. See Figure 5.5 for a skeleton example of this navigation.

It is often very helpful to see how other apps handle problems similar to yours. It's very valuable to see how the native apps that were designed by Google work because they tend to best reflect the current state of Android design and user experience. You should also look at popular third-party apps. For instance, Tweet Lanes, developed by Chris Lacy, also has to display multiple lists. It uses scrolling tabs to section off each of the lists of tweets. Users can tap the different tabs as well as scroll the tabs to find a specific section to jump to easily. Another very nice feature implemented in Tweet Lanes that's recommended when using tabs is that you can swipe the content to switch between tabs. This makes it easy for users to navigate through the app, especially on larger devices where the tabs can be more of a stretch. It also uses a drop-down for account selection.

Figure 5.5 The real estate app with tab navigation

Tweet Lanes also has the ability for the user to pick between a light and a dark theme. Although you do not need to be considering colors this early in the design process, it's a good idea to make note of apps to come back to for a closer look when you're ready. Figure 5.6 demonstrates two different screenshots of Tweet Lanes, which uses a very clean Holo-style design. This is a good opportunity to clearly see the structure of the app and how that structure does not change when the design (in this case, the theme) changes. Before jumping back to your app, also notice how you can immediately tweet from this screen (and most others); clearly one of the user goals in this app is to be able to tweet easily, and Tweet Lanes addresses that need beautifully.

Looking back at the real estate app, perhaps a drop-down for the lists would work in the real estate app? The main reason for using tabs is because the content is closely related and the user is likely to switch between tabs fairly frequently. Looking back at the three main sections for this app, they appear to be separate enough that a drop-down might work better, especially if you can toggle between a list and a map for the given section. Figure 5.7 demonstrates this drop-down navigation. It's a good idea to try a couple of options and see which works best.

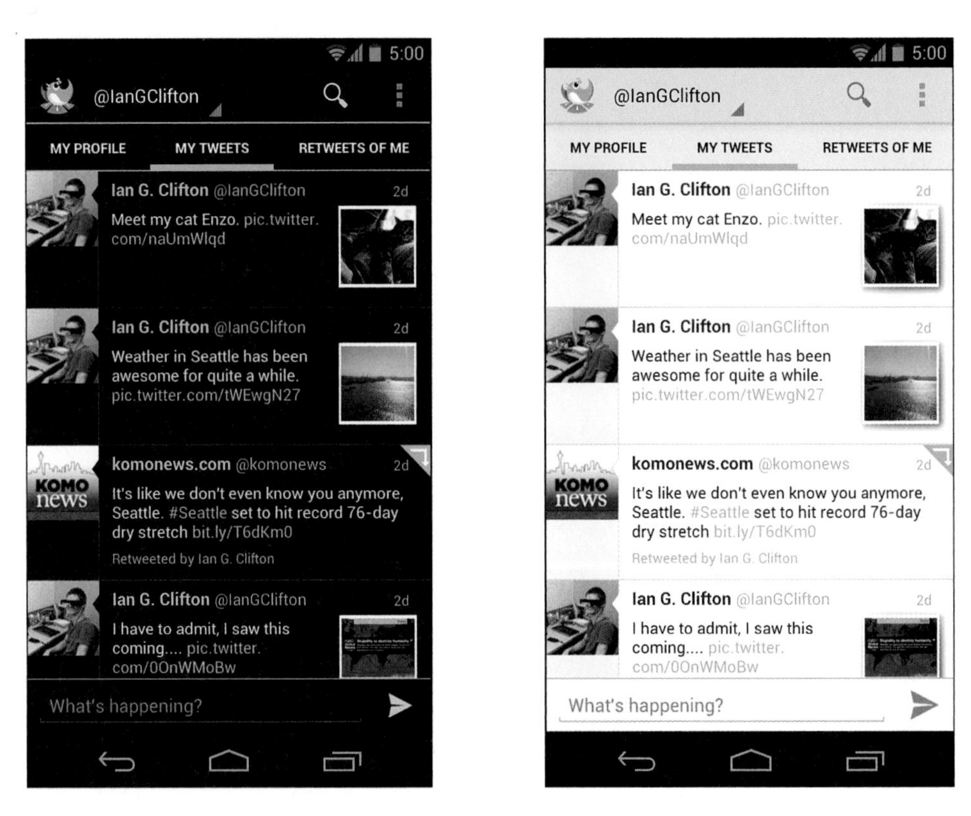

Figure 5.6 The Tweet Lanes app uses tabs for easy navigation and user-selectable themes.

Continuing with Content Pieces

Now that you have a couple of options for navigation done, it is time to get on to the content. Each of the main sections will contain property lists, so you need to have some way of succinctly representing each property in a list. That's a good place to start.

What aspects are most important when looking at a house? After thinking about it for a bit, you might say an image, the price, the address, the number of bedrooms and bathrooms, the total square footage, the year built, the type (for example, house, condominium, townhome, and so on), number of stories... and pretty soon your list is huge. By including the image, you can probably get away with excluding the type and number of stories. Plus, the property type is something a user is likely the filter out. Bedroom and bathroom count is important because even if a user filters it, the filter is likely to be a minimum rather than an exact amount (a user who specifies three bedrooms wants at least three, so a four bedroom house might be okay to display). The address is definitely important and can also serve as a hint as to the type (for example, "123 Main Street, Unit A"). The year is nice to know but probably not as vital because many houses are renovated and the user will likely specify a minimum, if that's a consideration. Square footage is pretty important. Looking back at the list, it is now down to image, price, address, bedroom and bathroom count, and probably the square footage. That is a lot more reasonable, so start there.

Figure 5.7 The real estate app with drop-down navigation

You have quite a few different considerations when deciding where to place images in an app, such as the quality of images and the frequency of images. Because this is for a list, the choices are the left side and the right side. If you frequently do not have images, the right side might be a better choice. That will ensure your text does not have a zigzagging reading line, as illustrated in Figure 5.8. If you have images for 80 percent of your items, then it might make more sense to have the images on the left and include a default image for items that do not have an image to keep a straight reading line. In the case of a real estate app, the vast majority of listings will include photos, so the left side should work.

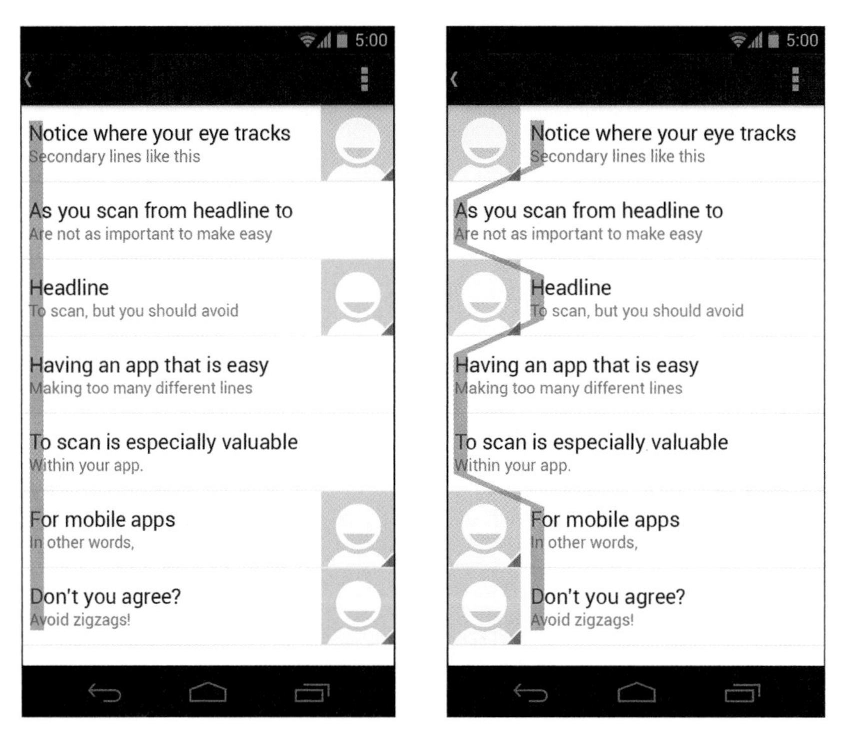

Figure 5.8 The blue highlight indicates the path of your eye when looking from item heading to item heading.

Of the remaining items, the address is likely to be the longest, so it should go next to the image at either the top or the bottom of the list item. The price is one of the most important pieces of info to scan through, so it should probably be separated from the other text, if possible. Perhaps the right side? The remaining bedroom and bathroom count as well as the square footage can probably be grouped together in text smaller than the price to reflect their importance. Sometimes it is best to try a few different layouts and see how they feel. See four different examples in Figure 5.9. Notice that each example has multiple copies below to get a feel for how they look in a list. The first (left-most) example shows a very typical layout. It is okay, but the information feels a bit crowded and the city gets lost in the mix. The second example seems okay at first glance, promoting the city, but then the street address is going to start in a different place on each item that is in a different city. The third example puts the city in the top right, which works surprisingly well. It feels a bit grouped with the price, but the price has a larger font, so it stays easy to scan. The final example is like the first, flipping the address and the numbers. It is probably a little better than the first, but not by much.

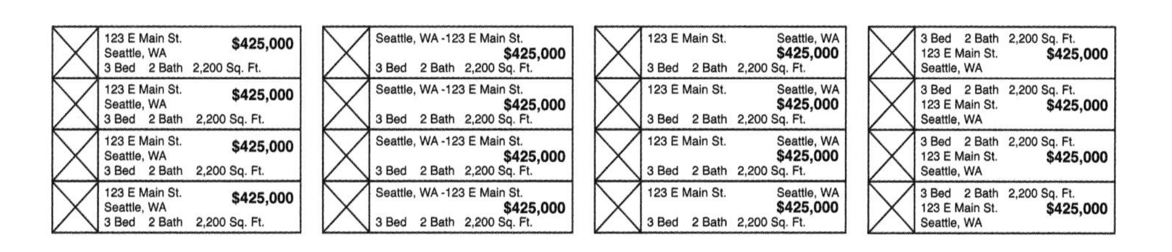

Figure 5.9 Wireframe examples of property list items

With the third choice sounding like the best bet, it is time to put it into the overall wireframe. Figure 5.10 demonstrates how the app looks with the property list items using tabbed navigation. It might seem a little strange to mix the Holo-style navigation skeleton with the sketch-like property items, but the point is to start getting a feel for how this works, and the important part is that the scales match. This lets you quickly see how much information will fit on the screen and whether content and navigation are visually fighting each other due to font size choices. This looks like a reasonable start for the main content. Because the other two tabs will have similar content, it's time to move on to the property detail screen.

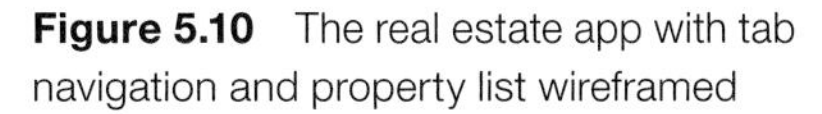

Figure 5.10 The real estate app with tab navigation and property list wireframed

Wireframing a Detail Page

Now that you have an idea of how the main pages could look, it is time to try a detail page. You should keep two things in mind for detail pages: They need to present enough additional information or capability to make them worth having, and they should generally present some of the information in a similar manner to the list presentation. The first of these is relatively obvious and generally easy, but occasionally you will come across an app where tapping on a list item just presents the exact same info but with a lot more whitespace—don't do that! The second point might seem a bit counterintuitive. If you have more screen space, shouldn't you take advantage of it? The answer is, of course, yes, but you also do not want to needlessly move content around. If the price is on the right side for the list item, it should probably be on the right side for the detail page.

Navigation for detail pages is usually easier to figure out. Looking at the property details page in the flowchart from Figure 5.2 shown earlier, you can see that the only way to get to a detail page is from the main screen, and the only place to go from there is the agent details screen. This is a good case for having an up indicator (shown as a left-facing chevron on the far left of the action bar), and the agent details can just be a button in the content area.

> note
>
> **THE UP INDICATOR** Many people are initially confused by the up indicator in Android. It shows as a left-facing chevron to the left of your app icon or logo in the action bar. In many cases, it has the same behavior as the back button, but there is a subtle—though important—difference. The back button should go back to the screen you were just viewing, but the up indicator should go up a level in the hierarchy.
>
> To make this clearer, imagine that you can see similar properties on the property details screen of the real estate app. Each time you tap a similar property, you go to a new detail screen showing all of its info, and that screen is at the same level as the previous one (that is, you are not drilling into deeper info; you're looking at something parallel to what you were just viewing). If you press back, you would go back to the previous detail screen. If you press up, you leave the property details and go to the previous level in the hierarchy, the main screen list.

Figure 5.11 shows a sample wireframe. The top of the page is dominated by a large photo of the property; this is probably a great opportunity to use `ViewPager` and allow swiping among photos. The next section of the detail page is very similar to what was on the list, with the difference being that the left thumbnail is gone because there is now a large photo above. The user has already learned how to interpret that information, and having a similar presentation reinforces the user's understanding. That information is sectioned off lightly with a horizontal divider, and then the description text appears, followed by the agent details button. Although a complete detail page for a real estate app would likely have a lot more content, this illustrates the important considerations: navigation, consistent information presentation, and additional content.

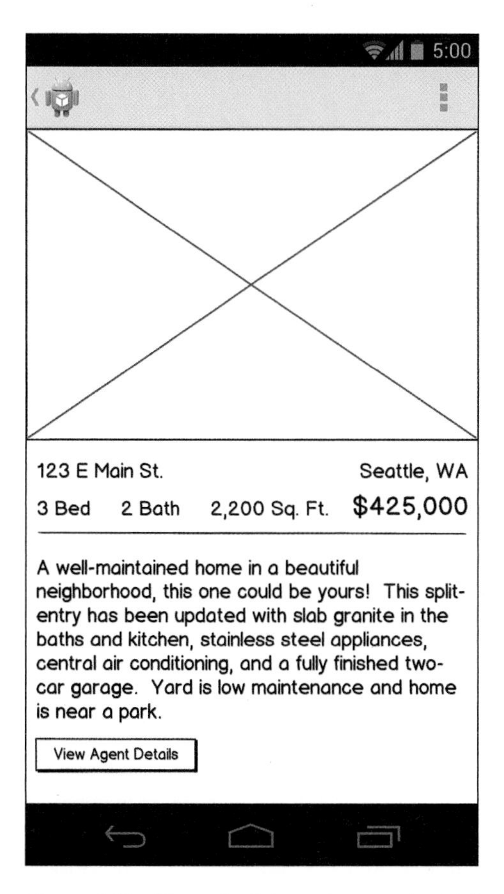

Figure 5.11 The real estate app's property detail screen

An important thing to consider when creating wireframes is what "real" content looks like. It is very easy to use text that just happens to be the right size to make everything work, but you really want to use realistic text. If 50 percent of the street addresses run all the way to the city name or beyond, then the wireframe should illustrate that. If most descriptions are just two sentences, that's what the wireframe should show. You want the wireframe to work for at least 80 percent of content, so it's a good idea to know ahead of time what the data looks like. Will a given bit of text fit on one line or will it spill onto a second line? Do you truncate that text if it's too long or do you let it flow? What do images look like if they're too small or the wrong aspect ratio? You do not necessarily have to wireframe every possibility, but it is a good idea to think about these situations ahead of time. Those details can go into the spec that is created later.

Supporting Multiple Devices

Early on in design considerations is the best time to start thinking about supporting different devices. A common mistake that designers make is to design with entirely one device in mind. It is a lot easier to balance the content on a screen when you design that content for one screen size only, but that is a bad practice to fall into. Besides, users can change font sizes, and that means views are going to be pushed around as needed.

Sometimes it can be helpful to do wireframing without any device borders to contain it. What does that UI look like in its natural form? How wide should a `TextView` be before you make the content wrap to the second line? Is the button connected to the bottom right of the content or the bottom right of the screen?

Playing around with the content positioning early on can make it clear how you can better support not only different devices but also landscape and portrait orientations specifically. Although many apps do not support landscape orientation on phones, there is little reason not to. The amount of work involved is not significant if you are already following best practices and planning to support a variety of device sizes.

One of the most common excuses for not supporting landscape for Android is that the app also has an iPhone version and that version won't support landscape; however, that's a poor reason. Android is built around the idea of consumer choice, and one of the choices that a fair number of Android users make is to buy a device with a hardware keyboard. Many of those keyboards are for landscape orientation, so forcing those users to bend their necks 90 degrees while using the keyboard because the iPhone version of the app does not support landscape orientation is a horrible excuse. Besides, if users want to use the app in landscape mode, why not let them? Ideally, you can make your app just as usable in landscape orientation as portrait, but it is not always possible. Oftentimes, time constraints prevent you from designing or developing a proper user experience for landscape orientations, but you should always consider them. Although phones with sliding keyboards are less common now than they once were, most large tablets are still used heavily in the landscape orientation. Consider what your user needs and prefers before ruling out support for landscape.

Naming Conventions

Following clear naming conventions will undoubtedly keep your resources easier to organize and track. Chances are, many of your assets will go through revisions, so you should consider that when naming. For instance, a name such as `red_background.png` is unclear. Where will it be used? What happens when the design changes and the background has to be blue? Instead, name assets based on function. Your `red_background.png` might be used on just one page and be named appropriately (for example, if it is only used on the settings screen, it might be called `settings_background.png`); if it's used for a group of pages, it should reflect that group (for example, an image used for all secondary pages might be called `secondary_background.png`).

Android also has conventions for specific assets (see http://developer.android.com/guide/practices/ui_guidelines/icon_design.html#design-tips). Icons, for instance, start with "`ic_`" and then the icon type. For example, `ic_dialog_warning.png` would be the icon used in a warning dialog. Typically, filenames have a suffix that indicates the state. For example, `button_primary_pressed.9.png` would be the primary button in its pressed state; chances are you'd also have a `button_primary_focused.9.png` and others. Usually the `StateDrawable` (see Chapter 4 "Adding App Graphics and Resources") is named either with no state (for example, `button_primary.xml`) or with a suffix to indicate that it's stateful (for example, `button_primary_stateful.xml` or `button_primary_touchable.xml`). This book will use the former, but remember that these are all just conventions, not requirements. Use what makes sense to you; just be consistent. See Table 5.1 for more examples.

Table 5.1 Asset Naming Conventions

Asset Type	Prefix	Examples
Action bar icons	`ic_action`	`ic_action_add.png` `ic_action_share.png`
Buttons	`button`	`button_primary.9.png` `button_subdued.9.png`
Dialog icons	`ic_dialog`	`ic_dialog_confirm.png` `ic_dialog_warning.png`
Dividers	`divider`	`divider_light.9.png` `divider_list.9.png`
Launcher icons	`ic_launcher`	`ic_launcher_main.png` `ic_launcher_map.png`
Map icons	`ic_map`	`ic_map_destination.png` `ic_map_pin.png`
Status bar/notification icons	`ic_stat_notify`	`ic_stat_notify_error.png` `ic_stat_notify_playing.png`
Tab icons	`ic_tab`	`ic_tab_list.png` `ic_tab_map.png`
Traditional menu icons	`ic_menu`	`ic_menu_help.png` `ic_menu_settings.png`

Crude Resources

Android is very adaptable to changes in assets, which means you can quickly throw a 50×50 image into a `ListView`, find out it feels too small, and try a 100×100 image. At this stage, resources are expected to be incomplete, but do not underestimate the value of creating some simple resources to start getting a feel for the grouping of content. Eventually, you'll have a nicely designed default thumbnail for images, but for now you can throw a box in there to help visualize how that space will be taken up.

If you follow naming conventions, such as those in Table 5.1, it will be much easier to swap out assets and see how something different looks. In most cases, it's enough to start by supplying just high-resolution assets such as all XHDPI assets. Later in the process, when the assets are closer to finalized, you can create files for each of the other densities.

Summary

You cannot overestimate the value of planning when it comes to app development. In this chapter you learned the need to define user goals and understand how product goals affect them. You learned about creating high-level flowcharts based on the goals and then jumped head-first into wireframes. If you have not done any wireframing before reading this chapter, you might still be feeling a little overwhelmed or are wondering which program you should use for your wireframes. Give a few of them a try. Try re-creating some of the wireframes shown in this chapter or build your own to get a feel for which program works best for you—and don't be afraid to break out your pen or pencil.

After reading this chapter, you should find navigation to be much clearer. It is particularly important that you understand the difference between the back button and "up" navigation, as discussed in this chapter. If you're still unsure, see how the native Android apps handle this. In the next chapter, you will see how to develop prototype apps using the wireframes from this chapter, and you will learn to implement tabs and drop-downs so that you can see which really will work best for this real estate app.

CHAPTER 6

DEVELOPING THE APP FOUNDATION

After having done the initial design work in the previous chapter, it is now time to start developing. This is often one of the most exciting parts of developing an app; you can go from no code to a working prototype very quickly. This chapter focuses on the process of breaking down a design into actual views within Android and implementing them. The key here is that you are not creating final code, but testing the theory of the initial design. It is important to remember that the design is just that—a theory—so testing it proves whether or not it will work. Because the design is not finalized, it is important to avoid spending significant time perfecting the code and layouts at this point. Instead, you want to get a prototype (an app that demonstrates a feature for testing) done as quickly as possible.

Organizing into Activities and Fragments

The first part of developing an app is breaking the design down into manageable chunks. What part is a full `Activity`? What about a `Fragment`? In an ideal world, you have been presented with (or created yourself) designs for phones and tablets, allowing you to easily see what part of the user interface is reused and how. In the real world, you are probably going to be starting on the app before even the phone wireframes are done.

Determining Your Fragments

To maintain flexibility, break everything into a `Fragment` first and then create each `Activity` that is needed to hold them together. If you have a flowchart to look at, usually each block can be a `Fragment`. If you have just wireframes, the job is a little trickier. You need to determine which screens have unique layouts. For instance, take a look at Figure 6.1; it's one of the real estate wireframes from the previous chapter.

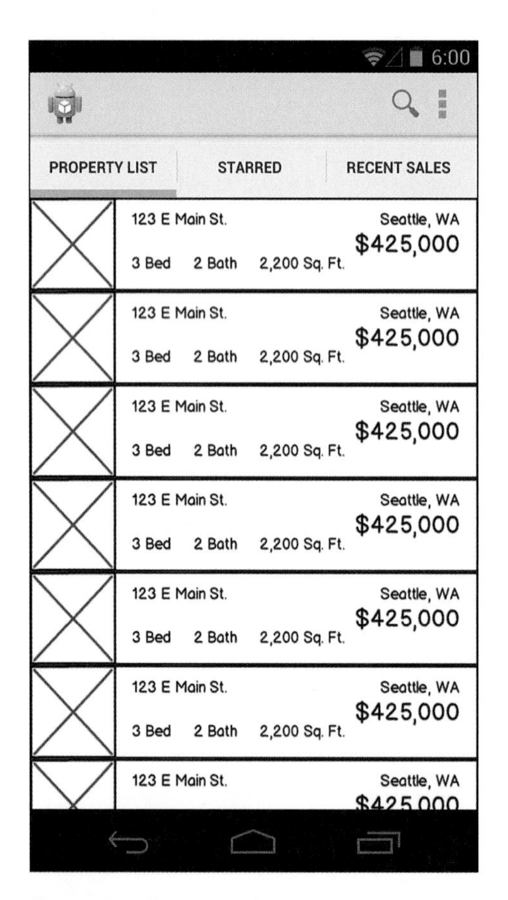

Figure 6.1 The real estate app with tab navigation and the property list wireframed

Chances are you will encounter wireframes like this quite frequently that only show one possible state of a given screen. You might be tempted to create a `Fragment` for each tab. In fact, that is likely the correct approach, except that each tab can be a separate instance of the same `Fragment`. Each one is listing properties. The properties listed might be different, but the display is (or should be) the same. That means this is one `Activity` that displays three instances of one `Fragment`.

You might also have a `Fragment` that displays a `MapView` and `Fragments` for displaying each of the other screens (property details and agent details). If you have wireframes for multiple different classifications of devices (for example, phones of normal size and 10" tablets), then you should create a single prototype app that can demonstrate each of the groups of wireframes. Start with the main device type that you will be targeting to quickly figure out if anything is clearly wrong when put on a device. You don't need to prototype every feature, but you should prototype primary navigation, important actions, and anything that isn't already proven in another app (such as a unique form of navigation). The general idea is that you spend a small portion of time prototyping to prove whether or not something is viable to avoid doing a huge amount of design and development for something that ends up not working.

> warning
>
> **LIMITATIONS OF `MapView`** Unfortunately, `MapView` has been one of the most problematic views in Android. The original version had to be within a `MapActivity`, which can only display one map at a time. If you try to display more than one, an exception will be thrown, likely crashing your app. In fact, you are expected to have only one `MapView` in a given process because the map tiles are fed to all `MapViews`, so panning in one `MapView` can affect the display in another `Activity` in the backstack. The solution of creating a separate process for each `Activity` that requires a `MapView` is heavy handed, wasteful, and far from ideal.
>
> Fortunately, Google released an entirely new version of the map library at the end of 2012 as part of the Google Play Services SDK. This updated version no longer suffers from the single instance limit and takes advantage of OpenGL ES 2.0 for better, faster rendering. For full details, see here: https://developers.google.com/maps/documentation/android/.
>
> Existing apps will continue to work with the original version of the maps library, but you should upgrade as soon as reasonably possible. All new apps should use Google Maps Android API V2 rather than the original version.

Creating the First Prototype

The initial screen shown in Figure 6.1 from the previous section is a great place to start. Templates were initially added to ADT version 20 and further improved in version 21, so creating something like the app layout in Figure 6.1 is an easy task. To check which version of ADT you have in Eclipse, go to Help then About Eclipse. You should see something similar to Figure 6.2. By clicking the Android icon, you will go to the details about the Android tools you have installed (see Figure 6.3), including the version number. If the first number is 21 or higher, then you can make use of the built-in templates, so you can begin by creating a new Android project. If not, you should go to Help, Check for Updates to update ADT.

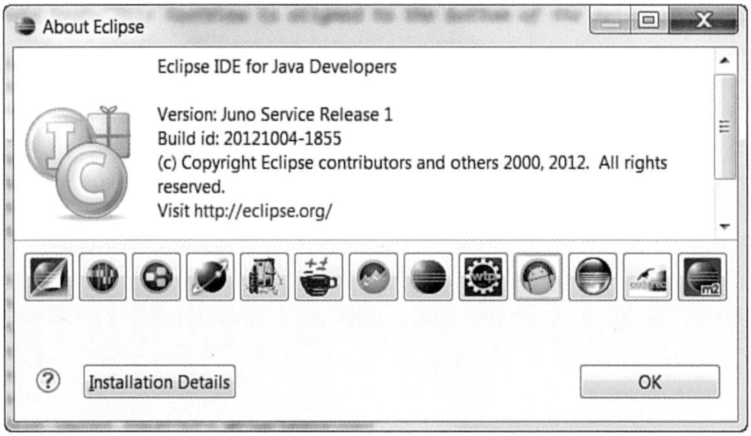

About Eclipse

Eclipse IDE for Java Developers

Version: Juno Service Release 1
Build id: 20121004-1855
(c) Copyright Eclipse contributors and others 2000, 2012. All rights reserved.
Visit http://eclipse.org/

Installation Details OK

Figure 6.2 The Eclipse About screen; note the selected Android icon.

Because this is a prototype, you can take some shortcuts to get things going more quickly. For example, in Figure 6.4, you can see that the minimum SDK is set at Android 4.0 (API 14). This lets you quickly test out the wireframes on new devices without worrying about compatibility for older devices. Once you have decided on a design direction, you can adjust the project as necessary to be compatible with as many devices as possible, but right now you are just testing the theory of the wireframes.

note

ADT SCREENSHOTS ADT is constantly being worked on and improved, which means that the screenshots you see in this book might vary from what you see, depending on the version you use. Do not be concerned if you see something completely different; just fill in the options that make sense and continue to the next step.

For more details about the development of ADT, see the website https://sites.google.com/a/android.com/tools/.

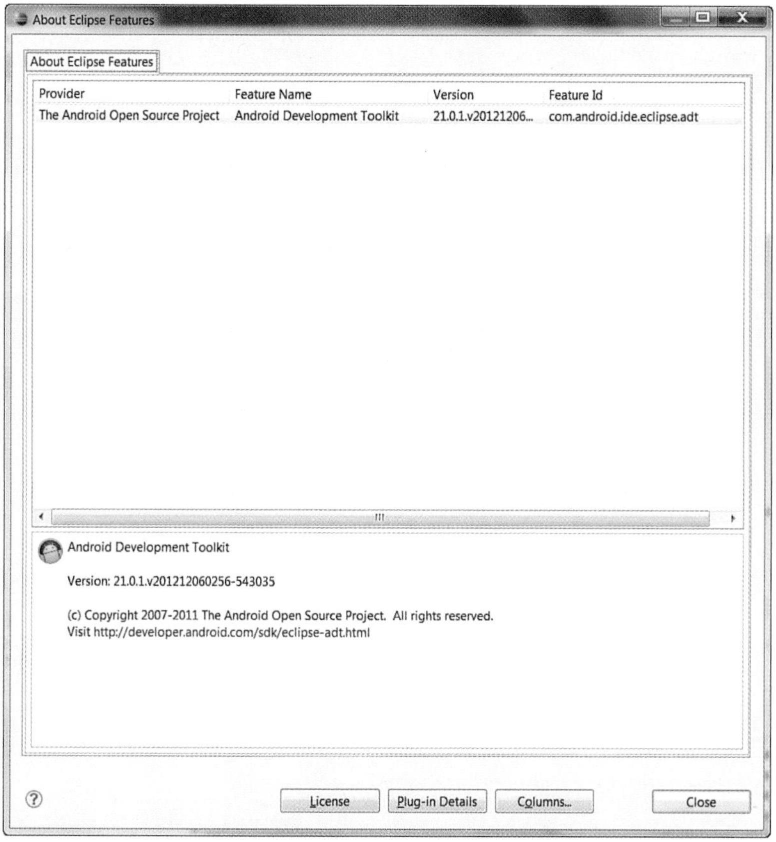

Figure 6.3 The details of the Android tools that are installed

Next, you are given the option to create a custom icon. Sometimes this is helpful if you're working on several apps at once, so you avoid having the default icon repeated multiple times on your device. This early in the process, you should not spend much time on the icon; it can even be a good idea to avoid colors (otherwise you may start to become accustomed to those colors even if they do not work for the app).

After creating or skipping the icon step, you should pick the BlankActivity template. This is just a simple template to set up the app with a single `Activity` and include the selected navigation, if chosen. Start with the Fixed Tabs + Swipe option (see Figure 6.5). As the name suggests, this includes tab-based navigation and also allows the user to swipe the content area to change tabs. If you are using two or three tabs, this is always the option to go with unless your content will include horizontally swipeable views.

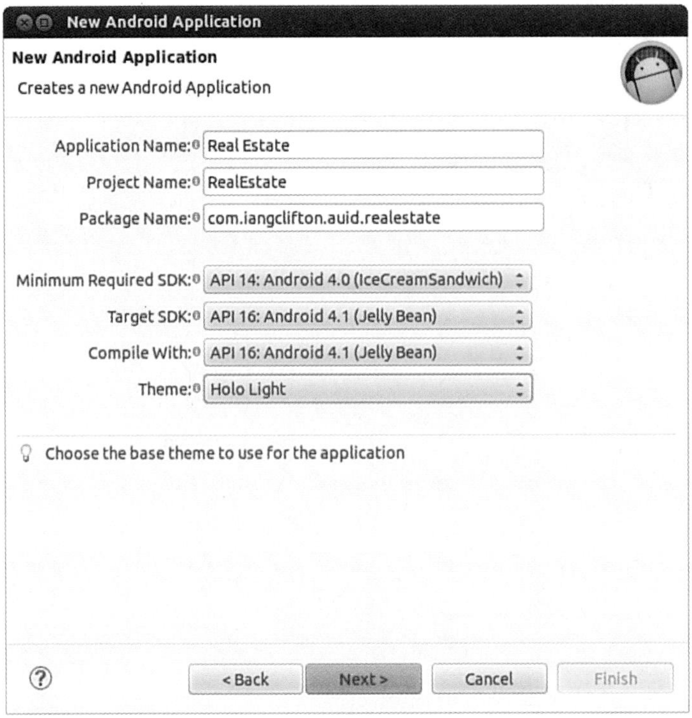

Figure 6.4 Creating a new Android project with API 14 as the minimum

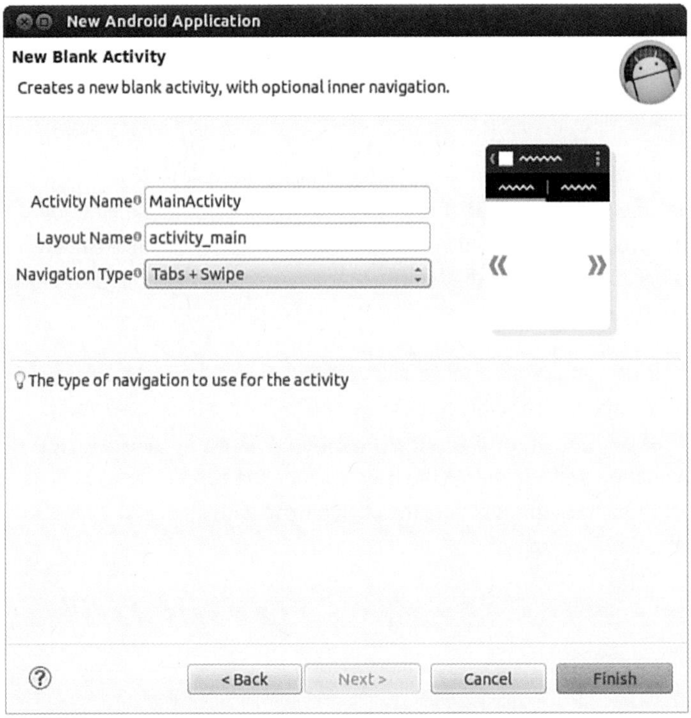

Figure 6.5 Creating a new `Activity` using tabs that support swiping

After clicking Finish, you should open `res/values/strings.xml` and update each of the title sections, giving you something like Listing 6.1. If you run the app now, it should look similar to Figure 6.6. If you see a dark action bar, chances are one of your `styles.xml` files is using `Theme.Holo.Light.DarkActionBar`. If you want to make sure the action bar is light, simply check each instance of `styles.xml` to ensure the parent style is `android:Theme.Holo.Light` in all cases. Oftentimes, the dark action bar looks better because it allows the chrome (that is, the graphical elements around the content) to recede and bring the brighter content to the foreground. Feel free to try either or both at this point.

Now is a great time to look through the code that was generated for you to make sure you understand it. You will see that it uses a `ViewPager` with a `FragmentPagerAdapter`. This lets you swipe between tabs to change which `Fragment` is being displayed.

Figure 6.6 Sample prototype supporting tabs and swiping

Listing 6.1 Sample `strings.xml` File

```
<?xml version="1.0" encoding="utf-8"?>
<resources>
    <string name="app_name">Real Estate</string>
    <string name="title_section3">Recent Sales</string>
    <string name="title_section2">Starred</string>
    <string name="title_section1">Property List</string>
    <string name="menu_settings">Settings</string>
</resources>
```

Creating the Second Prototype

After creating the first prototype using tab-based navigation, you need to create the second one using drop-down navigation. See Figure 6.7 to recall what this wireframe looked like. Fortunately, this is again extremely easy using ADT templates.

Figure 6.7 Wireframe showing drop-down navigation

By repeating the same steps you took to create the previous prototype, you can create the drop-down prototype by simply selecting Dropdown as the navigation type, as seen in Figure 6.8. You may also wish to use another package name so that you can install both apps onto a device for more easily testing the two prototypes.

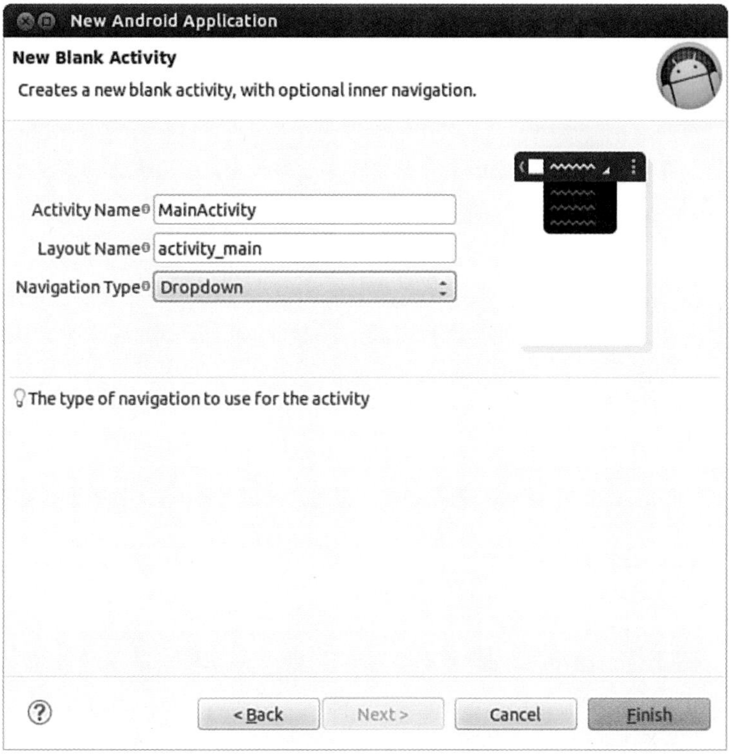

Figure 6.8 Creating a new `Activity` using drop-down navigation

Another option is to create the second prototype in the same app by picking File, New, Other..., Android Activity, BlankActivity and then entering the values you'd like on the resulting screen. If you make it a launcher activity, the app will create two icons, so you can launch either one.

note

ADT TEMPLATES If you are wondering where the ADT templates are coming from, they're in the SDK directory under `tools/templates/` and in a folder specific to the type (for example, `Activity`-based templates are in the `activities` folder). The developers behind ADT have included a few templates to start with and intend to create more, but you can also create templates for your own use.

If you want to know more information, Roman Nurik's Google+ post on ADT templates is a great place to start (see https://plus.google.com/113735310430199015092/posts/XTKTamk4As8). It is also helpful to take a look at examples created by others. For example, Jeff Gilfelt created several templates, including those that have support for ActionBarSherlock, making it much easier to create skeleton apps that support older versions of Android (see https://github.com/jgilfelt/android-adt-templates).

Breaking Wireframes into Views

Now that you have created the two navigation prototypes, it is time to start on actual views. Breaking apart a wireframe into views is a little bit different from converting comps (or comprehensive layouts, which are the visually complete layouts that include color, graphics, typography, and so on, that the final product should look like) to views. Because this is still early in the app's life, you can break the views apart in the easiest possible way. Do not worry about efficiency of the code or layout at this point because the theory put forth by the wireframe may turn out wrong, and this early code could get thrown out.

The Property List Item

The individual list item is a good place to start. Layouts like this can be a bit difficult to break out, especially when the wireframe does not illustrate what happens with a long address or city name or what happens if a house has 1.5 baths. At this point, you just need to make reasonable assumptions, because the design is likely to evolve more.

Because there are so many `TextView`s in this layout that are positioned based on the other `TextView`s, this layout is a good example of when a `RelativeLayout` can come in handy. The order in which you specify views for a `RelativeLayout` only determines the drawing order; because none of these views overlap, you can specify them in any order that makes sense. Create a new layout XML file with a `RelativeLayout` as its root. You can immediately add an `ImageView` that will be used for the thumbnail and align it to the top left of the parent `RelativeLayout`.

You should create a new resource file for storing dimensions by picking File, New, Other, and finally Android XML Values (within the Android folder). Type `dimens.xml` for the filename (remember, the name can be whatever you choose, but `dimens.xml` is a convention to let other Android developers know that the file contains various "dimens" in it, so you should generally stick with it), and click Finish. Add a new entry with a name of `default_spacing` and a value of 10dp. This is a placeholder size that can be changed later, but it's a good starting point for spacing (margins and padding). Set the `ImageView`'s `layout_marginRight` property to `@dimen/default_spacing`. This will push out any view that aligns to the right of the `ImageView` to give it breathing room.

You can specify any view next, but sometimes it's easiest to go to the next view that is positioned based on the parent alone, and that's the `TextView`, which displays the city and state at the top right. Set it to align to the parent's top and right (set `layout_alignParentTop` and `layout_alignParentRight` to `true`) and set the layout margin for the left, top, and right to your `default_spacing` value (again for breathing room). The street address should fit between the `ImageView` and the city, so set its `layout_toLeftOf` and `layout_toRightOf` properties accordingly. The margins that are specified for the other views will automatically adjust the position of the street address.

The price needs to be below the city, so create a `TextView` for it and make sure to align to the parent's right (`layout_alignParentRight`) and below the city (`layout_below`). Finally, align the beds `TextView` to the right of the `ImageView` and to the parent's bottom, the baths `TextView` to the right of that and to the parent's bottom, and the footage `TextView` to the right of the baths and to the parent's bottom.

This is not necessarily an ideal layout, depending on the content that might really fill these values, but you can do a few simple tricks to make this work well enough for the purpose of a prototype. For instance, if you set the gravity to right for both the baths and footage `TextViews` and give them a minimum width, you can reasonably align the text for all instances of these list items without doing extra work; if this layout proves to make sense visually, you can revisit how you want to ensure alignment. See Listing 6.2 for an example of the XML that you might have at this point. Note that each of the `TextViews` uses the built-in text appearances.

Listing 6.2 Possible Layout for a Property List Item

```
<?xml version="1.0" encoding="utf-8"?>
<RelativeLayout xmlns:android="http://schemas.android.com/apk/res/
➥android"
    android:layout_width="match_parent"
    android:layout_height="wrap_content" >

    <ImageView
        android:id="@+id/thumbnail"
        android:layout_width="wrap_content"
        android:layout_height="wrap_content"
        android:layout_alignParentLeft="true"
        android:layout_alignParentTop="true"
        android:layout_marginRight="@dimen/default_spacing"
        android:contentDescription="@null"
        android:src="@drawable/ic_thumbnail_placeholder" />
```

```
<TextView
    android:id="@+id/city"
    android:layout_width="wrap_content"
    android:layout_height="wrap_content"
    android:layout_alignParentRight="true"
    android:layout_alignParentTop="true"
    android:layout_marginLeft="@dimen/default_spacing"
    android:textAppearance="?android:attr/textAppearanceSmall" />

<TextView
    android:id="@+id/price"
    android:layout_width="wrap_content"
    android:layout_height="wrap_content"
    android:layout_alignParentRight="true"
    android:layout_below="@id/city"
    android:textAppearance="?android:attr/textAppearanceMedium" />

<TextView
    android:id="@+id/street"
    android:layout_width="wrap_content"
    android:layout_height="wrap_content"
    android:layout_alignParentTop="true"
    android:layout_toLeftOf="@id/city"
    android:layout_toRightOf="@+id/thumbnail"
    android:textAppearance="?android:attr/textAppearanceSmall" />

<TextView
    android:id="@+id/beds"
    android:layout_width="wrap_content"
    android:layout_height="wrap_content"
    android:layout_alignParentBottom="true"
    android:layout_toRightOf="@id/thumbnail"
    android:textAppearance="?android:attr/textAppearanceSmall" />

<TextView
    android:id="@+id/baths"
    android:layout_width="wrap_content"
    android:layout_height="wrap_content"
    android:layout_alignParentBottom="true"
    android:layout_marginLeft="@dimen/default_spacing"
    android:layout_toRightOf="@+id/beds"
    android:minWidth="70dp"
    android:gravity="right"
    android:textAppearance="?android:attr/textAppearanceSmall" />

<TextView
    android:id="@+id/footage"
    android:layout_width="wrap_content"
    android:layout_height="wrap_content"
```

```
        android:layout_alignParentBottom="true"
        android:layout_marginLeft="@dimen/default_spacing"
        android:layout_toRightOf="@+id/baths"
        android:minWidth="80dp"
        android:gravity="right"
        android:textAppearance="?android:attr/textAppearanceSmall" />

</RelativeLayout>
```

Putting the List Item in the App

The next step is to actually get this list item into the app to see if it looks similar to the wireframe. With just a little bit of extra work, you can create a simple "`Property`" object (as in a house or condominium) that can be used to populate the views. You can also create several instances of this `Property` object with different addresses and other attributes so that you can see what the layout looks like with some slightly more realistic data.

See Listing 6.3 for a sample class (called `Property` and stored in `property.java`) that can represent a single property. This class mimics what you might use when interacting with JSON from a server. Notice the use of `Parcelable`, which allows the object to be represented as a `Parcel`. This is a very efficient way to pass an object around, and it can be used to pass data in an `Intent` to another `Activity` or a `Service`. When working with more data than this, you may wish to implement the `Parcelable` interface more efficiently (that is, handle writing the relevant data to the `Parcel` and reading from it), but this is more than enough for testing out the prototype.

Another characteristic of this class is that all the values are final but it provides accessor methods for getting them from outside of the class. This pattern makes the class thread-safe with very little effort. Obviously, it is a bit early to be concerned with threading, but this pattern requires minimal time to implement and, if you know you will need this object regardless of the end visual design, putting the time in now is easier than halfway through the actual development of the app.

Listing 6.3 Property Class that Can Be Used to Populate Views

```
/**
 * Represents a single Property such as a house or a condo.
 *
 * This is thread-safe and implements Parcelable for passing between
 * Activities. In this case, the Property simply reuses the raw JSON
 * String to pass around so that the JSONObject can do the heavy
 * lifting.
 *
```

```
 * In the real world, the data for each of these objects would be
 * coming from a server somewhere, so this object is modeled after
 * a possible JSON representation.
 *
 * @author Ian G. Clifton
 */
public class Property implements Parcelable {
    private static final String TAG = "Property";

    public static final String JSON_KEY_BATHROOMS = "bathroomCount";
    public static final String JSON_KEY_BEDROOMS = "bedroomCount";
    public static final String JSON_KEY_CITY = "city";
    public static final String JSON_KEY_FOOTAGE = "footage";
    public static final String JSON_KEY_PRICE = "displayPrice";
    public static final String JSON_KEY_STATE = "state";
    public static final String JSON_KEY_STREET_ADDRESS = "address";

    /**
     * The number of bathrooms like "1.5"
     */
    private final float mBathroomCount;

    /**
     * The number of bedrooms
     */
    private final int mBedroomCount;

    /**
     * The name of the city like "Seattle"
     */
    private final String mCity;

    /**
     * Square footage of the property like "2200"
     */
    private final int mFootage;

    /**
     * The displayable price of the property like "$490,000"
     */
    private final String mPrice;

    /**
     * The raw JSON representation of the object
     */
    private final String mRawJson;

    /**
     * The abbreviated name of the state like "WA"
```

```
     */
    private final String mState;

    /**
     * The street address like "123 Main St."
     */
    private final String mStreetAddress;

    public Property(JSONObject json) throws JSONException {
        mBathroomCount = (float) json.getDouble(JSON_KEY_BATHROOMS);
        mBedroomCount = json.getInt(JSON_KEY_BEDROOMS);
        mCity = json.getString(JSON_KEY_CITY);
        mFootage = json.getInt(JSON_KEY_FOOTAGE);
        mPrice = json.getString(JSON_KEY_PRICE);
        mState = json.getString(JSON_KEY_STATE);
        mStreetAddress = json.getString(JSON_KEY_STREET_ADDRESS);
        mRawJson = json.toString();
    }

    @Override
    public int describeContents() {
        return 0;
    }

    /**
     * Returns the number of bathrooms like "1.5"
     *
     * @return the bathroomCount
     */
    public float getBathroomCount() {
        return mBathroomCount;
    }

    /**
     * Returns the number of bedrooms
     *
     * @return the bedroomCount
     */
    public int getBedroomCount() {
        return mBedroomCount;
    }

    /**
     * Returns the name of the city like "Seattle"
     *
     * @return the city
     */
    public String getCity() {
        return mCity;
```

```
    }

    /**
     * Returns the square footage of the property like "2200"
     *
     * @return the footage
     */
    public int getFootage() {
        return mFootage;
    }

    /**
     * Returns the displayable price of the property like "$490,000"
     *
     * @return the price
     */
    public String getPrice() {
        return mPrice;
    }

    /**
     * Returns the abbreviated name of the state like "WA"
     *
     * @return the state
     */
    public String getState() {
        return mState;
    }

    /**
     * Returns the street address like "123 Main St."
     *
     * @return the streetAddress
     */
    public String getStreetAddress() {
        return mStreetAddress;
    }

    @Override
    public void writeToParcel(Parcel dest, int flags) {
        dest.writeString(mRawJson);
    }

    /**
     * Parcelable.Creator required to construct a Property object
     * from a Parcel.
     */
    public static final Parcelable.Creator<Property> CREATOR = new
➥Parcelable.Creator<Property>() {
```

```
        @Override
        public Property createFromParcel(Parcel source) {
            final String rawJson = source.readString();
            try {
                final JSONObject jsonObject = new JSONObject(rawJson);
                return new Property(jsonObject);
            } catch (JSONException e) {
                // In theory, it's impossible to get here
                Log.e(TAG, "Failed to create Property from JSON String: "
➥+ e.getMessage());
                return null;
            }
        }

        @Override
        public Property[] newArray(int size) {
            return new Property[size];
        }

    };
}
```

Now, create a new class called `PropertyListFragment` that extends `ListFragment`, which is a `Fragment` that is intended to display a `ListView` and provides some helper methods. Create a `private static final String` called `ARGUMENT_KEY_PROPERTIES` with a value of "properties" (this will be used when saving and retrieving the `Property` objects that this `Fragment` displays). Add a `static public` method called `newInstance` that takes an `ArrayList` of `Property` objects and returns a `PropertyListFragment`. Within this method, you should create a new `Bundle` called `args`. On that `Bundle`, call `putParcelableArrayList`, passing in your `ARGUMENT_KEY_PROPERTIES` string and the `ArrayList` of `Property` objects. Next, create a new instance of your `PropertyListFragment` using the default constructor (that is, the constructor with no arguments) and call `setArguments` on it, passing in the `Bundle` you just created. Finally, return that `PropertyListFragment`.

If you are not particularly familiar with `Fragments`, you may be wondering why you would not just create a constructor that takes the `ArrayList` directly, but `Fragments` are required to have the default constructor. Android will use the default constructor to restore a `Fragment`; if that constructor is not available, a `RuntimeException` will be thrown. Using a `newInstance` method allows you to clearly specify exactly what the `Fragment` requires to work and set the arguments in one place, while avoiding the chance of accidentally removing the default constructor. By setting the arguments for a `Fragment`, you are giving it data that it can use to restore its state. A `Bundle` implements `Parcelable`, so Android can actually write that data anywhere (such as to disk) and retrieve it later.

Create an inner `private static class` called `PropertyListAdapter` and have it extend `ArrayAdapter<Property>`. Within it, you should create four class variables that are all private: `mInflater` (a `LayoutInflater`) as well as `Strings` called `mBath`, `mBed`, and `mSqFt`. Each of those variables will store classes for efficiency. Add a constructor that takes a `Context` and a `List` of `Property` objects. Your constructor should call through to the parent constructor that takes a `Context`, an `int`, and a `List` of `Objects`. The `int` that you pass should just be `-1`; it is used to specify a `TextView` layout resource ID, but you'll be using your custom layout, so you do not need to pass in a valid resource ID. Call `LayoutInflater.from(Context)` to set your `mInflater` variable. After that, you'll be setting each of those strings, so you should go into your `strings.xml` file and create three new values: `bath` ("Bath"), `bed` ("Bed") and `sq_ft` ("Sq. Ft."). Back in your constructor, get a local reference to `Resources` by calling `getResources()` on your `Context`. Set `mBath`, `mBed`, and `mSqFt` by using the `Resources.getString(int)` method, passing in the resource ID for each of the strings you just defined (for example, `R.string.bath`). Note, you may wish to add a space to the front of each of these strings to separate them slightly from the numbers.

The `ArrayAdapter` does most of the work for `PropertyListAdapter`, but you need to override `getView(int, View, ViewGroup)` to use a custom layout. First, get a reference to the `Property` for the passed position `int` by calling `getItem(position)` (the `ArrayAdapter` automatically maps this to the `List` that you passed to the super class constructor, retrieving that `Property` from the `List`). Now that you have the object that contains all your data, you need to make sure you have a layout to populate. Check if the `convertView` is `null` or not; remember that the `View` being passed to this method may be a `View` that was previously used, but it can also be `null`. If it's `null`, call `mInflater.inflate(R.layout.property_listitem, parent, false)` to inflate your custom layout and set the `convertView` to reference it. The first argument of the inflate method specifies the layout to inflate, the second is the `ViewGroup` that the inflated layout will be attached to, and the third says whether or not to actually attach the layout to the `ViewGroup` for you. You want to pass `false` because the `ListView` will handle adding the returned `View`.

You now have a `Property` object and a layout to populate with it. Get a reference to the `TextViews` in your layout one at a time by calling `convertView.findViewById(int)` and passing in the appropriate view ID (such as `R.id.city` for the city `TextView`). You'll have to cast the result to a `TextView`. After you have the `TextView`, update the text. For example, to set the square footage, you would call `setText(property.getFootage() + mSqFt)` on the footage `TextView`. You've created those strings so that you don't have to call `Resources.getString(int)` three times in this method, which makes it more efficient, but you will see how to make this even more efficient in the future.

See Listing 6.4 for a complete implementation of the `PropertyListFragment`, including the inner `PropertyListAdapter` class.

Listing 6.4 The `PropertyListFragment` with Adapter

```
/**
 * ListFragment that displays a List of Property objects.
 *
 * @author Ian G. Clifton
 */
public class PropertyListFragment extends ListFragment {

    private static final String ARGUMENT_KEY_PROPERTIES = "properties";

    /**
     * Static constructor to create a new Instance of a
➥PropertyListFragment
     *
     * @param properties ArrayList of Property objects to store in the
➥Fragment
     * @return PropertyListFragment with the passed Property objects
     * stored as args
     */
    public static PropertyListFragment newInstance(ArrayList<Property>
➥properties) {
        final Bundle args = new Bundle();
        args.putParcelableArrayList(ARGUMENT_KEY_PROPERTIES,
➥properties);

        final PropertyListFragment f = new PropertyListFragment();
        f.setArguments(args);
        return f;
    }

    @Override
    public void onActivityCreated(Bundle savedInstanceState) {
        super.onActivityCreated(savedInstanceState);

        final List<Property> properties =
➥getArguments().getParcelableArrayList(ARGUMENT_KEY_PROPERTIES);
        setListAdapter(new PropertyListAdapter(getActivity(),
➥properties));
    }

    /**
     * ArrayAdapter that displays Property objects.
     *
     * @author Ian G. Clifton
     */
```

```
    private static class PropertyListAdapter extends
➥ArrayAdapter<Property> {

        private final LayoutInflater mInflater;

        private final String mBath;
        private final String mBed;
        private final String mSqFt;

        public PropertyListAdapter(Context context, List<Property>
➥objects) {
            super(context, -1, objects);
            mInflater = LayoutInflater.from(context);
            final Resources res = context.getResources();
            mBath = " " + res.getString(R.string.bath);
            mBed = " " + res.getString(R.string.bed);
            mSqFt = " " + res.getString(R.string.sq_ft);
        }

        @Override
        public View getView(int position, View convertView, ViewGroup
➥parent) {
            final Property property = getItem(position);

            if (convertView == null) {
                convertView = mInflater.inflate(R.layout.
➥property_listitem, parent, false);
            }

            // This will be made more efficient in a future chapter
            TextView tv = (TextView) convertView.findViewById(
➥R.id.city);
            tv.setText(property.getCity() + ", " +
➥property.getState());
            tv = (TextView) convertView.findViewById(R.id.price);
            tv.setText(property.getPrice());
            tv = (TextView) convertView.findViewById(R.id.street);
            tv.setText(property.getStreetAddress());
            tv = (TextView) convertView.findViewById(R.id.beds);
            tv.setText(property.getBedroomCount() + mBed);
            tv = (TextView) convertView.findViewById(R.id.baths);
            tv.setText(property.getBathroomCount() + mBath);
            tv = (TextView) convertView.findViewById(R.id.footage);
            tv.setText(property.getFootage() + mSqFt);

            return convertView;
        }
    }
}
```

Now you have a `Property` class and a `PropertyListFragment`, which can display `Property` objects. Next, you need a way of creating `Property` objects that have simple test data in them. Create a new class to do that called `PropertyTestUtils`. This class will provide two methods: one to create an individual `Property` instance with test data and one to create an `ArrayList` of `Property` objects (it should return an `ArrayList` rather than just a `List` because an `ArrayList` can be easily used with `Parcelable`). There are countless ways to implement a class like this, and Listing 6.5 shows one of them. Another option is to create static JSON strings that serve as "fixtures" that your `Property` class parses. The advantage of Listing 6.5 is that it can more quickly yield a variety of outputs for testing visual design. The advantage of using fixtures is that they can be directly incorporated into unit tests.

This implementation of the class contains multiple static arrays of potential values for each of the attributes of the `Property` object. The important part here is that each of the values is representative of real-world data. Notice how certain values are repeated, such as three bedrooms, because these values are very common in real data sets. Having realistic data can help you to quickly see how well the wireframes can present actual data.

For now, this class will be used to populate `Property` objects to test the wireframes. Later on, you can pull it out and make it part of a unit test, so this code is not wasted.

Listing 6.5 The `PropertyTestUtils`, Which Can Easily Populate Sample `Property` Objects

```
/**
 * Creates Property objects with test data.
 *
 * @author Ian G. Clifton
 */
public class PropertyTestUtils {

    private static final float[] BATHROOMS = {
        1.0f, 1.25f, 1.5f, 1.5f, 1.75f, 1.75f, 2.0f, 2.25f,
    };

    private static final int[] BEDROOMS = {
        1, 2, 2, 3, 3, 3, 4, 4,
    };

    private static final String[] CITIES = {
        "Seattle", "Seattle", "Seattle", "Redmond",
        "Bellevue", "Bellevue", "Renton", "Kent",
    };

    private static final int FOOTAGE_MIN = 900;
    private static final int FOOTAGE_MAX = 3500;
```

```
    private static final String[] PRICES = {
        "$325,995", "$400,500", "$425,000", "$495,990",
        "$550,000", "$565,000", "$600,000", "$675,000"
    };

    private static final String STATE = "WA";

    private static final String[] STREET_ADDRESSES = {
        "20 First Court E.",
        "995 Fifth Avenue S.",
        "2557 Silly Loop SW.",
        "5959 Aggravated Drive NE. A905",
        "7010 Old Cedar Drive",
    };

    private final Random mRandom;

    /**
     * Constructs a new PropertyTestUtils object with the specified
➥seed
     *
     * @param seed
     *            long to seed the {@link Random} with
     */
    public PropertyTestUtils(long seed) {
        mRandom = new Random(seed);
    }

    /**
     * Returns ArrayList of Property objects
     *
     * @param count
     *            int number of Property objects to return
     * @return ArrayList of Property objects
     */
    public ArrayList<Property> getNewProperties(int count) {
        final ArrayList<Property> list = new ArrayList<Property>();
        for (int i = 0; i < count; i++) {
            list.add(getNewProperty());
        }
        return list;
    }

    /**
     * Returns new Property filled with test data
     *
     * @return new Property filled with test data
     */
    public Property getNewProperty() {
```

```
        final JSONObject json = new JSONObject();
        try {
            int randomValue = mRandom.nextInt(BATHROOMS.length);
            json.put(Property.JSON_KEY_BATHROOMS,
➥BATHROOMS[randomValue]);
            randomValue = mRandom.nextInt(BEDROOMS.length);
            json.put(Property.JSON_KEY_BEDROOMS,
➥BEDROOMS[randomValue]);
            randomValue = mRandom.nextInt(CITIES.length);
            json.put(Property.JSON_KEY_CITY, CITIES[randomValue]);
            randomValue = mRandom.nextInt(FOOTAGE_MAX - FOOTAGE_MIN) +
➥FOOTAGE_MIN;
            json.put(Property.JSON_KEY_FOOTAGE, randomValue);
            randomValue = mRandom.nextInt(PRICES.length);
            json.put(Property.JSON_KEY_PRICE, PRICES[randomValue]);
            json.put(Property.JSON_KEY_STATE, STATE);
            randomValue = mRandom.nextInt(STREET_ADDRESSES.length);
            json.put(Property.JSON_KEY_STREET_ADDRESS,
➥STREET_ADDRESSES[randomValue]);
            return new Property(json);
        } catch (JSONException e) {
            // This should never happen
            throw new RuntimeException(e);
        }
    }
}
```

Finally, you have all the classes you need, so you just have to modify `MainActivity` to use the `PropertyListFragment`. In the `getItem` method of `SectionsPagerAdapter`, instantiate a new `PropertyTestUtils`, get a list of properties, and create a new `PropertyListFragment` with them. The method will look like Listing 6.6. Now you can run the app.

Listing 6.6 The `getItem` Method Modified to Return a `PropertyListFragment`

```
@Override
public Fragment getItem(int position) {
    final PropertyTestUtils ptu = new PropertyTestUtils(position);
    final ArrayList<Property> properties = ptu.getNewProperties(30);
    final Fragment f = PropertyListFragment.newInstance(properties);
    return f;
}
```

Trying the app out on a couple of phones in portrait mode reveals some obvious problems. If you look at Figure 6.9, you can see how this looks on a Galaxy Nexus (720×1280 XHDPI resolution) and a Nexus S (480×800 HDPI resolution) with a dark action bar. Together, these two phones represent a reasonably large section of real-world devices. The display of the Nexus S is typical of the previous generation of screens, and the display of the Galaxy Nexus is fairly typical of the current generation (for example, the Nexus 4 has a 768×1280 display), but you may consider also looking at the output on a device with a 1080×1920 or similar display.

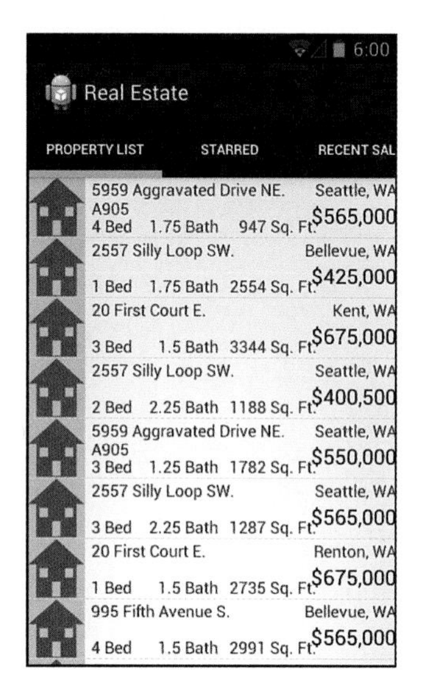

Figure 6.9 Prototype with properties listed (Galaxy Nexus on the left, Nexus S on the right)

Even on the larger screen of the Galaxy Nexus, the content looks too information dense. Despite text lining up, it is extremely hard to scan the listings. Although this can be alleviated with some styling, you can see that it is significantly worse on the Nexus S. Clearly, this first set of wireframes will need another revision, but that's okay. Iterating on the wireframes a few times is normal and one of the reasons you did not spend a huge amount of time getting everything just right.

Figure 6.10 demonstrates how the layout automatically adapts to landscape mode on a Galaxy Nexus. The tabs move into the action bar to give more vertical space; however, it's obvious that the list items could be better optimized for landscape mode.

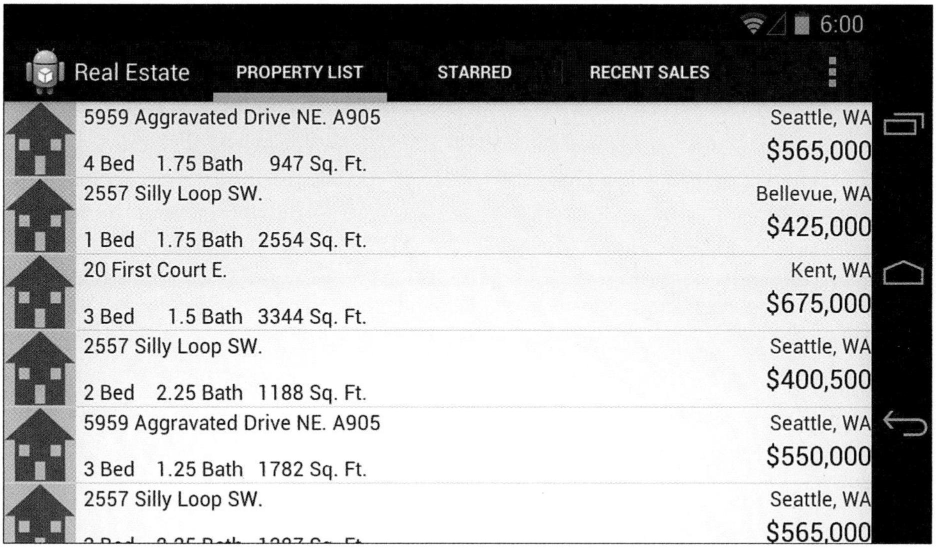

Figure 6.10 Prototype in landscape mode on the Galaxy Nexus

Creating Themes and Styles

Although you are not yet applying any significant color or visuals to your app, it is a good idea to consider what styles and themes you can apply. Styles are groups of properties that control what a view looks like. For instance, you can have a style that is used for header text that makes a `TextView` larger, colored a certain way, or even gives it a shadow. You can also extend styles, so you can add to or change the specified properties. If you have used CSS (cascading style sheets, used for specifying styles in HTML), you will find Android's styles to be similar.

A theme is a style that is applied to an `Activity`. All views in that `Activity` will use whichever properties from that style that apply to the given view. Typically, you'll extend another theme rather than creating your own from scratch. If you have been creating code along with this chapter, you can look at the `styles.xml` files that were generated for you to see this in action.

How does that help you at this point? Well, a good app should use a very limited set of styles. The user subconsciously learns these styles while using the app and can automatically register them (for example, "Okay, so this is a header") without conscious thought. Wireframes can very easily break out the styles that you need. For example, you are probably going to have three or four text sizes; more than that and the user will have difficulty discerning what the difference is between them. By specifying some of these styles early on, such as your style for body text or your style for headings, you can easily make changes in one place to update everything in the app. This is especially helpful while iterating on wireframes.

To inherit from a platform style, use the `parent` attribute. To inherit from your own styles, you can use the `parent` attribute, but you can instead use the style you're inheriting from as a prefix for the name. For example, if you have "MyTextStyle," you could extend it with "MyTextStyle.Blue," which will inherit all the styles from "MyTextStyle" (and presumably make the text blue).

You will see styles and themes applied more in future chapters, but you can also see details at http://developer.android.com/guide/topics/ui/themes.html. One note on naming: You should name your styles based on their purpose. For example "PrimaryHeading" is a good name but "BigGreenText" is not. The problem with the latter name is that the design of the app may change, so that the text becomes blue. Now you either have names that are inconsistent with their actual appearance or you rename the style and change each use of it.

Summary

In this chapter, you learned how to quickly create prototype apps based on wireframes. You should now feel confident creating layouts that can demonstrate wireframes on a real device, although you will get more practice in future chapters. The important thing to take away from this chapter is that the wireframe is a theory, and you create a prototype to test that theory. Sometimes you find that you have to completely throw out all the wireframes, but that's okay. Proving that something does not work is an important part of iterating on the app.

The next chapter shows how design can be applied to wireframes. The design retains the information hierarchy of the wireframes but can give the app a completely different feel.

CHAPTER 7

FINALIZING THE DESIGN

Now that you have completed wireframes and prototypes, you should have a good foundational knowledge upon which to build your designs. Good graphical design is a combination of art and science, understanding how to make something both beautiful and functional. Even if you're a developer reading this book who will have a designer handle creating comps, slices, and assets, it is very beneficial to understand the basics of what goes into a good design, and that is the focus of this chapter. There is countless more knowledge that aids in graphical design, such as color theory and typography, but this chapter serves to give you the basic understanding of what elements must be considered with a design and how to approach them for a mobile environment. After reading this chapter, you should have enough of an understanding of graphical design to be able to talk with your designer about the goals both of you have for the app and to follow along as the designer walks through his or her design to explain the decisions that went into each element.

Wireframes and Graphical Design

Although wireframes were primarily covered in Chapter 5, "Starting a New App," you should come back to them after trying to create prototypes and improve them. The cycle is iterative, like any development process, and having a solid set of wireframes will lead to a much better graphical design.

At this point, it may seem like the graphical design is just coloring between the lines created by the wireframes, but it is never that easy, nor should it be that limited. The wireframes serve as a logical grouping of content, an expectation of user interaction and user experience. They are intended to make the user expectations blatant. You would likely draw a box around related form elements in a wireframe, but the actual visual design might have just a background difference or even a common treatment to the form elements letting their visual proximity create the same grouping that the obvious box did in the wireframes.

Graphical design serves the two sides of the app: what the stakeholders want and what the users need. On one side, you have brand requirements. On the other, you have user expectations. The graphical design has to marry those together and, ideally, do it in a visually pleasing way.

Chances are you know what the brand requirements are. There is a certain logo to use, a specific color palette to work with, and other constraining factors. Knowing the user side of the equation is a little harder. Some of this comes out in the wireframes, where you can define the user interface based on what makes sense to the target audience. An interactive book aimed at young children should have large touch areas and large fonts, but a painting app for artists is going to have precise touch controls and an interface based largely on iconography. Other parts come out in the graphical design when considering the specific audience. Targeting teenagers? Maybe you should reconsider that floppy disk save icon. Targeting an international audience? You probably shouldn't use a thumbs-up icon to indicate a positive response.

App Visual Style and Personality

A lot of elements go into the style of an app. What does it look like? What does it feel like? What does it sound like? All of these aspects of the app should align to give the user a consistent and enjoyable experience. If your design is ultra-modern but your text screams Victorian throwback, the overall experience will feel disjointed. This harmony (or lack of) is something that the user will often feel but not necessarily be able to put a finger on. The designer is the one who puts conscious effort into ensuring a consistent visual experience.

Personality and Voice

The personality of your app is a combination of the design, the user interaction, and the text. If the design is clean and the user interaction is simple, then the voice is likely to be plainspoken and "to the point." If the design is robotic and the user interaction is deep, then the voice is probably more likely to sound, well, like a robot. Look at Table 7.1 for some basic examples of how the voice can vary based on the personality of the app. When in doubt, plain text is the best way to go.

Table 7.1 Examples of Different Types of Voice

Condition	Plain	Snarky	Robotic
Instruction for the user to type his/her name	Enter your name.	Type your name in the box or just stare at this screen for a while. Your choice.	TYPE YOUR NAME, HUMAN.
Loading new data	Updating...	Trying to update, but your connection is slooooow.	ACCESSING NEW DATA. PLEASE STAND BY.
Connection failure	Could not update. Please check your connection.	Failed to update. Maybe you should try paying your phone bill.	COULD NOT ACCESS DATA. PLEASE TRY AGAIN.

Lighting Angle

The traditional light source for graphical user interfaces is the top left (sometimes simplified to just the top for less depth). Unless you have an extremely good reason to break that tradition (and "to be different" isn't one), you should stick with it. Users have learned, whether consciously or not, that a button with lighter top and left edges and darker bottom and right edges is sticking up, and one with darker top and left edges and lighter bottom and right edges is depressed. The same is true for text. Text with a dark shadow above it will look like it is punched into the screen, whereas a light shadow above will make it look like it is sticking out. These subtle visuals can add depth to the design, but you should be careful to use them consistently and to avoid overusing them. If you use shadows as an indicator of something that is touchable, such as a button, you shouldn't use shadows to make groups of noninteractive content stand out as well.

Take a look at the sample button in Figure 7.1 to analyze the layers of lighting. Notice that the outer rim of the button catches the light at the top left and then casts a shadow just inside. The actual share icon is cut into the button, so a shadow is cast into the icon portion of the button from the top left as well. The bottom right of the rim of the button catches light and casts a shadow on the bottom right. Although most of your buttons will not be this detailed (and probably should not be since most mobile designs should focus on simplicity), this button style demonstrates the importance of a consistent lighting angle.

Figure 7.2 shows how minor adjustments that maintain the same lighting angle can create a pressed state for the same button. Notice how the inner shadow becomes darker and more pronounced around the top left. The center button portion moves very slightly to the bottom right and shrinks a small amount to reveal more of the outer rim.

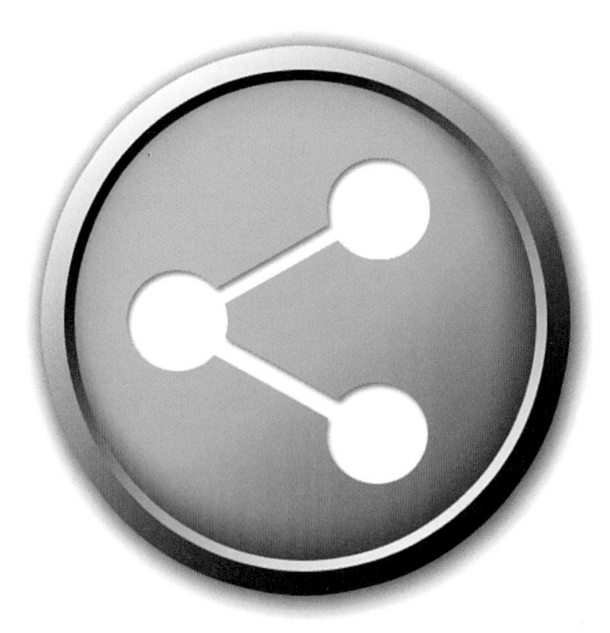

Figure 7.1 A detailed share button demonstrating a consistent lighting angle

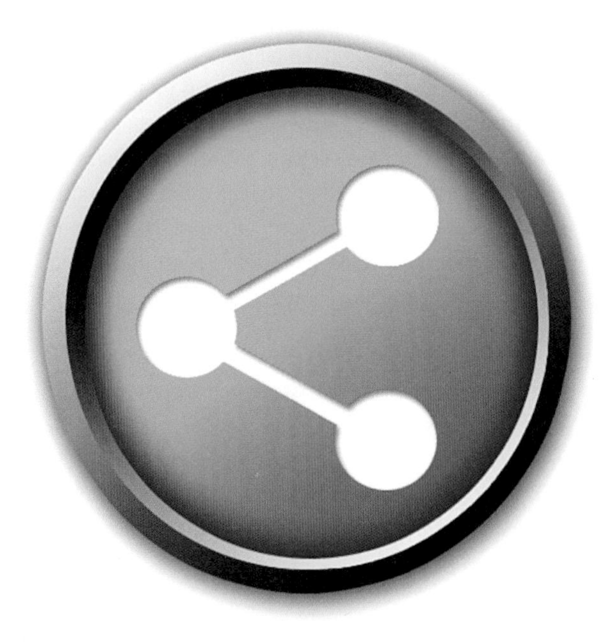

Figure 7.2 The share button in a pressed state

Colors

Color theory can be an entire book on its own, but some important aspects are especially beneficial in designing user interfaces. Most important is that you do not use color as the primary way of conveying information. Instead, rely on shape, positioning, proximity, and other methods. When you do use color, use it consistently. That means you need to consider both how the color is used in your app and outside of it. Don't use a dozen different colors just because you can.

Heavily saturated colors with medium luminosity imply a much stronger meaning than less saturated ones with a high or low luminosity. For instance, a strong red typically signifies an error or stop condition. Yellow is commonly used for warnings or UI updates that require attention. Green is usually reserved for good conditions and start buttons. Blue is sometimes used to indicate that something can be done or needs to be done.

Blacks, whites, and grays are interpreted as being very neutral and are often a good starting point, especially for backgrounds. A white background with black text may seem a bit simple, but the high contrast can be combined with good typography to make an extremely readable interface. Figure 7.3 shows the app Pocket, which demonstrates this very well. Pocket uses an action bar with lower contrast than typical to avoid drawing your eye away from the content. Figure 7.4 shows the app Currents, which has a slightly different take on the same overall theme of minimal visuals and clean typography. Currents hides the action bar at the top and subdues the UI at the bottom of the content for the same reason. This places all the focus on the content in a clean and beautiful display.

Apps that function primarily as image viewers typically have black backgrounds to make the images stand out without affecting the user's view of color. You may wonder why a photo-viewing app wouldn't use another color as the background. Why would it matter whether a photo is surrounded by black instead of red or blue? The answer comes from how human vision works. Instead of seeing absolute colors, the eye sees colors essentially as differences. You have a red-green difference channel and a yellow-blue difference channel (as seen in Figure 7.5), which can give you the feeling of those colors "fighting" each other when in close proximity. The higher the saturation, the more the colors fight, and the more users will be looking at your design instead of your content.

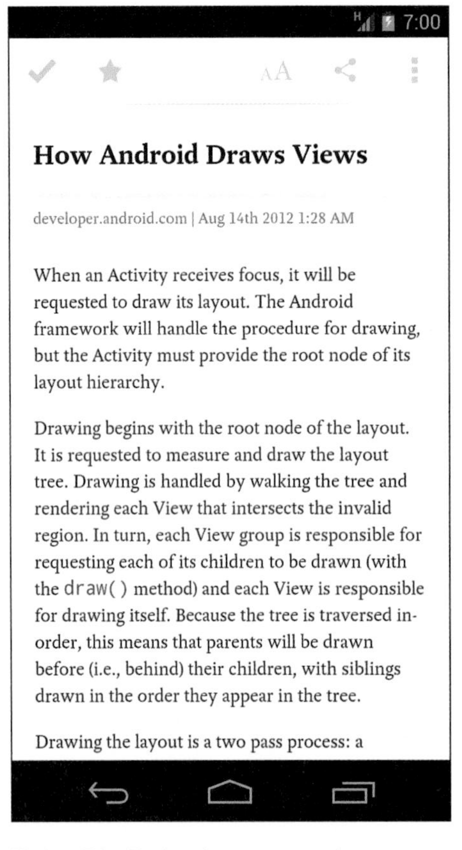

How Android Draws Views

developer.android.com | Aug 14th 2012 1:28 AM

When an Activity receives focus, it will be requested to draw its layout. The Android framework will handle the procedure for drawing, but the Activity must provide the root node of its layout hierarchy.

Drawing begins with the root node of the layout. It is requested to measure and draw the layout tree. Drawing is handled by walking the tree and rendering each View that intersects the invalid region. In turn, each View group is responsible for requesting each of its children to be drawn (with the `draw()` method) and each View is responsible for drawing itself. Because the tree is traversed in-order, this means that parents will be drawn before (i.e., behind) their children, with siblings drawn in the order they appear in the tree.

Drawing the layout is a two pass process: a

Figure 7.3 Pocket demonstrates clean typography and a subdued action bar.

10 Things You Should Never Say To Your Boss

CHERYL CONNER

I love the things Jenna Goudreau said in last week's article about the 10 Worst Communication Mistakes for your career – particularly her notes about what it takes to be viewed as a leader. As Jenna notes, it requires "executive presence," which includes having gravitas, excellent communication skills and a polished appearance.

While avoiding swearing, racial comments, flirting and off color jokes would seem fairly obvious, Jenna's points about "sounding

Figure 7.4 Currents hides the action bar and emphasizes the content.

Figure 7.5 Harsh contrast is distracting and even painful to look at.

Color vision deficiencies (colloquially referred to as "color blindness") are another consideration when choosing colors. The most common forms affect the ability to differentiate red and green hues from one another, but there are also color vision deficiencies that affect the ability to differentiate yellow and blue and even to differentiate color altogether (although quite rare). If you're using a recent version of Photoshop, you can preview your designs to get a feel for how they look to those with color vision deficiencies by going to View, Proof Setup, and picking one of the Color Blindness options. You can also go to Window, Arrange, New Window to create another view of the same document. Picking Window, Arrange, Tile All Vertically allows you to see both of these views side by side. You can then apply one of the color blindness proofs to easily compare full-color vision to either common color vision deficiency. See Figure 7.6 for an example. One quick check you can do to help ensure your design works is to convert it to grayscale and ensure all the essential elements are still obvious.

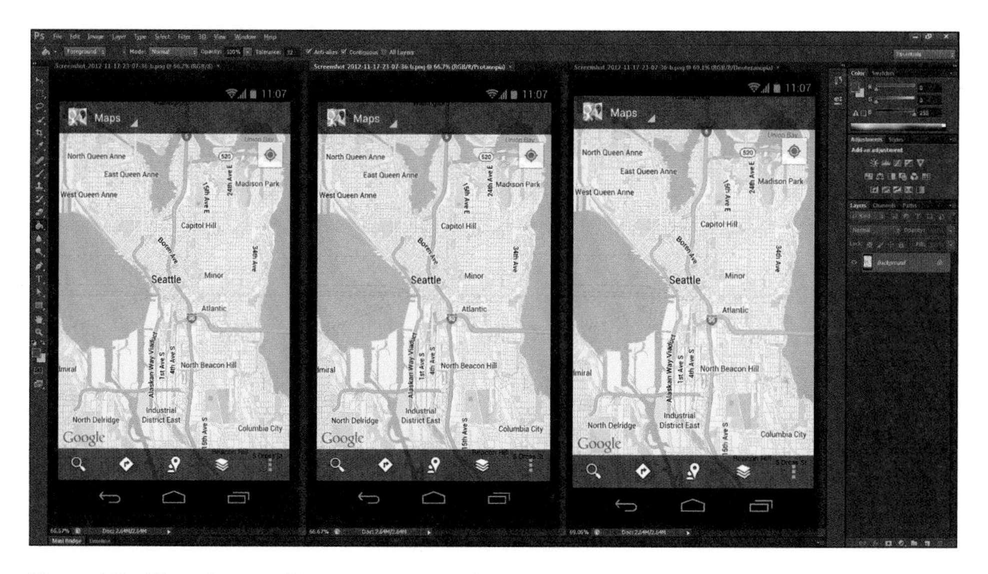

Figure 7.6 Photoshop enables you to use proofs for comparing color vision deficiencies.

Sizing and Density

As devices become larger, users interact with them from farther away. That means a 14pt font might be readable on a phone but less so on a 10" tablet. Fortunately, the easy solution is to have a separate `dimens.xml` file that specifies your dimensions for larger devices. For example, you might have a dimension specified called "heading_text" set to `22sp` that you use as the text size for your headings throughout the app. Listing 7.1 shows a simple `dimens.xml` file example of this that would go in `res/values/`. When you try the app on a large tablet, you may find that the font is a bit small because you hold the device farther away. For devices like that, you try some different sizes and find that `26sp` works much better. Instead of creating custom layouts or programmatically altering the text, you simply create a `values-sw600` directory in `res/` and put the `dimens.xml` file in it that looks like Listing 7.2. Any device that has a width and height that are at least 600 density independent pixels long will use the larger heading text; all other devices will use the smaller value.

Listing 7.1 A `dimens.xml` File Specifying Text Size for Most Devices

```
<?xml version="1.0" encoding="utf-8"?>
<resources>
    <dimen name="heading_text">22sp</dimen>
</resources>
```

Listing 7.2 A `dimens.xml` File Specifying Text Size for Larger Devices

```
<?xml version="1.0" encoding="utf-8"?>
<resources>
    <dimen name="heading_text">26sp</dimen>
</resources>
```

One more consideration with density is that you should always provide assets for the highest density you can and, ideally, you should include assets for each density you choose to support. Currently, XXHDPI is the highest density supported, representing about 480dpi. At the very least, you should provide an XXHDPI launcher icon (144×144) because 10" tablets (such as the Nexus 10) will use icons from one density "bucket" above their actual density. In other words, the Nexus 10 tablet is an XHDPI device, so it uses launcher icons from the XXHDPI density (if not found, it will scale from lower densities, but that results in a fuzzy icon).

If you come from an iOS background, it may help to think of the original few generations of the iPhone as being medium density (MDPI) devices. The iPhone 4 and above feature screens that are twice as dense in each direction, making them extra high density (XHDPI) devices. That means you can consider a Nexus 4 to be the same density as a newer iPhone, but you need to keep in mind that Android phones are often wider. For example, the Nexus 4 is 768 pixels wide as opposed to iPhone's 640 pixels wide.

If you need additional help understanding how you might design for a tablet instead of a phone, check out the blog post, "Designing for Tablets? We're Here to Help!" at http://android-developers.blogspot.com/2012/11/designing-for-tablets-were-here-to-help.html for some great tips and references to other resources.

Transparency and the 2.5× Rule

Transparency has many uses in design. It is a simple way of lowering contrast and blending parts of a user interface together. Transparency can also be used for visual effects such as cross-fading between two images. However, there is an important performance consideration with transparency. Many devices are fill-rate limited. That means they can only push so many pixels (typically due to a limited graphics pipeline). You might think that a device only needs to push as many pixels as are displayed on the screen, but that's not always the case. If you have several layers, you may have to draw pixels on top of pixels. In the case of software rendering, pixels are typically drawn using the painter's algorithm. The farthest/deepest layer is drawn first, then the next layer on top of that, and the next one, and so forth. Because of this drawing method, the device may be drawing pixels that are covered up entirely, thus wasting bandwidth. Hardware rendering can often be smarter, skipping pixels that aren't seen, which can optimize opaque layers.

The problem with transparency is that regardless of the rendering method, the pixels must be blended. That means having a black background and a white foreground with 50-percent transparency will draw all the pixels black and then the white pixels. If that is drawing 60 times per second, you have less than 17ms per frame to draw every pixel on the screen twice. Add more transparent pixels and suddenly you're drawing three times as many pixels as the screen displays in 17ms. It doesn't take long before the result is a choppy UI, particularly during animation and scrolling.

The general rule of thumb is to avoid drawing more than two-and-a-half times the total pixels on the screen. Some devices can handle more than this, but sticking to this limit means that your UI will appear smooth on a variety of devices.

Figure 7.7 shows a very simple UI that may appear to only have two or three layers at first glance; however, due to the way it is constructed, it actually has five layers. See Figure 7.8 for a breakdown of the five layers (note that the last layer is shown on black to make the light text visible, but just the light portion is drawn). As simple as this UI is, it's already at the edge of the 2.5× rule. By making the background image itself colored, you cut down the number of pixels that are drawn by nearly half. You might also consider not including the text shadows because they are barely visible here.

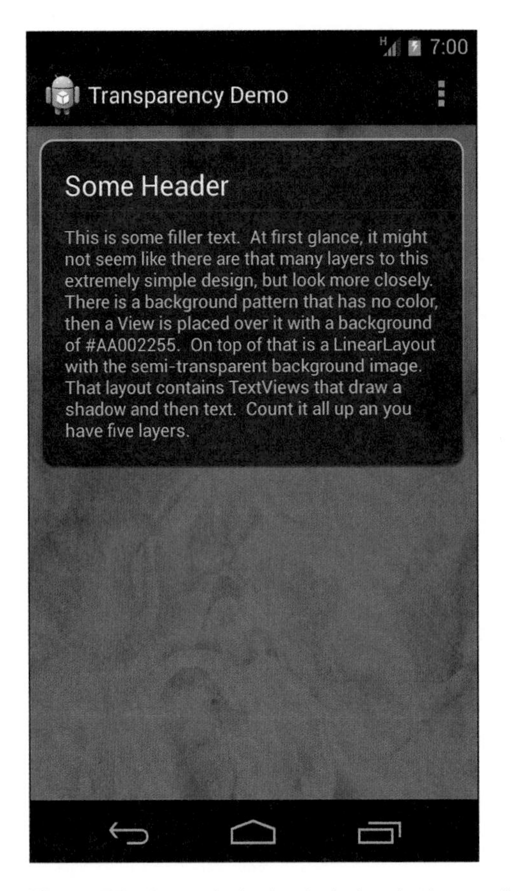

Figure 7.7 A seemingly simple design that is actually five layers

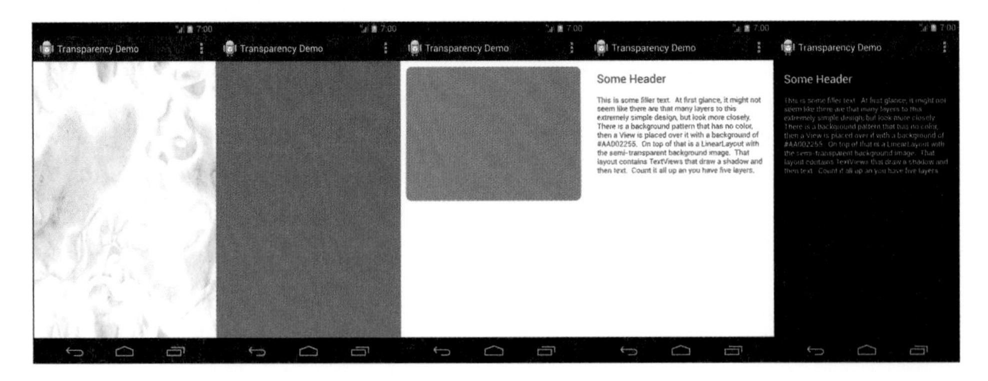

Figure 7.8 Each of the five layers that make up the design in Figure 7.7

Text Considerations

You will primarily communicate with your users through visuals and through text. Getting the text right is as important as getting your visuals right, so be sure to give text the proper level of consideration. Both the appearance of your text and its content influence how effectively a user can read and interpret what you're communicating.

When creating comps, use real text. It's easy to fall into the habit of using "lorem ipsum" filler text, but that can create a disconnect from the real content. How long are the titles? Is the text full of long, scientific terms or short capitalized acronyms? By using real text in your designs, you are forced to consider whether text should wrap and how full or empty the design will really be. This is one of the times when it is very useful for designers to work with the development team (including any server-side developers, when applicable) to get examples of real content. If a designer just creates a screen that shows a list of country names for the user to pick from, "U.S.A." might fit the design perfectly, but how does it look when the server actually returns "United States of America" instead?

In cases where you are designing for an app that does not yet have any real text defined, it's a little harder to make sure the comps are representative of the final product. Sometimes you can look at similar apps to get a feel for what kinds of text they handle. Other times you just have to take a stab at it and potentially revise once the real text is determined.

Text Contrast

To be easily read, your app's text must have enough contrast with its background. According to the WCAG (Web Content Accessibility Guidelines), your text should have a *minimum* 4.5-to-1 contrast ratio. There are a variety of online tools for determining contrast ratios such as the one at snook.ca (http://www.snook.ca/technical/colour_contrast/colour.html) and the one by Lea Verou (http://leaverou.github.com/contrast-ratio). There are also simple desktop programs that can make calculating contrast easy as well. Contrast Analyser for Windows and Mac is available at http://www.paciellogroup.com/resources/contrast-analyser.html and allows you to quickly check contrasts by using eyedropper tools for picking colors from anywhere on your screen.

Why should you care about maintaining this contrast ratio for text? After all, isn't this intended for people with visual impairments who actually represent a fairly small percentage of users? Although it's easy to dismiss the need for high contrast because it does not always let you create the visual design that you want, it's important to remember that this affects far more people than you might realize. Yes, there are the obvious users who benefit the most from higher contrast, such as those with color vision deficiencies and older users with presbyopia, but high-contrast text makes the app easier to use for everyone, even those with excellent vision. Consider also that your app may run on a variety of devices, each of a different size with a different screen technology. Add in that many devices are woefully reflective and users may be outside in the sun, and suddenly it seems everything is working against designs that don't ensure a high contrast in the text.

Hopefully you are doing your designing on a high-quality monitor that has been calibrated, but you still have to keep in mind that the app will be running on devices with AMOLEDs, which usually have high-contrast ratios and extremely oversaturated colors. It will also run on low-quality TFT LCDs, which often display only a fraction of the full color gamut. Throw some glare on top of a screen with lowered brightness because the user is trying to squeeze the last bit of battery life out of the device, and high contrast becomes vital.

One more consideration with text contrast is the pattern of the background. Whenever possible, the background should be a solid color or a simple gradient. A background with lines, zigzags, and other shapes will interfere with the user's ability to see the text. If it is okay to make the text difficult to read, then the text must not be very important. If the text is not important, why is it in your app?

Text Sizes, Styles, and Capitalization

Text sizes should be established very early on in the design process. It's too easy to decide on sizes for each individual screen and end up with a dozen different sizes in the app. By limiting the number of sizes, you allow the user to quickly learn what they mean. A good starting point is 22 points for a large font, 18 for a medium font, 14 for small, and 12 for very small (these would be implemented as scale independent pixels, or "sp," in the app). You can always adjust the font sizes as needed, but sticking to a small set of sizes will keep your design consistent. These sizes will be reasonably consistent across devices (for example, text that is 22dp will appear to be about the same size on multiple devices), with the caveat that the user can increase font sizes. In general, you do not need to design for each possible font size that the user could change to, but you should keep in mind that the sizes can be changed. For instance, try to avoid designing something that requires the text to be an exact height and breaks otherwise.

Android supports the typical range of styling for text such as bold, italic, and underline. As with any design, use these sparingly. If everything is bold, nothing is. If an entire paragraph is in italics, it is simply harder for the user to read. If every other word is underlined, there is a lot of visual clutter for the user to make sense of.

Avoid using all capitals whenever possible. If you send someone a message in all capital letters, it will be interpreted as yelling. If you create a design in all capitals, it will be interpreted as having poor readability. There are a lot of different theories about how text is read. One of the most prevalent has to do with word and letter shape where the approximate shape of letters and words is used for recognition. Another theory deals with parallel letter recognition in which several letters are being recognized at the same time. Regardless of which model is correct, the reality is that most people rarely read capitalized text. Because of that, reading capitalized text is harder and requires more effort.

Figure 7.9 demonstrates an app with some text in mixed casing and then all caps. The left side shows the app as is, and the right side shows it with the shapes emphasized. You can see that even when ignoring the spacing between letters, mixed casing creates much more detail in the shapes rather than everything looking like a rectangle.

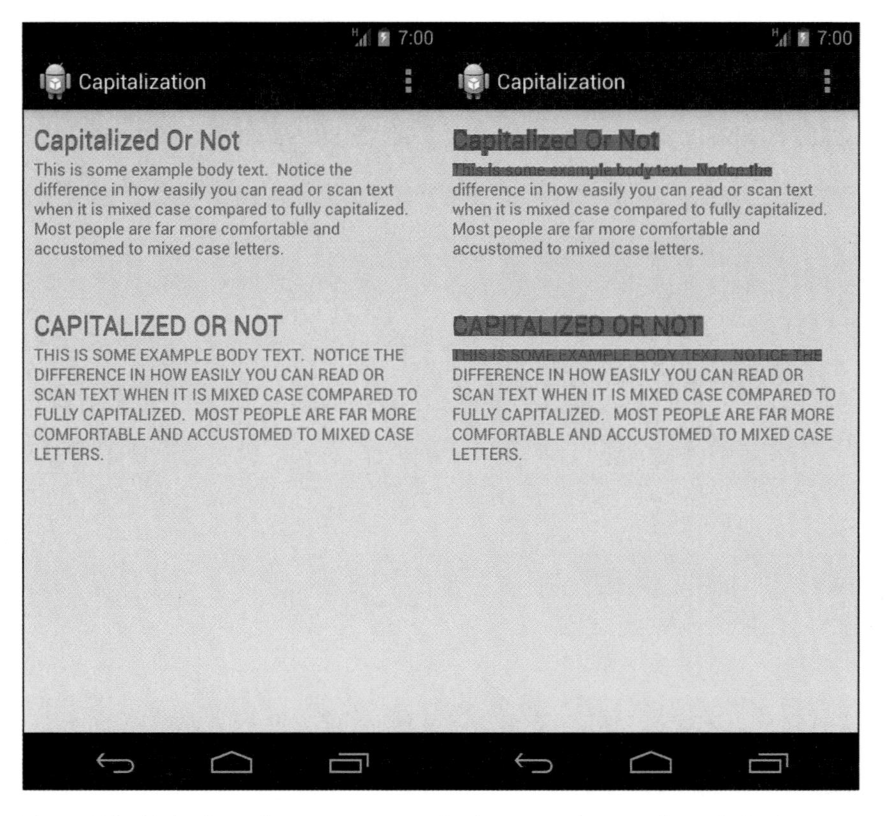

Figure 7.9 Notice how all caps creates text that is rectangular regardless of what it says.

Text Spacing

Unfortunately, Android is extremely limited when it comes to spacing in text. Line spacing, also called "leading," can be adjusted by a multiplier (for example, use 1 or 1.5) and an extra amount that's added or subtracted. For example, you can use a line spacing of 1.5 and add 2sp to each line, but you cannot do much more than that. One important thing to know is that if you are decreasing the line spacing, you may end up clipping descenders (the portion of a letter that goes below the baseline, such as the bottom of a *g*), so you may have to compensate with extra padding.

Android does not natively support adjusting kerning or tracking. Implementing custom kerning is a nontrivial effort, so it's best to pick a font that already has a default kerning that works for your design. The hours that would be spent developing a custom view to display a font with a slightly different kerning can be better spent on other aspects of the app.

Text Shadows

Text shadows can be used to give a little extra to some text. They're particularly useful when you want text to look pushed into the screen or pulled out. You can also use text shadows to help create more contrast around text or to draw users' eyes toward a particular part of the screen, such as a header. Consider carefully before using shadows on body text; smaller text can become more difficult to read with strong shadows. See Figure 7.10 for examples of text shadows.

Figure 7.10 Notice how the shadows work much better for heading text than body text.

Android has one particular quirk about the way it handles text shadows. Essentially the shadow is drawn and then the text is drawn on top of it. This sounds obvious and generally works, but having partially transparent text means that the shadow shows through the text. In some cases this can be what you want, but it often just works to muddy the text. You end up with your text color where the shadow isn't, a mix of your text color and the shadow where they overlap, and just the shadow outside of that. See Figure 7.11, which takes the same design as in Figure 7.10 and uses partially transparent text to let the shadow show through. The top-left section is blown up to help show the problem.

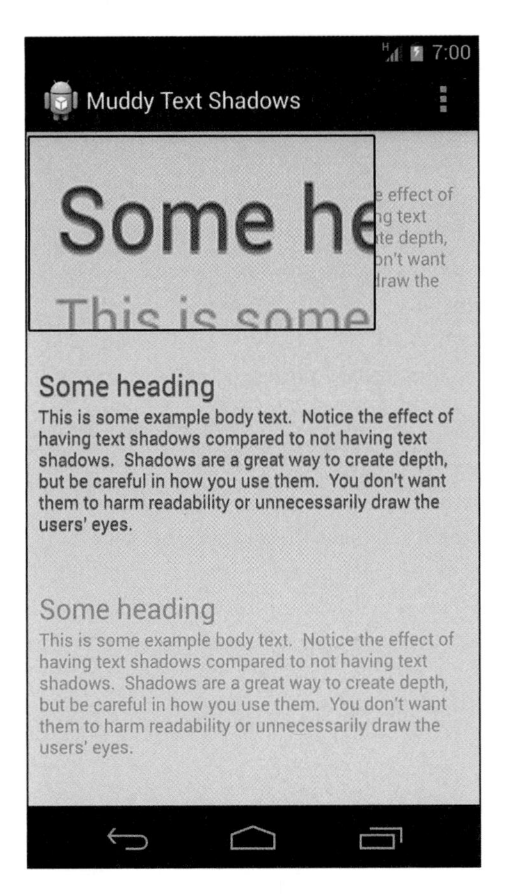

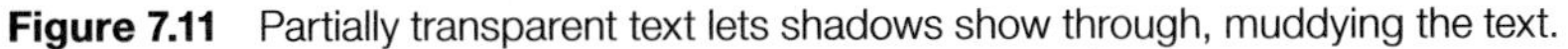
Figure 7.11 Partially transparent text lets shadows show through, muddying the text.

Custom Fonts

Traditionally, Android used the Droid family of fonts. The Droid fonts worked but they were not as clean as some more popular fonts such as Helvetica. Fortunately, the font Roboto was specifically designed for Android and added in Ice Cream Sandwich (Android 4.0). For most designs, this font should be considered first because it has been specifically built for mobile devices of varying densities and tends to render better across screen types, including those that don't use traditional RGB striping.

To better understand fonts, it's a good idea to learn about the basic classifications. The two primary types are serif and sans-serif. Serifs are little ends to strokes in each letter. For instance, an *H* would have three strokes to make up the letter but the two ends at the top and two ends at the bottom would also include horizontal strokes. Serif fonts are very common in print and are more "traditional" than sans-serif fonts. The word "sans" means without, so a sans-serif font is a font that does not have serifs. Serif fonts are sometimes referred to as Roman fonts (thus, you get fonts such as Times New Roman) and sans-serif fonts can be referred to as grotesk (or "grotesque") fonts. There are also other types such as script (a font that looks handwritten), but those are rarely used in functional design because they're extremely hard to read.

Of the sans-serif fonts, there are three main groups: grotesk, geometric, and humanist. Grotesk fonts make up a large number of sans-serif fonts and are the oldest of the sans-serif families (which is why sans-serif fonts are sometimes all grouped into the grotesk category). Geometric fonts use very obvious shapes and curves. Humanist fonts tend to more closely follow the lines a human would actually make when drawing a letter, so an *o* might not be a perfect circle. Humanist fonts are usually a bit more legible than geometric fonts, but they can also appear more visually complex. If you're curious, Roboto falls into the neo-grotesk (as in "new grotesk") font grouping. It also tends to have straight edges that allow it to render well across screen types and densities.

What does all this mean to you? Well, if you did not follow any of that, then you should use Roboto. It's available via http://developer.android.com/design/style/typography.html and includes a few varieties, so heavily consider using it. If you are dead set on using another font, be sure to test it on multiple screens (consider densities as well as sub-pixel layouts). Many thin/light fonts will not look good on AMOLEDs that use a PenTile matrix, so consider testing on devices such as the Nexus S.

Accessible Vocabulary

Text is not all about appearance. One of the important things to consider with text is how understandable it is to the end user. If you're targeting a general audience, that means you have to consider a variety of educational levels. Whenever possible, use plain, obvious language. For instance, don't say "reauthenticate" when you can say "log in again." Avoid technical jargon, use words consistently, and be succinct.

Standard Icons

The Android design site has a section specifically on iconography that is well worth reading (http://developer.android.com/design/style/iconography.html), and the main site also has an article about icons plus specific articles about each individual type of icon (http://developer.android.com/guide/practices/ui_guidelines/icon_design.html). Be sure to read these thoroughly before creating any icons for your app, whether they're launcher icons, notification bar icons, action bar icons, or something else entirely.

Android's launcher icons can be any shape you desire, so consider using shape to help users locate your app. For example, if your app is a world exploration app, your icon might be an image of the world, effectively a circle. Do not just create a rounded rectangle because it's common or can be used on iOS as well. Shape is one of the key visual indicators that people use to identify something, so use this flexibility of Android to your advantage.

Dynamic Content Considerations

It is easy to design for the ideal case, but you also have to consider each of the other states of the app. What does it look like when content is loading? What about when it fails to load? What if the content is longer or shorter than expected?

Varying Text Lengths

Although it was mentioned earlier, it's worth mentioning again: Use real content for your comps. Forcing yourself to use real content means your comps are much more likely to encounter the same scenarios that the developer will have to handle. If you design all your comps for ideal text sizes ("Hey, I've got enough room for a four-letter username, so 'Jake' would be perfect!"), you end up with great comps that don't help the development of the app as much as they should. The developer ends up trying to make reasonable guesses as to how to handle the real content and the developer probably has neither a background in design nor the time to really consider how the UI will be affected. Of course, that doesn't mean every case needs to be designed. Oftentimes, it is enough to design for the 80-percent case (in other words, pick text that is representative of 80 percent of use cases) and include details about how to handle others (for example, "limit text to one line and ellipsize").

Image Availability and Size

Include placeholder images for any images that will be loaded dynamically. The user experience becomes very jarring when images suddenly appear and text jumps around on the page to accommodate those images. Be sure to consider the aspect ratio of images. If you're connecting to a service that you have no control over for the images, you are going to need to take a representative sample and see how they look cropped in different ways. Do they need to fill the space or be fully displayed? Should they be enlarged if they're too small?

Navigation and Transitions

Considering navigation and transitions between UI early and often will help ensure that you create a better overall user experience. What does the UI look like while it is being interacted with? What about when swiping between lists? How does the next screen animate in? Just like the rest of the design, these considerations aren't just aesthetic. For example, the way in which the next view animates in affects whether the user perceives it as a new page and thus whether he or she thinks the back button will reverse the transition. Animations are covered more in Chapter 9, "Further Improving the App."

Error Cases

Do not forget your error cases. Do not forget your error cases. No, repeating that was not a mistake. Gracefully handling errors is a significant user experience consideration that should be well designed. This covers everything from the user entering an invalid email address to the device running out of storage space. It is very common to not design for these cases and to end up with a developer-designed result such as an ugly pop-up that just says, "No space available." That is neither good looking nor useful for the user. In fact, these nondesigned errors can feel rather jarring, which makes them much more troubling to the user. Instead of thinking, "Oh, I forgot the at symbol in my email address," the user might think, "What did I break?"

If an app is well designed, even the error states are designed and feel like they belong. Error messages should simply acknowledge a problem and give the user enough information to act upon the problem, without being judgmental. Sometimes you can use simple animation to draw the user's attention to an error (such as a minor shake of an `EditText` field). Other times it is enough to use color to indicate where a problem lies. See Figure 7.12 for an extremely simple example that uses color to indicate a problem, and both color and proximity to associate it with the applicable `EditText` view.

Summary

Designing an effective user interface is a lot of work. You have to consider what stakeholders want and what users need, somehow finding the balance between using existing patterns and visuals and creating a new, recognizable design. You also have to consider what is technically feasible, which brings up the importance of having the designer(s) and developer(s) communicate early and often. That communication is extremely valuable because it also forces the designer to talk through why the design is the way it is (what is it trying to accomplish) and allows the developer to understand what aspects are most important when the design might not be able to be perfectly met in code. Establish your patterns early (fonts, text sizes, color palette, touch states, and so on) and ensure they are consistent. Use color as a secondary indicator and follow conventions where applicable.

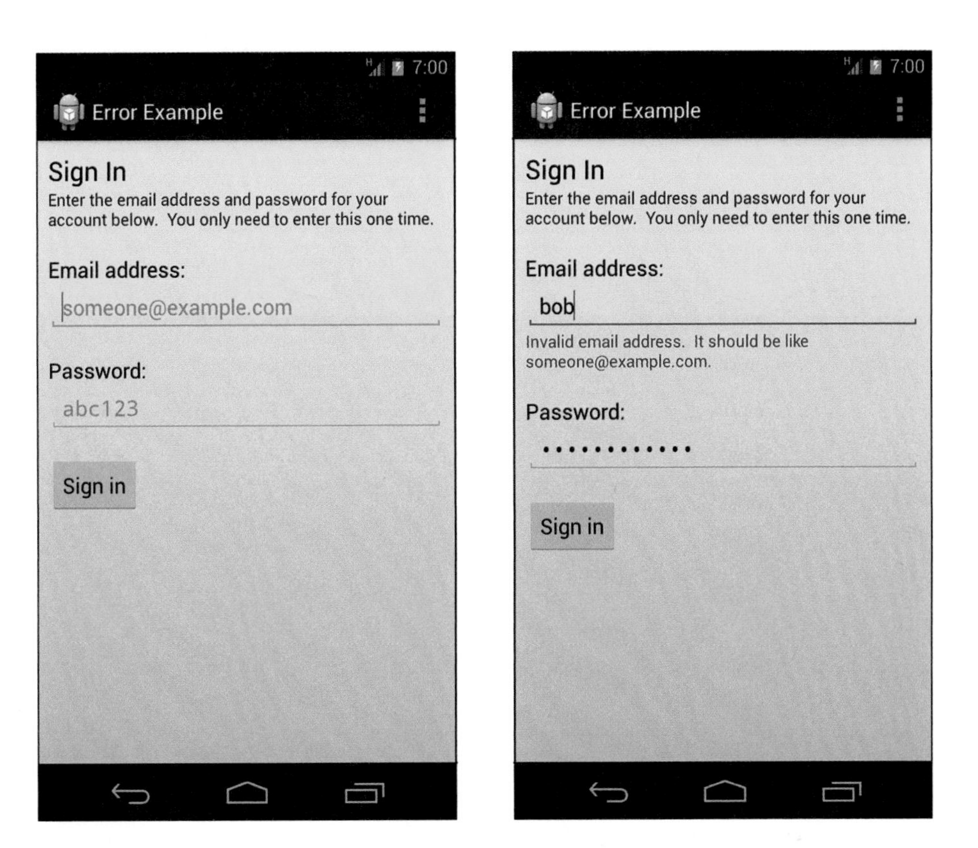

Figure 7.12 A simple error message associated with a specific `EditText`

In the next chapter, you will see how to begin implementing an actual design. You will also learn how a developer can communicate what he or she needs to the designer to get the right assets and stay true to the designer's vision.

CHAPTER 8

APPLYING THE DESIGN

Once you have a design ready to implement, you have to start breaking it apart into the various Android views needed to re-create the design as faithfully as possible. The first step to this is to really understand the design, and that means the designer and developer need to communicate early and often. Once the developer knows what the designer intends, the developer can communicate what assets are needed and begin implementing the design. This chapter focuses on both the communication between the developer and the designer and the techniques a developer can use to create the design in the app.

Working with the Designer

One of the challenges when applying design to an Android app is that developers and designers tend to speak different languages. Developers use Eclipse and ADT; designers use Photoshop and Illustrator. Developers speak in density independent pixels and scale independent pixels; designers speak in pixels and points. Developers typically focus on function and designers focus on form; the best designers and developers consider both form and function.

One other thing to consider in the differences between developers and designers is that there are specialties. Developers often don't realize that there are many types of design specialties such as graphic design (a focus on the visual elements of a design) and interactive design (a focus on how the user interacts with the visual elements of a design). Most designers, especially in the mobile environment, have experience with several of the design specialties, but they often have more expertise in one specialty. The same is true of developers. Many designers don't realize there are different specialties for developers. A developer can have extensive UI implementation experience, creating incredibly smooth user interfaces and yet balk at implementing the A-star algorithm. Similarly, a developer can implement low-level data transmission protocols with his or her eyes closed and yet have no idea how to use OpenGL.

The sooner you can get past the "designers make it pretty; developers make it work" mentality and acknowledge the subtleties of others' expertise, the sooner you can start working as a team. Learn the key parts of each other's vocabulary where your work directly interacts. For example, a developer should understand what the designer means by terms such as comps (comprehensive layouts are essentially the final design that most represent what the product should look like on device) and slices (the individual graphics assets that make up the design, such as the image for a button). Designers should understand the basic idea of a view and an action bar, for instance. A designer who really understands what a fragment is can design in a way that is easier for a developer to work with.

Once you have started to work with each other, ask questions. A designer should not be afraid to ask questions such as "Can this interaction be made smoother?" or "Do we have control over the alignment of this text?" A developer should not be afraid to ask, "What does this look like when scrolling between items?" or "What's the goal of this font style?" Speaking of goals, it's a great idea to have the designer explain to the developer the overarching theme and reasoning behind choices. There are going to be times when the developer has to do some interpretation of the design, such as when handling an obscure edge case, and knowing the intent of the designer can help ensure a cohesive visual experience for the user.

Stay in constant communication. If you want a broken app, a great way to develop it is to have the designer create something in a dark corner and then hand it off to the developer to implement in a different dark corner. Designers often like to push the limits of what can be done to create an exciting user experience, so having developer feedback early can help. The designer also won't know the level of effort behind most development. Without communication, you can end up in a situation like this: The developer spends two weeks with his or her head down in RenderScript creating a fabulous scrolling carousel and neglecting the other features. Then the designer sees it and wonders why everything else looks terrible. The developer explains how much effort the carousel was and how the other parts didn't seem as significant, and then the designer says, "Oh, well that's not really an important part of the design. I just thought it'd be cool if the items curved slightly as they went off the screen."

Slicing the Graphics Assets

One of the important parts of going from gorgeous comps to an amazing UI is "slicing," which refers to cutting the pieces of the comps into specific assets that the app needs. Sometimes this process is easy, such as saving out the background for a page. Other times it involves some work, such as when a given asset actually spans several layers in Photoshop (or whatever graphical tool is used). Designers frequently use layers to achieve various visual effects, from multiplying colors to adding gloss, so it is not always just the case of cropping a portion of the screen and saving to a new file. Additionally, many assets will work best as nine-patch images. To best slice the assets, the designer needs to explain the effect that is desired and the developer has to explain how to cut up the pieces to get that effect, keeping in mind the device constraints.

The Easy Slices

Some slices are just plain easy to create. Things such as the background can often just be used as is or with some minimal resizing. Assets that should be tiled just need to be sliced into pieces that can be tiled either by repeating the tile or by mirroring it. See Figure 8.1 for an example of a background that has been tiled by simply repeating the same image (red lines added to show where the edges of the tiles are). Figure 8.2 demonstrates tiling by mirroring (that is, it flips the image to align the edges). These tiled assets as well as simple gradients work well for backgrounds because they can support a variety of screen sizes without appearing distorted. See Listing 8.1 for an example of an XML drawable that tiles an image via mirroring (change "mirror" to "repeat" for standard tiling).

Listing 8.1 An XML Drawable That Tiles an Image

```
<?xml version="1.0" encoding="utf-8"?>
<bitmap xmlns:android="http://schemas.android.com/apk/res/android"
    android:src="@drawable/bg_tile"
    android:tileMode="mirror" />
```

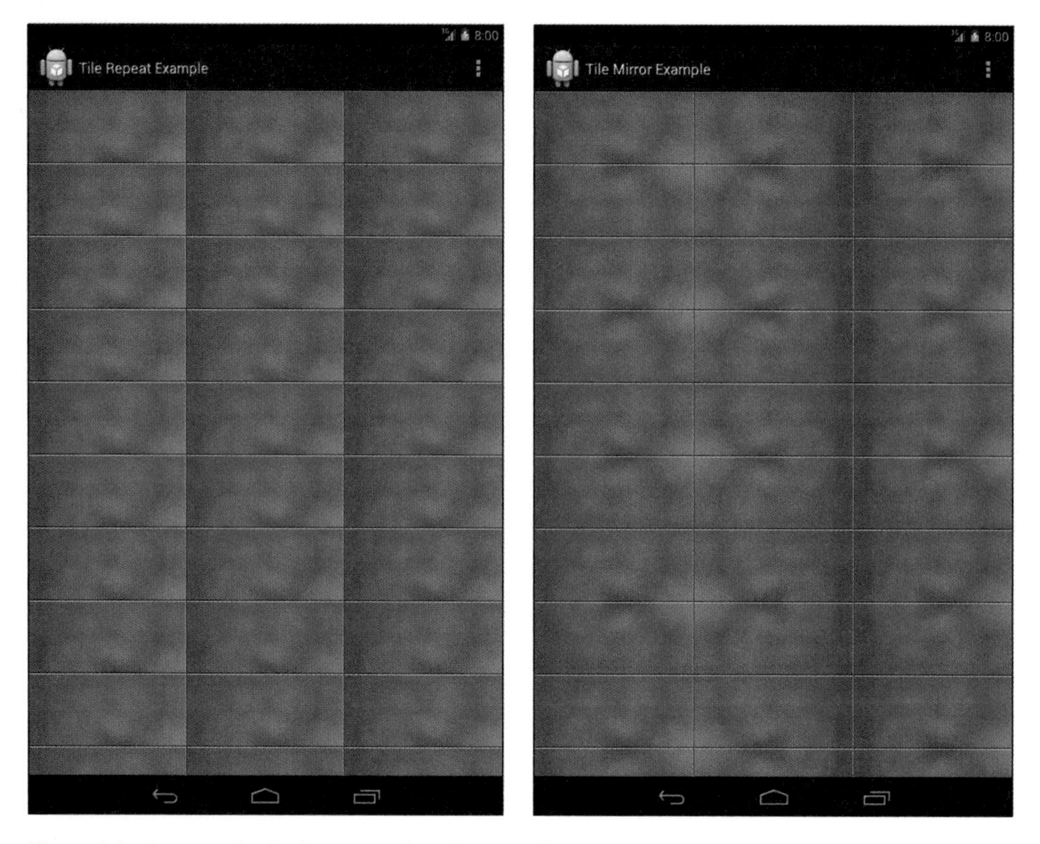

Figure 8.1 An example of using a repeating tile background

Figure 8.2 An example of using a mirrored tile background

Other easy slices are placeholder images, logos, and images that can basically be used as is, such as existing icons. You can download a large array of Android action bar icons via the design site (http://developer.android.com/design/downloads/index.html), which saves you work and ensures you are using the standard icons your users will already understand. If you still need something else, consider using the Android Asset Studio to generate your icons (http://android-ui-utils.googlecode.com/hg/asset-studio/dist/index.html).

Nine-Patch Images

Containers are commonly able to be sliced into nine-patch images because they are intended to fit variably sized content while giving some sense of edges or grouping. A nine-patch image is simply an image that has some extra pixels specifying what portion of the image can stretch and where content can go within the image. For example, buttons are usually containers that have text or an icon in them. The middle portion of a button needs to be big enough to fit whatever the text is in it (keeping in mind that the amount of space required to explain the button's action will vary for different languages and for different font sizes). The defining feature of a button is usually the edge, which lets it stand out as something touchable by casting a shadow or catching the light. The corners are sometimes rounded, so you want to preserve that radius but extend the flat sides to fit the content.

The two main ways that designers create nine-patch images are the `draw9patch` tool that comes with the Android SDK and the program they already use for creating images (for example, Photoshop). The `draw9patch` tool has the advantage of giving previews of the image being resized horizontally, vertically, and in both directions. Despite the fact that a specialized tool exists for creating nine-patch images, they are actually extremely easy to create in Photoshop, GIMP, or any other image manipulation software, which is sometimes preferable because creating nine-patches this way more easily fits into a typical design workflow.

If you have an existing asset that you want to make into a nine-patch image, open it in a separate file. For example, you might have a button such as the one in Figure 8.3. Although all you need to do to make an image into a nine-patch is to add pixels to the outside, it's best to first eliminate any redundancy in the image. For example, this image is wider than it needs to be. The center pixels are repeated, so they can be eliminated. See Figure 8.4 to see the pixels that can be removed highlighted in red. If you look at the vertical row of pixels immediately to the left of the reddened section, you can see each of these pixels is just repeated for the entire red section. By deleting the red section and bringing the two ends together, you can save a lot of wasted space and you also make sure that the button will work well in a variety of situations (such as when the string on it might be short, such as "on").

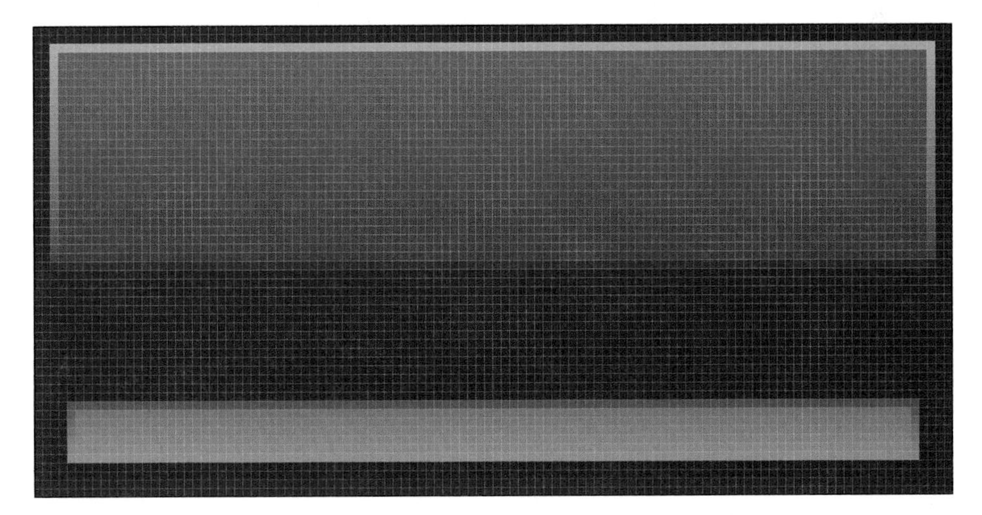

Figure 8.3 An enlarged example of a custom toggle button

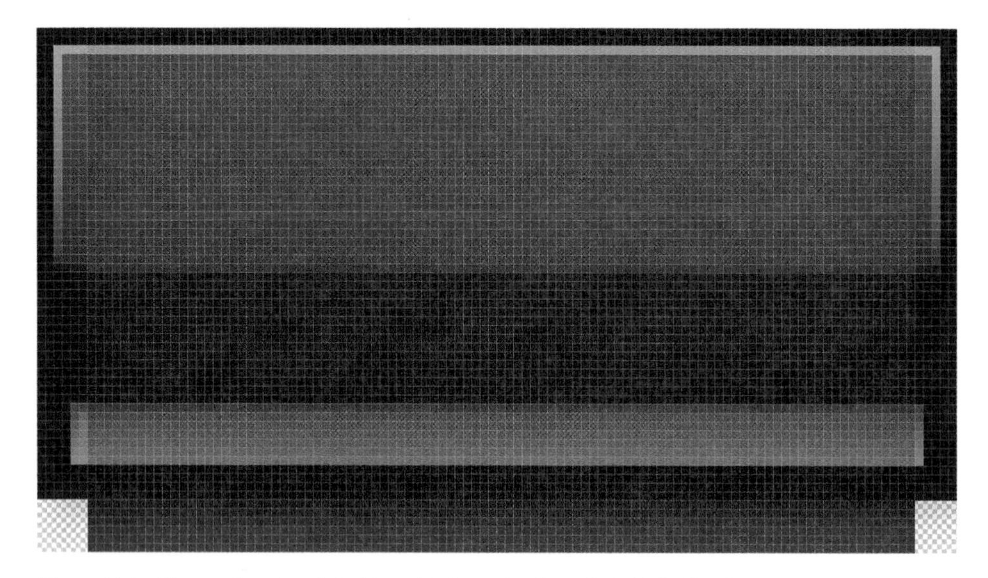

Figure 8.4 The previous toggle button with the redundant pixels highlighted in red

After eliminating any extra pixels in the image, you want to crop it tightly so there are no wasted pixels (the example image is cropped right up to the button and to the end of the drop shadow at the bottom). Then, expand the canvas by two pixels vertically and horizontally, ensuring that your content is centered. Create fully opaque black pixels on the left where the image can stretch vertically and black pixels on the top where it can stretch horizontally. Black pixels added to the right and bottom indicate where content can be placed (such as the "on" text). Frequently, the pixels indicating content location will be directly across from the pixels that indicate where the image can stretch, but that's not always the case. In the end, you should have something like Figure 8.5.

Generating Alternate Sizes

Although Android will scale images for you, it is much better to supply correctly sized assets for each density you will support. Not only does this keep your app looking better, but it also improves performance and decreases processing and memory overhead.

Generally, assets should be created at a resolution much higher than what will ultimately be used. They can then be resized for each of the densities you will support. At the very least, your assets should be created with XHDPI in mind (if not XXHDPI) and resized for each of the other densities you intent to support. A variety of tools are available online that can do this for you. For example, "9Patch Resizer" is a simple Java application that you can drag XHDPI files onto to create HDPI, MDPI, and LDPI assets (it works on nine-patch images and regular images alike). It's freely available at http://code.google.com/p/9patch-resizer/. The Android Asset Studio (http://android-ui-utils.googlecode.com/hg/asset-studio/dist/index.html) also has several tools available for generating alternate densities and specific assets.

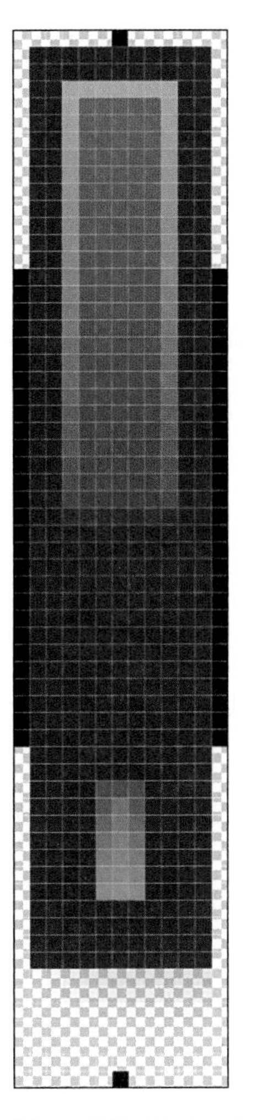

Figure 8.5 The toggle button with redundant pixels removed and nine-patch indicators added

Unfortunately, there are times when you'll find a certain asset is not resized well by one of the automated tools and you need to resize it by hand. There is no simple step-by-step guide for resizing images because it depends on the content of the image and how much you're shrinking it, but there are a few tips to consider. If the image is based on a vector asset, work with the vector asset again instead of shrinking the image that's already rasterized the vector asset. Try different scaling algorithms. For shrinking images, Photoshop's "Bicubic Sharper" works the best in most cases, but not all. In cases where you are dealing with shrinking an image to exactly half the size in each dimension (such as when going from XHDPI to MDPI), bi-linear can give good results. Keep in mind that other software has other algorithms (for example, GIMP has Lanczos3 but Photoshop does not), so you may need to try other tools if you're not satisfied with what your usual software is giving you.

Updating Themes and Styles

Hopefully you have been developing your app with themes and styles. Once you've received a design, work with the designer to understand the visual patterns. In some cases, the patterns will have already been established by the wireframes, so you just need to update the colors or font treatment and everything will look good; however, most of the time the design is different enough from the wireframes (or the wireframes were never actually created) that you need to do quite a bit of work.

Create an overall app theme that extends the system theme that is closest to what you want. The recent versions of ADT will automatically generate version-specific themes for you, so this process is a lot easier than it used to be. If you are making a change that's not version specific, put it in the base `styles.xml` file (in `res/values`). If you are referencing resources that are not available in the `minSdkVersion` you have specified in your manifest, be sure to put those references in version-specific folders.

Try to group styles based on function rather than appearance. For instance, you should have a "Header" style as opposed to a "BigRedText" style. What if you really do have two headers, one with big red text and one with big blue text? Ask the designer why. Is it because one is a top-level header and one is a subheader? Is one used for the main page and another for the detail page? If nothing else, try to break them up without exact color. For example, you might have a header that is dark text and one that is light. Something like "Header.Light" is a much better name than "Header.Red" because it's more likely to be true even after design updates. The red color might have shifted to orange or even green, but it's probably still going to be dark text if the background is light or light text if the background is dark.

Ideally, the designer creates a style guide that explains all the styles, but that is not commonly the case. Sometimes styles are called out in the "redlines" (typically a document containing multiple comps that have been marked up to specify spacing, assets, and so on) for specific screens instead of in a full guide. And other times the developer has to interpret the comps to figure out what is intended. Looking at Figure 8.6, you can see an enlarged version of some header text. The important parts are that this is the default Roboto font and it is bold; also, a small text shadow appears directly below the text. After learning the details of this header, the developer would create something like Listing 8.2.

Figure 8.6 Enlarged sample header text from a comp

Listing 8.2 A Sample Style for a Simple Heading

```
<style name="Heading">
  <item name="android:shadowColor">#FF221100</item>
  <item name="android:shadowDx">0</item>
  <item name="android:shadowDy">1</item>
  <item name="android:shadowRadius">.1</item>
  <item name="android:textAppearance">?android:attr/
➥textAppearanceLarge</item>
  <item name="android:textColor">#FF663300</item>
  <item name="android:textStyle">bold</item>
</style>
```

Breaking Comps into Views

In Chapter 6, "Developing the App Foundation," you learned how to break wireframes into views. Wireframes are often very easy to split into views because each piece of information being presented tends to map to a specific view. Breaking comps into views can be a little more challenging, especially if you did not have the advantage of seeing any wireframes.

Take a look at Figure 8.7, which shows a fairly simple design. How many views are in this design? Look closely at the image to note that it has the image of the flowers, a 1px black border around the image, and an overly strong shadow. What would you do to create that effect?

This design is actually extremely simple inside of a `LinearLayout` that has a tiled background (the background is very subtle to give it a hint of texture without drawing your eyes). There is a `TextView` for the header, a `View` for the horizontal line, a `TextView` for the intro text, a single `ImageView` for the flowers, and a final `TextView`. The `ImageView` has a background nine-patch image that is basically a black square with a transparent center and a shadow. The transparent center is marked as where the content goes. See Listing 8.3 for one possible implementation of this layout.

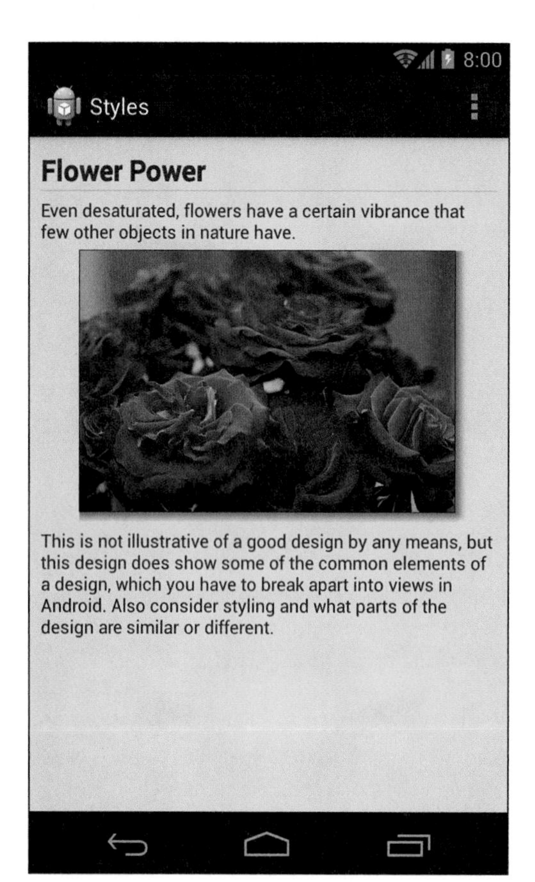

Figure 8.7 Simple example of a comp with just a few views

Listing 8.3 A Sample Implementation of the Layout in Figure 8.7

```
<LinearLayout
    xmlns:android="http://schemas.android.com/apk/res/android"
    xmlns:tools="http://schemas.android.com/tools"
    android:layout_width="match_parent"
    android:layout_height="match_parent"
    android:background="@drawable/bg"
    android:orientation="vertical"
    android:padding="10dp"
    tools:context=".MainActivity" >
```

```
    <TextView
        android:id="@+id/heading"
        style="@style/Heading"
        android:layout_width="match_parent"
        android:layout_height="wrap_content"
        android:layout_marginBottom="1dp"
        android:text="@string/flower_power" />

    <View style="@style/Divider" />

    <TextView
        android:id="@+id/intro"
        android:layout_width="match_parent"
        android:layout_height="wrap_content"
        android:text="@string/intro_text"
        android:layout_marginBottom="5dp"
        android:layout_marginTop="5dp"
        android:textAppearance="?android:attr/textAppearanceSmall" />

    <ImageView
        android:id="@+id/image"
        android:layout_width="wrap_content"
        android:layout_height="wrap_content"
        android:layout_gravity="center_horizontal"
        android:background="@drawable/dropshadow"
        android:contentDescription="@string/flowers"
        android:layout_marginLeft="5dp"
        android:src="@drawable/flowers" />

    <TextView
        android:id="@+id/body"
        android:layout_width="match_parent"
        android:layout_height="wrap_content"
        android:layout_marginTop="5dp"
        android:text="@string/body_text"
        android:textAppearance="?android:attr/textAppearanceSmall" />

</LinearLayout>
```

In some cases, you do have the advantage of seeing wireframes and then the final comps. Consider Figure 8.8, which shows a simple wireframe from a profile page on a photography app. You can see it essentially has a header section that describes the person with a thumbnail, name, and title/descriptor. Below that is the content area, which is just a scrollable list of photos (demonstrated on the right side of Figure 8.8).

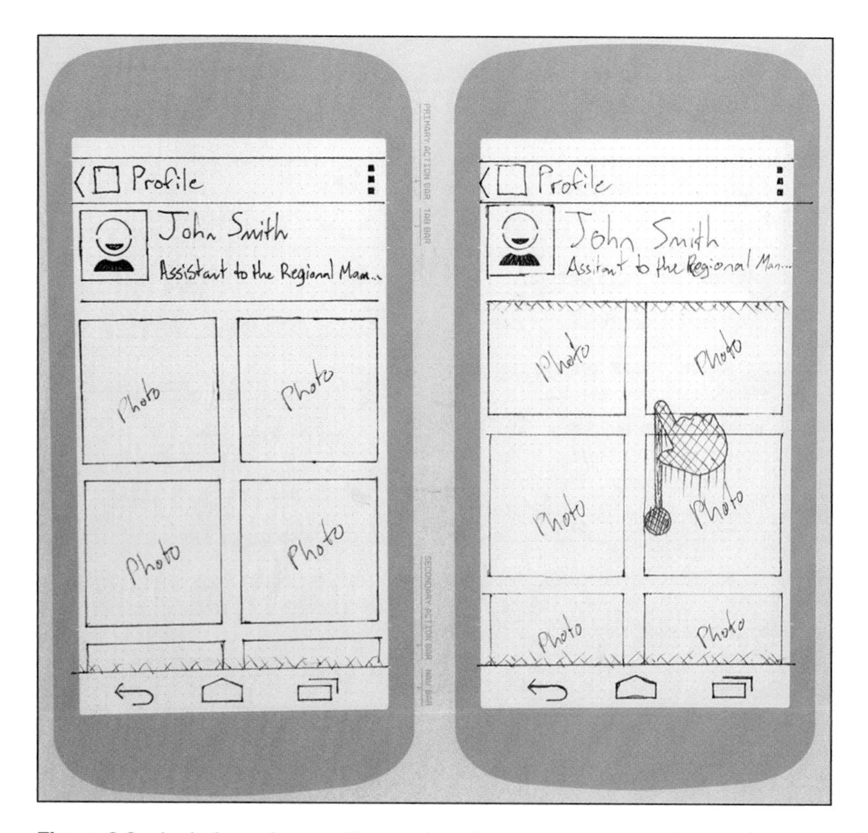

Figure 8.8 A wireframe for a profile page in a photography app showing the default view (left) and the view as it is scrolled (right)

Now look at Figure 8.9. This is one possible design interpretation of the previous wireframe. The action bar is dark, but it has a hint of red to it. The header section is mostly kept in line with the wireframe, except that the title/descriptor is clearly pulled up to the name here. The thumbnail and text have an etched appearance to give them a little bit of depth. The content area is very similar to the wireframe with just a slight border added to each image and an abstract background. A thin red line marks the top and bottom of the content and helps separate the content from the onscreen navigation buttons at the bottom of newer devices.

This example is a bit more interesting than the previous one because it clearly does not fit into a single `LinearLayout` or even a pair of `LinearLayouts`. Look at Figure 8.8 and Figure 8.9 for a moment and consider how you would implement it.

Figure 8.9 One sample design created based on the wireframe in Figure 8.8

If you put this in a vertical `LinearLayout`, you have two sections: the header and the content. The header can be a `RelativeLayout` containing an `ImageView` and two `TextViews`. The content is a `GridView`. See Figure 8.10 for a visual breakdown of the views.

Some developers default to `LinearLayouts` for everything and would have made a horizontal `LinearLayout` for the header that contained a vertical `LinearLayout` for the two `TextViews`. You should avoid making a similar mistake. Any time you nest `LinearLayouts`, consider whether a `RelativeLayout` would make more sense. A `RelativeLayout` doesn't always make more sense (for example, when you have a few rows of views), but it can often simplify your layouts and make them more efficient. If you have nested `LinearLayouts` that go from vertical to horizontal to vertical, you almost definitely have a case for a `RelativeLayout`.

Figure 8.10 A visual breakdown of the views you could use to create the design

Improving Efficiency

You have several techniques for improving the efficiency of your app with regard to your layouts. The most obvious one is to simplify your layouts, as mentioned briefly previously (this is also covered in more detail in Chapter 11, "Combining Views for Custom Components"). Other techniques for improving efficiency are controlling garbage collection, decreasing the number of methods and amount of view traversal you do, and controlling how much you draw onscreen.

Controlling Garbage Collection

One of the great things about Java is you are mostly removed from the monotonous task of memory management. Computers, including smartphones, are amazingly powerful and should be able to handle most memory management themselves. When this burden is taken off the developer, the developer can focus on features instead of tracking down pointer errors and memory leaks. The problem is that it is very easy to become accustomed to not thinking about memory at all. Then suddenly the garbage collector has to clean up your mess and the UI freezes. Android 2.3 added concurrent garbage collection, so the 100+ms garbage collector pauses have been eliminated, but even fast garbage collection in the 5ms range can cause hiccups.

Consider the user scrolling through a long list of items. To perform at 60fps (the ideal frame rate), you need to do all your calculations and drawing in about 16ms. If garbage collection is taking one-third of that, it becomes a lot harder to keep your UI feeling smooth. The clear solution is to avoid instantiating new objects or removing references in performance-sensitive code. That means any code that handles laying out views, animating, drawing to the screen, or interpreting user interactions (for example, touch events) needs to be efficient. This is covered in depth in the later chapters of this book, but an important consideration early on is with `AdapterView`s such as `ListView`.

`AdapterView`s use an `Adapter` to create their views. The `getView(int, View, ViewGroup)` method is called each time a new view needs to be displayed. Well-behaved `AdapterView`s such as `ListView` will pass in an existing "convert view" that can (and should) be reused (this convert view is a view that was displayed but has since been pushed off the screen). Look at Listing 8.4, which is a truncated version of the code from Listing 6.4 that you developed as part of the prototype in Chapter 6. In particular, look at the `getView` method and notice that the layout is only inflated if the `convertView` is null; otherwise, the existing `convertView` is reused to avoid inflation and extra garbage collection.

Listing 8.4 The `PropertyListAdapter` from Chapter 6

```
/**
 * ListFragment that displays a List of Property objects.
 *
 * @author Ian G. Clifton
 */
public class PropertyListFragment extends ListFragment {

    ... other code ...

    /**
     * ArrayAdapter that displays Property objects.
     *
     * @author Ian G. Clifton
     */
    private static class PropertyListAdapter extends
➥ArrayAdapter<Property> {

        private final LayoutInflater mInflater;
```

```
        private final String mBath;
        private final String mBed;
        private final String mSqFt;

        public PropertyListAdapter(Context context, List<Property>
➥objects) {
            super(context, -1, objects);
            mInflater = LayoutInflater.from(context);
            final Resources res = context.getResources();
            mBath = " " + res.getString(R.string.bath);
            mBed = " " + res.getString(R.string.bed);
            mSqFt = " " + res.getString(R.string.sq_ft);
        }

        @Override
        public View getView(int position, View convertView, ViewGroup
➥parent) {
            final Property property = getItem(position);

            if (convertView == null) {
                convertView = mInflater.inflate
➥(R.layout.property_listitem, parent, false);
            }

            TextView tv = (TextView) convertView.findViewById
➥(R.id.city);
            tv.setText(property.getCity() + ", " +
➥property.getState());
            tv = (TextView) convertView.findViewById(R.id.price);
            tv.setText(property.getPrice());
            tv = (TextView) convertView.findViewById(R.id.street);
            tv.setText(property.getStreetAddress());
            tv = (TextView) convertView.findViewById(R.id.beds);
            tv.setText(property.getBedroomCount() + mBed);
            tv = (TextView) convertView.findViewById(R.id.baths);
            tv.setText(property.getBathroomCount() + mBath);
            tv = (TextView) convertView.findViewById(R.id.footage);
            tv.setText(property.getFootage() + mSqFt);

            return convertView;
        }
    }
}
```

`ViewHolder` Pattern

Continuing to improve the `ListView`, consider what all is happening for each view that is being displayed. The layout inflation has been eliminated, but each `getView` call traverses the view to find the six `TextViews` that need to be updated. Assuming a simple linear search and only six views, the first view lookup checks one view, the next checks two views, and the last has to look at all six. In total, you perform more than 20 view checks for every single view that gets added to the screen! The more complex the view, the longer it takes to traverse the hierarchy and find the views you are looking for.

The ideal solution would be to only have to find the views one time and then just retain the references, and that's what the `ViewHolder` pattern does. Because you are reusing views (via the convert view), you have to traverse a finite number of views before you have found every view you care about in the list. By creating a class called `ViewHolder` that has references to each of the views you care about, you can instantiate that class once per view in the `ListView` and then reuse that class as much as needed. This class is always implemented as a static inner class, so it is really just acting as a container for view references. See Listing 8.5 for a simple example of a class that takes the view and sets all the necessary references.

Listing 8.5 An Example of a `ViewHolder` Class

```
/**
 * A class that holds view references.
 *
 * @author Ian G. Clifton
 */
private static class ViewHolder {

    /* package */ final TextView baths;
    /* package */ final TextView beds;
    /* package */ final TextView city;
    /* package */ final TextView footage;
    /* package */ final TextView price;
    /* package */ final TextView street;

    /* package */ ViewHolder(View v) {
        baths = (TextView) v.findViewById(R.id.baths);
        beds = (TextView) v.findViewById(R.id.beds);
        city = (TextView) v.findViewById(R.id.city);
        footage = (TextView) v.findViewById(R.id.footage);
        price = (TextView) v.findViewById(R.id.price);
        street = (TextView) v.findViewById(R.id.street);
    }
}
```

Now, you can go back to your `getView` method and make some changes. If `convertView` is null, inflate a new view as you already have and then create a new `ViewHolder`, passing in the view you just created. To keep the `ViewHolder` with this view, call the `setTag` method, which allows you to associate an arbitrary object with any view. If `convertView` is not null, simply call `getTag` and cast the result to your `ViewHolder`.

Now that you have the `ViewHolder`, you can just reference the views directly, so the rest of your `getView` code is not only much simpler than before but also better performing and easier to read. See Listing 8.6 for the updated `getView` call. Any time you use an `Adapter` and you use the child views in the `getView` method, you should use this `ViewHolder` pattern.

Listing 8.6 The `getView` Method Using a `ViewHolder`

```
@Override
public View getView(int position, View convertView, ViewGroup parent) {
    final Property property = getItem(position);
    final ViewHolder holder;
    if (convertView == null) {
        convertView = mInflater.inflate(R.layout.property_listitem,
➥parent, false);
        holder = new ViewHolder(convertView);
        convertView.setTag(holder);
    } else {
        holder = (ViewHolder) convertView.getTag();
    }

    holder.city.setText(property.getCity() + ", " +
➥property.getState());
    holder.price.setText(property.getPrice());
    holder.street.setText(property.getStreetAddress());
    holder.beds.setText(property.getBedroomCount() + mBed);
    holder.baths.setText(property.getBathroomCount() + mBath);
    holder.footage.setText(property.getFootage() + mSqFt);

    return convertView;
}
```

Eliminating Overdraw

Overdraw is when your app causes pixels to be drawn on top of each other. For example, imagine a typical app with a background, whether plain or an image. Now you put an opaque button on it. First, the device draws the background; then it draws the button. The background under the button was drawn but is never seen, so that processing and data transfer are wasted.

You might wonder how you can actually eliminate overdraw then, and the answer is that you do not need to. You only need to eliminate excessive overdraw. What "excessive" means is different for each device, but the general rule of thumb is that you should not be drawing more than 2.5x the number of pixels on the screen (as detailed in Chapter 7, "Finalizing the Design"). When you go above 3x the number of pixels, performance almost always suffers.

It's worth noting that some devices are better than others at efficiently avoiding drawing pixels when opaque pixels would be drawn right on top of them. GPUs that use deferred rendering are able to eliminate overdraw in cases where fully opaque pixels are drawn on fully opaque pixels, but not all Android devices have GPUs that use deferred rendering. Further, if pixels have any amount of transparency, that overdraw cannot be eliminated because the pixels have to be combined. That is why designs that contain a significant amount of transparency are inherently more difficult to make smooth and efficient than designs that do not.

Overdraw is easiest to eliminate when you can see it. Android 4.2 offers a developer option to show GPU overdraw by coloring the screen differently based on how many times a pixel has been drawn and redrawn. To enable it, go to the device settings and then Developer options and scroll to the "drawing" section to enable the Show GPU Overdraw option (see Figure 8.11). When this option is checked, any application that starts up will be colored to show the amount of overdraw. That means if your app is already running, you need to kill it (you can most easily do this by pressing the recent apps key and swiping your app horizontally off the screen).

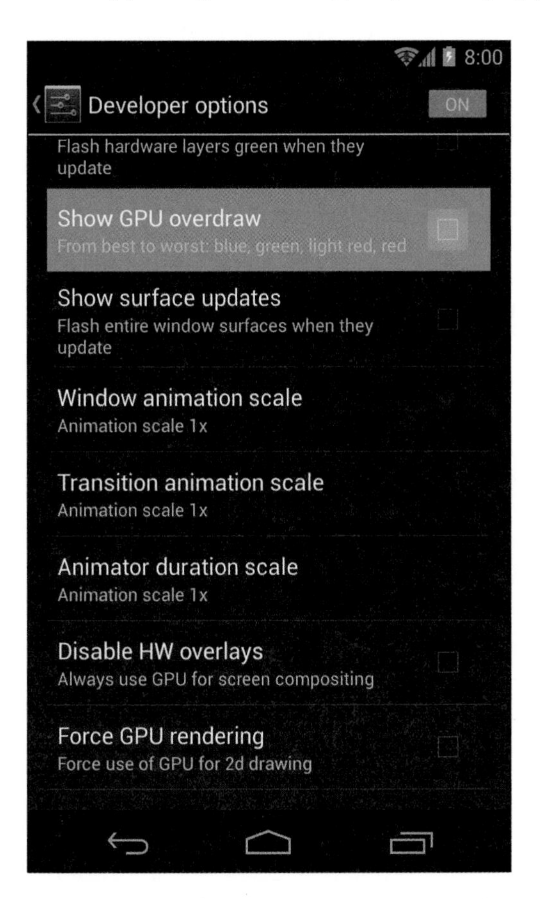

Figure 8.11 The Show GPU Overdraw option in Android's developer options

First, you should understand what the color tints mean. If there is no tint, there is no overdraw, and this is the ideal situation. A blue tint indicates a single overdraw (meaning the pixel was drawn once and then drawn again), and you can think of it as being "cold" because your device can easily handle a single level of overdraw (so the processor is not overheating). When something is tinted green, it has been overdrawn twice. Light red indicates an overdraw of three times, and dark red indicates an overdraw of four (or more) times (red, hot, bad!).

Large sections of blue are acceptable as long as the whole app is not blue. Medium-sized sections of green are okay, but you should avoid having more than half of the screen green. Light red is much worse, but it's still okay for small areas such as text or a tiny icon. Dark red should make you cry. Well, maybe not cry, but you should definitely fix any dark red. These areas are drawn five times (or more), so just imagine your single device powering five screens and you should realize how bad this is.

Looking at an implementation of the design from Figure 8.7, you can get a feel for how this tool works. Figure 8.12 shows one possible implementation of the design and the level of overdraw it creates. Keep in mind that this is just a `LinearLayout` with some simple views. There isn't another `ViewGroup` within it, so overdraw should be minimal.

Then why is the whole app overlaid with blue (making it look slightly purple due to the red styling) to signify that it has been overdrawn? There isn't a single part of the app that wasn't at least drawn twice, and that means something is wrong. If you've verified the layout isn't drawing a background twice, then the most likely cause is your theme. In this case, the app is using a variant of the light theme, depending on the version of Android. All versions of that theme paint a white background. That means the app is painting a white background and then painting the action bar and `LinearLayout` background on top of that. No part of that background shows through, so everything is overdrawn at least one time, and that's why it is all overlaid with blue (or worse).

Your first inclination might be to eliminate the background of the theme. After all, why not null it out if the app is painting over it? Android actually uses that background to generate previews of your app to keep visuals smoother (for example, when you switch back to your app from the recent apps menu, but it is no longer in memory), so you do not want to remove it in XML. The answer is to remove that background once you have added your layout. See Listing 8.7 for an example that removes this in the `onCreate` method of an `Activity`.

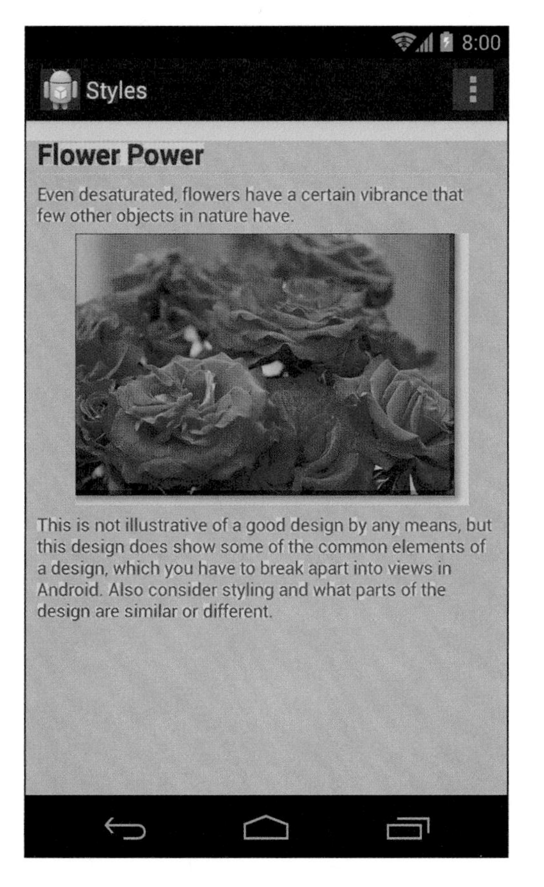

Figure 8.12 Example of an app with overdraw shown

Listing 8.7 Removing the Theme Background

```
@Override
protected void onCreate(Bundle savedInstanceState) {
    super.onCreate(savedInstanceState);
    setContentView(R.layout.activity_main);
    getWindow().setBackgroundDrawable(null);
}
```

Now that the background isn't being redrawn, it's worth looking at the app again and seeing what the overdraw looks like. Figure 8.13 illustrates this. Notice that there is some blue/purple, which is nothing to worry about, and a tiny bit of green (also insignificant). The red has been eliminated. You might be wondering why the header text is green but the body text is blue/purple—that's because the header has a shadow that has to also be drawn, which is another reason to avoid shadows on body text.

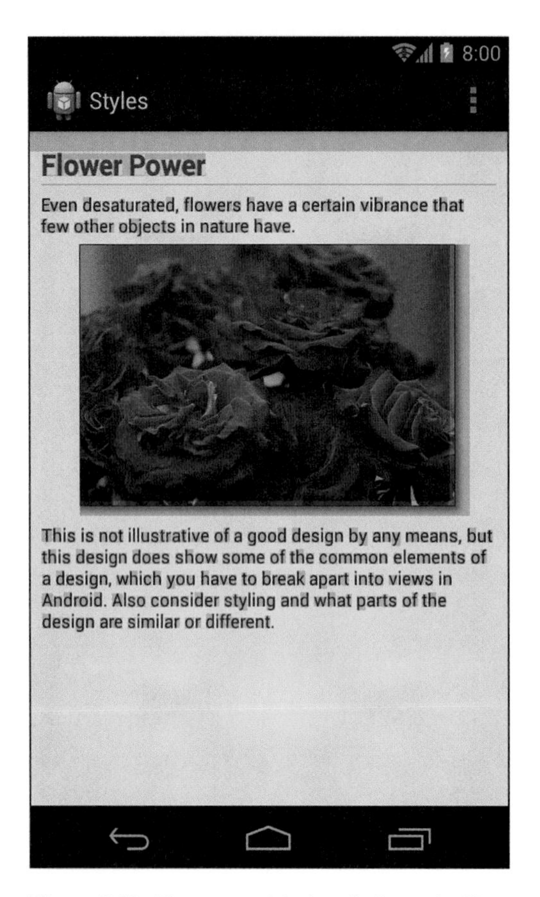

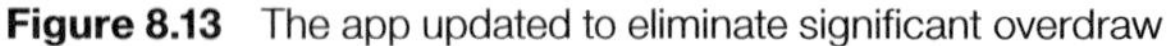

Figure 8.13 The app updated to eliminate significant overdraw

Basic Testing Across Device Types

There are countless variations of Android devices out there, so it's nearly impossible to really test your app against them all. Fortunately, it is relatively easy to test against groups of devices that you intend to support, especially if you are not doing anything complex with the GPU (in other words, not using any manufacturer- or chip-specific features). Typically, only graphically intense games have to consider what GPU is on a given device, and a regular app can more or less ignore the GPU. That means you can focus on device sizes and device densities. For "normal"-sized devices (that is, phone-sized), you should primarily test against HDPI and XHDPI screens. Because many users get their devices on contract, the life span of a device is typically considered to be two or three years, so you can't discount HDPI devices just yet, even though many phones sold today are XHDPI devices.

You should also consider testing against the Nexus 7 as the de facto large device. The Nexus 7 is a great device, but it presents a bit of a challenge. In portrait mode, it is very similar to a phone. The screen is larger, but it does not quite feel tablet sized. That means many apps will work pretty well with little to no modification. Switch it to landscape though, and you suddenly have a device that feels much more like a tablet. It's wide enough to have two panes of content, so you have to consider what that means for your design.

Finally, you should test against "xlarge" or 10" tablets. These tablets do not represent a substantial portion of the Android market right now, but their sales are growing. Most apps are not optimized for 10" tablets, so that means optimizing your app lets you stand out. People tend to like using one app across their devices, so if your app is the only one of its kind that works well across all devices, you just earned yourself some additional installs and users who are likely to be loyal. Just remember than these tablets almost always require changes to the layouts to make efficient use of their extra space, whereas the Nexus 7 can frequently work fine with apps designed for phones.

Summary

This chapter focused on the communication between designers and developers and how to go from comps to designed apps. In particular, you have learned the considerations necessary for slicing assets, how to create styles that reflect the comps, and how to break the comps into Android layouts. You also got a taste of how to optimize your layouts to avoid garbage collection and overdraw.

In the next chapter, you will add more polish to your apps. Instead of focusing on static layouts, you will consider how to simplify your layouts to efficiently animate them. You will also learn how to use custom assets such as fonts to add a bit of personality to your apps.

CHAPTER 9

FURTHER IMPROVING THE APP

Beginning with Chapter 5, "Starting a New App," you followed the real process behind designing and developing an app. You've seen what goes into the ideas, leading to the wireframes. You tested those wireframes with simple prototypes in Chapter 6, "Developing the App Foundation." In Chapter 7, "Finalizing the Design," you learned how to design the app and what considerations go into the design. The previous chapter, "Applying the Design," showed you how to interpret a design and create an app out of it. Most developers stop there, but still some work remains. In this chapter, you will learn how to perfect the visual aspects of the app by making your layouts more efficient and analyzing the resulting display. You'll also add animations using both view animations and property animations to give your app the extra polish that helps it stand out.

Hierarchy Viewer

Hierarchy Viewer is an excellent tool for understanding the complexity of your layouts. Although it can be used as a standalone application, the intent now is to use it as a perspective in Eclipse. To use it, open the Window menu, select Open Perspective, and then click Other.... Select Hierarchy View from the list. You will see something like Figure 9.1.

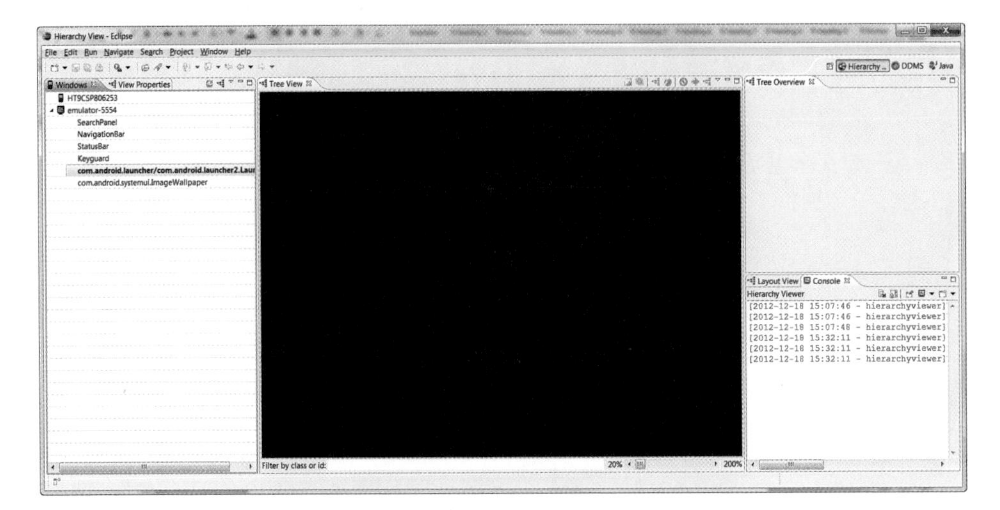

Figure 9.1 The initial Hierarchy View perspective

On the left side, you will see the Windows tab, which lists devices that you can see view hierarchies for. If you plug in another device or start another emulator, you may need to click refresh to add that device to the list. If you expand any device, you can see the foreground window will be in bold. Click it and then click the load button above (the one that looks like a hierarchy of blue squares). Sit back for a while; it can take quite some time to load your hierarchy.

> **warning**
>
> Hierarchy Viewer only works on devices that are unlocked and on emulators. To use it in your app on a locked device, you should include the `ViewServer` class from https://github.com/romainguy/ViewServer that Romain Guy (a software engineer on the Android team at Google) wrote. Be sure to remove it from the project when you make a build that will go to an app store.

Once the view hierarchy has loaded, the left window will show view properties, the center of the screen will be the detailed view hierarchy, the top right will be an overview, and the bottom right is the layout view that lets you see what portion of the screen the selected view is responsible for. Your screen should look like Figure 9.2.

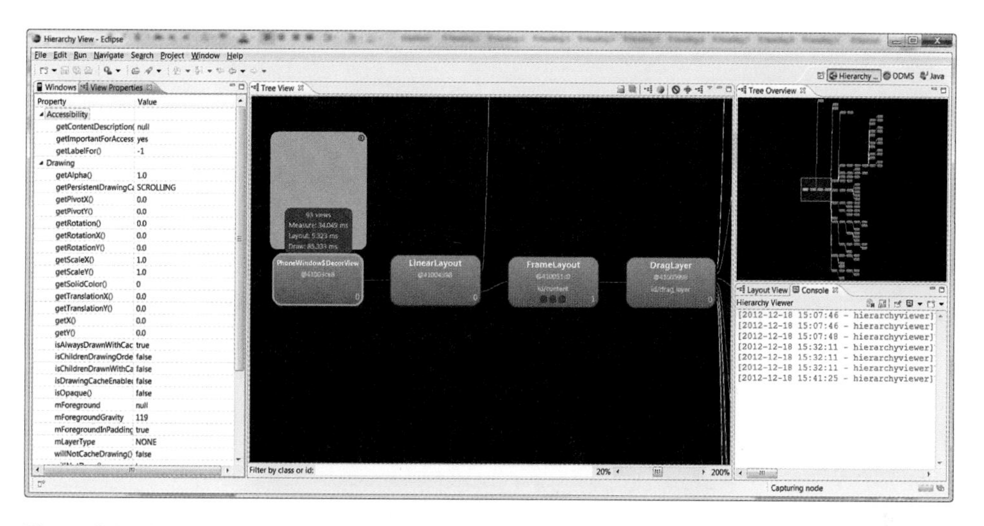

Figure 9.2 After the view hierarchy has been loaded, this is what you should see.

Each gray box in the tree view (the center window) represents a view. The boxes can have the class type (for example, `LinearLayout`), the memory address, the ID (for example, `id/content`), performance indicators, and a view index. The view index shows you the view's position within the parent, where the first child is position 0. The performance indicators are simply colored circles that indicate the time it took to measure the view, the time it took for the layout pass, and the time it took to draw the view. These indicators are broken into three groups. If a view is within the fastest 50 percent of views for the given indicator (for example, draw time), that view will be green for that circle. If it's in the 50 percent of slow views, it will be yellow. If it is the slowest of all the views, it is red.

By clicking a gray box, you can see an image of the view, a count of how many views this view represents (a 1 indicates the view itself; a 2 indicates the view plus a child view), and the exact times for measuring, laying out, and drawing the view. In the view properties (the left window), you can see virtually everything you could want to know about a view. This is extremely helpful when troubleshooting, for example, views that do not appear on the screen when you think they should.

Eliminating Views

One helpful use of the Hierarchy View is to identify where your layout is overly complex. One example that was given in Chapter 8 is nested `LinearLayouts`. When you have nested `LinearLayouts` of alternating orientations, you can commonly eliminate them with a `RelativeLayout`. Figure 9.3 illustrates what this can look like in the Hierarchy View perspective.

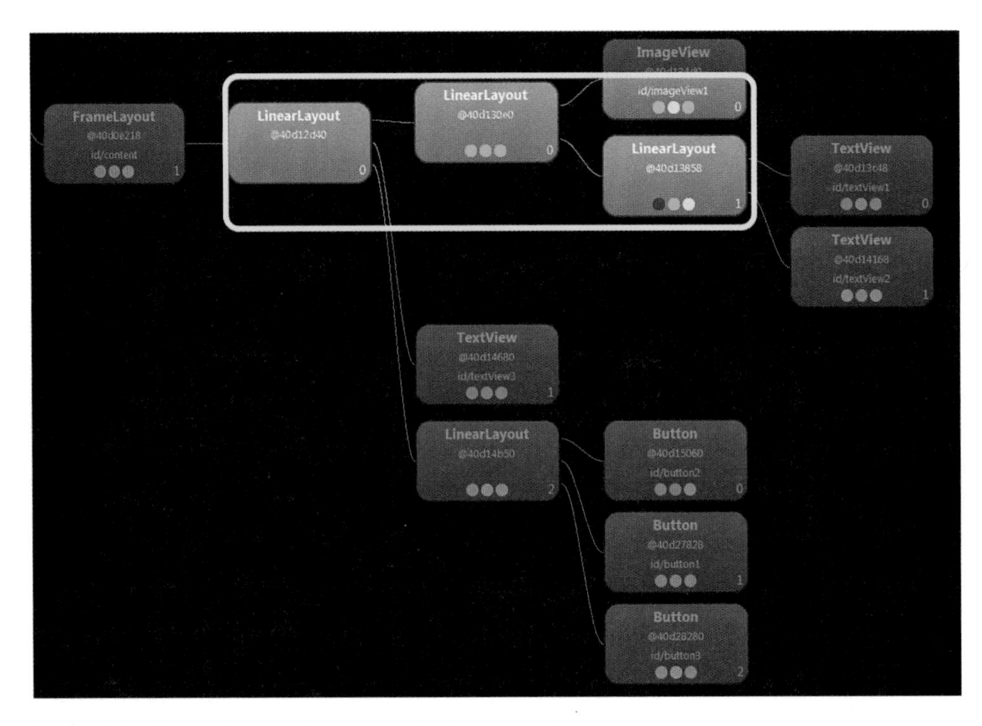

Figure 9.3 Nested `LinearLayouts` in the Hierarchy View

`TextViews` can also often be combined and eliminated because they actually support a wide array of styles even within a single `TextView`. Chapter 10, "How to Handle Common Components," discusses using "spans" to create complex styles without the need for multiple `TextViews`.

Another time when you can eliminate views is when they are purely decorative and tied to another view. For example, look at Figure 9.4, which shows one of the sample designs from the previous chapter. Notice the green horizontal line just below the header. This line is specifically tied to the header, so it would make sense for the line to be part of that view. There are multiple ways to accomplish this, but one in particular is extremely easy. If you create the divider as a nine-patch image, you can define transparent pixels above the divider where the text will go (remember that transparent pixels in a nine-patch are optimized by Android and not drawn). See Figure 9.5 for an enlarged example of the nine-patch image.

Listing 9.1 shows the layout as it was implemented in the previous chapter. The divider is a view that just has a set height and a specific background color. It's a fairly simple use of a view, but it is a bit of a waste. By deleting the view acting as the divider and changing the `TextView` to use the nine-patch as a background (see Listing 9.2), you have simplified the hierarchy and now you can actually define that background as part of a style, so the line will automatically be included in other places you have header text.

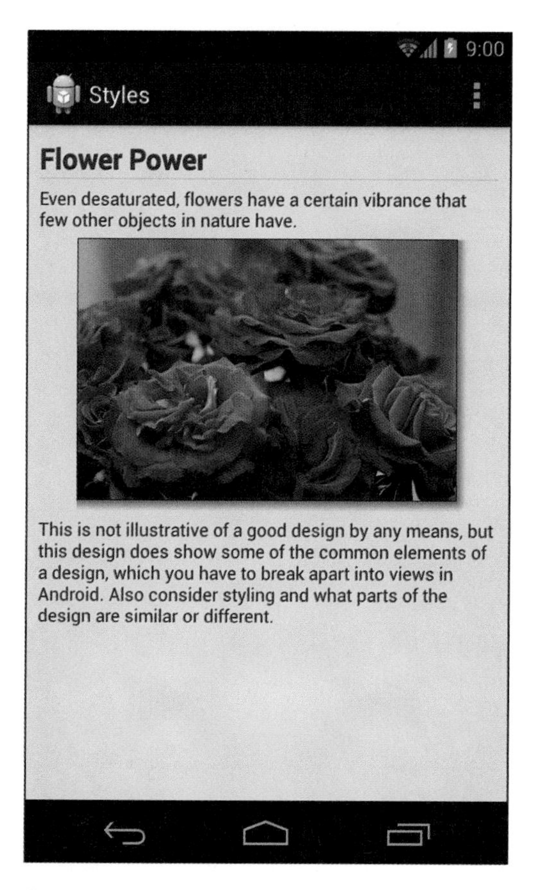

Figure 9.4 One of the previous example designs; note the line under the header.

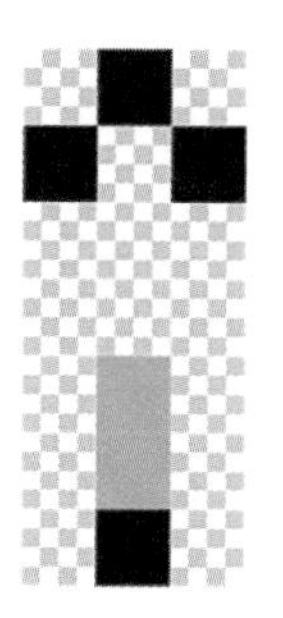

Figure 9.5 An enlarged version of a nine-patch that can create the line in Figure 9.4

Listing 9.1 The Layout Implementation with a View for the Divider

```
<LinearLayout xmlns:android="http://schemas.android.com/apk/res/
➥android"
    xmlns:tools="http://schemas.android.com/tools"
    android:layout_width="match_parent"
    android:layout_height="match_parent"
    android:background="@drawable/bg"
    android:orientation="vertical"
    android:padding="10dp"
    tools:context=".MainActivity" >

    <TextView
        android:id="@+id/heading"
        style="@style/Heading"
        android:layout_width="match_parent"
        android:layout_height="wrap_content"
        android:layout_marginBottom="1dp"
        android:text="@string/flower_power" />

    <View style="@style/Divider" />

    <TextView
        android:id="@+id/intro"
        android:layout_width="match_parent"
        android:layout_height="wrap_content"
        android:text="@string/intro_text"
        android:layout_marginBottom="5dp"
        android:layout_marginTop="5dp"
        android:textAppearance="?android:attr/textAppearanceSmall" />

    <ImageView
        android:id="@+id/image"
        android:layout_width="wrap_content"
        android:layout_height="wrap_content"
        android:layout_gravity="center_horizontal"
        android:background="@drawable/dropshadow"
        android:contentDescription="@string/flowers"
        android:layout_marginLeft="5dp"
        android:src="@drawable/flowers" />

    <TextView
        android:id="@+id/body"
        android:layout_width="match_parent"
        android:layout_height="wrap_content"
        android:layout_marginTop="5dp"
        android:text="@string/body_text"
        android:textAppearance="?android:attr/textAppearanceSmall" />

</LinearLayout>
```

Listing 9.2 The Updated `TextView` with the Nine-Patch Background

```
<TextView
    android:id="@+id/heading"
    style="@style/Heading"
    android:layout_width="match_parent"
    android:layout_height="wrap_content"
    android:background="@drawable/divider"
    android:text="@string/flower_power" />
```

Export to a Photoshop Document (PSD)

One of the extremely powerful but often overlooked features of Hierarchy Viewer is the ability to export a layout hierarchy as a Photoshop Document (a PSD file). This can be hugely valuable to designers, so make sure they are aware of this functionality. There is a rather forgettable-looking button above the tree view that appears to be three overlapping squares. That's the Capture Layers button. If you do not see it, you can also click the downward-facing triangle to get the list of options and select it from there. The resulting PSD can take a while to be generated, so be patient. If it fails, you will see an error in the console and can try again (occasionally it helps to reconnect the hardware device or restart the emulator).

Each view in your hierarchy will be given an individual layer in the PSD file with visibility of the layer turned on or off, depending on the visibility of the view itself. See Figure 9.6 for an example of what this looks like.

Because this PSD is not using any advanced features such as layer masks, you can actually open it in GIMP and other tools as well. Along with the techniques discussed in the previous chapter, this is an excellent method of detecting overdraw.

Exporting to a PSD is a great way for a developer and a designer to speak the same language. The designer can inspect in detail exactly what is going on with a layout by tweaking the layers and then tell the developer which layer has an issue (the layers are named after the view IDs when present, making it extra easy to associate a layer with a view). This also gives the designer the opportunity to make changes to further optimize the design. Perhaps initially a view seemed best at 50-percent opacity, but now the designer can tweak how opaque a view is just like any layer in Photoshop and determine that 40 percent is actually better.

One thing to note is that the layers are all rasterized. In simplistic terms, the pixels that each view creates are what are actually exported as layers. `TextViews` do not create actual text layers, for instance. That also means that if you have a complex view that's drawing shapes, text, and images, only the resulting pixels are exported, so you can't see what each "layer" of that view looks like.

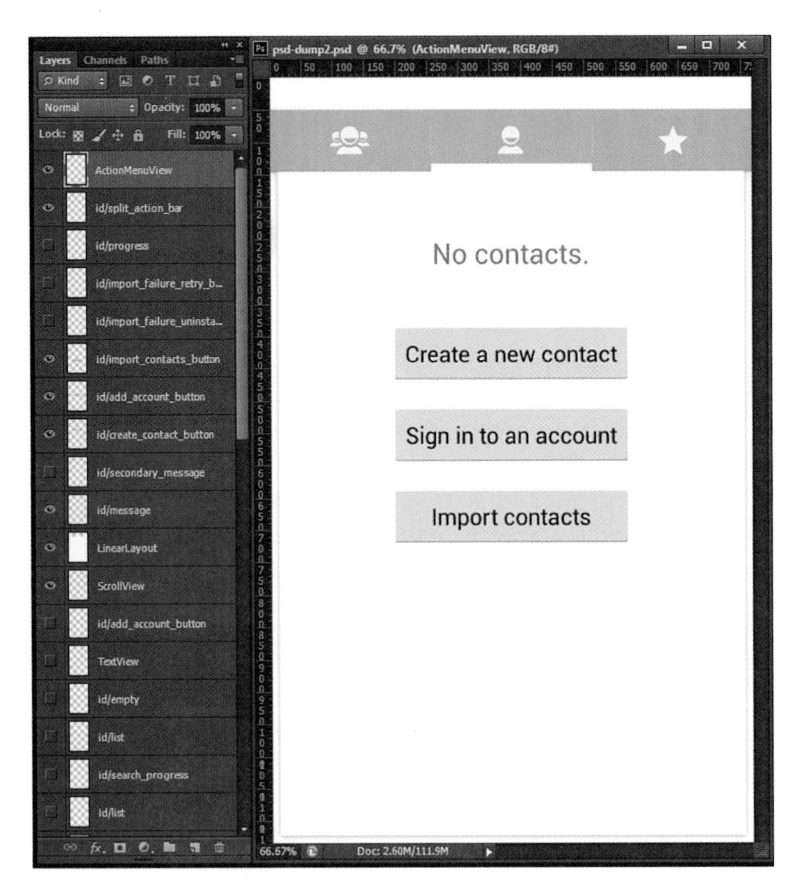

Figure 9.6 A sample PSD dump from Hierarchy Viewer

Animations

Animations are a great way to make an app feel more professional and complete. When done correctly, animations improve the user experience by helping transition between different states of the app. They can draw the users' eyes toward the important part of the app, such as something that changed, and they can also be used to indicate navigation. People's minds look for things that are different from those around them and for breaks in patterns, so animations are an excellent way to take advantage of that to influence where the user looks.

In early versions of Android, a transition from one `Activity` to the next was shown with an animation that made it appear like the next `Activity` came in from the right. This told users that they were progressing into the app and that the back button would take them to the previous screen. That default animation has since changed so that it appears like the next screen fades in and grows from the center, with the back button causing it to shrink and fade out to the center. This change allows you to have horizontally scrolling content (such as a `ViewPager`) without causing user confusion, and it also makes more sense as Android better supports right-to-left languages. See Figure 9.7 for a three-frame version of this animation.

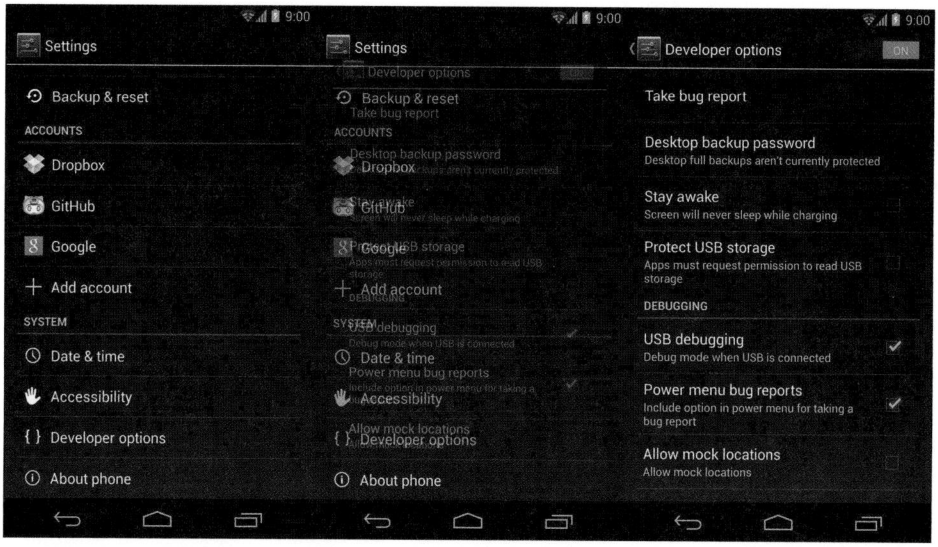

Figure 9.7 Three frames of the standard `Activity` transition

Another common animation is one that shows transition from one app to another. For example, you tap a link in an app that goes to the browser. This animation has the current app fade out as it shrinks upward and the new app fades in as it grows from the bottom. See Figure 9.8 for a five-frame version of this animation. This significant difference from the in-app animation is purposeful and a good example of what you want animation to achieve: The animation tells the user something obvious without being intrusive. If neither of these situations animated or if they used the same animation, the user experience would be confusing.

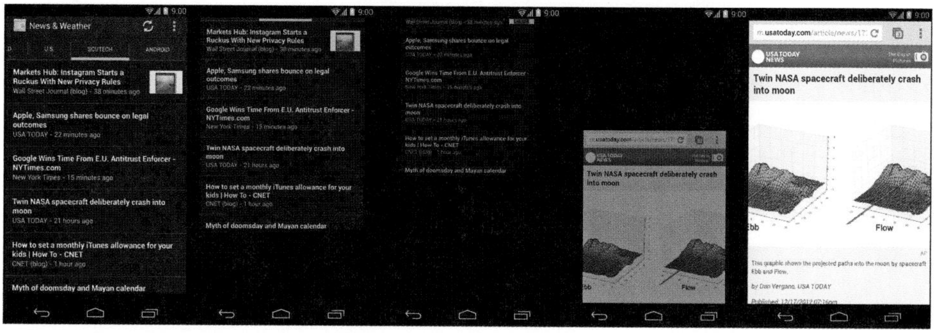

Figure 9.8 Five frames from the standard animation between apps

There are two important reasons for understanding these default animations before creating your own custom animations. First, do not change the animations you use for these situations unless you have a really good reason. Users have learned these animations and understand what they mean. If you decide that your animation should slide in from the left just to be different, you're creating user confusion. The other reason to understand these default animations is because you do not want any of your custom animations to appear similar to these. If you decide that as the user browses photos in your app, the old photos will fade out as they shrink to the top and new photos will fade in as they grow from the bottom, users will be confused (not to mention probably annoyed at the excessive animating). Besides, if you do not have a good reason for using custom animations, sticking with the defaults saves you time.

View Animations

View animations were the primary animation method in Android originally and they're supported by all versions of Android. They basically work as tween animations, which means you specify a start and an end state and the states in be*tween* are calculated. For instance, you might specify that a view starts fully transparent and ends as a fully opaque view. With a linear animation, your view would be about halfway transparent at the midpoint. These tween animations support changes in transparency (alpha), size (scale), position (translate), and rotation (rotate).

With view animations, you can also supply an interpolator, which adjusts how far along an animation is at a given time. Interpolators work by taking a float as an input that is between 0 (the start of the animation) and 1.0 (the end of the animation) and returning a float that is the modified position. The returned float can return values outside of the start and end position, which can allow the animation to undershoot and overshoot the start and end points. For example, you might have a view that's supposed to move 100dp to the right. An interpolator might cause the view to go to 120dp and then come back to the left 20dp.

To see the various interpolators in action, you can run the API Demos app. (If you don't already have API Demos installed on your device, you can create a new project in Eclipse and select Android Sample Project. After changing the API level, if desired, pick API Demos from the list and a project will be created for you that contains all the API demos.). You need to pick Views from the main menu (*not* Animations) and then Animation and Interpolators. From there, you can pick each interpolator and watch the effect on the animation.

> **note**
>
> View animations affect the drawing of the view, not the actual positioning. That means if you animate a button from the left side of the screen to the right side, the click listening will still be happening on the left side despite the fact that the button appears to be on the right side. To avoid that problem, either use property

animations or adjust the layout positioning within the parent after the animation has completed.

View animations are also limited to the bounds of the parent view. That means if you are animating an image that exists inside a `ViewGroup` that takes up the upper half of the screen, the image cannot animate to the bottom half of the screen (the view will be clipped if it exceeds the bounds of the parent).

To try out animations, create a new Android project. Your layout should be a vertically oriented `LinearLayout` that contains a 50dp-by-50dp colored view with an ID of `animation_target` (as you can probably guess, this is the view that you will animate) and a `Button` that will trigger the animation. Your layout should look like Listing 9.3.

Listing 9.3 The Layout to Test Animations With

```
<LinearLayout xmlns:android="http://schemas.android.com/apk/res/
➥android"
    xmlns:tools="http://schemas.android.com/tools"
    android:layout_width="match_parent"
    android:layout_height="match_parent"
    android:gravity="center"
    android:orientation="vertical"
    android:padding="10dp"
    tools:context=".MainActivity" >

    <View
        android:id="@+id/animation_target"
        android:layout_width="50dp"
        android:layout_height="50dp"
        android:background="#FF33AAAA" />

    <Button
        android:id="@+id/button_animate"
        android:layout_width="wrap_content"
        android:layout_height="wrap_content"
        android:text="@string/animate" />

</LinearLayout>
```

Now, you need to create the actual animation. Right-click in your project and pick New, Other..., and then select "Android XML File" from the list. You should select Tween Animation for the resource type (see Figure 9.9). Name the file `rotate.xml`, select "rotate" for the root element, and then click Finish.

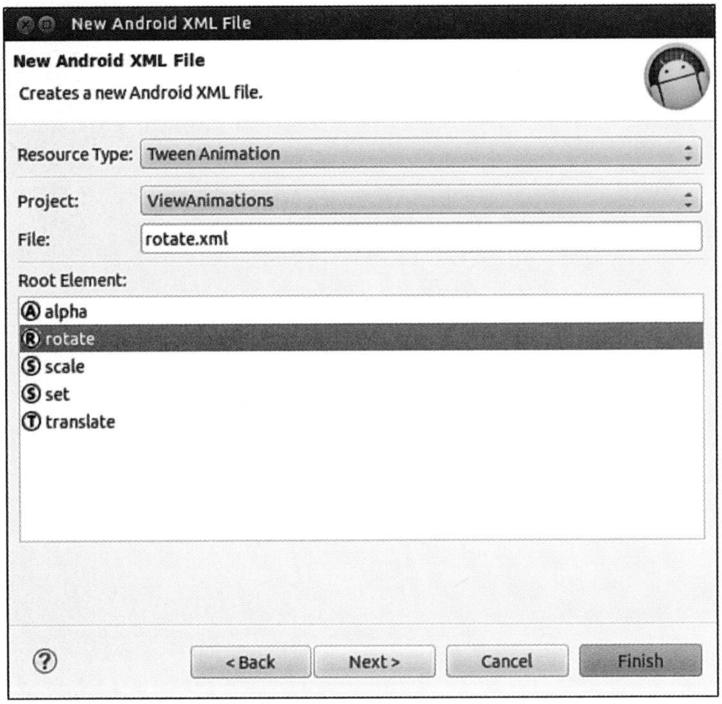

Figure 9.9 The dialog for creating a new view animation

The Android XML file generator does not always correctly put the namespace in there (the "xmlns:android..." part), so add it to the rotate node if it is missing. You need to add several attributes. First, add a `duration`, which specifies how many milliseconds this animation will last. Then, because it is a rotation animation, you need to specify `fromDegrees` and `toDegrees` attributes (use 0 and 90 to make the square view appear to rotate from one side to the next). Specify an interpolator using any that are built in; this example uses `overshoot_interpolator`. Finally, you need to specify the x and y coordinates of the point on which the view will pivot with `pivotX` and `pivotY`. The pivot point can be specified in raw pixels (discouraged), percentage of the view itself (here we use 50% to mean it should rotate from the center of the view), or a percentage relative to the parent (specified like "10%p"). See Listing 9.4 for the sample rotation animation.

Listing 9.4 The XML Rotate Animation

```
<?xml version="1.0" encoding="utf-8"?>
<rotate xmlns:android="http://schemas.android.com/apk/res/android"
    android:duration="500"
    android:fromDegrees="0"
    android:interpolator="@android:anim/overshoot_interpolator"
```

```
    android:pivotX="50%"
    android:pivotY="50%"
    android:toDegrees="90" />
```

Next, you need to update the `Activity` (obviously you can, and generally should, use a `Fragment`, but this example just uses the `Activity` to limit the lines of code not related to the animation). In `onCreate(Bundle)`, you need to use `AnimationUtils` to load the `Animation` object. Then, get a reference to the view that will animate. Finally, set an `OnClickListener` on the button.

The `Activity` should implement `OnClickListener`, and the `onClick(View)` method simply needs to start the animation by calling `startAnimation(Animation)` on the view that you want to animate. See Listing 9.5 for a sample implementation.

Listing 9.5 The `MainActivity` That Triggers the Animation

```
public class MainActivity extends Activity implements OnClickListener {

    private Animation mAnimation;
    private View mAnimationTarget;

    @Override
    public void onClick(View v) {
        mAnimationTarget.startAnimation(mAnimation);
    }

    @Override
    protected void onCreate(Bundle savedInstanceState) {
        super.onCreate(savedInstanceState);
        setContentView(R.layout.activity_main);

        // Load the Animation
        mAnimation = AnimationUtils.loadAnimation(this, R.anim.rotate);

        // Get a reference to the target
        mAnimationTarget = findViewById(R.id.animation_target);

        // Set OnClickListener on the button
        findViewById(R.id.button_animate).setOnClickListener(this);
    }
}
```

This code is fairly simple. When the `Activity` is created, you inflate the `Animation` object to keep a reference to it. You grab a reference to the target view and set an `OnClickListener` on the button to manually trigger the animation. After running the app, simply tap the button to trigger the animation. You can tap it several times, but notice that each time you tap it, the view skips back to the starting position and begins the animation from the start. You should see something like Figure 9.10 when you click the button.

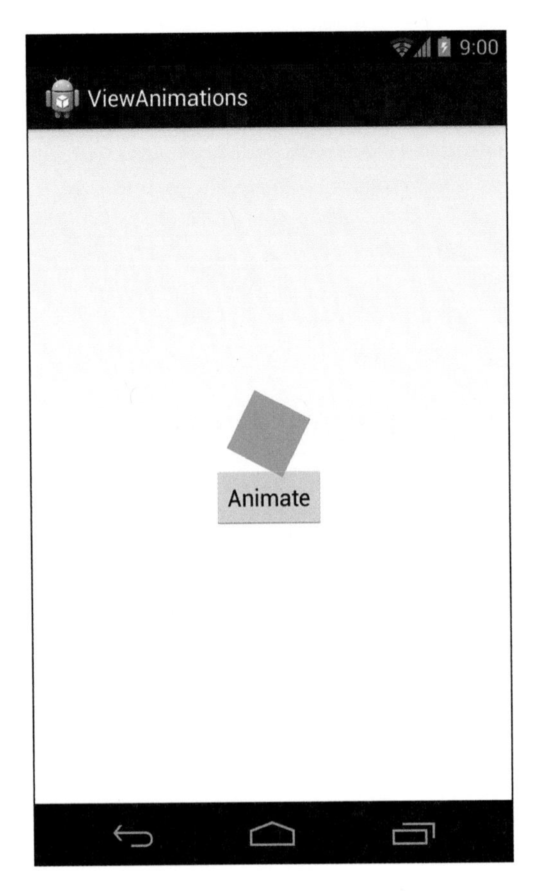

Figure 9.10 An example of the view being rotated after the button has been pressed

You can also create sets of animations in XML and even animations that happen after other animations. Look at Listing 9.6 for an example of what an XML file looks like that performs one animation and then performs a pair of animations at the same time.

First, this animation moves (translates) the view 40 percent of the parent's width to the right (remember that the *p* indicates the value is a percentage of the parent's width). This animation takes half of a second (500ms). Next is a set of two animations: one that scales and one that rotates. Both of those animations have a `startOffset` of 500ms, so they begin after that first translate animation ends. The scale animation goes from the full size to zero over the course of 500ms. The rotate animation rotates 90 degrees counterclockwise and shares the decelerate interpolator.

Listing 9.6 A Compound Animation Defined in XML

```
<?xml version="1.0" encoding="utf-8"?>
<set xmlns:android="http://schemas.android.com/apk/res/android"
    android:shareInterpolator="false" >

    <translate
        android:interpolator="@android:anim/
➥accelerate_decelerate_interpolator"
        android:duration="500"
        android:fromXDelta="0%p"
        android:toXDelta="40%p" />

    <set android:interpolator="@android:anim/decelerate_interpolator" >
        <scale
            android:duration="500"
            android:fromXScale="1.0"
            android:fromYScale="1.0"
            android:pivotX="50%"
            android:pivotY="50%"
            android:startOffset="500"
            android:toXScale="0.0"
            android:toYScale="0.0" />

        <rotate
            android:duration="500"
            android:fromDegrees="0"
            android:pivotX="50%"
            android:pivotY="50%"
            android:startOffset="500"
            android:toDegrees="-90" />
    </set>

</set>
```

If you update the `Activity` to use this animation resource instead of the basic rotation one, you will see something like Figure 9.11 (though hopefully you'll see a few more frames). The view slides to the right before it begins to rotate and shrink. The second part of the animation happens as the view is returning to its starting position, so it almost appears to jump back at an arc.

For significantly more detail about view animations, see the resource on the developer site at http://developer.android.com/guide/topics/resources/animation-resource.html#View.

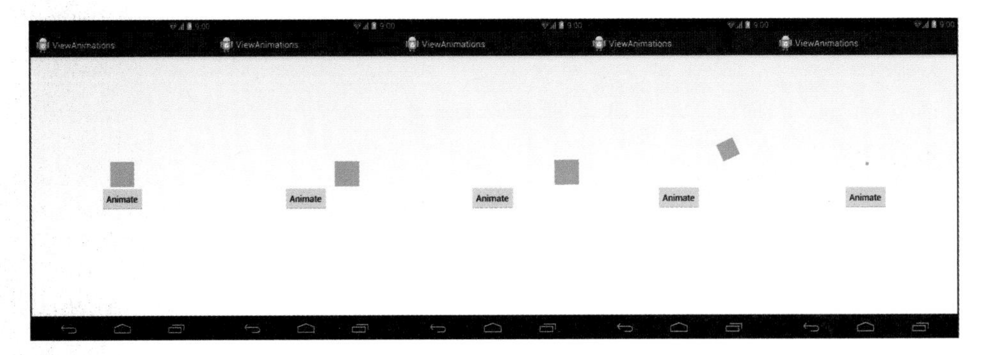

Figure 9.11 Five frames of the animation defined in Listing 9.6

Property Animations

View animations have several limitations. They work only on a few specific pieces of aspects of views and they only affect where the view is drawn (not where the view actually is, an important distinction for views with click listeners). In many cases, those limitations aren't a problem. Many views take advantage of view animations, such as the `ViewAnimator` class and its subclasses. These classes make it easy to crossfade between a loading indicator and the content view, for example, but they cannot do things such as animate the background of a view between two colors or affect objects that aren't views.

In Android 3.0 (Honeycomb), the property animation system was introduced. The idea is that you can animate any property (a field or class variable) of any object, so they can do the same things as view animations and a whole lot more.

> **note**
>
> The property animation system was introduced in API level 11, so that means you need to avoid using any of these classes on previous versions of Android. If your app supports older versions of Android, consider using the NineOldAndroids library by Jake Wharton (available at http://nineoldandroids.com/), which makes these objects available for Android 1.0 apps and up.

The first class to know for property animation is the `ValueAnimator`. This class handles all the timing and the value computations. It also keeps track of whether the animation repeats, what listeners should be notified of the new values, and more. This class does not directly modify any properties; it just supplies the mechanism for doing so. You can call `addUpdateListener` to provide an `AnimatorUpdateListener` to be notified of each "frame" being finished. The `AnimatorUpdateListener` would call `getAnimatedValue` on the `ValueAnimator` to get the value at that time and adjust whatever property needs to be adjusted.

The next class to know about will make your life a lot easier. The `ObjectAnimator` is a subclass of `ValueAnimator` that allows you to specify an object that has properties to animate. This object needs a setter method for that property (so if you want to animate "alpha," the object needs a `setAlpha` method) that can be called for each update. If you do not specify a starting value, it also needs a getter method (for example, `getAlpha()`) to determine the starting point and the range of animation.

Taking a look at a simple example will help clarify how to use an `ObjectAnimator`. If you wanted to animate a view from fully opaque to fully transparent and back again over the course of five seconds, how much code would be required? See Listing 9.7 for the answer.

Listing 9.7 A Simple `ObjectAnimator` Example

```
final ObjectAnimator anim = ObjectAnimator.ofFloat(myView, "alpha",
➥1f, 0f, 1f);
anim.setDuration(5000);
anim.start();
```

As you can see, the code required is quite small. You create an `ObjectAnimator` by using the static `ofFloat` method. The first value passed is the object to animate. The second value is the name of the property to animate. The rest of the values are the floats to animate among. You can specify just one float, in which case the value is assumed to be the end animation value and the begin value will be looked up by calling `getAlpha` in this case. The `setDuration` method takes a long to tell it the number of milliseconds to animate for.

You can also combine multiple animations. For instance, you might want to animate a view to the right 200 pixels and down 50 pixels at the same time. In this case, you create the two `ObjectAnimator` instances and combine them with an `AnimatorSet` by calling the `playTogether` method with both animations (alternatively, you could call `playSequentially` to play one and then the other). The code looks like Listing 9.8.

Listing 9.8 Combining Animations with `AnimationSet`

```
ObjectAnimator animX = ObjectAnimator.ofFloat(myView, "x", 200f);
ObjectAnimator animY = ObjectAnimator.ofFloat(myView, "y", 50f);
AnimatorSet animationSet = new AnimatorSet();
animationSet.setDuration(5000);
animationSet.playTogether(animX, animY);
animationSet.start();
```

You can actually make this a bit more efficient by using `PropertyValueHolder` objects, but there is an even better way. In Android 3.1, the Android team introduced the `ViewPropertyAnimator`. By calling `animate()` on any `View` object, you get a `ViewPropertyAnimator` that has simple methods for changing alpha, rotation, scale, translation, and so on. Each of these methods returns the `ViewPropertyAnimator`, so you can easily chain several methods together. Take a look at Listing 9.9 to see how simple the code can become.

Listing 9.9 Using `ViewPropertyAnimator`

```
myView.animate()
        .setDuration(5000)
        .x(200f)
        .y(50f)
        .start();
```

The animation that was already impressive at just six lines can now be just one (shown on multiple lines here for readability). What's even more impressive is that, behind the scenes, this super-concise code is even more efficient than the previous example!

There is a lot more that the property animation framework can do, including support for choreographing several animations, specifying custom keyframes, and controlling animations based on views being added or removed to a `ViewGroup`. To see more detail, check out the property animation page http://developer.android.com/guide/topics/graphics/prop-animation.html.

Custom Fonts

There are times when using a custom font can improve your app. Some apps designed for reading provide additional font choices for users; other apps might use fonts specific to their brand. When deciding on whether to use an additional font, consider how it helps the user experience. Don't include a font just because it's popular or makes the app look different from others; include a font because a usability study has shown that your app is easier to read with the font or because your brand requires it and you want to avoid using images for custom text.

The Roboto font family was built specifically for Android and is the default font for Android 4.0 (Ice Cream Sandwich) and above. Whenever possible, it is the font you should use. You can download the font from the Android design site (https://developer.android.com/design/style/typography.html), and it includes multiple variations. In addition to Roboto regular, there is a thin version, light version, medium version, black version, and condensed version (as well as bold and italic versions where applicable). See Figure 9.12 for some examples of Roboto.

Roboto Condensed
Roboto Thin
Roboto Light
Roboto Regular
Roboto Medium
Roboto Black

Figure 9.12 The various styles of the Roboto font family

Because this font was built for Android specifically, it displays very well on a variety of densities and screen types. Many of the most commonly used fonts today were designed for print, which is a very different medium than an electronic display, so some of the fonts that look great on paper do not reproduce well onscreen. In particular, if you are considering light or thin fonts, be sure to test them on medium- and high-density displays and test them against AMOLEDs like the one on the Nexus S.

If you do decide to use an alternate font, you need to put it in a directory called `assets` within the root directory of your project. The easiest way to use a custom font in your app is to extend `TextView` to create your own class. Listing 9.10 shows an example.

Listing 9.10 A Custom `TextView` for Displaying a Font

```
public class TextViewRobotoThin extends TextView {

    /**
     * This is the name of the font file within the assets folder
     */
    public static final String FONT_LOCATION = "roboto_thin.ttf";
```

```
    private static Typeface sTypeface;

    public TextViewRobotoThin(Context context) {
        super(context);
        init(context);
    }

    public TextViewRobotoThin(Context context, AttributeSet attrs) {
        super(context, attrs);
        init(context);
    }

    public TextViewRobotoThin(Context context, AttributeSet attrs, int
➥defStyle) {
        super(context, attrs, defStyle);
        init(context);
    }

    /**
     * Returns the Typeface for Roboto thin
     *
     * @param context Context to access the app's assets
     * @return Typeface for Roboto thin
     */
    public static Typeface getTypeface(Context context) {
        if (sTypeface == null) {
            sTypeface = Typeface.createFromAsset(context.getAssets(),
➥FONT_LOCATION);
        }
        return sTypeface;
    }

    /**
     * Initializes this TextView to the Roboto thin font
     *
     * @param context Context to access AssetManager
     */
    private void init(Context context) {
        if (isInEditMode()) {
            if (TextUtils.isEmpty(getText())) {
                setText("Roboto thin");
            }
            return;
        }

        setTypeface(getTypeface(context));
    }
}
```

At the top of the class is a static string specifying the name of the font file. Each of the normal constructors calls through to the custom `init(Context)` method, which will set the `Typeface`. Notice that there is a check of `isInEditMode()`. This call returns `true` when the code is running in an editor (such as the preview mode in ADT) and exists specifically to let you make changes that help display the view in those cases (for example, because a `ListView` requires an `Adapter`, it would never show anything while just previewing the layout it exists in, so it shows a series of sample items to give some sense of how it will look). The whole `if` block can be removed with no effect on the code running on a device.

A public static method called `getTypeface()` will create the `Typeface` from the font file in the assets directory if it hasn't already been created and then return the `Typeface`. This is useful for times when you might access the `Typeface` for other uses (perhaps you do some custom drawing using this `Typeface` elsewhere). By having this public static method, anywhere in your code that needs this custom `Typeface` has one place to go, and you can just change the `FONT_LOCATION` if you need to change the font everywhere in the app. Lastly, the `init` method checks if the view is in edit mode (which means it is being viewed in ADT rather than while running on a device). If that's the case, it checks if text has been set. If not, it creates some default text. Either way, it returns early because ADT does not support loading custom fonts from your assets directory for previews. If the app is running on a real device, the method's only purpose is to set the `Typeface`.

You can now use this class anywhere you would use an ordinary `TextView`. For instance, you can replace the default "hello world" `TextView` with this in a new project. See Listing 9.11 for a sample layout. Figure 9.13 shows how this custom `TextView` looks on an actual device.

Listing 9.11 A Layout That Utilizes the Custom `TextView`

```
<RelativeLayout xmlns:android="http://schemas.android.com/apk/res/
➥android"
    xmlns:tools="http://schemas.android.com/tools"
    android:layout_width="match_parent"
    android:layout_height="match_parent"
    tools:context=".MainActivity" >

    <com.iangclifton.auid.customfont.TextViewRobotoThin
        android:id="@+id/textViewRobotoThin1"
        android:layout_width="wrap_content"
        android:layout_height="wrap_content"
        android:layout_centerHorizontal="true"
        android:layout_centerVertical="true"
        android:text="@string/hello_world"
        android:textAppearance="?android:attr/textAppearanceLarge" />

</RelativeLayout>
```

Figure 9.13 The custom `TextView` being displayed on a device

Summary

In this chapter you learned how to use Hierarchy Viewer to understand your layouts and make them more efficient. You will use that knowledge further in Chapter 11, "Combining Views for Custom Components." You also learned how to export a layout to a PSD document for inspection. Then you focused on animations—understanding the default transition animations and the differences between view animations and property animations. Finally, you saw how to implement a simple `TextView` that utilizes a custom font.

This chapter marks the end of the usual Android design and development process. At this point you should feel confident implementing an app and using all the views and the layout-specific tools provided by the SDK. In the next few chapters, you will be focusing on advanced techniques, learning how to load data across configuration changes, create custom views, and even work with image compositing.

CHAPTER 10

HOW TO HANDLE COMMON COMPONENTS

A lot of different UI components are common to apps. Splash screens and loading indicators, for example, are very common but have several different implementations. There are times when you need to include complex styling for text or even inline images, but do not want to create several views. You may want to improve the user experience by loading content just before the user needs it. In this chapter, you will learn about these common app components and the best way to develop them.

Splash Screen

Splash screens are typically still images that fill the screen of a mobile device. On a desktop computer, they can be full screen (such as for an operating system) or a portion of the screen (for example, Photoshop, Eclipse, and so on). They give feedback that the system has responded to the user's action of opening the application. Splash screens can include loading indicators but are often static images.

Do You Really Need It?

Looking back at the previous examples (operating systems, Photoshop, and Eclipse), you should notice something in common with desktop uses of splash screens: The applications are large. They need to show the user something while they are loading so that the user will not feel like the computer has locked up or failed to respond to the user's actions.

Compared to massive applications such as Photoshop, your Android app is very small and likely loading from flash storage rather than a slower, spinning disk. Many people also have the mistaken conception that because iOS apps require splash screens that Android apps do, too. Related, when an app already exists on iOS and is being built for Android afterward, many people think that it should have a splash screen in both places to be consistent, but you should play to the strengths of each platform and take advantage of how fast Android apps load. So, does your app really need a splash screen?

The correct answer to start with is no, until you have proven it a necessity. Splash screens are often abused as a way of getting branding in front of the user, but they should only be used if loading is going on in the background. An app that artificially displays a splash screen for a few seconds is preventing the user from actually using the app, and that is the whole reason the user has the app in the first place. Mobile apps are especially designed for quick, short uses. You might have someone pushing for more heavy-handed branding, but that can ultimately hurt the app and the brand itself if users find they have two wait a few extra seconds when they open the app but they don't have to wait with a competitor's app.

That said, there are genuine times when a splash screen is needed. If you cannot show any UI until some loading takes place that could take a while, then it makes sense to show a splash screen. A good example of this is a game running in OpenGL that needs to load several textures into memory, not to mention sound files and other resources. Another example is an app that has to load data from the Web. For the first run, the app might not have any content to display, so it can show a splash screen while the web request is made, making sure to give an indication of progress. For subsequent loads, the cached data can be displayed while the request is made. If that cached data takes any significant amount of time, you might opt to show the splash screen there too until the cached content has loaded, then have a smaller loading indicator that shows the web request is still in progress. If you want to display a splash screen because your layout takes a long time to display, you should first consider making your layout more efficient.

Keep in mind that the user might want to take an action immediately and does not care about the main content. You would not want the Google Play app to show a splash screen for five seconds because it is loading the top content when you are actually just opening it to search for a specific app.

Ultimately, you should opt to skip on the splash screen unless you have developed the app and it is absolutely necessary. When in doubt, it is not needed.

Using a `Fragment` for a Splash Screen

If you have determined that your app is one of the few that does truly require a splash screen, one approach for displaying it is to use a `Fragment`. You immediately show it in your `onCreate(Bundle)` method, start your loading on a background thread, and replace the `Fragment` with your actual UI `Fragment` when your loading has completed. That sounds easy enough, but what does it really look like?

First, create the `Fragment` that you will use for the splash screen. You'll probably have some kind of branded background, but this example will just use a simple XML-defined gradient for the background (see Listing 10.1).

Listing 10.1 A Simple Gradient Saved as `splash_screen_bg.xml`

```
<?xml version="1.0" encoding="utf-8"?>
<shape xmlns:android="http://schemas.android.com/apk/res/android"
    android:shape="rectangle" >

    <gradient
        android:angle="90"
        android:centerColor="#FF223333"
        android:endColor="@android:color/black"
        android:startColor="@android:color/black" />

</shape>
```

Next, create a layout for the splash screen. This example will use a really simple layout that just shows the text "Loading" and a `ProgressBar`. Notice that the style is specifically set on the `ProgressBar` to make this a horizontal indicator (instead of an indeterminate indicator) in Listing 10.2.

Listing 10.2 The Splash Screen Layout

```
<?xml version="1.0" encoding="utf-8"?>
<LinearLayout xmlns:android="http://schemas.android.com/apk/res/
➥android"
    android:layout_width="match_parent"
```

```
    android:layout_height="match_parent"
    android:background="@drawable/splash_screen_bg"
    android:gravity="center"
    android:orientation="vertical" >

    <TextView
        android:layout_width="wrap_content"
        android:layout_height="wrap_content"
        android:text="@string/loading"
        android:textAppearance="@android:style/
➥TextAppearance.Medium.Inverse" />

    <ProgressBar
        android:id="@+id/progress_bar"
        style="?android:attr/progressBarStyleHorizontal"
        android:layout_width="200dp"
        android:layout_height="wrap_content"
        android:max="100" />

</LinearLayout>
```

The last piece of the splash screen portion is to create a simple `Fragment` that displays that layout. The one requirement of this `Fragment` is that it has a way of updating the `ProgressBar`. In this example, a simple `setProgress(int)` method is tied directly to the `ProgressBar` in the layout. See Listing 10.3 for the full class and Figure 10.1 for what this will look like in use.

Listing 10.3 The Fragment That Displays the Splash Screen

```
public class SplashScreenFragment extends Fragment {

    private ProgressBar mProgressBar;

    @Override
    public View onCreateView(LayoutInflater inflater, ViewGroup
➥container, Bundle savedInstanceState) {
        final View view = inflater.inflate(R.layout.splash_screen,
➥container, false);
        mProgressBar = (ProgressBar) view.findViewById
➥(R.id.progress_bar);
        return view;
    }

    /**
     * Sets the progress of the ProgressBar
     *
     * @param progress int the new progress between 0 and 100
     */
```

```
    public void setProgress(int progress) {
        mProgressBar.setProgress(progress);
    }
}
```

Figure 10.1 The simple splash screen with loading indicator

Now that the easy part is done, you need to handle loading the data. Prior to the introduction of the `Fragment` class, you would do this with a simple `AsyncTask` in your `Activity` that you would save and restore during config changes (attaching and detaching the `Activity` to avoid leaking the `Context`). This is actually easier now with a `Fragment`. All you have to do is create a `Fragment` that lives outside of the `Activity` lifecycle and handles the loading. The `Fragment` does not have any UI because its sole purpose is to manage loading the data.

Take a look at Listing 10.4 for a sample `Fragment` that loads data. First, it defines a public interface that can be used by other classes to be notified of progress with loading the data. When the `Fragment` is attached, it calls `setRetainInstance(true)` so that the `Fragment` is kept across configuration changes. When the user rotates the device, slides out a keyboard, or otherwise affects the device's configuration, the `Activity` will be re-created but this `Fragment` will continue to exist. It has simple methods to check if loading is complete and to get the result of loading the data (which is stored as a `Double` for this example, but it could be anything for your case). It can also set and remove the `ProgressListener` that is notified of updates to the loading.

The `Fragment` contains an `AsyncTask` that does all the hard work. In this case, the background method is combining some arbitrary square roots (to mimic real work) and causing the `Thread` to sleep for 50ms per iteration to create a delay similar to what you might see with real use. This is where you would grab assets from the Web, load them from the disk, parse a complex data structure, or do whatever you needed to finish before the app is ready.

On completion, the `AsyncTask` stores the result, removes its own reference, and notifies the `ProgressListener` (if one is available).

Listing 10.4 A Fragment That Handles Loading Data Asynchronously

```
public class DataLoaderFragment extends Fragment {

    /**
     * Classes wishing to be notified of loading progress/completion
     * implement this.
     */
    public interface ProgressListener {
        /**
         * Notifies that the task has completed
         *
         * @param result Double result of the task
         */
        public void onCompletion(Double result);

        /**
         * Notifies of progress
         *
         * @param value int value from 0-100
         */
        public void onProgressUpdate(int value);
    }

    private ProgressListener mProgressListener;
    private Double mResult = Double.NaN;
    private LoadingTask mTask;

    @Override
    public void onAttach(Activity activity) {
        super.onAttach(activity);
```

```
        // Keep this Fragment around even during config changes
        setRetainInstance(true);
    }

    /**
     * Returns the result or {@value Double#NaN}
     *
     * @return the result or {@value Double#NaN}
     */
    public Double getResult() {
        return mResult;
    }

    /**
     * Returns true if a result has already been calculated
     *
     * @return true if a result has already been calculated
     * @see #getResult()
     */
    public boolean hasResult() {
        return !Double.isNaN(mResult);
    }

    /**
     * Removes the ProgressListener
     *
     * @see #setProgressListener(ProgressListener)
     */
    public void removeProgressListener() {
        mProgressListener = null;
    }

    /**
     * Sets the ProgressListener to be notified of updates
     *
     * @param listener ProgressListener to notify
     * @see #removeProgressListener()
     */
    public void setProgressListener(ProgressListener listener) {
        mProgressListener = listener;
    }

    /**
     * Starts loading the data
     */
    public void startLoading() {
        mTask = new LoadingTask();
        mTask.execute();
    }
```

```
    private class LoadingTask extends AsyncTask<Void, Integer,
➥Double>
{

        @Override
        protected Double doInBackground(Void... params) {
            double result = 0;
            for (int i = 0; i < 100; i++) {
                try {
                    result += Math.sqrt(i);
                    Thread.sleep(50);
                    this.publishProgress(i);
                } catch (InterruptedException e) {
                    return null;
                }
            }
            return Double.valueOf(result);
        }

        @Override
        protected void onPostExecute(Double result) {
            mResult = result;
            mTask = null;
            if (mProgressListener != null) {
                mProgressListener.onCompletion(mResult);
            }
        }

        @Override
        protected void onProgressUpdate(Integer... values) {
            if (mProgressListener != null) {
                mProgressListener.onProgressUpdate(values[0]);
            }
        }
    }
}
```

To tie everything together, you need an `Activity`. Listing 10.5 shows an example of such an `Activity`. It implements the `ProgressListener` from the `DataLoaderFragment`. When the data is done loading, the `Activity` simply displays a `TextView` with the result (that's where you would show your actual app with the necessary data loaded in). When notified of updates to loading progress, the `Activity` passes those on to the `SplashScreenFragment` to update the `ProgressBar`.

In `onCreate(Bundle)`, the `Activity` checks whether or not the `DataLoaderFragment` exists by using a defined tag. If this is the first run, it won't exist, so the `DataLoaderFragment` is instantiated, the `ProgressListener` is set to the `Activity`, the `DataLoaderFragment` starts loading, and the `FragmentManager` commits a `FragmentTransaction` to add the

DataLoaderFragment (so it can be recovered later). If the user has rotated the device, the DataLoaderFragment will be found, so the app has to check whether or not the data has already loaded. If it has, the method is done; otherwise, everything falls through to checking if the SplashScreenFragment has been instantiated, creating it if it hasn't.

The onStop() method removes the Activity from the DataLoaderFragment so that your Fragment does not retain a Context reference and the app avoids handling the data result if it's not in the foreground. Similarly, onStart() checks if the data has been successfully loaded.

The last method, checkCompletionStatus(), checks if the data has been loaded. If it has, it will trigger onCompletion(Double) and remove the reference to the DataLoader Fragment. By removing the reference, the Activity is able to ensure that the result is only handled once (which is why onStart() checks if there is a reference to the DataLoaderFragment before handling the result). Figure 10.2 shows what the app looks like once it has finished loading the data.

Listing 10.5 The Activity That Ties Everything Together

```
public class MainActivity extends Activity implements
➥ProgressListener {

    private static final String TAG_DATA_LOADER = "dataLoader";
    private static final String TAG_SPLASH_SCREEN = "splashScreen";

    private DataLoaderFragment mDataLoaderFragment;
    private SplashScreenFragment mSplashScreenFragment;

    @Override
    public void onCompletion(Double result) {
        // For the sake of brevity, we just show a TextView with the
➥result
        TextView tv = new TextView(this);
        tv.setText(String.valueOf(result));
        setContentView(tv);
        mDataLoaderFragment = null;
    }

    @Override
    public void onProgressUpdate(int progress) {
        mSplashScreenFragment.setProgress(progress);
    }

    @Override
    protected void onCreate(Bundle savedInstanceState) {
        super.onCreate(savedInstanceState);

        final FragmentManager fm = getFragmentManager();
```

```
        mDataLoaderFragment = (DataLoaderFragment)
➥fm.findFragmentByTag(TAG_DATA_LOADER);
        if (mDataLoaderFragment == null) {
            mDataLoaderFragment = new DataLoaderFragment();
            mDataLoaderFragment.setProgressListener(this);
            mDataLoaderFragment.startLoading();
            fm.beginTransaction().add(mDataLoaderFragment,
➥TAG_DATA_LOADER).commit();
        } else {
            if (checkCompletionStatus()) {
                return;
            }
        }

        // Show loading fragment
        mSplashScreenFragment = (SplashScreenFragment)
➥fm.findFragmentByTag(TAG_SPLASH_SCREEN);
        if (mSplashScreenFragment == null) {
            mSplashScreenFragment = new SplashScreenFragment();
            fm.beginTransaction().add(android.R.id.content,
➥]mSplashScreenFragment, TAG_SPLASH_SCREEN).commit();
        }
    }

    @Override
    protected void onStart() {
        super.onStart();
        if (mDataLoaderFragment != null) {
            checkCompletionStatus();
        }
    }

    @Override
    protected void onStop() {
        super.onStop();
        if (mDataLoaderFragment != null) {
            mDataLoaderFragment.removeProgressListener();
        }
    }

    /**
     * Checks if data is done loading, if it is, the result is handled
     *
     * @return true if data is done loading
     */
    private boolean checkCompletionStatus() {
        if (mDataLoaderFragment.hasResult()) {
```

```
                onCompletion(mDataLoaderFragment.getResult());
                FragmentManager fm = getFragmentManager();
                mSplashScreenFragment = (SplashScreenFragment)
➥fm.findFragmentByTag(TAG_SPLASH_SCREEN);
                if (mSplashScreenFragment != null) {
                    fm.beginTransaction().remove(mSplashScreenFragment).
➥commit();
                }
                return true;
            }
            mDataLoaderFragment.setProgressListener(this);
            return false;
        }
    }
```

Figure 10.2 The resulting app after data has loaded

Quite a bit is going on in this small bit of code, so it's a good idea to review it. On a high level, you are using `DataLoaderFragment` to load all the data, and it exists outside of configuration changes. The `Activity` checks `DataLoaderFragment` each time it is created and started to handle the result. If it's not done yet, the `SplashScreenFragment` is shown to indicate progress.

Loading Indication

Immediate feedback is one of the most important parts of a good UI. If a button does not have a touch state and the resulting action takes some time, the user will feel like the app is unresponsive. Unfortunately, whether the app needs to run complex image analysis algorithms or just access web resources, there are times when it will not be able to immediately show the users what they want to see. In these instances, you use a loading indicator to give the user a sense that something is happening. Ideally, you use a loading indicator that can show progress such as when downloading a file, but sometimes you have to fall back on the indeterminate loading indicator, which just tells the user, "Hey, something is happening, but who knows how long it will take."

Dialogs versus Inline

Using dialogs to indicate loading is the go-to solution for a lot of developers. In fact, Android's `ProgressDialog` class makes this extremely easy. Just create an instance using one of the static `show()` methods and then update it if possible. When your task is done, you just `dismiss()` the dialog. Simple enough, right?

The problem is that these dialogs are modal. That means the user can do nothing else in your app while looking at one of these dialogs, so they don't make sense unless there really is nothing else the user can do (for example, the previously explained splash screen). You may have allowed the user to back out of the dialog, but that just results in the user being confused as to whether the task actually stopped or not (and further confused when the UI suddenly changes when it does complete). Instead, consider using inline loading indicators.

An inline loading indicator is basically a loading indicator that is a part of your regular view hierarchy. It goes where the content that is loading will go and serves as a placeholder as well as a visual indication of activity. Not only is this significantly less disruptive than a dialog, it lets the user interact with other content immediately. If you go to Google Play to search for a particular app, you don't want to wait while the front page loads before you can actually search. An additional advantage of inline indicators is that they allow you to load different sections of a screen and display them independently. You might go to someone's profile page in an app and see the basic info. At the same time, one section is loading that displays recent content posted by that person and another section loads people who are similar to that person. Neither of these pieces is dependent on the other.

Using an Inline Loading Indicator

Using inline loading indicators in your app is actually extremely easy. The simplest way is to just include a `ProgressBar` in your layout somewhere and then hide or remove it when the loading is complete and add the new views. There are several ways to make this easier to manage. If the extra content is almost always available (for example, you might go from a list of articles to a detailed article page, and you just need to fetch the body text), then an easy approach is to use a `ViewSwitcher`. A `ViewSwitcher` is a `ViewGroup` that contains two child `Views` and can animate between them. In this case, you use it to display a loading indicator and then switch to the other `View` when it is ready.

First, define a couple of animations in XML. These go in `res/anim`. Listing 10.6 defines a simple fade-in animation, and Listing 10.7 defines a fade-out animation.

Listing 10.6 A Simple Fade-in Animation Saved as `fade_in.xml`

```
<?xml version="1.0" encoding="utf-8"?>
<alpha xmlns:android="http://schemas.android.com/apk/res/android"
    android:duration="300"
    android:fromAlpha="0.0"
    android:interpolator="@android:anim/decelerate_interpolator"
    android:toAlpha="1.0" />
```

Listing 10.7 A Simple Fade-out Animation Saved as `fade_out.xml`

```
<?xml version="1.0" encoding="utf-8"?>
<alpha xmlns:android="http://schemas.android.com/apk/res/android"
    android:duration="300"
    android:fromAlpha="1.0"
    android:interpolator="@android:anim/accelerate_interpolator"
    android:toAlpha="0.0" />
```

With those animations defined, all you need now is a `ViewSwitcher` that is displaying a loading indication and a second child `View` that is the content you have finished loading. You set the animations and then simply call `showNext()`, as shown in Listing 10.8.

Listing 10.8 Using a `ViewSwitcher` to Animate Between Views

```
ViewSwitcher viewSwitcher = (ViewSwitcher) findViewById
➥(R.id.view_switcher);
viewSwitcher.setInAnimation(this, R.anim.fade_in);
viewSwitcher.setOutAnimation(this, R.anim.fade_out);
viewSwitcher.showNext();
```

Sometimes you'll have some chunk of content that is frequently not there or that has a complex view hierarchy. In these cases, it's a good idea to make use of `ViewStubs`. A `ViewStub` is an extremely simple implementation of `View` that essentially acts as a placeholder for other content. It takes up no space and draws nothing, so it has minimal impact on your layout complexity. Think of it like an `include` tag that does not actually include another layout until you say to do so.

Listing 10.9 shows what a `ViewStub` will look like in your XML layout. The regular ID is used for finding the `ViewStub`, but it can also specify an `inflatedID` for finding the layout after it has been inflated. The layout that will be inflated is specified by the `layout` property the same as it is in an `include` tag.

Listing 10.9 An XML `ViewStub`

```
<ViewStub
    android:id="@+id/view_stub"
    android:layout_width="match_parent"
    android:layout_height="wrap_content"
    android:inflatedId="@+id/dynamic_content"
    android:layout="@layout/other_layout" />
```

All that is left to do is to find a reference to your `ViewStub`, inflate it, and do whatever you need to with the resulting layout. See Listing 10.10 for the basic code involved.

Listing 10.10 Inflating a `ViewStub` in Java

```
ViewStub stub = (ViewStub) findViewById(R.id.view_stub);
View otherLayout = stub.inflate();
// Do something with otherLayout...
```

Complex `TextViews`

`TextViews` in Android are extremely powerful. Obviously, they're able to display text, but they can also display several styles of text, different fonts or colors, and even inline images, all within a single `TextView`. You can have specific portions of text respond to click events and really associate any object you want with any portion of text. These ranges of text are generically referred to as "spans," as in a span (range) of bold text or a span of subscript.

Existing Spans

Android has a large number of prebuilt spans you can take advantage of. Because you can assign any object as a span, there isn't an actual span class. That's great in that it gives you a huge amount of flexibility, but it also means you have to dig a little to figure out what is supported.

First, you should know about the two main types of spans: `CharacterStyle` and `ParagraphStyle`. As you can probably guess, these interfaces refer to spans that affect one or more characters and spans that affect entire paragraphs. Most spans will implement one of these two interfaces (although many implement more than just these). See the following list of built-in spans to get an idea about what is already supported:

`AbsoluteSizeSpan`—A span that allows you to specify an exact size in pixels or density independent pixels.

`AlignmentSpan.Standard`—A span that attaches an alignment (from `Layout.Alignment`).

`BackgroundColorSpan`—A span that specifies a background color (the color behind the text, such as for highlighting).

`ClickableSpan`—A span that has an `onClick` method that is triggered. (This class is abstract, so you can extend it with a class that specifies the `onClick` behavior.)

`DrawableMarginSpan`—A span that draws a `Drawable` plus the specified amount of spacing.

`DynamicDrawableSpan`—A span that you can extend to provide a `Drawable` that may change (but the size must remain the same).

`EasyEditSpan`—A span that just marks some text so that the `TextView` can easily delete it.

`ForegroundColorSpan`—A span that changes the color of the text (basically just called `setColor(int)` on the `TextPaint` object).

`IconMarginSpan`—A span that draws a `Bitmap` plus the specified amount of spacing.

`ImageSpan`—A span that draws an image specified as a `Bitmap`, `Drawable`, `URI`, or resource ID.

`LeadingMarginSpan.Standard`—A span that adjusts the margin.

`LocaleSpan`—A span that changes the locale of text (available in API level 17 and above).

`MaskFilterSpan`—A span that sets the `MaskFilter` of the `TextPaint` (such as for blurring or embossing).

`MetricAffectingSpan`—A span that affects the height and/or width of characters (this is an abstract class).

`QuoteSpan`—A span that puts a vertical line to the left of the selected text to indicate it is a quote; by default the line is blue.

`RasterizerSpan`—A span that sets the `Rasterizer` of the `TextPaint` (generally not useful to you).

RelativeSizeSpan—A span that changes the text size relative to the supplied float (for instance, setting a 0.5 float will cause the text to render at half size).

ReplacementSpan—A span that can be extended when something custom is drawn in place of the spanned text (for example, ImageSpan extends this).

ScaleXSpan—A span that provides a multiplier to use when calling the `TextPaint`'s `setTextScaleX(float)` method. (In other words, setting this to 0.5 will cause the text to be scaled to half size along the x axis, thus appearing squished.)

StrikethroughSpan—A span that simply passes `true` to the `TextPaint`'s `setStrikeThruText(boolean)` method, causing the text to have a line through it (useful for showing deleted text, such as in a draft of a document).

StyleSpan—A span that adds bold and/or italic to the text.

SubscriptSpan—A span that makes the text subscript (below the baseline).

SuggestionSpan—A span that holds possible replacement suggestions, such as for a incorrectly spelled word (available in API level 14 and above).

SuperscriptSpan—A span that makes the text superscript (above the baseline).

TabStopSpan.Standard—A span that allows you to specify an offset from the leading margin of a line.

TextAppearanceSpan—A span that allows you to pass in a `TextAppearance` for styling.

TypefaceSpan—A span that uses a specific typeface family (`monospace`, `serif`, or `sans-serif` only).

UnderlineSpan—A span that underlines the text.

URLSpan—A `ClickableSpan` that attempts to view the specified URL when clicked.

Using Spans for Complex Text

One of the simplest ways to use spans is with the `HTML` class. If you have some HTML in a string, you can simply call `HTML.fromHtml(String)` to get an object that implements the `spanned` interface that will have the applicable spans applied. You can even supply an `ImageGetter` and a `TagHandler`, if you'd like. The styles included in the HTML will be converted to spans so, for example, "b" (bold) tags are converted to `StyleSpans` and "u" (underline) tags are converted to `UnderlineSpans`. See Listing 10.11 for a brief example of how to set the text of a `TextView` from an HTML string and enable navigating through and clicking the links.

Listing 10.11 Using HTML in a `TextView`

```
textView.setText(Html.fromHtml(htmlString));
textView.setMovementMethod(LinkMovementMethod.getInstance());
textView.setLinksClickable(true);
```

Another easy method for implementing spans is to use the `Linkify` class. The `Linkify` class allows you to easily create links within text for web pages, phone numbers, email addresses, physical addresses, and so on. You can even use it for custom regular expressions, if you're so inclined.

Finally, you can also manually set spans on anything that implements the `Spannable` interface. If you have an existing `String` or `CharSequence` that you'd like to make `Spannable`, use the `SpannableString` class. If you are building up some text, you can use the `SpannableStringBuilder`, which works like a `StringBuilder` but can attach spans. To the untrained eye, the app in Figure 10.3 is using two `TextViews` and an `ImageView`, but it actually has just a single `TextView`. See Listing 10.12 to understand how you can do this with one `TextView` and a few spans.

Figure 10.3 An app that seemingly uses more views than it really does

Listing 10.12 Using Spans with a `SpannableStringBuilder`

```
public class MainActivity extends Activity {

    @Override
    protected void onCreate(Bundle savedInstanceState) {
        super.onCreate(savedInstanceState);

        final SpannableStringBuilder ssb = new
➥SpannableStringBuilder();
        final int flag = Spannable.SPAN_EXCLUSIVE_EXCLUSIVE;
        int start;
        int end;

        // Regular text
        ssb.append("This text is normal, but ");

        // Bold text
        start = ssb.length();
        ssb.append("this text is bold");
        end = ssb.length();
        ssb.setSpan(new StyleSpan(Typeface.BOLD), start, end, flag);

        // Inline image
        ssb.append('\n');
        start = end++;
        ssb.append('\uFFFC'); // Unicode replacement character
        end = ssb.length();
        ssb.setSpan(new ImageSpan(this, R.drawable.ic_launcher), start,
➥end, flag);

        // Stretched text
        ssb.append('\n');
        start = end++;
        ssb.append("This text is wide");
        end = ssb.length();
        ssb.setSpan(new ScaleXSpan(2f), start, end, flag);

        // Assign to TextView
        final TextView tv = new TextView(this);
        tv.setText(ssb);
        setContentView(tv);
    }
}
```

Autoloading ListViews

Using a ListView is a great way to display an extensive data set. For instance, you might show a list of news articles. For this to load quickly, you only request the first 10 or 20 news articles to show in the list; however, the user may want to see more. Older user experiences would have a button at the end of the list that the user could tap that would begin loading the next set. That works, but you can do better.

Concept and Reasoning

To improve the user experience, it's a good idea to anticipate the user's actions. Scrolling through a list is a great example where you can easily make reasonable assumptions. If the user has scrolled to the bottom of the list, there is a good chance that the user wants to continue scrolling. Instead of waiting for the user to press a button, you can immediately begin loading more items. So, now you've managed to save the user a little bit of work, but you can go a step further.

When the user has scrolled to near the bottom of the list, you can start loading more. Say you display 20 items and the user has scrolled down to where the device is showing items 12 through 17. The user is very close to the bottom of the list, so you can begin loading more items ahead of time. If your data source and connection are fast, the next 10 or 20 items can be loaded by the time the user gets to the bottom of the list. Now the user can scroll without effort through a large data set, and you can still have the benefits of loading a smaller set of data to speed up the initial user experience.

Autoloading Near the Bottom of a List

Although you are going to start loading before getting to the bottom of a list, you will want to have a loading indicator at the bottom because the user can get there before the loading completes. So, to start, create a simple loading view called loading_view.xml like the one in Listing 10.13.

Listing 10.13 A Simple Loading Layout

```
<?xml version="1.0" encoding="utf-8"?>
<LinearLayout xmlns:android="http://schemas.android.com/apk/res/
➥android"
    android:layout_width="match_parent"
    android:layout_height="wrap_content"
    android:gravity="center"
    android:orientation="horizontal" >
```

```
    <ProgressBar
        android:layout_width="wrap_content"
        android:layout_height="wrap_content"
        android:layout_marginRight="10dp" />

    <TextView
        android:layout_width="wrap_content"
        android:layout_height="wrap_content"
        android:text="@string/loading"
        android:textAppearance="?android:attr/textAppearanceMedium" />

</LinearLayout>
```

Next, create an `Adapter` that will provide fake data to test out this technique. Listing 10.14 shows an example. This sample `Adapter` just keeps a count representing the number of fake items to show. You can simulate adding more items with the `addMoreItems(int)` method. For the purposes of testing this autoloading technique, this is adequate.

Listing 10.14 An `Adapter` That Can Mimic Real Content

```
private static class SimpleAdapter extends BaseAdapter {

    private int mCount = 20;
    private final LayoutInflater mLayoutInflater;
    private final String mPositionString;
    private final int mTextViewResourceId;

    /*package*/ SimpleAdapter(Context context, int textViewResourceId)
{
        mLayoutInflater = LayoutInflater.from(context);
        mPositionString = context.getString(R.string.position) + " ";
        mTextViewResourceId = textViewResourceId;
    }

    public void addMoreItems(int count) {
        mCount += count;
        notifyDataSetChanged();
    }

    @Override
    public int getCount() {
        return mCount;
    }

    @Override
    public String getItem(int position) {
        return mPositionString + position;
    }
```

```
    @Override
    public long getItemId(int position) {
        return position;
    }

    @Override
    public View getView(int position, View convertView, ViewGroup
➥parent) {
        final TextView tv;
        if (convertView == null) {
            tv = (TextView) mLayoutInflater.inflate
➥(mTextViewResourceId, null);
        } else {
            tv = (TextView) convertView;
        }

        tv.setText(getItem(position));
        return tv;
    }
}
```

The last piece is the actual `Fragment` that does the hard work. It is a `ListFragment` that listens to the position of the `ListView` and loads more items if necessary. The `AUTOLOAD_THRESHOLD` value determines how close to the bottom of the list the user has to be before loading. The `MAXIMUM_ITEMS` value is an arbitrary limit to the size of our list, so you can see how to handle removing the loading `View` when all data has been loaded.

The `mAddItemsRunnable` object simulates adding additional items after a delay, similarly to how you would add more items after fetching them from a data source. In `onActivityCreated(Bundle)`, a `Handler` is created (for posting the `Runnable` with a delay), the `Adapter` is created, a footer view is instantiated and added to the `ListView`, the `Adapter` is set, and the `Fragment` is added as the `OnScrollListener`. It's important that you add the footer before setting your `Adapter` because the `ListView` is actually wrapping your `Adapter` with one that supports adding header and footer `Views`.

When the user scrolls, the `Fragment` checks if data is not currently loading and if there is more data to load. If that is the case, it checks if the `Adapter` has already added at least the maximum number of items (remember, this is arbitrary to simulate having a finite data set like you would in a real use). If there is no more data, the footer is removed. If there is more data, the `Fragment` checks to see if the user has scrolled far enough to load more data and triggers the load.

The `onScrollStateChanged` method has to be implemented as part of `OnScrollListener`, but it is not needed in this code, so it does nothing.

The onStart and onStop methods handle stopping and starting the loading of data, so the load does not continue when the app is no longer visible. This is not particularly necessary in the sample code, but it is useful in the real world when you might be loading or processing a large amount of data and don't want it to be done if the user has changed apps.

For a complete implementation, see Listing 10.15.

Listing 10.15 A ListFragment That Automatically Loads More Content

```
public class AutoloadingListFragment extends ListFragment implements
➥OnScrollListener {

    private final int AUTOLOAD_THRESHOLD = 4;
    private final int MAXIMUM_ITEMS = 52;
    private SimpleAdapter mAdapter;
    private View mFooterView;
    private Handler mHandler;
    private boolean mIsLoading = false;
    private boolean mMoreDataAvailable = true;
    private boolean mWasLoading = false;

    private Runnable mAddItemsRunnable = new Runnable() {
        @Override
        public void run() {
            mAdapter.addMoreItems(10);
            mIsLoading = false;
        }
    };

    @Override
    public void onActivityCreated(Bundle savedInstanceState) {
        super.onActivityCreated(savedInstanceState);
        final Context context = getActivity();
        mHandler = new Handler();
        mAdapter = new SimpleAdapter(context,
➥android.R.layout.simple_list_item_1);
        mFooterView = LayoutInflater.from(context).inflate(
➥R.layout.loading_view, null);
        getListView().addFooterView(mFooterView, null, false);
        setListAdapter(mAdapter);
        getListView().setOnScrollListener(this);
    }

    @Override
    public void onScroll(AbsListView view, int firstVisibleItem,
            int visibleItemCount, int totalItemCount) {
```

```
        if (!mIsLoading && mMoreDataAvailable) {
            if (totalItemCount >= MAXIMUM_ITEMS) {
                mMoreDataAvailable = false;
                getListView().removeFooterView(mFooterView);
            } else if (totalItemCount - AUTOLOAD_THRESHOLD <=
➥firstVisibleItem + visibleItemCount) {
                mIsLoading = true;
                mHandler.postDelayed(mAddItemsRunnable, 1000);
            }
        }
    }

    @Override
    public void onScrollStateChanged(AbsListView view,
➥int scrollState) {
        // Ignore
    }

    @Override
    public void onStart() {
        super.onStart();
        if (mWasLoading) {
            mWasLoading = false;
            mIsLoading = true;
            mHandler.postDelayed(mAddItemsRunnable, 1000);
        }
    }

    @Override
    public void onStop() {
        super.onStop();
        mHandler.removeCallbacks(mAddItemsRunnable);
        mWasLoading = mIsLoading;
        mIsLoading = false;
    }
}
```

Now that you have it all finished, give it a try. Notice that when you are scrolling slowly, the content loads before you ever know that it was loading. If you fling to the bottom quickly, you'll have the experience shown in Figure 10.4, where the list shows the loading footer just before the content loads in. Notice, too, that your position in the list is not changed when new content loads in. The user is not disturbed even if he or she was unaware that content was loading, and the loading view being replaced by content makes it clear that something new has loaded (without the loading view, the user might think he or she is at the bottom of the list, even after new content has been loaded).

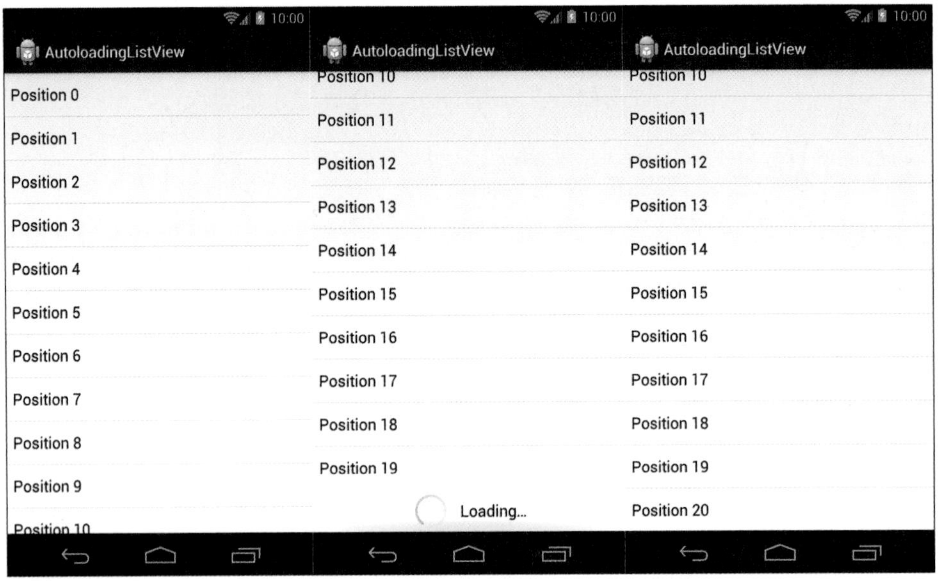

Figure 10.4 Scrolling quickly from the top (left) to the bottom (middle) results in content loading in automatically (right).

Summary

Although there are countless techniques for developing better apps, this chapter has introduced you to a few of the more common ones. By now, you should hate splash screens, but you should also know how to implement them correctly. You should be annoyed by modal loading dialogs and have experience implementing more user-friendly inline dialogs. Your experience with `TextView` spans will allow you to avoid creating several `TextView`s for minor style changes, and you should know how to implement autoloading `ListView`s.

CHAPTER 11

COMBINING VIEWS FOR CUSTOM COMPONENTS

In Chapter 10, "How to Handle Common Components," you learned to apply existing Android classes to solve common challenges in Android. The best approach is generally to use the existing classes unless you have a compelling reason to do something different. Sometimes existing classes do not quite solve your problem, especially when it comes to views. When you do need to create a custom view, there are two main approaches: modify one or more existing views to do what you want, or create your own. This chapter focuses on the first solution. Chapter 12, "Developing Fully Custom Views," does the latter to create a view from scratch.

When to Combine Views

Deciding exactly when to combine views for a custom component is a challenge for new Android developers. They typically don't know most of the views that are available, so they're trapped between researching what can be done with the existing views and creating their own. In general, you should favor using existing views. They have been thoroughly tested against a variety of edge cases and are generally very efficient. If you research all the views currently out there and do not find one that matches your needs, at least you have become more familiar with what is available and can rely on that knowledge in the future. You may even discover a view that does 90 percent of what you need, so you can extend it and make some minor modifications to get your desired functionality.

The most common reasons for combining views to create a custom component are to simplify interaction with multiple views (such as when you represent an object with a set of views and want to easily be able to pass that object to one place and have the views populate themselves) and to join multiple views that each do a piece of what you would like. In this chapter, you will learn how to do both.

Combining Views to Simplify Working with Them

Oftentimes you will use several views to represent a single object. For example, in Chapter 6, "Developing the App Foundation," you created a `Property` class that could represent a house with a specific number of bedrooms and bathrooms, an address, square footage, and so on. In that chapter, you created a simple `ListView` and an `Adapter` to populate the views with the `Property` objects' data. In this chapter, you're going to reuse that `Property` class and create a custom view that can populate itself based on a `Property` object. Create a new project and copy the `Property` class and `PropertyTestUtils` into the project.

Start by creating a new `RelativeLayout` called `property.xml`. You want to create something like Figure 11.1, where you have an `ImageView` for a thumbnail on the left, a `TextView` for the price on the right, a `TextView` for the street address in the middle, and a `TextView` for the city and state below that. See Listing 11.1 for an example of the resulting XML file.

Figure 11.1 Outlines of the views to create for displaying a property

Listing 11.1 The Initial `property.xml` Layout File

```
<?xml version="1.0" encoding="utf-8"?>
<RelativeLayout xmlns:android="http://schemas.android.com/apk/res/
➥android"
    android:layout_width="match_parent"
    android:layout_height="wrap_content" >

    <ImageView
        android:id="@+id/thumbnail"
        android:layout_width="@dimen/thumbnail"
        android:layout_height="@dimen/thumbnail"
        android:layout_alignParentLeft="true"
        android:layout_centerVertical="true"
        android:layout_margin="@dimen/half_default_spacing"
        android:contentDescription="@null" />
```

```
    <TextView
        android:id="@+id/street_address"
        android:layout_width="match_parent"
        android:layout_height="wrap_content"
        android:layout_alignParentTop="true"
        android:layout_marginTop="@dimen/default_spacing"
        android:layout_toLeftOf="@+id/price"
        android:layout_toRightOf="@+id/thumbnail"
        android:textAppearance="?android:attr/textAppearanceSmall" />

    <TextView
        android:id="@+id/city_state_address"
        android:layout_width="match_parent"
        android:layout_height="wrap_content"
        android:layout_below="@+id/street_address"
        android:layout_marginBottom="@dimen/default_spacing"
        android:layout_marginTop="@dimen/default_spacing"
        android:layout_toLeftOf="@+id/price"
        android:layout_toRightOf="@+id/thumbnail"
        android:textAppearance="?android:attr/textAppearanceSmall" />

    <TextView
        android:id="@+id/price"
        android:layout_width="wrap_content"
        android:layout_height="wrap_content"
        android:layout_alignParentRight="true"
        android:layout_centerVertical="true"
        android:layout_marginLeft="@dimen/default_spacing"
        android:layout_marginRight="@dimen/default_spacing"
        android:textAppearance="?android:attr/textAppearanceLarge" />

</RelativeLayout>
```

Now that you have a layout, you need to create a class that populates the layout with a `Property` class. Create a new view that extends `RelativeLayout`. Be sure to check the box to create the "Constructors from superclass" so that the three standard `View` class constructors will be in place for you. You should then create an `init` method that takes the `Context` and call it from each constructor (the `View` class has a `getContext()` method that allows you to get the `Context` that way, but you already have an instance of it in each constructor, so just pass it along). The `init` method needs to inflate the property layout and then get a reference to each of the views.

Now, just add a `setProperty` method that takes a `Property` object and updates each view with its data. Because there isn't an image associated with the `Property` objects, just set the `ImageView` for the thumbnail to any `Drawable`. Listing 11.2 shows what the `PropertyView` class should look like so far.

Listing 11.2 The Initial `PropertyView` Class

```
public class PropertyView extends RelativeLayout {
    private TextView mCityStateTextView;
    private TextView mPriceTextView;
    private TextView mStreetTextView;
    private ImageView mThumbnailImageView;

    public PropertyView(Context context) {
        super(context);
        init(context);
    }

    public PropertyView(Context context, AttributeSet attrs) {
        super(context, attrs);
        init(context);
    }

    public PropertyView(Context context, AttributeSet attrs, int
➥defStyle) {
        super(context, attrs, defStyle);
        init(context);
    }

    /**
     * Updates this View to display the passed Property
     *
     * @param property Property to display
     */
    public void setProperty(Property property) {
        final String cityState = property.getCity() + ", " +
➥property.getState();
        mCityStateTextView.setText(cityState);
        mPriceTextView.setText(property.getPrice());
        mStreetTextView.setText(property.getStreetAddress());
        mThumbnailImageView.setImageResource(R.drawable.house);
    }

    private void init(Context context) {
        inflate(context, R.layout.property, this);
        mCityStateTextView = (TextView) findViewById
➥(R.id.city_state_address);
        mPriceTextView = (TextView) findViewById(R.id.price);
        mStreetTextView = (TextView) findViewById(R.id.street_address);
        mThumbnailImageView = (ImageView) findViewById(R.id.thumbnail);
    }
}
```

The last piece before you can give it a try is to update the `Activity` or `Fragment` you are running this from (this example uses an `Activity` to keep things simple). Set the content view to a `LinearLayout` that is vertically oriented and obtain a reference to that `LinearLayout`. Next, get an instance of the `PropertyTestUtils` class to generate sample `Property` objects from (the example passes it `1` as the `long` in the constructor; you can pass the same to get the exact same results or something else to experiment with different values for the views to display).

Create a loop and iterate three times, instantiating a `PropertyView` each time and populating it with a test instance of a `Property` object. In this example, a background is assigned so that you can more clearly see where each `PropertyView` is laid out, but it's optional. Finally, just add the `PropertyView` to the `LinearLayout` and run the app. Your code should look like Listing 11.3. (Note that `onCreateOptionsMenu(Menu)` is not required; it is automatically generated by ADT.)

Listing 11.3 The Initial `Activity` That Tests the `PropertyViews`

```
public class MainActivity extends Activity {

    @Override
    protected void onCreate(Bundle savedInstanceState) {
        super.onCreate(savedInstanceState);
        setContentView(R.layout.activity_main);
        final ViewGroup rootLayout = (ViewGroup) findViewById(
➥R.id.root);

        // Create Property and PropertyView
        final PropertyTestUtils ptu = new PropertyTestUtils(1);
        for (int i = 0; i < 3; i++) {
            final Property property = ptu.getNewProperty();
            final PropertyView propertyView = new PropertyView(this);
            propertyView.setProperty(property);
            propertyView.setBackgroundResource(R.drawable.gradient);
            rootLayout.addView(propertyView);
        }
    }

    @Override
    public boolean onCreateOptionsMenu(Menu menu) {
        // Inflate the menu; this adds items to the action bar if it is
➥present.
        getMenuInflater().inflate(R.menu.activity_main, menu);
        return true;
    }
}
```

If you run the app on your device or an emulator, you should see something like Figure 11.2. Easy enough, right? You have now created a custom `RelativeLayout` that populates multiple views just by being passed a `Property` object. You can use this same `PropertyView` class in an `Adapter` and you won't need to do the `ViewHolder` pattern because the `PropertyView` already keeps a reference to each of the necessary views.

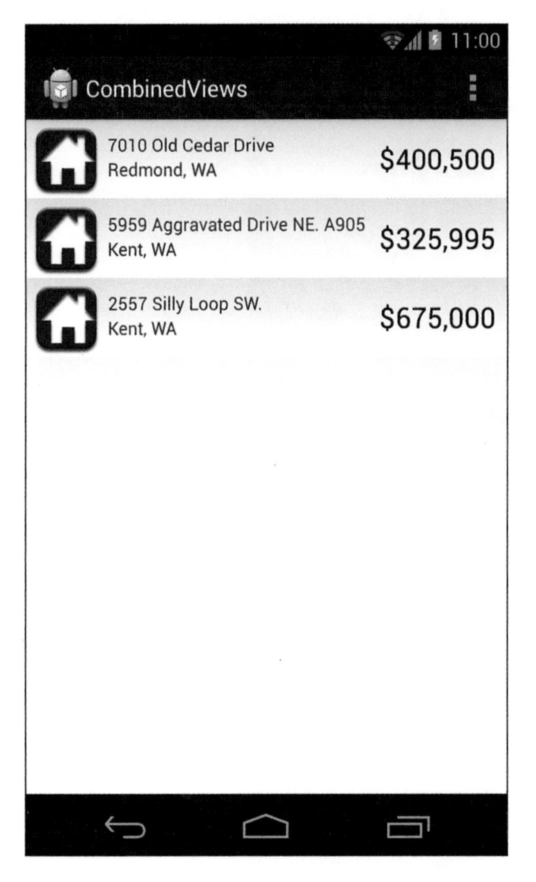

Figure 11.2 Displaying three sample `PropertyViews`

If you were paying close attention, you might notice that it looks like the `PropertyView`, which extends `RelativeLayout`, is inflating a `RelativeLayout`, so wouldn't that make two `RelativeLayouts`? Yes, it does! In fact, if you take a look at the Hierarchy View (in Eclipse go to Window, Open Perspective, Other..., Hierarchy View), you will notice the `PropertyView` contains the child `RelativeLayout` that was defined in XML. See the circled layouts in Figure 11.3.

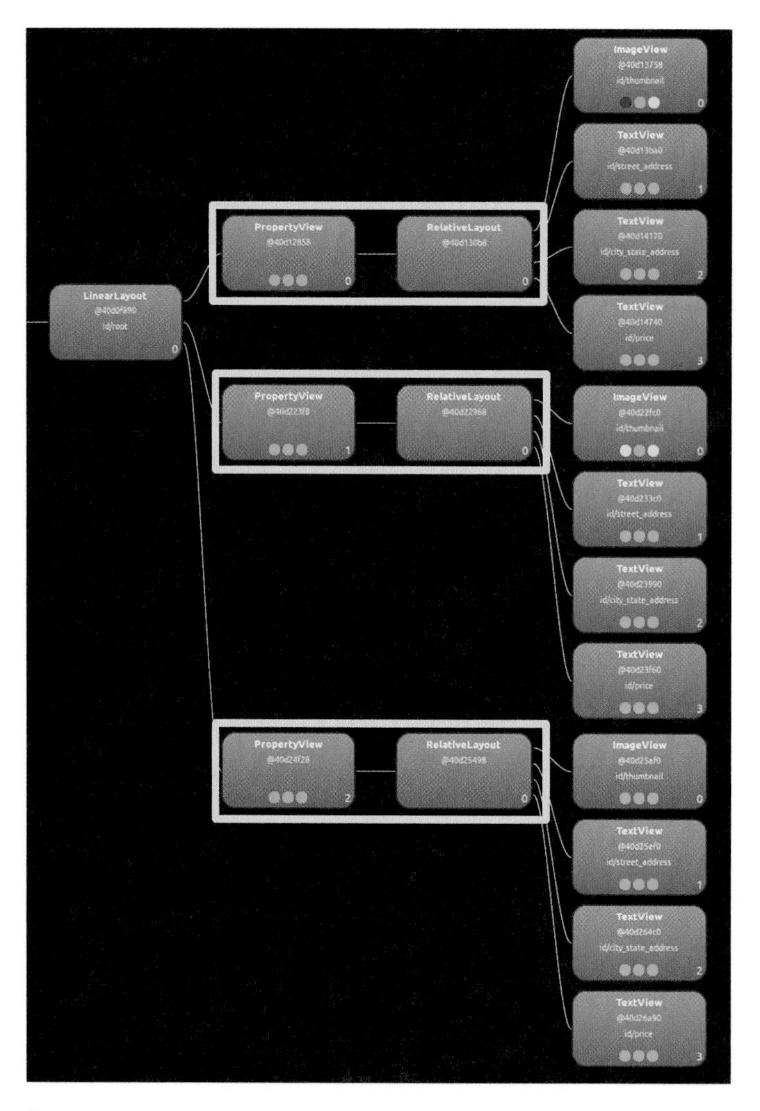

Figure 11.3 Hierarchy View shows that layouts are being wasted.

Although this sample code is going to be plenty fast, the extra `RelativeLayout` is wasteful and can be impactful in other situations, such as when you're using a `ListView`. Fortunately, the solution is extremely simple. Change the `property.xml` layout to have a `merge` root; it should look like Listing 11.4. XML requires a root node, but sometimes you do not want one (such as in this case, where the `PropertyView` would be the root but is created programmatically). In such cases, use `merge`. It essentially acts as a placeholder and does not represent an actual view. Instead, when this layout is inflated in the `init(Context)` method, all the child views within the `merge` node are added directly to the `PropertyView`.

Listing 11.4 The Updated `property.xml` Layout File That Uses a Merge Node

```
<?xml version="1.0" encoding="utf-8"?>
<merge xmlns:android="http://schemas.android.com/apk/res/android">

    <ImageView
        android:id="@+id/thumbnail"
        android:layout_width="@dimen/thumbnail"
        android:layout_height="@dimen/thumbnail"
        android:layout_alignParentLeft="true"
        android:layout_centerVertical="true"
        android:layout_margin="@dimen/half_default_spacing"
        android:contentDescription="@null" />

    <TextView
        android:id="@+id/street_address"
        android:layout_width="match_parent"
        android:layout_height="wrap_content"
        android:layout_alignParentTop="true"
        android:layout_marginTop="@dimen/default_spacing"
        android:layout_toLeftOf="@+id/price"
        android:layout_toRightOf="@+id/thumbnail"
        android:textAppearance="?android:attr/textAppearanceSmall" />

    <TextView
        android:id="@+id/city_state_address"
        android:layout_width="match_parent"
        android:layout_height="wrap_content"
        android:layout_below="@+id/street_address"
        android:layout_marginBottom="@dimen/default_spacing"
        android:layout_marginTop="@dimen/default_spacing"
        android:layout_toLeftOf="@+id/price"
        android:layout_toRightOf="@+id/thumbnail"
        android:textAppearance="?android:attr/textAppearanceSmall" />

    <TextView
        android:id="@+id/price"
        android:layout_width="wrap_content"
        android:layout_height="wrap_content"
        android:layout_alignParentRight="true"
        android:layout_centerVertical="true"
        android:layout_marginLeft="@dimen/default_spacing"
        android:layout_marginRight="@dimen/default_spacing"
        android:textAppearance="?android:attr/textAppearanceLarge" />

</merge>
```

Run Hierarchy View again. Now you should see something similar to Figure 11.4. Notice that the extra layouts are no longer being created and the whole hierarchy is one level less deep. Needlessly complex view hierarchies are one of the main causes of performance problems in Android (two others are GPU overdraw and slow code on the main thread).

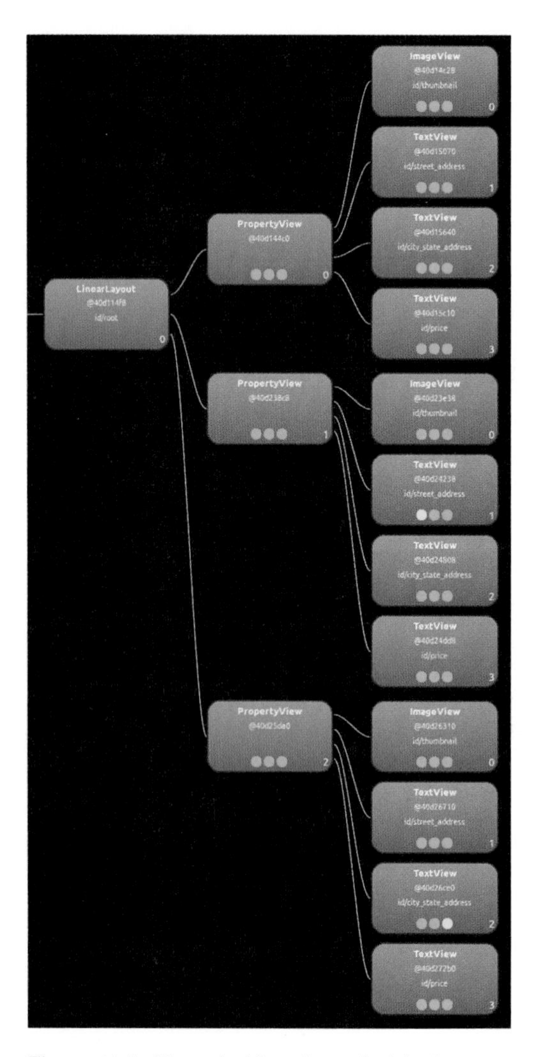

Figure 11.4 Hierarchy View shows that the layouts are more efficient now.

Well, that was an easy optimization. Done, right? Actually, with just a little more work, this code can be even further optimized. The street address and the city/state `TextView`s have identical styling and, more importantly, they line up on the left and right sides. That means these views could really just be one `TextView`. First, update the layout so that you have a single "address" `TextView`. The layout should look like Listing 11.5.

Listing 11.5 The Updated `property.xml` Layout with Only One Address `TextView`

```
<?xml version="1.0" encoding="utf-8"?>
<merge xmlns:android="http://schemas.android.com/apk/res/android">

    <ImageView
        android:id="@+id/thumbnail"
        android:layout_width="@dimen/thumbnail"
        android:layout_height="@dimen/thumbnail"
        android:layout_alignParentLeft="true"
        android:layout_centerVertical="true"
        android:layout_margin="@dimen/half_default_spacing"
        android:contentDescription="@null" />

    <TextView
        android:id="@+id/address"
        android:layout_width="match_parent"
        android:layout_height="wrap_content"
        android:layout_alignParentTop="true"
        android:layout_marginTop="@dimen/default_spacing"
        android:layout_toLeftOf="@+id/price"
        android:layout_toRightOf="@+id/thumbnail"
        android:textAppearance="?android:attr/textAppearanceSmall" />

    <TextView
        android:id="@+id/price"
        android:layout_width="wrap_content"
        android:layout_height="wrap_content"
        android:layout_alignParentRight="true"
        android:layout_centerVertical="true"
        android:layout_marginLeft="@dimen/default_spacing"
        android:layout_marginRight="@dimen/default_spacing"
        android:textAppearance="?android:attr/textAppearanceLarge" />

</merge>
```

Next, update your `PropertyView` class. Now it just needs one address `TextView` reference. When setting the text after being passed a `Property` object, use a `StringBuilder` to construct the text to display. `StringBuilder` is an efficient way of combining several strings and/or characters. When it's ready, you can just call its `toString()` method and pass that string to the `TextView` (if you're wondering how you can style the street address different from the city/state, or vice versa, you should take a look at `SpannableStringBuilder`, which will allow you to assign spans to the text as you build it up). The code should look like Listing 11.6.

Listing 11.6 The Final `PropertyView` Class

```
public class PropertyView extends RelativeLayout {
    private TextView mAddressTextView;
    private TextView mPriceTextView;
    private ImageView mThumbnailImageView;

    public PropertyView(Context context) {
        super(context);
        init(context);
    }

    public PropertyView(Context context, AttributeSet attrs) {
        super(context, attrs);
        init(context);
    }

    public PropertyView(Context context, AttributeSet attrs, int
➥defStyle) {
        super(context, attrs, defStyle);
        init(context);
    }

    /**
     * Updates this View to display the passed Property
     *
     * @param property Property to display
     */
    public void setProperty(Property property) {
        StringBuilder sb = new StringBuilder();
        sb.append(property.getStreetAddress())
          .append('\n')
          .append(property.getCity())
          .append(", ")
          .append(property.getState());
        mAddressTextView.setText(sb.toString());

        mPriceTextView.setText(property.getPrice());
        mThumbnailImageView.setImageResource(R.drawable.house);
    }

    private void init(Context context) {
        inflate(context, R.layout.property, this);
        mAddressTextView = (TextView) findViewById(R.id.address);
        mPriceTextView = (TextView) findViewById(R.id.price);
        mThumbnailImageView = (ImageView) findViewById(R.id.thumbnail);
    }
}
```

Running Hierarchy View once more, you can see that the layout is even simpler. Compare Figure 11.5 to Figure 11.3, and you can see that with just a few minutes of extra work, the layout complexity decreased by one level and the child views per `PropertyView` decreased by 25 percent.

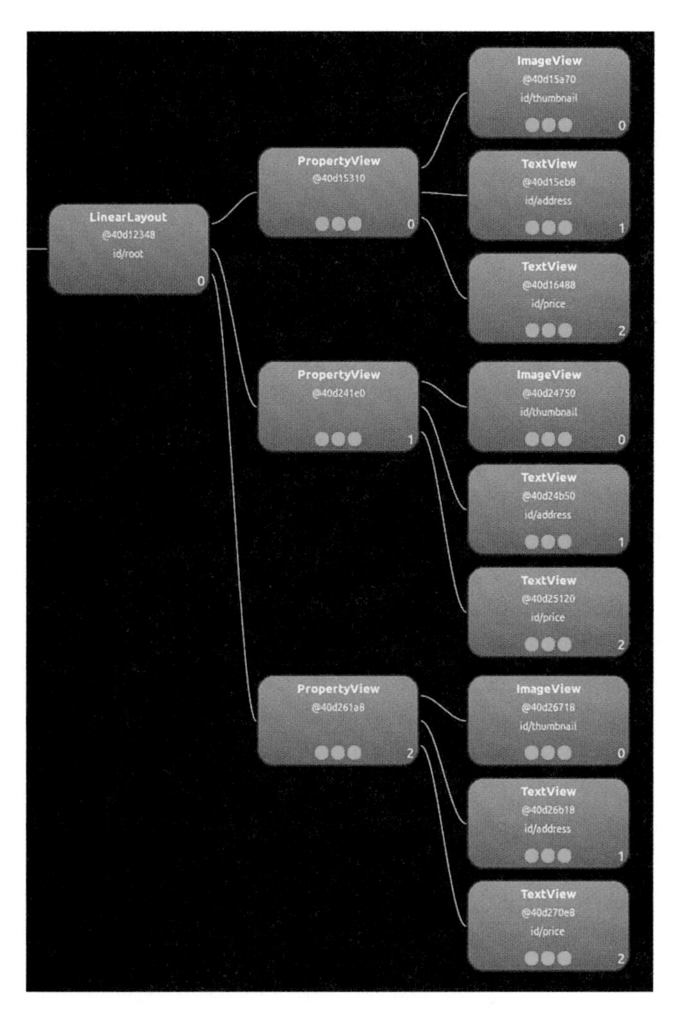

Figure 11.5 Hierarchy View shows that the layouts are even more efficient now.

Now the `PropertyView` is efficient and easy to use. You could spend more time further improving the efficiency, but this should be enough to demonstrate some of the simple gotchas when combining views. Always keep an eye out for `ViewGroups` that have only a single child that is a `ViewGroup` with one or more child views. Except in the case of overlaying graphics, that is nearly always a sign of a wasted layout. Further, keep in mind that `TextView` is an extremely versatile class and multiple `TextViews` can often be combined.

Implementing a Multibutton Toggle

Now that you know how to combine views to make them much easier to work with, the next step is learning how to create a custom component where the combined views interact. The concept is similar to the previous section, "Combining Views to Simplify Working with Them," but instead of just being used to display some data easily, the views will affect one another. For the purpose of this example, you will create a multibutton toggle.

This multibutton toggle has a few requirements. The first is that only one button in the group can be selected at a time. Second, the strings displayed on the buttons should be specified in XML. Finally, to make it reusable, the component should take a listener that is used to notify other classes when a button has been selected and which button was deselected.

Creating the Initial Java Class

This component can most easily be implemented by starting with a `LinearLayout`. It has the ability to easily put components side by side and size them evenly by using weighting, if desired. When you are first learning about creating compound views like this, it is often helpful to create a proof-of-concept that has all the core pieces in place without any custom XML, styling, or external dependencies. So start with that.

Create a new class called `MultiButton` that extends `LinearLayout` and be sure to implement all three of the constructors. It should also implement the `View.OnClickListener` interface (see Figure 11.6 for what the New Java Class dialog should look like). To do the bulk of the work, create a private `init` method that takes the `Context` and `AttributeSet` and call it from each constructor. This method will be what sets everything up (eventually from XML). The `init` method should create three `ToggleButton` instances (which extend `CompoundButton`) and add them to the `LinearLayout` with `addView(View)`.

It also needs to assign an `OnClickListener` to each of them, so you should call `setOnClickListener(this)` on each button. Because only one `CompoundButton` is going to be selected at a time, it's a good idea to keep a reference to the currently selected view, so create a private variable called `mSelectedButton` and assign the first button you create to `mSelectedButton`. At this point, you should have something similar to Listing 11.7.

Figure 11.6 The New Java Class dialog for creating the `MultiButton` class

Listing 11.7 The Initial `MultiButton` Class

```
public class MultiButton extends LinearLayout implements
➥OnClickListener {

    private CompoundButton mSelectedButton;

    public MultiButton(Context context) {
        super(context);
        init(context, null);
    }

    public MultiButton(Context context, AttributeSet attrs) {
        super(context, attrs);
        init(context, attrs);
    }
```

```
    @SuppressLint("NewApi")
    public MultiButton(Context context, AttributeSet attrs, int
➥defStyle) {
        super(context, attrs, defStyle);
        init(context, attrs);
    }

    @Override
    public void onClick(View v) {
        // TODO Auto-generated method stub

    }

    /**
     * Initializes the Buttons inside this View
     *
     * @param context Context to create Buttons with
     * @param attrs AttributeSet or null
     */
    private void init(Context context, AttributeSet attrs) {

        for (int i = 0; i < 3; i++) {
            final CompoundButton button = new ToggleButton(context);
            addView(button);
            button.setOnClickListener(this);

            if (i == 0) {
                mSelectedButton = button;
            }
        }
    }
}
```

note

If your `minSdkVersion` is set below 11 in your manifest, you may get a lint warning on your constructor that calls `super(context, attrs, defStyle)`. You can safely suppress this warning with the `@SuppressLint("NewApi")` annotation, as long as you do not programmatically call that constructor (and there is no need to programmatically call it in any of the sample code or most Android apps).

Create a simple layout that includes your `MultiButton` class. Remember that when including a custom view in XML, you need to use the full package plus class name. See Listing 11.8 for a simple layout example that just puts the `MultiButton` class in a vertically oriented `LinearLayout`.

Listing 11.8 The Simple `activity_main.xml` Layout File

```
<?xml version="1.0" encoding="utf-8"?>
<LinearLayout xmlns:android="http://schemas.android.com/apk/res/
➥android"
    xmlns:tools="http://schemas.android.com/tools"
    android:layout_width="match_parent"
    android:layout_height="match_parent"
    android:orientation="vertical"
    tools:context=".MainActivity" >

    <com.iangclifton.auid.multibutton.MultiButton
        android:id="@+id/multi_button"
        android:layout_width="wrap_content"
        android:layout_height="wrap_content"
        android:orientation="horizontal" />

</LinearLayout>
```

Running the app as is should give you something like Figure 11.7. It isn't very inspiring at this point—you just have three `ToggleButton` instances. They're totally independent, but they won't be for long.

Handling Clicks

Before going on to making the `MultiButton` view work with custom XML attributes, you need to make it, well, work. It should only allow one `ToggleButton` to be on at a time. It should also define a listener interface to allow other classes to respond to buttons being toggled on or off.

Create an interface within the class called `OnMultiButtonCheckedListener` and have it define a single method called `onMultiButtonChecked` that takes two arguments: the `CompoundButton` that was just checked and the `CompoundButton` that was just unchecked. Then, add a method to set a listener called `setOnMultiButtonCheckedListener` that takes an `OnMultiButtonCheckedListener` and assigns it to a class variable.

Now you can finally implement `onClick(View)`. Because this method is only used for the created `CompoundButton`s, you can immediately cast the passed view to a `CompoundButton`. The `MultiButton` should not ever allow the situation of no `CompoundButton` being selected, so call `setChecked(true)` on the passed `CompoundView`. Next, check if the passed `CompoundView` is different from the last `CompoundButton` that was selected. If so, uncheck the previous button, notify the `OnMultiButtonCheckedListener` (if set), and then update the reference to the last selected `CompoundButton`.

Figure 11.7 The `MultiButton` view so far

One more good method to have is one that will allow you to get the selected `CompoundButton`. This allows code to check the previously selected `CompoundButton` to restore state or respond at a later time. Go ahead and add a get `getCheckedButton()` method that returns the `mSelectedButton`.

Once you have all this done, your `MultiButton` class should look like Listing 11.9.

Listing 11.9 The Updated `MultiButton` Class That Controls Button Selection

```
public class MultiButton extends LinearLayout implements
➥OnClickListener {

    private OnMultiButtonCheckedListener mListener;
    private CompoundButton mSelectedButton;
```

```
    /**
     * Interface that listens to the MultiButton being checked
     */
    public interface OnMultiButtonCheckedListener {

        /**
         * Notifies the interface that a new button has been checked
         *
         * @param checked CompoundButton that is now checked
         * @param unchecked CompoundButton that was checked previously
         */
        public void onMultiButtonChecked(CompoundButton checked,
➥CompoundButton unchecked);
    }

    public MultiButton(Context context) {
        super(context);
        init(context, null);
    }

    public MultiButton(Context context, AttributeSet attrs) {
        super(context, attrs);
        init(context, attrs);
    }

    @SuppressLint("NewApi")
    public MultiButton(Context context, AttributeSet attrs, int
➥defStyle) {
        super(context, attrs, defStyle);
        init(context, attrs);
    }

    /**
     * Returns the currently checked button
     *
     * @return CompoundButton that is currently checked
     */
    public CompoundButton getCheckedButton() {
        return mSelectedButton;
    }

    @Override
    public void onClick(View v) {
        final CompoundButton button = (CompoundButton) v;
        button.setChecked(true);

        if (v != mSelectedButton) {
            mSelectedButton.setChecked(false);
            if (mListener != null) {
```

```
                    mListener.onMultiButtonChecked(button,
➥mSelectedButton);
                }
                mSelectedButton = button;
            }
        }

        /**
         * Sets the listener to be notified of a new button being checked
         *
         * @param listener OnMultiButtonCheckedListener to notify, can be
➥null
         */
        public void setOnMultiButtonCheckedListener(
➥OnMultiButtonCheckedListener listener) {
            mListener = listener;
        }

        /**
         * Initializes the Buttons inside this View
         *
         * @param context Context to create Buttons with
         * @param attrs AttributeSet or null
         */
        private void init(Context context, AttributeSet attrs) {

            for (int i = 0; i < 3; i++) {
                final CompoundButton button = new ToggleButton(context);
                addView(button);
                button.setOnClickListener(this);

                if (i == 0) {
                    mSelectedButton = button;
                    mSelectedButton.setChecked(true);
                }
            }
        }
    }
```

Add a simple `TextView` to the main layout so that you can indicate which `CompoundButton` was pressed. Then you can begin updating the `MainActivity`. It should now implement `OnMultiButtonCheckedListener`. The `onMultiButtonChecked` method should simply update the added `TextView` with the text from the checked `CompoundButton`. Implement `onResume`, calling through to the super method and updating the `TextView`. This will allow the `TextView` to be updated even after the state has been restored (such as on orientation change). Listing 11.10 shows what `MainActivity` should look like with the updates.

Listing 11.10 The Updated `Activity` That Uses the `MultiButton` Class

```
public class MainActivity extends Activity implements
➥OnMultiButtonCheckedListener {

    private MultiButton mMultiButton;
    private TextView mTextView;

    @Override
    protected void onCreate(Bundle savedInstanceState) {
        super.onCreate(savedInstanceState);
        setContentView(R.layout.activity_main);

        mTextView = (TextView) findViewById(R.id.text_view);
        mMultiButton = (MultiButton) findViewById(R.id.multi_button);
        mMultiButton.setOnMultiButtonCheckedListener(this);
    }

    @Override
    public boolean onCreateOptionsMenu(Menu menu) {
        // Inflate the menu; this adds items to the action bar if it is
➥present.
        getMenuInflater().inflate(R.menu.activity_main, menu);
        return true;
    }

    @Override
    public void onResume() {
        super.onResume();
        mTextView.setText(mMultiButton.getCheckedButton().getText());
    }

    @Override
    public void onMultiButtonChecked(CompoundButton checked,
➥CompoundButton unchecked) {
        mTextView.setText(checked.getText());
    }

}
```

At this point, your custom view works as it should. Tapping one of the buttons will trigger the `onClick` method of `MultiButton`. That method will set the clicked button to selected and deselect the previously selected button (assuming it is not the same button). When it deselects the previously selected button, it will trigger the `OnMultiButtonCheckedListener` (if one has been applied). In this case, `MainActivity` is notified of the change and it gets the text value of the newly selected button and updates a `TextView` with it. Now `MultiButton` just needs to handle saving and restoring state.

Saving and Restoring State

You may have noticed that rotating the phone causes the selected CompoundButton to be forgotten. There are three things you have to do to save state. The first thing you have to do is tell Android that you want to save state so that it knows to trigger the state-saving and -restoring methods on your view. The next is to make sure that the view you want to maintain state has an ID (meaning your MultiButton view). Finally, you have to actually implement the methods. It's a little work, but it doesn't take long to get the hang of it.

First, you need to call setSaveEnabled(true) at the beginning of the init method. Without calling this, Android will not make any attempt to save your state and you will be wondering why nothing seems to work. By requiring views to declare that they will save state, Android can avoid calling the state-saving and -restoring methods on views that will not handle them for efficiency.

Now, implement an inner class that can maintain the state of your MultiButton. The best way to do so is to extend BaseSavedState. This is a Parcelable class, so it can efficiently be passed around when your Activity is torn down and rebuilt. Create a private static inner class called SavedState that extends BaseSavedState. All it needs to do is keep track of the selected button, so create an int called selectedPosition. Any class that implements Parcelable must create a public field called CREATOR that implements the Parcelable.Creator interface.

One constructor takes a Parcelable, which will represent the super class saved state and is what you use when you are saving state. The other constructor takes a Parcel; that's the one that is used when the system is restoring your class, so pull your int out of the Parcel. In the writeToParcel method, write the int to the Parcel after calling the super method. See Listing 11.11 for the complete SavedState class.

Listing 11.11 The SavedState Inner Class of MultiButton

```
public class MultiButton extends LinearLayout implements
➥OnClickListener {

...other code...

    private static class SavedState extends BaseSavedState {

        private int selectedPosition;

        public static final Parcelable.Creator<SavedState> CREATOR =
➥new Parcelable.Creator<SavedState>() {
            public SavedState createFromParcel(Parcel in) {
                return new SavedState(in);
            }
```

```
            public SavedState[] newArray(int size) {
                return new SavedState[size];
            }
        };

        public SavedState(Parcelable superState) {
            super(superState);
        }

        private SavedState(Parcel in) {
            super(in);
            selectedPosition = in.readInt();
        }

        @Override
        public void writeToParcel(Parcel dest, int flags) {
            super.writeToParcel(dest, flags);
            dest.writeInt(selectedPosition);
        }
    }
}
```

Now that you have a container to save state with, you need to implement the `onRestore-InstanceState` and `onSaveInstanceState` methods of your `MultiButton` view. When restoring state, you are passed a `Parcelable`. First, see if it's an instance of the `SavedState` class you just created. If it isn't, just pass it through to the super method and return. If it is, you can call `getSuperState()` and pass the returned `Parcelable` to the super method. Uncheck the currently selected `CompoundButton` and update the reference with the child at the position specified by the `SavedState` object. Then, check that `CompoundButton`.

To save state, call through to the parent method to get its `Parcelable`. Construct your `SavedState` object by passing in the super class saved state. Loop through the child views until you find the position of the currently selected `CompoundButton` and updated the `SavedState` with the position. Break out of the loop and return the `SavedState` object. Listing 11.12 shows the two methods in detail, and Figure 11.8 shows an example of what this can look like so far.

Listing 11.12 The Updated `MultiButton` Class That Controls Button Selection

```
public class MultiButton extends LinearLayout implements
➥OnClickListener {

...other code...

    @Override
    protected void onRestoreInstanceState(Parcelable state) {
```

```
        if (!(state instanceof SavedState)) {
            // Not our SavedState, so call super and be done with it
            super.onRestoreInstanceState(state);
            return;
        }

        final SavedState ourState = (SavedState) state;
        super.onRestoreInstanceState(ourState.getSuperState());
        mSelectedButton.setChecked(false);
        mSelectedButton = (CompoundButton) getChildAt(
➥ourState.selectedPosition);
        mSelectedButton.setChecked(true);
    }

    @Override
    protected Parcelable onSaveInstanceState() {
        final Parcelable superState = super.onSaveInstanceState();
        final SavedState ourState = new SavedState(superState);
        final int childCount = getChildCount();
        for (int i = 0; i < childCount; i++) {
            if (getChildAt(i) == mSelectedButton) {
                ourState.selectedPosition = i;
                break;
            }
        }
        return ourState;
    }

...other code...

}
```

Defining Custom XML Attributes

The last remaining things to do to finish off the `MultiButton` are to create the `CompoundButton`s based on strings specified in XML, instead of hardcoding the creation of three, and to allow customization. Start by creating an `arrays.xml` file in your `res/values` directory (note that you can actually put it in your `strings.xml` file or any XML file containing a `resources` node, but it's a good idea to separate out the different types of resources into separate files to keep them organized). This file should contain a single sample array of a few strings that can be used as button labels. See Listing 11.13 for an example that uses "Map," "List," and "Hybrid" as the strings (do not worry about the exact string names at this point).

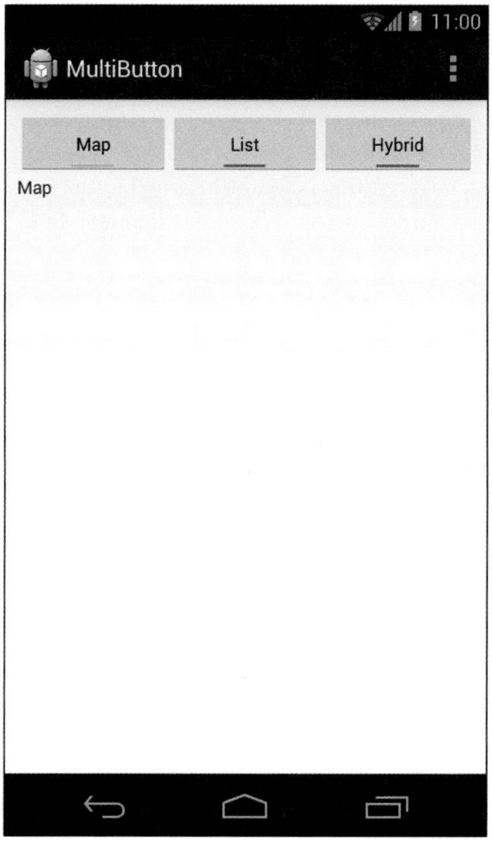

Figure 11.8 The `MultiButton` updated with click handling and state saving/restoring

Listing 11.13 The `arrays.xml` File with a Simple Sample Array

```
<?xml version="1.0" encoding="utf-8"?>
<resources>
    <array name="sample_array">
        <item>Map</item>
        <item>List</item>
        <item>Hybrid</item>
    </array>
</resources>
```

Now you need to tell Android what attributes your custom view supports. To do so, create an `attrs.xml` file also in `res/values`. The root of this file is also a `resources` node. Within a `declare-styleable` node, create `item` nodes. The first two are `buttonBackground` and `buttonBackgroundEnd`. They are references to `Drawables` that can be used for the backgrounds of the `CompoundButtons`. Sometimes the last button in a series has a different design, so this allows you to specify a different background for it. Next, you need to create an `attr` node with a `name` of "textArray," and that will be a reference to the array you just created in `arrays.xml`. Finally, if you're able to change the button backgrounds, you need to be able to change the text color. Android already has an attribute for this, so you use the android namespace prefix and do not specify a format (for a more thorough explanation of custom attributes, the available formats, and implementation details, see Appendix C, "Common Task Reference"). The file should look like Listing 11.14.

Listing 11.14 The `attrs.xml` File with Custom Attributes

```
<?xml version="1.0" encoding="utf-8"?>
<resources>
    <declare-styleable name="MultiButton">
        <attr name="buttonBackground" format="reference"/>
        <attr name="buttonBackgroundEnd" format="reference"/>
        <attr name="textArray" format="reference" />
        <attr name="android:textColor"/>
    </declare-styleable>
</resources>
```

Next, update the `activity_main.xml` layout file to pass in the `sample_array` from `arrays.xml`. You can also pass in the custom backgrounds for the buttons and a text color. The important thing to know is that you have to specify a new XML namespace. You're already used to specifying the android namespace with `xmlns:android="http://schemas.android.com/apk/res/android"` as an attribute in the root node; to add a namespace for your own app, copy that and change the first instance of "android" to "app" and the last instance to your package name. Your custom attributes should be preceded by "app," just as the default ones are preceded by "android" (note, you can use whatever namespace makes sense but "app" is a common convention). See Listing 11.15 for an example of what your layout should look like.

Listing 11.15 The Updated `activity_main.xml` Layout with Custom Attribute

```
<?xml version="1.0" encoding="utf-8"?>
<LinearLayout xmlns:android="http://schemas.android.com/apk/res/
➥android"
    xmlns:app="http://schemas.android.com/apk/
➥res/com.iangclifton.auid.multibutton"
    xmlns:tools="http://schemas.android.com/tools"
    android:layout_width="match_parent"
    android:layout_height="match_parent"
    android:orientation="vertical"
    android:padding="10dp"
    tools:context=".MainActivity" >
```

```
    <com.iangclifton.auid.multibutton.MultiButton
        android:id="@+id/multi_button"
        android:layout_width="match_parent"
        android:layout_height="wrap_content"
        android:orientation="horizontal"
        android:textColor="@android:color/white"
        app:buttonBackground="@drawable/toggle_button"
        app:buttonBackgroundEnd="@drawable/toggle_button_right"
        app:textArray="@array/sample_array" />

    <TextView
        android:id="@+id/text_view"
        android:layout_width="wrap_content"
        android:layout_height="wrap_content" />

</LinearLayout>
```

Now it's time to update the `MultiButton` class. This time you will mostly be updating the `init` method. Add an `int` argument to the `init` method so that a custom resource ID for a string array can be passed in and then update the first constructor to take and pass the same argument. The other constructors can pass any value because the `AttributeSet` takes priority.

Define a private static final `int` of `DEFAULT` that is equal to `-1`. This will be used to tell when a custom background was not specified in XML for the buttons. If the `AttributeSet` passed to the `init` method is null, attempt to get the text array using the passed resource ID. Otherwise, get the styled attributes from the passed `AttributeSet`. This is a `TypedArray` (basically a container that can map resource IDs) from which you can get the values of your custom attributes. You should load the resource ID for the custom button background and custom end button background, if specified. If only the custom button background is specified (and not the background for the end button), it should be used for all buttons. Load the text color as a `ColorStateList` (this allows you to have colors that change based on the button's state, although this example just uses white) and load the text array.

Do not forget to recycle the `TypedArray`. Calling recycle allows the system to reuse the style attributes for greater efficiency.

If you do not have a text array at this point, throw an `InflateException` to help catch the problem early. Finally, loop through the text array, creating a `CompoundButton` for each `CharSequence`, setting text color and backgrounds when needed. For a full example of the `MultiButton`, see Listing 11.16.

Listing 11.16 The Updated `attrs.xml` File with Additional Custom Attributes

```
public class MultiButton extends LinearLayout implements
➥OnClickListener {

    private static final int DEFAULT = -1;

    private OnMultiButtonCheckedListener mListener;
    private CompoundButton mSelectedButton;

    /**
     * Interface that listens to the MultiButton being checked
     */
    public interface OnMultiButtonCheckedListener {

        /**
         * Notifies the interface that a new button has been checked
         *
         * @param checked CompoundButton that is now checked
         * @param unchecked CompoundButton that was checked previously
         */
        public void onMultiButtonChecked(CompoundButton checked,
➥CompoundButton unchecked);
    }

    public MultiButton(Context context, int textArrayResourceId) {
        super(context);
        init(context, null, textArrayResourceId);
    }

    public MultiButton(Context context, AttributeSet attrs) {
        super(context, attrs);
        init(context, attrs, -1);
    }

    @SuppressLint("NewApi")
    public MultiButton(Context context, AttributeSet attrs, int
➥defStyle) {
        super(context, attrs, defStyle);
        init(context, attrs, -1);
    }

    /**
     * Returns the currently checked button
     *
     * @return CompoundButton that is currently checked
     */
    public CompoundButton getCheckedButton() {
        return mSelectedButton;
    }
```

```
    @Override
    public void onClick(View v) {
        final CompoundButton button = (CompoundButton) v;
        button.setChecked(true);

        if (v != mSelectedButton) {
            mSelectedButton.setChecked(false);
            if (mListener != null) {
                mListener.onMultiButtonChecked(button,
➥mSelectedButton);
            }
            mSelectedButton = button;
        }
    }

    /**
     * Sets the listener to be notified of a new button being checked
     *
     * @param listener OnMultiButtonCheckedListener to notify, can be
➥null
     */
    public void setOnMultiButtonCheckedListener(
➥OnMultiButtonCheckedListener listener) {
        mListener = listener;
    }

    @Override
    protected void onRestoreInstanceState(Parcelable state) {
        if (!(state instanceof SavedState)) {
            // Not our SavedState, so call super and be done with it
            super.onRestoreInstanceState(state);
            return;
        }

        final SavedState ourState = (SavedState) state;
        super.onRestoreInstanceState(ourState.getSuperState());
        mSelectedButton.setChecked(false);
        mSelectedButton = (CompoundButton) getChildAt(
➥ourState.selectedPosition);
        mSelectedButton.setChecked(true);
    }

    @Override
    protected Parcelable onSaveInstanceState() {
        final Parcelable superState = super.onSaveInstanceState();
        final SavedState ourState = new SavedState(superState);
        final int childCount = getChildCount();
        for (int i = 0; i < childCount; i++) {
            if (getChildAt(i) == mSelectedButton) {
                ourState.selectedPosition = i;
```

```
                    break;
                }
            }
            return ourState;
        }

        /**
         * Initializes the Buttons inside this View
         *
         * @param context Context to create Buttons with
         * @param attrs AttributeSet or null
         */
        private void init(Context context, AttributeSet attrs, int
➥textArrayResourceId) {
            setSaveEnabled(true);

            final CharSequence[] textArray;
            int buttonBackground = DEFAULT;
            int buttonBackgroundEnd = DEFAULT;
            ColorStateList textColors = null;
            if (attrs == null) {
                textArray = context.getResources()
➥.getTextArray(textArrayResourceId);
            } else {
                // Load custom attributes
                final TypedArray customAttrs = context
➥.obtainStyledAttributes(attrs, R.styleable.MultiButton);
                buttonBackground = customAttrs.getResourceId(
➥R.styleable.MultiButton_buttonBackground, DEFAULT);
                buttonBackgroundEnd = customAttrs.getResourceId(
➥R.styleable.MultiButton_buttonBackgroundEnd, DEFAULT);
                if (buttonBackgroundEnd == DEFAULT) {
                    buttonBackgroundEnd = buttonBackground;
                }
                textColors = customAttrs.getColorStateList(
➥R.styleable.MultiButton_android_textColor);
                textArray = customAttrs.getTextArray(
➥R.styleable.MultiButton_textArray);
                customAttrs.recycle();
            }

            if (textArray == null) {
                throw new InflateException("MultiButton requires a
➥textArray");
            }

            // Loop through CharSequences to create ToggleButtons
            for (int i = 0; i < textArray.length; i++) {
                final CharSequence text = textArray[i];
                final ToggleButton button = new ToggleButton(context);
                addView(button);
```

```
            button.setOnClickListener(this);
            button.setText(text);
            button.setTextOff(text);
            button.setTextOn(text);

            // Add weight
            LayoutParams lp = (LayoutParams) button.getLayoutParams();
            lp.weight = 1f;

            // Assign text color
            if (textColors != null) {
                button.setTextColor(textColors);
            }

            // Assign custom backgrounds
            if (i == textArray.length - 1) {
                if (buttonBackgroundEnd != DEFAULT) {
                    button.setBackgroundResource(buttonBackgroundEnd);
                }
            } else {
                if (buttonBackground != DEFAULT) {
                    button.setBackgroundResource(buttonBackground);
                }
            }

            // Obtain reference to first button
            if (mSelectedButton == null) {
                mSelectedButton = button;
                mSelectedButton.setChecked(true);
            }
        }
    }

    private static class SavedState extends BaseSavedState {

        private int selectedPosition;

        @SuppressWarnings("unused")
        public static final Parcelable.Creator<SavedState> CREATOR =
➥new Parcelable.Creator<SavedState>() {
            public SavedState createFromParcel(Parcel in) {
                return new SavedState(in);
            }

            public SavedState[] newArray(int size) {
                return new SavedState[size];
            }
        };

        public SavedState(Parcelable superState) {
            super(superState);
```

```
        }

        private SavedState(Parcel in) {
            super(in);
            selectedPosition = in.readInt();
        }

        @Override
        public void writeToParcel(Parcel dest, int flags) {
            super.writeToParcel(dest, flags);
            dest.writeInt(selectedPosition);
        }
    }
}
```

If everything looks good, run the app on your device or emulator and see the changes. The examples here use a custom button background for each state. The end button has a slight shadow, so it uses a different set of assets. Figure 11.9 demonstrates one example of how this could look. If you are unsure how to create a `Drawable` (selector) that has a different `Drawable` for each possible button state, see the example in Listing 11.17.

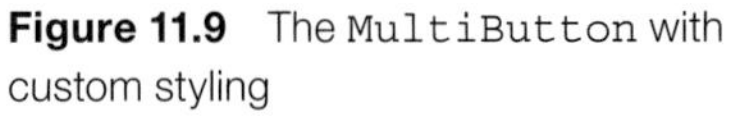
Figure 11.9 The `MultiButton` with custom styling

Listing 11.17 A Sample Drawable with Custom `Drawable`s for Each State

```
<?xml version="1.0" encoding="utf-8"?>
<selector xmlns:android="http://schemas.android.com/apk/res/android">

    <item android:drawable="@drawable/toggle_button_on_disabled"
       android:state_checked="true"
       android:state_enabled="false"
       android:state_window_focused="false"/>
    <item android:drawable="@drawable/toggle_button_on_pressed"
        android:state_checked="true"
        android:state_pressed="true"/>
    <item android:drawable="@drawable/toggle_button_on_focused"
        android:state_checked="true"
        android:state_enabled="true"
        android:state_focused="true"/>
    <item android:drawable="@drawable/toggle_button_on"
        android:state_checked="true"
        android:state_enabled="true"/>
    <item android:drawable="@drawable/
➥toggle_button_on_disabled_focused"
        android:state_checked="true"
        android:state_focused="true"/>
    <item android:drawable="@drawable/toggle_button_on_disabled"
        android:state_checked="true"/>
    <item android:drawable="@drawable/toggle_button_off_disabled"
        android:state_enabled="false"
        android:state_window_focused="false"/>
    <item android:drawable="@drawable/toggle_button_off_pressed"
        android:state_pressed="true"/>
    <item android:drawable="@drawable/toggle_button_off_focused"
        android:state_enabled="true"
        android:state_focused="true"/>
    <item android:drawable="@drawable/toggle_button_off"
        android:state_enabled="true"/>
    <item android:drawable="@drawable/
➥toggle_button_off_disabled_focused"
        android:state_focused="true"/>
    <item android:drawable="@drawable/toggle_button_off"/>

</selector>
```

Summary

In this chapter, you learned how to combine multiple views to make them easier to work with and to add new functionality. You now know how to combine views to clean up your code and present information in a consistent, clean way. You also know how to combine views that can interact. An important part of creating custom views is supporting custom attributes to keep your layout presentation in XML, separate from your code. This chapter gave you an example of how that can work. Finally, you learned how to use a `Parcelable` for saving and restoring state for views. This subtle difference to custom views allows your app to better handle orientation and other configuration changes efficiently and keeps the behavior predictable.

In the next chapter, you will take your knowledge of views even further. Instead of using existing views in new ways, you will create entirely custom views; however, keep in mind what you have learned in this chapter. Make use of existing views where you can because they've been thoroughly tested and require much less effort to combine than creating views from scratch.

CHAPTER 12

DEVELOPING FULLY CUSTOM VIEWS

Android has a significant number of views already created for your use. Throughout this book, you've learned how to work with many of them, and in the previous chapter, "Combining Views for Custom Components," you learned how to combine multiple existing views to make them easier to work with and to add new functionality. Many apps will never need more than what you have learned so far, but sometimes you need to create your own views or significantly modify existing ones. This chapter will teach you the concepts behind how views actually work and then show you the details of actually creating your own custom view.

General Concepts

Before you can start developing your own custom views, it's a good idea to understand the general concepts behind views. Views must know how to measure themselves, lay themselves (and any children) out, and draw themselves (although some views do not actually draw anything). They also have to handle various input events such as clicks and long presses.

When you are first creating a view, you will find it very useful to look at the source code for views that are similar to what you want. The source code for views is available online at https://android.googlesource.com/platform/frameworks/base/+/refs/heads/master/core/java/android/view and available via git (http://source.android.com/source/downloading.html). Note that many of the fields stored in views have package visibility, so you will see subclasses often accessing these fields directly, such as `mPaddingLeft`. In general, you should avoid doing the same to ensure that your code remains compatible with any changes to the Android classes outside of your control. You can nearly always store copies of the values in your own class when you need the performance benefit of avoiding a method call.

Measurement

The first part to understand about views is how measurement happens. Measurement is when a view says how big it would like to be given certain constraints. For instance, a view might be asked how tall it would like to be given a width of 300 pixels.

The parent view will call each child view's `measure(int, int)` method, passing in two integers that represent the measurement specification for the width and height, respectively. This triggers the child's `onMeasure(int, int)` method with the same parameters, which is required to call `setMeasuredDimensions(int, int)` with the actual pixel values for the width and height of the view. After that has happened, the view's `getMeasuredWidth()` and `getMeasuredHeight()` methods will return those dimensions.

The measurement specification is an integer packed with `MeasureSpec` (https://developer.android.com/reference/android/view/View.MeasureSpec.html) that has both a mode and a size (an int is used instead of an object for efficiency). The mode can be one of `AT_MOST`, `EXACTLY`, and `UNSPECIFIED`. The `AT_MOST` mode means the child can specify any size for this dimension up to the size provided in the `MeasureSpec`. The `EXACTLY` mode says that the view must be the exact number of pixels passed in as the size (note that this is actual pixels and not density independent pixels, so you do not need to convert the value based on density). The `UNSPECIFIED` mode means that the parent has not provided any restrictions on the size of the child, so the child should determine its own ideal size.

The parent usually considers the `LayoutParams` of the child to determine what measurement specifications to pass down. For instance, a view's `LayoutParams` might specify

MATCH_PARENT for the width, and the parent might then pass down a MeasureSpec that says the child will be exactly 768px (a possible exact width of the parent). However, regardless of what is requested by the LayoutParams, the MeasureSpec that is passed from the parent to the child is what must be obeyed.

Layout

The method layout(int, int, int, int) is called on each view, triggering onLayout(boolean, int, int, int, int)—just as the measure(int, int) method triggers onMeasure(int, int). In the onLayout method, each parent view can position its child views according to the sizes determined in the measurement phase. Once the positions for a given child are determined, its layout(int, int, int, int) method is called. For instance, a vertically oriented LinearLayout might go through its children, positioning one, and using its height to position the next one (LinearLayout actually does significantly more than this, but this is the basic idea).

The four ints passed to the layout method are the left, top, right, and bottom pixel positions relative to the parent. The onLayout method receives a boolean that indicates if this is a new size and/or position along with those four ints.

There are times when a view determines that it needs to be laid out again because its size has changed. In this case, it calls the requestLayout() method. For example, if you call setImageDrawable(Drawable) on an ImageView with a Drawable that is not the same size as the current Drawable, it will call requestLayout() so that it can be given the right amount of space for the new Drawable.

Drawing

The drawing phase is when the view actually creates the pixels that it will display. This all happens in the onDraw(Canvas) method. The view should avoid allocating any objects in this method and should be as efficient as possible to keep the UI smooth.

If a view has determined that its drawing state has changed (such as when you give an ImageView a new Drawable), then it can call invalidate() to request that onDraw(Canvas) is called. The invalidate() call is asynchronous; it merely flags the view as needing to be redrawn. That means you can safely call it multiple times. For example, if you set the text of a TextView, invalidate() will be called. If you then change the color of the text, invalid() will be called again. None of the drawing will happen until the next drawing pass. When you need to invalidate a view from a background thread, you can use postInvalidate().

> **note**
>
> When views do not need to draw anything (such as `ViewGroups` that just lay out other views), they can call `setWillNotDraw(boolean)`, passing in `true`. This allows Android to do some extra optimization. When extending existing views, be aware that some set this value to `true`, which means your `onDraw(Canvas)` method will never be called. For instance, a `LinearLayout` without dividers sets this to true. To check the current value, call `willNotDraw()` on your view.

Canvas

The `Canvas` object that is passed in the `onDraw` method can be thought of as the tool that handles drawing. It is backed by a mutable `Bitmap` object that actually holds all the pixels. To draw, you need a `Paint` (described shortly) and something to draw, such as another `Bitmap` or a rectangle. The `Canvas` class has a large number of methods for drawing and simplifying drawing. `Canvas` supports clipping (a clip is a portion of the `Bitmap` that can be drawn onto, similar to using a marquee in an image program), drawing `Bitmaps`, drawing shapes (arcs, rectangles, circles, and so on), adjusting the `Canvas` with matrixes (including helper methods to simplify translation, rotation, scaling, and skewing), saving and restoring state (used for saving and restoring the state of the clip and matrixes), and some other helper methods.

You can also instantiate your own `Canvas` object by supplying it with a mutable `Bitmap` object. This is very useful when you need to perform some kind of drawing only once and want to retain the results.

Paint

The `Paint` class holds information about how to draw, such as the color, styles for filling and ending lines, and even complex `XferModes` (discussed in Chapter 13, "Working with the Canvas and Advanced Drawing"). Nearly all the drawing calls performed by a `Canvas` object require a `Paint` object. A `Canvas` object will do something like draw a rectangle, but the `Paint` object will determine if it is anti-aliased, filled in, and so on.

Remember that you should avoid allocating objects in your `onDraw(Canvas)` method, so you should generally allocate your `Paint` objects elsewhere. Another option is to allocate them the first time `onDraw(Canvas)` is called and then retain the reference for future calls.

Bitmaps

As you know, a bitmap is a type of image. The original term was literally a map of bits to be displayed since the pixels were either on or off (there was no color or intensity to consider), but it has since acquired a more generalized meaning that really just means it's an image defined by pixels. The `Bitmap` object is a representation of pixels with various helper methods. Generally you will use the static `Bitmap` methods, such as `createBitmap`, to instantiate a new `Bitmap` object, but there is also a `BitmapFactory` that can be helpful.

Bitmaps can be mutable or immutable. If a Bitmap is mutable, you can change the values of its pixels; immutable Bitmaps cannot have their pixels changed. If you are supplying a Bitmap to a Canvas, it must be mutable.

> **warning**
>
> Prior to Android 3.0 (Honeycomb), the raw pixels of a Bitmap object were actually stored in a different heap. That caused a lot of problems with managing memory, especially because the pixels were not necessarily freed when the Bitmap object itself was destroyed (or even shortly after). If you develop any code that quickly allocates and deallocates Bitmaps and can run on older versions of Android, be sure to heavily test it to make sure you do not run into OutOfMemoryExceptions.

Drawables

You have used Drawables throughout this book and probably in every app you've written. Now that you have a basic understanding of how a view draws and what a Canvas is, you can apply that knowledge to Drawables. They have a draw(Canvas) method that you can call directly in your custom views. You can control where the Drawable draws by using its setBounds method (there is one for supplying a Rect and one for supplying four int coordinates).

If you load a Drawable with the Resources class via getDrawable(int), it will return a specific type of Drawable (such as a NinePatchDrawable or ShapeDrawable), but you can generally use all these through the methods available in the abstract Drawable class. You can get the ideal size for a Drawable with the getIntrinsicWidth() and getIntrinsicHeight() methods. For example, a BitmapDrawable will return the dimensions of the actual image it represents, but you can still use setBounds to provide other dimensions.

Drawables will be covered more in the next chapter as well.

Touch Input

Touch input is the primary means of interacting with views in Android. In most cases, you can use the standard listeners, such as OnClickListener and OnLongClickListener, to handle the interactions. In some cases, you need to handle custom, more complex touches. If a view already meets your needs but you just need to handle custom touches, then consider using the OnTouchListener to avoid having to subclass the view.

Touch events are reported with the MotionEvent object (which can also be used for other input types such as a trackball). MotionEvents track pointers (such as a user's fingers on the screen), and each pointer receives a unique ID; however, most interactions with pointers actually use the pointer index—that is, the position of the pointer within the array of pointers tracked by a given MotionEvent. A pointer index is not guaranteed to be the same, so you must get the index with findPointerIndex(int) (where the int argument is the unique pointer ID).

There are a lot of types of MotionEvents (you can see details at https://developer.android.com/reference/android/view/MotionEvent.html), but a few in particular you should know. ACTION_DOWN indicates that a new pointer is being tracked, such as when you first touch the screen. ACTION_MOVE indicates that the pointer has changed, usually location, such as when you drag your finger on the screen. ACTION_UP indicates that the pointer has finished, such as when you lift your finger from the screen. ACTION_POINTER_DOWN and ACTION_POINTER_UP indicate when a secondary pointer is starting to be tracked and is finishing respectively, such as when you touch the screen with a second finger. ACTION_CANCEL indicates that the gesture has been aborted.

Android has several classes that simplify working with input. GestureDetector can be used to listen for common touch gestures. To use it, you simply pass the MotionEvent from your onTouchEvent(MotionEvent) method in the view to onTouchEvent(MotionEvent) on the GestureDetector. It specifies the OnGestureListener interface that defines various gesture-based methods such as onFling and onLongPress. You can use a GestureDetector to determine when any of these predefined gestures has taken place and then trigger your OnGestureListener. Because you often only need to handle a subset of the gestures available, there is a SimpleOnGestureListener that implements all the methods of OnGestureListener as empty methods or methods that simply return false. If you wanted to listen to just flings, you would override onDown(MotionEvent) to return true (returning false from this method will prevent the other methods from triggering because the touch event will be ignored) and override onFling(MotionEvent, MotionEvent, float, float) to handle the fling. Note that a compatibility version of GestureDetector appears in the support library called GestureDetectorCompat.

To simplify working with MotionEvents, there is a MotionEventCompat class in the support library. It provides static methods for working with MotionEvents so that you don't have to deal with masks manually. For instance, you can call getActionMasked(MotionEvent) to get just the action portion of the int (such as ACTION_DOWN) that is returned by a MotionEvent's getAction() method.

Android also provides two classes for working with scrolling. The original is called Scroller and has been available since the beginning of Android's public release. The newer version is called OverScroller and was added in API level 9. Both of them allow you to do things such as animate a fling gesture. The main difference between the two is that OverScroller allows you to overshoot the bounds of the scrolling container. This is what happens when you fling a list quickly in Android and then the list stops and the edge glows. The OverScroller determines how far beyond the list you have scrolled and converts that "energy" into the glow. EdgeEffect was introduced in API level 14 (Ice Cream Sandwich) to standardize working with visual indicators of overscrolling. If you decide to create a custom view and want to have an `EdgeEffect` while still supporting older versions of Android, you can use the `EdgeEffectCompat` class from the support library. When running on pre-ICS versions of Android, it will simply have no effect.

Other Forms of Input

When Android was originally developed, it was designed to support a variety of form factors, and that meant it had to support multiple input types. Many of the original phones had touchscreens along with alternate input methods such as scroll wheels and directional pads. Although many Android devices today do not use these other input methods, it's still worth considering how users can interact with your views without touch input. In most cases, supporting other forms of input requires very little effort. Plus, supporting a directional pad, for instance, allows your app to run on Google TV or to be better used by devices with keyboards.

In general, you simply need to override `onKeyDown(int, KeyEvent)` to handle alternate forms of input. The first parameter is an `int` identifying which key was pressed (the `KeyEvent` object has constants for all the keys; for example, `KeyEvent.KEYCODE_ENTER` is the `int` representing the Enter key). The second parameter is the actual `KeyEvent` object that contains details such as whether another key is being pressed (to let you do things like check if Alt is being pressed while this key is being pressed) and what device this event originated from (for example, an external keyboard).

Trackball events can be handled with your `onKeyDown(int, KeyEvent)` method and, in most cases, that is all you want to do. For instance, if you do not specifically handle trackball events, a scroll to the right on a trackball will end up triggering `onKeyDown(int, KeyEvent)` with the "key" being `KEYCODE_DPAD_RIGHT`. In the case where you do want to handle trackball events differently (such as to handle flings), you will do so in `onTrackballEvent(MotionEvent)`. Be sure to return `true` to consume the event.

Developing the Custom View

To better understand all the details of a custom view, it's time to make your own view. You're going to make a simple view that takes an array of icons (`Drawables`) and draws them. It will assume they are all the same size and draw them from left to right. That doesn't sound too exciting, but you will learn how to handle positioning each of the `Drawables` to be drawn, how to keep things efficient, how to handle scrolling and overscrolling, and how to detect when a `Drawable` is touched. This view actually requires a fairly significant amount of code, so it may be a good idea to jump back to the first part of this chapter to review the general concepts of each stage (for example, measuring the view) before diving into the actual implementation.

Creating the Initial Custom View Files

To get started, create a new project called `HorizontalIconView` and set the target to API level 17 and the minimum to 16 (for now). Create a new `dimens.xml` file in `res/values` that has two dimensions. The first dimension is `icon_size` and represents the width and height of the icons; set it to 48dp. The second dimension is `icon_spacing` and represents the space between icons; set it to 10dp. Your file should look like Listing 12.1.

Listing 12.1 The Simple `dimens.xml` File

```
<?xml version="1.0" encoding="utf-8"?>
<resources>
    <dimen name="icon_size">48dp</dimen>
    <dimen name="icon_spacing">10dp</dimen>
</resources>
```

Create the `HorizontalIconView` class next that extends `View` and be sure the check the box to implement all three parent constructors. Each constructor should call through to `init(Context)`, which you'll be making shortly. There are also several class variables to create. See Listing 12.2 for what the class should initially look like with all the variables included. These are all the variables that will be used throughout the next few sections, so don't worry about understanding all of them just yet; they'll be explained as you build each method that requires them.

Listing 12.2 The Initial `HorizontalIconView`

```
public class HorizontalIconView extends View {
    private static final String TAG = "HorizontalIconView";

    private static final int INVALID_POINTER =
➥MotionEvent.INVALID_POINTER_ID;

    /**
     * int to track the ID of the pointer that is being tracked
     */
    private int mActivePointerId = INVALID_POINTER;

    /**
     * The List of Drawables that will be shown
     */
    private List<Drawable> mDrawables;

    /**
     * EdgeEffect or "glow" when scrolled too far left
     */
    private EdgeEffectCompat mEdgeEffectLeft;
```

```
    /**
     * EdgeEffect or "glow" when scrolled too far right
     */
    private EdgeEffectCompat mEdgeEffectRight;

    /**
     * List of Rects for each visible icon to calculate touches
     */
    private final List<Rect> mIconPositions = new ArrayList<Rect>();

    /**
     * Width and height of icons in pixels
     */
    private int mIconSize;

    /**
     * Space between each icon in pixels
     */
    private int mIconSpacing;

    /**
     * Whether a pointer/finger is currently on screen that is being
➥tracked
     */
    private boolean mIsBeingDragged;

    /**
     * Maximum fling velocity in pixels per second
     */
    private int mMaximumVelocity;

    /**
     * Minimum fling velocity in pixels per second
     */
    private int mMinimumVelocity;

    /**
     * How far to fling beyond the bounds of the view
     */
    private int mOverflingDistance;

    /**
     * How far to scroll beyond the bounds of the view
     */
    private int mOverscrollDistance;

    /**
     * The X coordinate of the last down touch, used to determine when
     * a drag starts
```

```
     */
    private float mPreviousX = 0;

    /**
     * Number of pixels this view can scroll (basically width - visible
➥width)
     */
    private int mScrollRange;

    /**
     * Number of pixels of movement required before a touch is "moving"
     */
    private int mTouchSlop;

    /**
     * VelocityTracker to simplify tracking MotionEvents
     */
    private VelocityTracker mVelocityTracker;

    /**
     * Scroller to do the hard work of scrolling smoothly
     */
    private OverScroller mScroller;

    /**
     * The number of icons that are left of the view and therefore not
➥drawn
     */
    private int mSkippedIconCount = 0;

    public HorizontalIconView(Context context) {
        super(context);
        init(context);
    }

    public HorizontalIconView(Context context, AttributeSet attrs) {
        super(context, attrs);
        init(context);
    }

    public HorizontalIconView(Context context, AttributeSet attrs, int
➥defStyle) {
        super(context, attrs, defStyle);
        init(context);
    }
}
```

Now it's time to create the `init(Context)` method. It's a private method that does not return anything and just sets up some values for the view. Get a reference to the `Resources` by calling `context.getResources()`. Use `getDimensionPixelSize(int)` to set both the `mIconSize` and the `mIconSpacing` using the two dimensions you previously created (`R.dimen.icon_size` and `R.dimen.icon_spacing`). Next, get a `ViewConfiguration` reference by calling its static `get(Context)` method. The `ViewConfiguration` class can give you values to use in your views to make sure your custom views behave in the same way as all other views. For instance, set `mTouchSlop` to the value returned by `ViewConfiguration`'s `getScaledTouchSlop()` method. This value is the number of pixels a pointer/finger must travel on the screen before being considered "moving" and is scaled to the device's density. If you did not consider touch slop, it would be extremely hard to touch down on an exact pixel and lift your finger without moving to another pixel on accident. Once a pointer has moved the touch slop amount, it's moving, so it can become a gesture such as a drag or a fling (and is no longer possible for the touch to be a "click" or "long click" because of the distance it has traveled). You should also set `mMinimumVelocity` via `getScaledMinimumFlingVelocity()` (which represents the minimum pixels per second a pointer has to move to initiate a fling gesture), `mMaximumVelocity` via `getScaledMaximumFlingVelocity()` (which represents the maximum pixels per second that a fling can travel at), `mOverflingDistance` via `getScaledOverflingDistance()` (which represents the maximum distance to fling beyond the edge of the view; you'll convert that value into the glow at the edge of the view instead of scrolling beyond), and `mOverscrollDistance` via `getScaledOverscrollDistance()` (which represents the same thing as the overfling distance but when you are dragging or scrolling the view instead of flinging it).

To be explicit, call `setWillNotDraw(false)` on your view to ensure that the `onDraw(Canvas)` method will be called. It's good to get into the habit of calling this method in an initialization method for all your custom views that draw so that you don't forget to do so when extending a view that will not draw unless you call this method; otherwise, you could be in for a few hours of frustrating troubleshooting.

Set up the `mEdgeEffectLeft` and `mEdgeEffectRight` by instantiating a new `EdgeEffectCompat` from the support library. This class is where you put all the extra "energy" when scrolling beyond the bounds of the view. The more that you scrolled beyond the view, the brighter it glows. You should also set `mScroller` as a new `OverScroller`. That will be used to do the hard work of animating flings.

When you're done with the `init(Context)` method, it should look like Listing 12.3.

Listing 12.3 The Complete `init` Method

```
/**
 * Perform one-time initialization
 *
```

```
     * @param context Context to load Resources and ViewConfiguration data
     */
    private void init(Context context) {
        final Resources res = context.getResources();
        mIconSize = res.getDimensionPixelSize(R.dimen.icon_size);
        mIconSpacing = res.getDimensionPixelSize(R.dimen.icon_spacing);

        // Cache ViewConfiguration values
        final ViewConfiguration config = ViewConfiguration.get(context);
        mTouchSlop = config.getScaledTouchSlop();
        mMinimumVelocity = config.getScaledMinimumFlingVelocity();
        mMaximumVelocity = config.getScaledMaximumFlingVelocity();
        mOverflingDistance = config.getScaledOverflingDistance();
        mOverscrollDistance = config.getScaledOverscrollDistance();

        // Verify this View will be drawn
        setWillNotDraw(false);

        // Other setup
        mEdgeEffectLeft = new EdgeEffectCompat(context);
        mEdgeEffectRight = new EdgeEffectCompat(context);
        mScroller = new OverScroller(context);
    }
```

Now that your view sets up all the basic values it will need, there's just one thing remaining before measuring and drawing your view: You need to be able to set the `Drawables`. Create a public method called `setDrawables(List<Drawable>)`. It's not quite as straightforward as just updating `mDrawables`. First, you can check if `mDrawables` is `null`; if it is, check if the passed-in `List` is `null`. If both are `null`, you can just return because nothing needs to be updated. If `mDrawables` was `null` but the passed-in `List` was not, call `requestLayout()` because there is a new `List` of `Drawables` to measure. If `mDrawables` was not `null` but the passed-in `List` was, call `requestLayout()`, set `mDrawables` to `null`, and return. If `mDrawables` and the passed-in `List` of `Drawables` are the same size, the view simply needs to be redrawn (remember, all of the "icons" or `Drawables` are being drawn at the size specified in `dimens.xml`, so only the number of them has to be compared), so call `invalidate()`. If the two `Lists` are a different size, you need to `requestLayout()`. Anything that didn't return needs to update `mDrawables`, so create a new `List` containing the `Drawables`. The reason for creating a new `List` is because the view should not have to handle the case of the `List` being modified by external code that adds or removes `Drawables`. See Listing 12.4 for the complete method.

Listing 12.4 The Complete `setDrawables` Method

```
    /**
     * Sets the List of Drawables to display
     *
     * @param drawables List of Drawables; can be null
```

```
     */
    public void setDrawables(List<Drawable> drawables) {
        if (mDrawables == null) {
            if (drawables == null) {
                return;
            }
            requestLayout();
        } else if (drawables == null) {
            requestLayout();
            mDrawables = null;
            return;
        } else if (mDrawables.size() == drawables.size()) {
            invalidate();
        } else {
            requestLayout();
        }
        mDrawables = new ArrayList<Drawable>(drawables);
        mIconPositions.clear();
    }
```

You could make this also check for empty `Lists` being passed in, if you believe that is a use case that will happen frequently. Without explicitly checking for empty lists, the view will just treat them like a non-empty `List`, but it will never draw anything.

Measuring View Dimensions

The first challenge of creating your custom view is to handle the measuring. Some custom views are extremely easy to measure; others take a bit of work. If your view is being used internally only (that is, it's not going to be in a library or repository that other developers can use), you can take some shortcuts to simply make it support the layouts you will use it in; otherwise, you need to make sure your view handles whatever the parent asks of it.

It's very common to create private methods called `measureHeight(int)` and `measureWidth(int)` to split up measuring the two dimensions, so do that now. Both should return an `int` that represents the measured size. The height is the easier of the two to measure, so start there. Declare an `int` called `result` and set it to 0; it will be the measured size. Get the mode portion of the `int` that was passed in by using `MeasureSpec.getMode(int)` and get the size portion by calling `MeasureSpec.getSize(int)`. If the mode is `MeasureSpec.EXACTLY`, you can set your result to the size and you're done. In all other cases, you want to determine your size. Add the top padding size and the bottom padding size (you can use `getPaddingTop()` and `getPaddinBottom()`, respectively) plus the `mIconSize` to set `result` to the desired height. Next, check if the mode is `MeasureSpec.AT_MOST`. If it is, the parent view is saying your view needs to be no bigger than the passed size. Use `Math.min(int, int)` to set `result` to the smaller of the passed-in size and your calculated size and then return the result. Your method should look like Listing 12.5.

Listing 12.5 The Simple `measureHeight` Method

```
/**
 * Measures height according to the passed measure spec
 *
 * @param measureSpec int measure spec to use
 * @return int pixel size
 */
private int measureHeight(int measureSpec) {
    int specMode = MeasureSpec.getMode(measureSpec);
    int specSize = MeasureSpec.getSize(measureSpec);

    int result = 0;
    if (specMode == MeasureSpec.EXACTLY) {
        result = specSize;
    } else {
        result = mIconSize + getPaddingTop() + getPaddingBottom();
        if (specMode == MeasureSpec.AT_MOST) {
            result = Math.min(result, specSize);
        }
    }

    return result;
}
```

Copy and paste the method you just made and rename it to `measureWidth(int)`. You need to calculate the full size of the view with all `Drawables` in place to know how much it needs to scroll regardless of the size of the visible portion of the view. Just after pulling the mode and size out of the passed `int`, you will calculate the maximum size. Retrieve the number of icons by getting the size of `mDrawables` (remember that it can be `null`). Multiply the icon count by the `mIconSize` to get the amount of space needed just for drawing the icons. Calculate the amount of space needed for the dividers (the space between the icons). If the icon count is one or less, there will be no divider space; otherwise, there will be `mIconSpacing` times one less than the icon count (for example, if there are three icons, there are two spaces; one between the first and second item and one between the second and third). Now add the divider space, the icon space, and the padding to get the maximum size needed for this view.

Down in the code you copied in, you need to adjust the `else` statement. If the spec mode is `AT_MOST`, set the result to the smaller of the maximum size and the passed spec size. In all other cases, set the result to the maximum size you calculated.

Finally, you need to determine how much scrolling should be possible. If the maximum size you calculated is greater than the result (that is, there is more to draw than will fit in the allowed space), set `mScrollRange` to the difference; otherwise, set it to 0. See Listing 12.6 for the complete method.

Listing 12.6 The Complete `measureWidth` Method

```
/**
 * Measures width according to the passed measure spec
 *
 * @param measureSpec int measure spec to use
 * @return int pixel size
 */
private int measureWidth(int measureSpec) {
    int specMode = MeasureSpec.getMode(measureSpec);
    int specSize = MeasureSpec.getSize(measureSpec);

    // Calculate maximum size
    final int icons = (mDrawables == null) ? 0 : mDrawables.size();
    final int dividerSpace;
    if (icons <= 1) {
        dividerSpace = 0;
    } else {
        dividerSpace = (icons - 1) * mIconSpacing;
    }
    final int iconSpace = mIconSize * icons;
    final int maxSize = dividerSpace + iconSpace + getPaddingLeft() +
➥getPaddingRight();

    // Calculate actual size
    int result = 0;
    if (specMode == MeasureSpec.EXACTLY) {
        result = specSize;
    } else {
        if (specMode == MeasureSpec.AT_MOST) {
            result = Math.min(maxSize, specSize);
        } else {
            result = maxSize;
        }
    }

    if (maxSize > result) {
        mScrollRange = maxSize - result;
    } else {
        mScrollRange = 0;
    }

    return result;
}
```

You can now implement the actual `onMeasure(int, int)` method with ease. Simply override the method to call `setMeasuredDimension(int, int)`, passing in the values from the two methods you created. It should look like Listing 12.7.

Listing 12.7 The Complete `onMeasure` Method

```
    @Override
    protected void onMeasure(int widthMeasureSpec, int
➥heightMeasureSpec) {
        setMeasuredDimension(measureWidth(widthMeasureSpec),
➥measureHeight(heightMeasureSpec));
    }
```

That's all there is for measuring. If you're making a view for a library, you should consider how you will handle undesirable sizes. For instance, obviously we only want to use this view where it fits the desired height (vertical padding plus the icon), but what if a user gives a different height? Should you adjust the measuring by seeing how much vertical room there actually is for the icon? Yes and no are both acceptable answers, as long as they are documented.

A `ViewGroup` would also implement `onLayout` at this point to position each of its children. The `ViewGroup` needs to simply call `layout` on each of the children, passing in the left, top, right, and bottom pixel positions. Because this custom view does not have any children, you do not need to implement that method and can move on to the drawing phase.

Drawing to the Canvas

Now that you have measured your view, you need to implement the drawing step. All of this will be done in the view's `onDraw(Canvas)` call, so start implementing that now. First, check if you have anything to draw. If `mDrawables` is `null` or `mDrawables` is an empty `List`, you can immediately return.

Next, get the dimensions you need to work with. First, get a local copy of the width by calling `getWidth()`. Then, create a copy of the bottom, left, and top padding with the `getPadding` calls. You need to determine the portion of the overall view that is visible. Although your view may be a few thousand pixels wide, it could just be showing 200 pixels, so you do not want to draw more than you need to. See Figure 12.1 for a visual explanation (and note that this example uses several numeric `Drawable`s to make it easy to see the scroll position). This shows the full view width, but the `onDraw(Canvas)` method should only draw the portion displayed by the device.

To get the left edge of the display, call `getScrollX()`, which returns the horizontal offset caused by scrolling. For now, this will always be 0, but it will change once you've added in support for scrolling. To keep the code clear, also determine the right edge of the display by adding the width to the left edge. Now you can easily check if your `Drawable`s are within these coordinates.

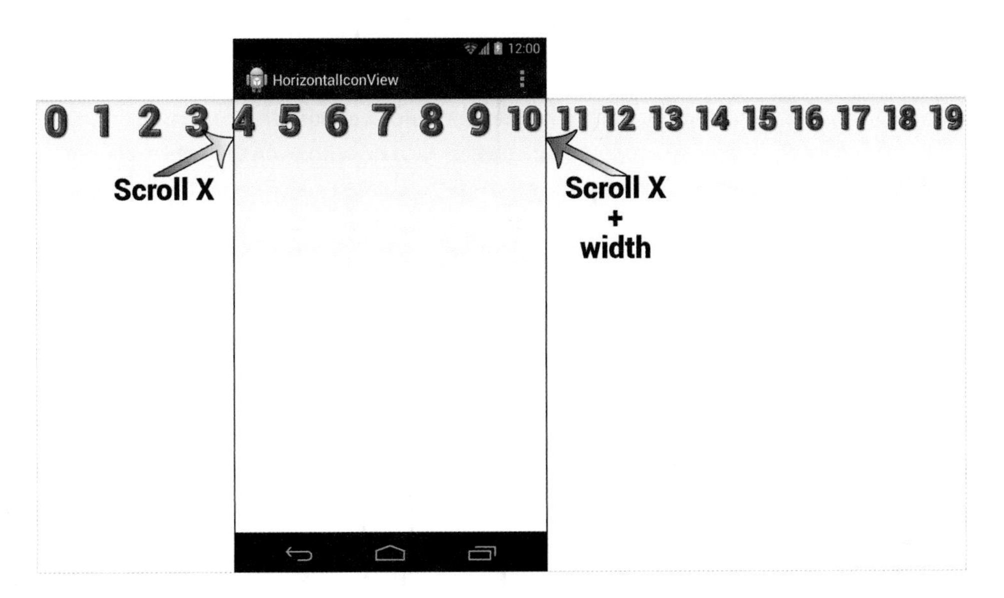

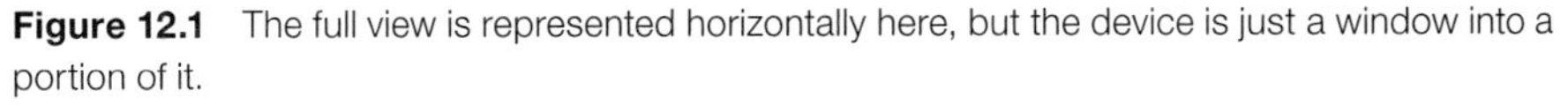

Figure 12.1 The full view is represented horizontally here, but the device is just a window into a portion of it.

Create a `left` and a `top` non-final `int`. This is a common technique for tracking where you are drawing to next, so set the `left` to `paddingLeft` and set the `top` to `paddingTop`. In this example, everything is drawn in a straight line, so `top` won't change, but you will be increasing `left`. Keep in mind the `left` value is using the coordinate system for the view, not the currently shown portion of the view. In other words, it's based on the full horizontal image from Figure 12.1 and not just the portion shown on the screen.

Update the `mSkippedIconCount` to 0. This keeps track of how many icons you skipped before starting to draw. The value of tracking this will be more apparent soon. Loop through the `mDrawables List`, checking if the icon is onscreen. If the current `left` position plus the width of the icon (in other words, the right-most pixel of the `Drawable`) is less than the `leftEdge` of the screen, then add the icon size and spacing to `left`, increment the skipped icon count, and continue—there is no need to draw it. If the current value for `left` is greater than the right edge, you have drawn everything that will go on the screen and you can break out of the loop and skip all the icons to the right of the screen.

For all icons that are actually displayed on the screen, you will get the `Drawable`, set the bounds, and draw the `Drawable` with the `Canvas`. The bounds will have the left and top set to the `left` and `top` variables, respectively. The right and bottom will be set to `left` plus icon size and `top` plus icon size, respectively.

Before continuing on with the next `Drawable`, you want to store the bounds of the `Drawable` as a `Rect` in `mIconPositions`. This can later be used to see if you tap within the bounds of a given `Drawable`. Note that you want to keep as few objects as possible, so you don't create a `Rect` for every single `Drawable`; you create one for each `Drawable` on the screen. Looking back at Figure 12.1, you can see that the 4 is the first `Drawable`, so it would be the `Rect` at position 0. The 10 would be the `Rect` at position 6. If the `mIconPositions List` already contains a `Rect` for that position, the bounds can simply be copied from the `Drawable` to that `Rect`; otherwise, a new `Rect` can be created by using the `Drawable`'s `copyBounds()` method without any arguments and added to the `List`.

Before continuing on with the next `Drawable`, don't forget to increase `left` by the icon width plus the icon spacing. At this point, your `onDraw(Canvas)` method should look like Listing 12.8.

Listing 12.8 The `onDraw` Method So Far

```
@Override
protected void onDraw(Canvas canvas) {
    if (mDrawables == null || mDrawables.isEmpty()) {
        return;
    }

    final int width = getWidth();
    final int paddingBottom = getPaddingBottom();
    final int paddingLeft = getPaddingLeft();
    final int paddingTop = getPaddingTop();

    // Determine edges of visible content
    final int leftEdge = getScrollX();
    final int rightEdge = leftEdge + width;

    int left = paddingLeft;
    int top = paddingTop;
    mSkippedIconCount = 0;

    final int iconCount = mDrawables.size();
    for (int i = 0; i < iconCount; i++) {
        if (left + mIconSize < leftEdge) {
            // Icon is too far left to be seen
            left = left + mIconSize + mIconSpacing;
            mSkippedIconCount++;
            continue;
        }
        if (left > rightEdge) {
            // All remaining icons are right of the view
            break;
        }
```

```
            // Get a reference to the icon to be drawn
            final Drawable icon = mDrawables.get(i);
            icon.setBounds(left, top, left + mIconSize, top + mIconSize);
            icon.draw(canvas);

            // Icon was drawn, so track position
            final int drawnPosition = i - mSkippedIconCount;
            if (drawnPosition + 1 > mIconPositions.size()) {
                final Rect rect = icon.copyBounds();
                mIconPositions.add(rect);
            } else {
                final Rect rect = mIconPositions.get(drawnPosition);
                icon.copyBounds(rect);
            }

            // Update left position
            left = left + mIconSize + mIconSpacing;
        }

}
```

Now that you've managed to create all this drawing code, it's a good idea to test it. For now, just create a `List` of `Drawables` in your `Activity`, instantiate a new instance of your custom view, set the `List` of `Drawables`, and then call `setContentView(View)` with your `HorizontalIconView`. See Listing 12.9 for a simple example of what your `Activity`'s `onCreate(Bundle)` method can look like at this point, and see Figure 12.2 for what the output might look like.

Listing 12.9 A Simple `onCreate` Method in an `Activity`

```
@Override
protected void onCreate(Bundle savedInstanceState) {
    super.onCreate(savedInstanceState);

    // Get a List of Drawables
    final Resources res = getResources();
    final List<Drawable> list = new ArrayList<Drawable>();
    list.add(res.getDrawable(R.drawable.icon_00));
    list.add(res.getDrawable(R.drawable.icon_01));
    list.add(res.getDrawable(R.drawable.icon_02));
    list.add(res.getDrawable(R.drawable.icon_03));
    list.add(res.getDrawable(R.drawable.icon_04));
    list.add(res.getDrawable(R.drawable.icon_05));
    list.add(res.getDrawable(R.drawable.icon_06));
    list.add(res.getDrawable(R.drawable.icon_07));
    list.add(res.getDrawable(R.drawable.icon_08));
    list.add(res.getDrawable(R.drawable.icon_09));
    list.add(res.getDrawable(R.drawable.icon_10));
```

```
        list.add(res.getDrawable(R.drawable.icon_11));
        list.add(res.getDrawable(R.drawable.icon_12));
        list.add(res.getDrawable(R.drawable.icon_13));
        list.add(res.getDrawable(R.drawable.icon_14));
        list.add(res.getDrawable(R.drawable.icon_15));
        list.add(res.getDrawable(R.drawable.icon_16));
        list.add(res.getDrawable(R.drawable.icon_17));
        list.add(res.getDrawable(R.drawable.icon_18));
        list.add(res.getDrawable(R.drawable.icon_19));

        final HorizontalIconView view = new HorizontalIconView(this);
        view.setDrawables(list);

        setContentView(view);
    }
```

Figure 12.2 This is the view so far.

Preparing for Touch Input

Touch input can be one of the most challenging aspects of creating a view due to the many places you can make mistakes that cause bizarre behavior, missed interactions, or sluggishness. Also, a lot of interactions and considerations go into making touch behavior feel right. This custom view will give you the opportunity to see how to handle touches, drags, flings, over-scrolling, and edge effects.

First, start with some of the easier methods to get prepared for the heavy work. Start with overriding and implementing `computeScroll()`, which updates scrolling during flings. Check if `mScroller`'s `computeScrollOffset` returns `true`. If it does, the `OverScroller` hasn't finished animating and you need to continue scrolling the view (if not, you don't need to do anything else in this method). Get the X position by calling `getScrollX()`. It represents the current X position but not what it should be after the scroll is complete, so it's commonly called `oldX`. Get what the X position should be by calling `mScroller`'s `getCurrX()` (just called `x`). If these are not the same, you should call `overScrollBy(int, int, int, int, int, int, int, int, boolean)`. Yes, that method takes a *lot* of `int`s. They are in pairs, starting with the change in X (`x` minus `oldX`) and the change in Y (0) position, then the current scroll positions for X (`oldX`) and Y (0), followed by the X scroll range (`mScrollRange`) and Y scroll range (0), and the last `int`s are the maximum overscroll distance for X (`mOverflingDistance`) and Y (0). The last value is a `boolean` that indicates if this is a touch event (pass `false` because this is triggered when the view is still scrolling after a fling).

Now you call `onScrollChanged(x, 0, oldX, 0)` to notify the view that you scrolled it. If `x` is less than zero and `oldX` is not, then the fling has gone beyond the left end, so `mEdgeEffectLeft` should react. Call its `onAbsorb(int)` method, passing in the current velocity (get it from the `mScroller`'s `getCurrVelocity()` method). Similarly, if `x` is greater than `mScrollRange` and `oldX` is not, then the fling went beyond the right edge, so `mEdgeEffectRight` should react. See Listing 12.10 for the full method.

Listing 12.10 The Complete `computeScroll` Method

```
@Override
public void computeScroll() {
    if (mScroller.computeScrollOffset()) {
        int oldX = getScrollX();
        int x = mScroller.getCurrX();

        if (oldX != x) {
            overScrollBy(x - oldX, 0, oldX, 0, mScrollRange, 0,
➥mOverflingDistance, 0, false);
            onScrollChanged(x, 0, oldX, 0);

            if (x < 0 && oldX >= 0) {
                mEdgeEffectLeft.onAbsorb((int)
➥mScroller.getCurrVelocity());
```

```
            } else if (x > mScrollRange && oldX <= mScrollRange) {
                mEdgeEffectRight.onAbsorb((int)
➥mScroller.getCurrVelocity());
            }
        }
    }
}
```

Any time you create a view that calls the `overScrollBy` method, you should also override `onOverScrolled(int, int, boolean, boolean)`, so do that next. This one is actually very easy. If `mScroller`'s `isFinished()` method returns `true`, just call through to the super method. If not, call `setScrollX(scrollX)` to update the scroll position. If `clamped` is `true`, you need to call the `mScroller`'s `springBack(int, int, int, int, int, int)` method. This method brings the `OverScroller` back to a valid position and, more specifically, allows the glow at the edge of the view when you fling it. Be careful with this method; the `int`s are not quite in X/Y pairs. The first two are the start for X (`scrollX`) and Y (0), the next two are the minimum (0) and maximum (`mScrollRange`) values for X (*not* the minimum for X and Y), and the last two are the minimum and maximum values for Y. You are probably starting to notice how easy it can be to mix up one of these `int`s and end up with bugs and strange behavior. See Listing 12.11 for the full method.

Listing 12.11 The Complete `onOverScrolled` Method

```
@Override
protected void onOverScrolled(int scrollX, int scrollY, boolean
➥clampedX, boolean clampedY) {
    if (mScroller.isFinished()) {
        super.scrollTo(scrollX, scrollY);
    } else {
        setScrollX(scrollX);
        if (clampedX) {
            mScroller.springBack(scrollX, 0, 0, mScrollRange, 0, 0);
        }
    }
}
```

Another method to implement that's relatively short is `fling(int)`. You will use this internally to trigger a fling. If `mScrollRange` is 0, just return because there is nowhere to fling. Otherwise, calculate an `int` called `halfWidth` by subtracting the horizontal padding from the width of the view and dividing the result by 2. This value will be used for the overfling range. Call `mScroller`'s `fling(int, int, int, int, int, int, int, int)` method. This is another one that's easy to make a mistake on. The first two `int`s are for the starting position for X (`getScrollX()`) and Y (0). The second pair is the velocity for X (`velocity`) and Y (0). After that, you have the min X position (0) and max X position (`mScrollRange`), followed by the min Y position (0) and max Y position (0). The last pair is the overfling range for X (`halfWidth`) and Y (0). See Listing 12.12 for the full method.

Listing 12.12 The Complete `fling` Method

```
/**
 * Flings the view horizontally with the specified velocity
 *
 * @param velocity int pixels per second along X axis
 */
private void fling(int velocity) {
    if (mScrollRange == 0) {
        return;
    }

    final int halfWidth = (getWidth() - getPaddingLeft() -
➥getPaddingRight()) / 2;
    mScroller.fling(getScrollX(), 0, velocity, 0, 0, mScrollRange, 0,
➥0, halfWidth, 0);
    invalidate();
}
```

You need to update the `onDraw(Canvas)` method to draw the overscroll glow. At the end of the method, check if `mEdgeEffectLeft` is not `null` (it shouldn't be, but at some point you might want your view to support disabling the edge glow). If `mEdgeEffectLeft.isFinished()` returns `false`, you need to rotate the canvas 270 degrees and then translate (move) it back by the height of the view so that you can draw the effect. When you call the `mEdgeEffectLeft`'s `draw(Canvas)` method, it returns `true` if the effect hasn't yet faded out (meaning you need to invalidate the view). You then restore the canvas to its state prior to your rotation and translation. The work is similar for `mEdgeEffectRight`. See Listing 12.13 for the detailed code. This code is taken from the `HorizontalScrollView` with minor modification.

Listing 12.13 The Code for Drawing the Edge Effects in `onDraw(Canvas)`

```
if (mEdgeEffectLeft != null) {
    if (!mEdgeEffectLeft.isFinished()) {
        final int restoreCount = canvas.save();
        final int height = getHeight() - paddingTop - paddingBottom;

        canvas.rotate(270);
        canvas.translate(-height + paddingTop, Math.min(0, leftEdge));
        mEdgeEffectLeft.setSize(height, getWidth());
        if (mEdgeEffectLeft.draw(canvas)) {
            postInvalidateOnAnimation();
        }
```

```
            canvas.restoreToCount(restoreCount);
        }
        if (!mEdgeEffectRight.isFinished()) {
            final int restoreCount = canvas.save();
            final int height = getHeight() - paddingTop - paddingBottom;

            canvas.rotate(90);
            canvas.translate(-paddingTop, -(Math.max(mScrollRange,
➥leftEdge) + width));
            mEdgeEffectRight.setSize(height, width);
            if (mEdgeEffectRight.draw(canvas)) {
                postInvalidateOnAnimation();
            }
            canvas.restoreToCount(restoreCount);
        }
    }
```

One final helper method to create before you can start diving into the gritty touch code is `onSecondaryPointerUp(MotionEvent)`. This is called when the user has two (or more) fingers down on the view and lifts one of them up. The `MotionEvent` passed into this method was triggered by the finger that lifted, so you need to check to see if its pointer ID matches the one you are tracking (well, the one you will be tracking soon when you do the heavy touch code). If it does, you need to get another pointer to track. Although there can be many different pointers, it is good enough (for this view at least) to simply switch to the second pointer if the first was lifted or the first pointer if the second was lifted. You also need to clear the velocity because you're tracking a new pointer. See Listing 12.14 for the full method; this is another one that comes mostly from `HorizontalScrollView`.

Listing 12.14 The Complete `onSecondaryPointerUp` Method

```
private void onSecondaryPointerUp(MotionEvent ev) {
    final int pointerIndex = MotionEventCompat.getActionIndex(ev);
    final int pointerId = MotionEventCompat.getPointerId(ev,
➥pointerIndex);
    if (pointerId == mActivePointerId) {
        final int newPointerIndex = pointerIndex == 0 ? 1 : 0;
        mPreviousX = ev.getX(newPointerIndex);
        mActivePointerId = ev.getPointerId(newPointerIndex);
        if (mVelocityTracker != null) {
            mVelocityTracker.clear();
        }
    }
}
```

Handling Touch Input

You've done all the preparatory work for handling touch events, so now it's time to dive in and tackle the hard part. Override the `onTouchEvent(MotionEvent)` method. If `mVelocityTracker` is `null`, get a new reference by calling `VelocityTracker.obtain()`. Add the movement represented in this `MotionEvent` to the tracker by calling `addMovement(MotionEvent)` on it. Get the action `int`, which tells you what this `MotionEvent` represents (was it a touch or a movement or something else), by calling `MotionEventCompat.getActionMasked(MotionEvent)`. The `MotionEventCompat` class comes in the support library and has a few static methods to help work with `MotionEvents`. Now, switch on the action.

The first case to tackle is `MotionEvent.ACTION_DOWN`. This is only ever triggered by the first pointer (the pointer with index 0) touching the view; it will never be triggered by a second pointer touching the view when a pointer is already touching it. That means if the `mScroller` has not finished animating (check `isFinished()`), you need to stop it (`mScroller.abortAnimation()`). In other words, if the view is flinging and the user touches the view, it should stop flinging as if grabbed. Store the X coordinate of the motion event in `mPreviousX` by calling `MotionEventCompat.getX(MotionEvent, 0)`. Store the pointer ID in `mActivePointerId`. This is the identifier for the pointer you will be watching for movements. If another pointer touches the view and starts sliding around, you don't care about it.

The next case is the hardest one, and that's `MotionEvent.ACTION_MOVE`. First, you find the index of the pointer you care about (remember the difference between index and ID, as explained earlier in the chapter) and get its X coordinate. If `mIsBeingDragged` is not `true`, it means the user has touched the view but has not yet moved the finger enough to be considered a drag, so you need to check if the difference between this X coordinate and `mPreviousX` that you updated in the `ACTION_DOWN` case is greater than the touch slop. If it is, the user is now dragging the view, so set `mIsBeingDragged` to `true` and remove the touch slop from the delta between the previous X position and the current one. This subtle change to the delta prevents the view from feeling like it suddenly skips the amount the pointer had moved. Think of sliding your finger across something slightly slick in real life, such as a magazine cover. Your finger might slide a little before there is enough friction to move that object, then the object continues to move from the point where there was enough friction as opposed to the object suddenly jumping as if your first point of contact had enough friction.

If the user is dragging the view, you need to call `overScrollBy` (and get all those `int`s just right). The return result indicates if it scrolls beyond the bounds, so clear the velocity tracker if it does. If `mEdgeEffectLeft` is not `null`, you should check if the view is being scrolled beyond its bounds. For example, if the view is being scrolled beyond the left edge (0), you need to call the `onPull(float)` method of `mEdgeEffectLeft`. If that's the case, you should also call `abortAnimation()` on `mEdgeEffectRight` if it's not already finished because you're done pulling on that edge. Do the same for if the view is being scrolled beyond the right edge (pulled past mScrollRange). The abortAnimation() call will tell you if the view is still animating, so you can check it to see if you need to invalidate the view, but you're potentially dealing with two edge effects (one that might be starting to glow now and one that might have already been glowing), so it's easier to just check if either edge is not finished after doing everything else.

The next case to handle is MotionEvent.ACTION_UP, and it signifies that there are no more pointers touching the view. That means you need to check whether this results in a fling of the view or a touch that didn't drag. If mIsBeingDragged is true, you need to calculate the velocity stored in mVelocityTracker by calling computeCurrentVelocity(1000, mMaximumVelocity), where the first value is the units (1000 means velocity in pixels per second) and the second is the maximum velocity you care about. This actually calls through to a native method to calculate the velocity because it can be a complex calculation. After triggering that method, you can get the result by calling getXVelocity(int). If the result is greater than mMinimumVelocity, call fling with the inverse of your velocity. The reason you pass the inverse is because you're actually moving the displayed portion of the view in the opposite direction of the fling. For example, if your finger slides to the right very fast, you have a fling with a positive velocity; however, the view is supposed to look like it is scrolling left. If the velocity was not enough to be a fling, call the mScroller's springBack method to make sure you stay within the bounds of the view. You should now recycle the VelocityTracker and remove your reference to it. By recycling it, you return it to the pool that can be handed out to another view, so you must not interact with it after that. If mEdgeEffectLeft is not null, you should call onRelease() on both mEdgeEffectLeft and mEdgeEffectRight.

Still in ACTION_UP, if mIsBeingDragged is false, you should check if it was just a touch of a Drawable. Get the X and Y coordinates for the pointer and then loop through mIcon Positions, checking each Rect's contains(int, int) method to see if the pointer is within that view. If it is, just use a Toast to indicate which position you touched and indicate how many Rects are in the mIconPositions List (so you can see that it does not grow excessively). If you were really going to do something significant with the touch, you would want to check whether it was a regular touch or a long press and you would want to update the Drawable states to let them know when they were being touched. You can determine the amount of time needed before a touch is a long press by comparing the time it has been touched with ViewConfiguration.getLongPressTimeout(), which will return the number of milliseconds (usually 500).

The case after that is MotionEvent.ACTION_CANCEL, and it's relatively easy. Because this indicates that the gesture has been aborted (for example, if a parent view started to intercept the touch events). The general goal of this method is to do what you do when it's an ACTION_UP, but do not trigger any events (no flinging, no selecting, and so on). If the view wasn't being dragged, do nothing. If it was, spring back to valid coordinates, recycle the VelocityTracker and remove your reference to it, and call onRelease() on both of your EdgeEffectCompats.

Finally, the last case to worry about: `MotionEvent.ACTION_POINTER_UP`. This indicates that a pointer other than the primary one went up. Now you can call that handy `onSecondaryPointerUp(MotionEvent)` method you created earlier. That's it! See Listing 12.15 for the complete class, including the full `onTouchEvent(MotionEvent)` method.

> **note**
>
> Listing 12.15 is quite lengthy because it contains the entire custom `HorizontalIconView`. You should spend time reviewing it to make sure that it makes sense and consider re-reading any sections of this chapter that are not quite clear to you.
>
> Remember that the code examples for this book are all available at http://auidbook.com, so you can access all of the code from Chapter 12 to run it yourself and experiment. Sometimes changing existing code to see how it affects the resulting app is the best way to understand it.

Listing 12.15 The Complete `HorizontalIconView` Class

```
public class HorizontalIconView extends View {
    private static final String TAG = "HorizontalIconView";

    private static final int INVALID_POINTER =
➥MotionEvent.INVALID_POINTER_ID;

    /**
     * int to track the ID of the pointer that is being tracked
     */
    private int mActivePointerId = INVALID_POINTER;

    /**
     * The List of Drawables that will be shown
     */
    private List<Drawable> mDrawables;

    /**
     * EdgeEffect or "glow" when scrolled too far left
     */
    private EdgeEffectCompat mEdgeEffectLeft;

    /**
     * EdgeEffect or "glow" when scrolled too far right
     */
    private EdgeEffectCompat mEdgeEffectRight;

    /**
     * List of Rects for each visible icon to calculate touches
     */
    private final List<Rect> mIconPositions = new ArrayList<Rect>();
```

```
/**
 * Width and height of icons in pixels
 */
private int mIconSize;

/**
 * Space between each icon in pixels
 */
private int mIconSpacing;

/**
 * Whether a pointer/finger is currently on screen that is being
 * tracked
 */
private boolean mIsBeingDragged;

/**
 * Maximum fling velocity in pixels per second
 */
private int mMaximumVelocity;

/**
 * Minimum fling velocity in pixels per second
 */
private int mMinimumVelocity;

/**
 * How far to fling beyond the bounds of the view
 */
private int mOverflingDistance;

/**
 * How far to scroll beyond the bounds of the view
 */
private int mOverscrollDistance;

/**
 * The X coordinate of the last down touch, used to determine when
 * a drag starts
 */
private float mPreviousX = 0;

/**
 * Number of pixels this view can scroll (basically width - visible
➥width)
 */
private int mScrollRange;

/**
 * Number of pixels of movement required before a touch is "moving"
 */
```

```
    private int mTouchSlop;

    /**
     * VelocityTracker to simplify tracking MotionEvents
     */
    private VelocityTracker mVelocityTracker;

    /**
     * Scroller to do the hard work of scrolling smoothly
     */
    private OverScroller mScroller;

    /**
     * The number of icons that are left of the view and therefore not
➥drawn
     */
    private int mSkippedIconCount = 0;

    public HorizontalIconView(Context context) {
        super(context);
        init(context);
    }

    public HorizontalIconView(Context context, AttributeSet attrs) {
        super(context, attrs);
        init(context);
    }

    public HorizontalIconView(Context context, AttributeSet attrs, int
➥defStyle) {
        super(context, attrs, defStyle);
        init(context);
    }

    @Override
    public void computeScroll() {
        if (mScroller.computeScrollOffset()) {
            int oldX = getScrollX();
            int x = mScroller.getCurrX();

            if (oldX != x) {
                overScrollBy(x - oldX, 0, oldX, 0, mScrollRange, 0,
➥mOverflingDistance, 0, false);
                onScrollChanged(x, 0, oldX, 0);

                if (x < 0 && oldX >= 0) {
                    mEdgeEffectLeft.onAbsorb((int)
➥mScroller.getCurrVelocity());
                } else if (x > mScrollRange && oldX <= mScrollRange) {
                    mEdgeEffectRight.onAbsorb((int)
➥mScroller.getCurrVelocity());
```

```
                }
            }
        }
    }

    @Override
    public boolean onTouchEvent(MotionEvent ev) {
        if (mVelocityTracker == null) {
            mVelocityTracker = VelocityTracker.obtain();
        }
        mVelocityTracker.addMovement(ev);

        final int action = MotionEventCompat.getActionMasked(ev);
        switch (action) {
            case MotionEvent.ACTION_DOWN: {
                if (!mScroller.isFinished()) {
                    mScroller.abortAnimation();
                }

                // Remember where the motion event started
                mPreviousX = (int) MotionEventCompat.getX(ev, 0);
                mActivePointerId = MotionEventCompat.getPointerId(ev,
➥0);
                break;
            }

            case MotionEvent.ACTION_MOVE: {
                final int activePointerIndex =
➥MotionEventCompat.findPointerIndex(ev, mActivePointerId);
                if (activePointerIndex == INVALID_POINTER) {
                    Log.e(TAG, "Invalid pointerId=" + mActivePointerId
➥+ " in onTouchEvent");
                    break;
                }

                final int x = (int) MotionEventCompat.getX(ev, 0);
                int deltaX = (int) (mPreviousX - x);
                if (!mIsBeingDragged && Math.abs(deltaX) > mTouchSlop) {
                    mIsBeingDragged = true;
                    if (deltaX > 0) {
                        deltaX -= mTouchSlop;
                    } else {
                        deltaX += mTouchSlop;
                    }
                }
                if (mIsBeingDragged) {
                    // Scroll to follow the motion event
                    mPreviousX = x;

                    final int oldX = getScrollX();
                    final int range = mScrollRange;
```

```
                    if (overScrollBy(deltaX, 0, oldX, 0, range, 0,
➥mOverscrollDistance, 0, true)) {
                        // Break our velocity if we hit a scroll
➥barrier.
                        mVelocityTracker.clear();
                    }

                    if (mEdgeEffectLeft != null) {
                        final int pulledToX = oldX + deltaX;
                        if (pulledToX < 0) {
                            mEdgeEffectLeft.onPull((float) deltaX /
➥getWidth());
                            if (!mEdgeEffectRight.isFinished()) {
                                mEdgeEffectRight.onRelease();
                            }
                        } else if (pulledToX > range) {
                            mEdgeEffectRight.onPull((float) deltaX /
➥getWidth());
                            if (!mEdgeEffectLeft.isFinished()) {
                                mEdgeEffectLeft.onRelease();
                            }
                        }
                        if (!mEdgeEffectLeft.isFinished() ||
➥!mEdgeEffectRight.isFinished()) {
                            postInvalidateOnAnimation();
                        }

                    }

                }
                break;
            }
            case MotionEvent.ACTION_UP: {
                if (mIsBeingDragged) {
                    mVelocityTracker.computeCurrentVelocity(1000,
➥mMaximumVelocity);
                    int initialVelocity = (int)
➥mVelocityTracker.getXVelocity(mActivePointerId);

                    if ((Math.abs(initialVelocity) > mMinimumVelocity)) {
                        fling(-initialVelocity);
                    } else {
                        if (mScroller.springBack(getScrollX(), 0, 0,
➥mScrollRange, 0, 0)) {
                            postInvalidateOnAnimation();
                        }
                    }

                    mActivePointerId = INVALID_POINTER;
                    mIsBeingDragged = false;
                    mVelocityTracker.recycle();
```

```
                    mVelocityTracker = null;

                    if (mEdgeEffectLeft != null) {
                        mEdgeEffectLeft.onRelease();
                        mEdgeEffectRight.onRelease();
                    }
                } else {
                    // Was not being dragged, was this a press on an
➥icon?
                    final int activePointerIndex =
➥ev.findPointerIndex(mActivePointerId);
                    if (activePointerIndex == INVALID_POINTER) {
                        return false;
                    }
                    final int x = (int) ev.getX(activePointerIndex) +
➥getScrollX();
                    final int y = (int) ev.getY(activePointerIndex);
                    int i = 0;
                    for (Rect rect : mIconPositions) {
                        if (rect.contains(x, y)) {
                            final int position = i + mSkippedIconCount;
                            Toast.makeText(getContext(), "Pressed icon
➥" + position + "; rect count: " + mIconPositions.size(),
➥Toast.LENGTH_SHORT).show();
                            break;
                        }
                        i++;
                    }
                }
                break;
            }
            case MotionEvent.ACTION_CANCEL: {
                if (mIsBeingDragged) {
                    if (mScroller.springBack(getScrollX(), 0, 0,
➥mScrollRange, 0, 0)) {
                        postInvalidateOnAnimation();
                    }
                    mActivePointerId = INVALID_POINTER;
                    mIsBeingDragged = false;
                    if (mVelocityTracker != null) {
                        mVelocityTracker.recycle();
                        mVelocityTracker = null;
                    }

                    if (mEdgeEffectLeft != null) {
                        mEdgeEffectLeft.onRelease();
                        mEdgeEffectRight.onRelease();
                    }
                }
                break;
            }
            case MotionEvent.ACTION_POINTER_UP: {
```

```
                onSecondaryPointerUp(ev);
                break;
            }
        }
        return true;
    }

    /**
     * Sets the List of Drawables to display
     *
     * @param drawables List of Drawables; can be null
     */
    public void setDrawables(List<Drawable> drawables) {
        if (mDrawables == null) {
            if (drawables == null) {
                return;
            }
            requestLayout();
        } else if (drawables == null) {
            requestLayout();
            mDrawables = null;
            return;
        } else if (mDrawables.size() == drawables.size()) {
            invalidate();
        } else {
            requestLayout();
        }
        mDrawables = new ArrayList<Drawable>(drawables);
        mIconPositions.clear();
    }

    @Override
    protected void onDraw(Canvas canvas) {
        if (mDrawables == null || mDrawables.isEmpty()) {
            return;
        }

        final int width = getWidth();
        final int paddingBottom = getPaddingBottom();
        final int paddingLeft = getPaddingLeft();
        final int paddingTop = getPaddingTop();

        // Determine edges of visible content
        final int leftEdge = getScrollX();
        final int rightEdge = leftEdge + width;

        int left = paddingLeft;
        int top = paddingTop;
        mSkippedIconCount = 0;

        final int iconCount = mDrawables.size();
        for (int i = 0; i < iconCount; i++) {
            if (left + mIconSize < leftEdge) {
```

```
                // Icon is too far left to be seen
                left = left + mIconSize + mIconSpacing;
                mSkippedIconCount++;
                continue;
            }

            if (left > rightEdge) {
                // All remaining icons are right of the view
                break;
            }

            // Get a reference to the icon to be drawn
            final Drawable icon = mDrawables.get(i);
            icon.setBounds(left, top, left + mIconSize, top +
➥mIconSize);
            icon.draw(canvas);

            // Icon was drawn, so track position
            final int drawnPosition = i - mSkippedIconCount;
            if (drawnPosition + 1 > mIconPositions.size()) {
                final Rect rect = icon.copyBounds();
                mIconPositions.add(rect);
            } else {
                final Rect rect = mIconPositions.get(drawnPosition);
                icon.copyBounds(rect);
            }

            // Update left position
            left = left + mIconSize + mIconSpacing;
        }

        if (mEdgeEffectLeft != null) {
            if (!mEdgeEffectLeft.isFinished()) {
                final int restoreCount = canvas.save();
                final int height = getHeight() - paddingTop
➥- paddingBottom;

                canvas.rotate(270);
                canvas.translate(-height + paddingTop, Math.min(0,
➥leftEdge));
                mEdgeEffectLeft.setSize(height, getWidth());
                if (mEdgeEffectLeft.draw(canvas)) {
                    postInvalidateOnAnimation();
                }
                canvas.restoreToCount(restoreCount);
            }
            if (!mEdgeEffectRight.isFinished()) {
                final int restoreCount = canvas.save();
                final int height = getHeight() - paddingTop
➥- paddingBottom;
```

```
                canvas.rotate(90);
                canvas.translate(-paddingTop, -(Math.max(mScrollRange,
➥leftEdge) + width));
                mEdgeEffectRight.setSize(height, width);
                if (mEdgeEffectRight.draw(canvas)) {
                    postInvalidateOnAnimation();
                }
                canvas.restoreToCount(restoreCount);
            }
        }
    }

    @Override
    protected void onMeasure(int widthMeasureSpec, int
➥heightMeasureSpec) {
        setMeasuredDimension(measureWidth(widthMeasureSpec),
➥measureHeight(heightMeasureSpec));
    }

    @Override
    protected void onOverScrolled(int scrollX, int scrollY, boolean
➥clampedX, boolean clampedY) {
        if (mScroller.isFinished()) {
            super.scrollTo(scrollX, scrollY);
        } else {
            setScrollX(scrollX);
            if (clampedX) {
                mScroller.springBack(scrollX, 0, 0, mScrollRange,
➥0, 0);
            }
        }
    }

    /**
     * Flings the view horizontally with the specified velocity
     *
     * @param velocity int pixels per second along X axis
     */
    private void fling(int velocity) {
        if (mScrollRange == 0) {
            return;
        }

        final int halfWidth = (getWidth() - getPaddingLeft() -
➥getPaddingRight()) / 2;
        mScroller.fling(getScrollX(), 0, velocity, 0, 0, mScrollRange,
➥0, 0, halfWidth, 0);
        invalidate();
    }
```

```
    /**
     * Perform one-time initialization
     *
     * @param context Context to load Resources and ViewConfiguration
➥data
     */
    private void init(Context context) {
        final Resources res = context.getResources();
        mIconSize = res.getDimensionPixelSize(R.dimen.icon_size);
        mIconSpacing = res.getDimensionPixelSize(R.dimen.icon_spacing);

        // Cache ViewConfiguration values
        final ViewConfiguration config = ViewConfiguration.get(
➥ context);
        mTouchSlop = config.getScaledTouchSlop();
        mMinimumVelocity = config.getScaledMinimumFlingVelocity();
        mMaximumVelocity = config.getScaledMaximumFlingVelocity();
        mOverflingDistance = config.getScaledOverflingDistance();
        mOverscrollDistance = config.getScaledOverscrollDistance();

        // Verify this View will be drawn
        setWillNotDraw(false);

        // Other setup
        mEdgeEffectLeft = new EdgeEffectCompat(context);
        mEdgeEffectRight = new EdgeEffectCompat(context);
        mScroller = new OverScroller(context);
        setFocusable(true);
    }

    /**
     * Measures height according to the passed measure spec
     *
     * @param measureSpec
     *            int measure spec to use
     * @return int pixel size
     */
    private int measureHeight(int measureSpec) {
        int specMode = MeasureSpec.getMode(measureSpec);
        int specSize = MeasureSpec.getSize(measureSpec);

        int result = 0;
        if (specMode == MeasureSpec.EXACTLY) {
            result = specSize;
        } else {
            result = mIconSize + getPaddingTop() + getPaddingBottom();
            if (specMode == MeasureSpec.AT_MOST) {
                result = Math.min(result, specSize);
            }
        }
```

```
        return result;
    }

    /**
     * Measures width according to the passed measure spec
     *
     * @param measureSpec
     *            int measure spec to use
     * @return int pixel size
     */
    private int measureWidth(int measureSpec) {
        int specMode = MeasureSpec.getMode(measureSpec);
        int specSize = MeasureSpec.getSize(measureSpec);

        // Calculate maximum size
        final int icons = (mDrawables == null) ? 0 : mDrawables.size();
        final int iconSpace = mIconSize * icons;
        final int dividerSpace;
        if (icons <= 1) {
            dividerSpace = 0;
        } else {
            dividerSpace = (icons - 1) * mIconSpacing;
        }
        final int maxSize = dividerSpace + iconSpace + getPaddingLeft()
➥+ getPaddingRight();

        // Calculate actual size
        int result = 0;
        if (specMode == MeasureSpec.EXACTLY) {
            result = specSize;
        } else {
            if (specMode == MeasureSpec.AT_MOST) {
                result = Math.min(maxSize, specSize);
            } else {
                result = maxSize;
            }
        }

        if (maxSize > result) {
            mScrollRange = maxSize - result;
        } else {
            mScrollRange = 0;
        }

        return result;
    }

    private void onSecondaryPointerUp(MotionEvent ev) {
        final int pointerIndex = MotionEventCompat.getActionIndex(ev);
        final int pointerId = MotionEventCompat.getPointerId(ev,
➥pointerIndex);
```

```
            if (pointerId == mActivePointerId) {
                final int newPointerIndex = pointerIndex == 0 ? 1 : 0;
                mPreviousX = ev.getX(newPointerIndex);
                mActivePointerId = ev.getPointerId(newPointerIndex);
                if (mVelocityTracker != null) {
                    mVelocityTracker.clear();
                }
            }
        }
    }
```

Test out your new view. Make sure it can scroll (see Figure 12.3) through the full range of `Drawables`, left and right. Also, make sure the overscroll visuals on the left work (see Figure 12.4) and the overscroll visuals on the right work (see Figure 12.5).

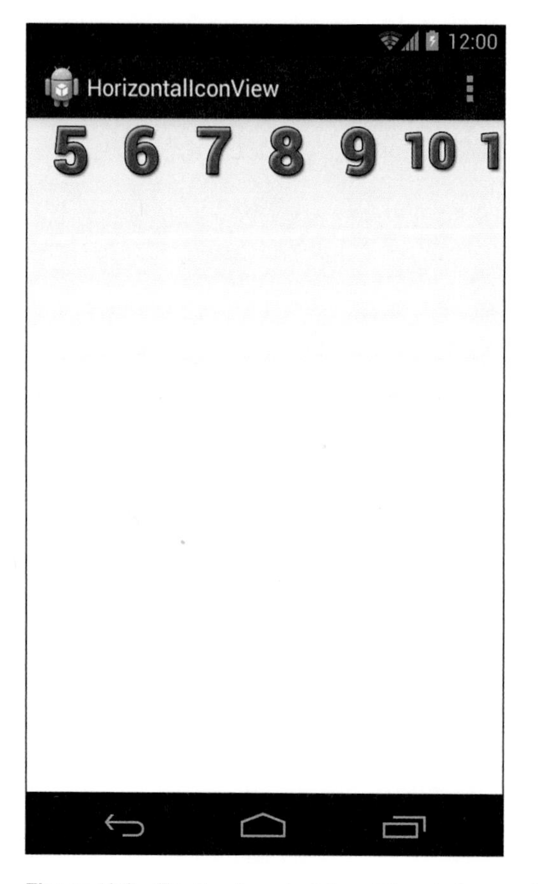

Figure 12.3 The `HorizontalIconView` being scrolled

Figure 12.4 The `HorizontalIconView`'s left edge effect being tested

You might be wondering why the overscroll glow appears over the entire `Activity` area. That's because the custom view was passed in with `setContentView(View)`. To verify it really works how it should, try putting it in a layout. You might also consider adding padding or other attributes that may affect the way it draws. See Listing 12.16 for a sample layout.

Figure 12.5 The `HorizontalIconView`'s right edge effect being tested

Listing 12.16 A Simple Layout for Testing the Custom View

```
<RelativeLayout
    xmlns:android="http://schemas.android.com/apk/res/android"
    xmlns:tools="http://schemas.android.com/tools"
    android:layout_width="match_parent"
    android:layout_height="match_parent"
    tools:context=".MainActivity" >

    <com.iangclifton.auid.horizontaliconview.HorizontalIconView
        android:id="@+id/horizontal_icon_view"
        android:layout_width="match_parent"
        android:layout_height="wrap_content"
        android:layout_centerVertical="true"
        android:background="#FFBBFFBB"
        android:padding="10dp" />

</RelativeLayout>
```

Updating the `Activity` to use that layout and running it on a Nexus 4 gives the result in Figure 12.6. Notice that the glow on the left side is contained within the view itself. The view is correctly centered and has the correct background.

Figure 12.6 The custom view being tested within a layout

Now is a great time to go back through the code and make sure you understand each method. Don't be afraid to experiment. See what happens if you comment out certain lines or change the values. That's one of the best ways to understand what is really happening with the code and why you pass certain values to methods.

Other Considerations

This view is far from perfect, but it does demonstrate the challenging parts of creating a custom view. It also has a potential bug in that the number of `Rect`s that are kept for hit detection can actually be one greater than the number of views on the screen. It's not a major problem, but it's something that would be worth fixing before making this part of some library. Of course, if you were to make this part of a library, you would want to finish the hit handling for the icons and use a custom listener interface to report touches instead of directly handling them.

Another problem with this view is that it only works on Android 4.2 and above (API level 16) because of the use of `postInvalidateOnAnimation()`, which causes `invalidate` to happen on the next frame. To improve compatibility with older versions of Android, you can use reflection to see if this method exists. If not, the standard `invalidate()` method will work. The `OverScroller`'s `getCurrVelocity()` method is used, which was added in Android 4.0 (API level 14). You can instead use the velocity from your `mVelocityTracker`'s last report, calculate the velocity yourself, use reflection, use a fixed value, or even just comment out those lines (in which case a fling just won't cause the glow). If you wanted to add support for significantly older versions of Android such as Android 2.2, you would have to do a bit more work. Instead of `OverScroller`, the pre-2.3 versions of Android would have to use `Scroller` (or you could implement your own `OverScroller` class). That means you couldn't trigger any of the edge effects and you would need to avoid calling any overscroll-related methods in the view for those versions because the concept of overscrolling was not introduced until Android 2.3.

Summary

This is definitely the most challenging and the deepest chapter of the book. If you feel like you don't quite understand all of it, that's okay. The important part is understanding the concepts so you can start to work on custom views yourself. The first few views you make on your own are likely to have bugs or cause some frustration. There are a lot of places to mix up an `int` or forget to call a method, so don't be surprised if you have to spend effort troubleshooting. That's a great way to learn. Hopefully by reading this book, you've learned to avoid some of the common pitfalls, such as not calling `setWillNotDraw(false)` and wondering for hours why your drawing code isn't working.

When you're ready to learn more about custom views, the Android developer site has some good documentation on additional ways to work with touch input at http://developer.android.com/training/gestures/index.html. Of course, there's rarely a better place to learn than the code itself, so don't be afraid to pull up the source for one of the SDK's views. You'll start to see many repeating patterns, and that's when your understanding really starts to come together.

Now that you've learned all the important parts about creating views, it's time to learn more about drawing. Chapter 13 will teach you how to do image compositing, and you can apply your new knowledge about drawing to create custom `Drawables`, including one that uses a `BitmapShader` for drawing an image with rounded corners.

CHAPTER 13

WORKING WITH THE CANVAS AND ADVANCED DRAWING

Now that you understand how to create completely custom views, it is helpful to understand some advanced drawing techniques. This chapter will show different methods of image compositing using a custom view as well as a method for using a custom `Shader` to change the shape of an image by using a custom `Drawable`. Both the image compositing techniques and the `Shader` techniques can be used in your own views, `Drawable`s, and even custom utility classes to achieve effects that aren't readily supported by Android's default classes.

PorterDuff Image Compositing

Behind the scenes, Android is using Skia, an excellent 2D C++ graphics library. Most of the drawing-related code you use in Android directly mirrors code from Skia. This also means that Android supports PorterDuff image compositing. Thomas Porter and Tom Duff wrote a seven-page paper titled "Compositing Digital Images" that explained methods of combining two or more images that have become extremely common in applications for mobile and desktop.

Android identifies the specific compositing method by using an `enum`, which is really just telling the native code which method to call. Unfortunately, the Android documentation for `PorterDuff.Mode` `enum`s is very limited. It gives you the name and a formula, and you're expected to understand the rest. At first, the formulas look a bit foreign, but most are not too bad once you understand what the letters mean and what the goal is.

For all the formulas, an *S* represents the source image and a *D* represents the destination image. An *a* represents the alpha channel and a *c* represents the color channels (a color being made of a red channel, a green channel, a blue channel, and an optional alpha channel). For all these composition modes, the color channels are treated individually and do not interact with other channels. If you are adding the source color to the destination color, you are adding the red channel of the source to the red channel of the destination, the green channel of the source to the green channel of the destination, and the blue channel of the source to the blue channel of the destination. Obviously, that's a bit wordy, so it can be expressed as "Sc + Dc" instead.

Multiplication is not too much different, except you can better understand it by thinking of individual channels as `float`s. If 0 represents the minimum value of the channel and 1 represents the maximum value of the channel, you have infinite values (in reality it is limited by the precision of the data type, but that's an implementation detail). In fact, this is how OpenGL works. These values can be converted to a specific bit depth when needed (for example, if you represent color with 256 values per channel, a value of `.25f` would be about 64). These channels can also be multiplied. For instance, you can take a green value of `.2f` and a green value of `.5f` and multiply them together you have a value of `.1f`, which equates to a color value of about 26.

Some of the modes to follow refer to the inverse of a channel. The inverse is what you get when you take the maximum value (`1f`) and subtract the current value. For instance, the inverse of `.25f` would be `.75f (1f – .25f)`. This is not the opposite color (also called complementary color) because it is for a single channel. If you had a fully green color (`0f` red, `1f` green, `0f` blue), the inverse would be magenta (`1f` red, `0f` green, `1f` blue).

Modes

Each of the PorterDuff methods is referred to as a `Mode` in Android. When using a `Paint` object, you can give it an `Xfermode` ("transfer mode") that is used when drawing. To give it a `PorterDuff.Mode`, you have to use the `PorterDuffXfermode` object, passing in the `Mode` `enum` that you want to use. Keep in mind that you do not want to construct objects during an `onDraw(Canvas)` method, so it's best to instantiate your `PorterDuffXfermode` object before you need to draw.

In some explanations of PorterDuff compositing, you might see the two images referred to as "A" and "B," but Android calls them the source ("SRC") image and the destination ("DST") image. In Android, the destination image is the one you are drawing the source into. Several of the methods have both a source image version and a destination image version, which can be helpful if the `Bitmap` backing your `Canvas` for one of your images is mutable but the other one is not. For example, `SRC_OVER` draws the source image over the top of the destination image. `DST_OVER` draws the destination image over the source image. To simplify the explanations, this book describes only the source versions in detail, but both types are included in the sample images.

`Clear`

Formula: [0, 0]

"Clear" simply means that nothing will be drawn in the completed image. This is typically used to "erase" some portion of an image. See the example in Figure 13.1.

Figure 13.1 The PorterDuff `Clear` mode shows neither the source nor the destination image.

SRC and DST

Formula: [Sa, Sc]

These two modes are fairly simple. If you use SRC, then only the source image is drawn. Similarly, if you use DST, only the destination image is drawn. You will probably rarely (if ever) use these because you can usually eliminate the need to create one of the two images earlier, if you are able to determine it is not needed. See the example of SRC and DST in Figure 13.2.

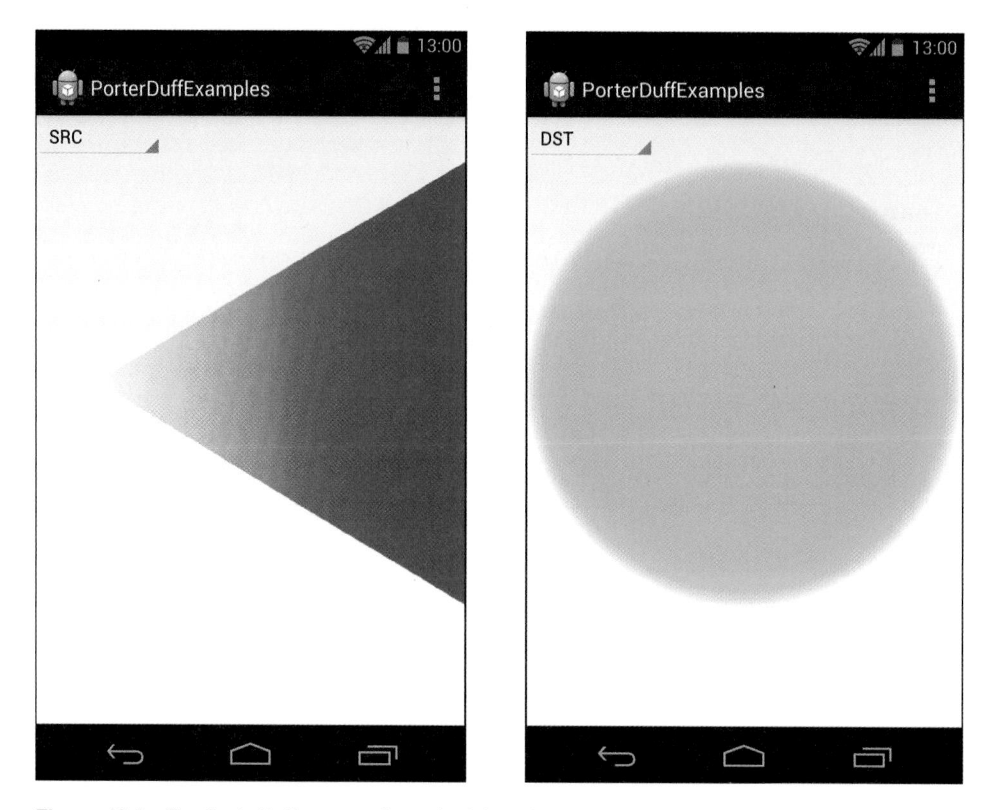

Figure 13.2 The PorterDuff SRC mode on the left and DST on the right

SRC_IN and DST_IN

Formula: [Sa × Da, Sc × Da]

"Source in" multiplies the source's alpha and color by the destination's alpha. This means that you're replacing the destination with the source where they overlap. Because both the color and alpha are multiplied, anywhere they don't overlap is cleared. In other words, the *source* is *in* place of the destination. See Figure 13.3 for an example.

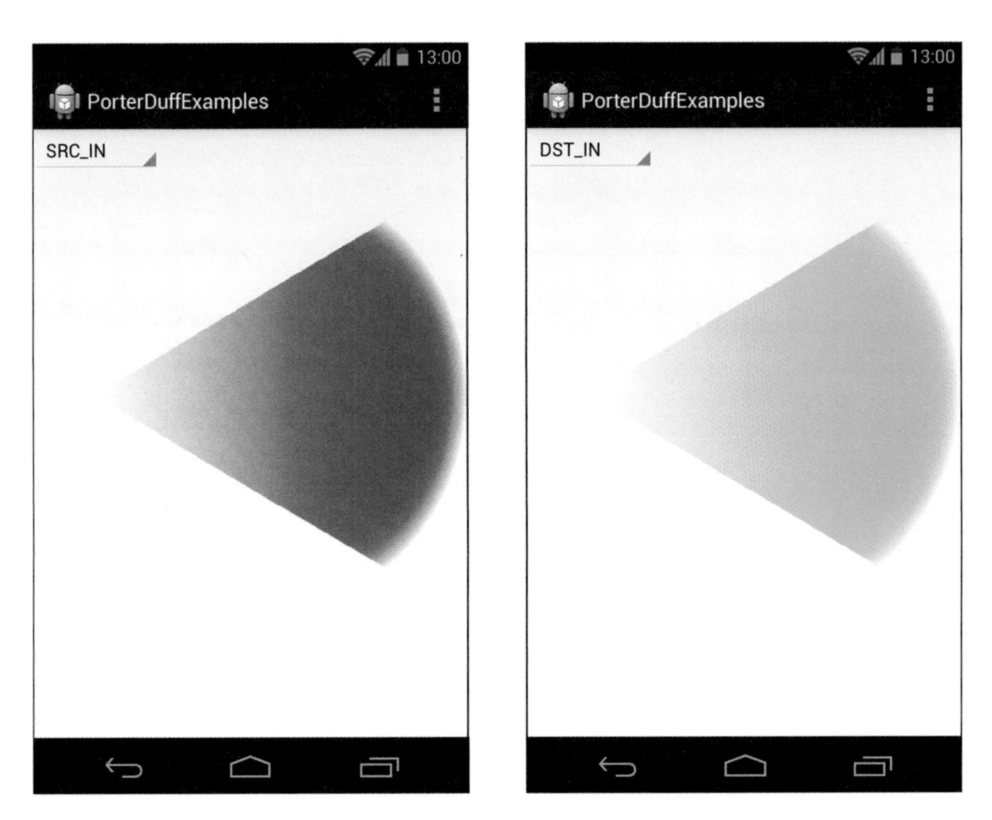

Figure 13.3 The PorterDuff `SRC_IN` mode on the left and `DST_IN` on the right

`SRC_OUT` and `DST_OUT`

Formula: [Sa × (1 – Da), Sc × (1 – Da)]

The "out" methods are basically the opposite of the "in" methods. When you're using `SRC_OUT`, only the part of the source image that does not overlap the destination image will be drawn. "Source out" multiplies the source's alpha and color by the inverse of the destination's alpha. Anywhere that the destination is fully transparent, the source will be fully opaque. If the destination is fully opaque somewhere, the source will not be visible. You are placing the *source out*side of the destination's alpha channel. See Figure 13.4 for an example.

`SRC_OVER` and `DST_OVER`

Formula: [Sa + (1 – Sa) × Da, Sc + (1 – Sa) × Dc]

"Source over" is a bit trickier to understand in terms of the math, but the end result is easy to understand. The *source* is placed *over* the top of the destination. The inverse of the source's alpha channel is multiplied by the destination's alpha channel and then the source's alpha is added back to it. The color is also modified in a similar manner. The inverse of the source's alpha is multiplied by the destination's color and then the sources color is added. See Figure 13.5 for an example.

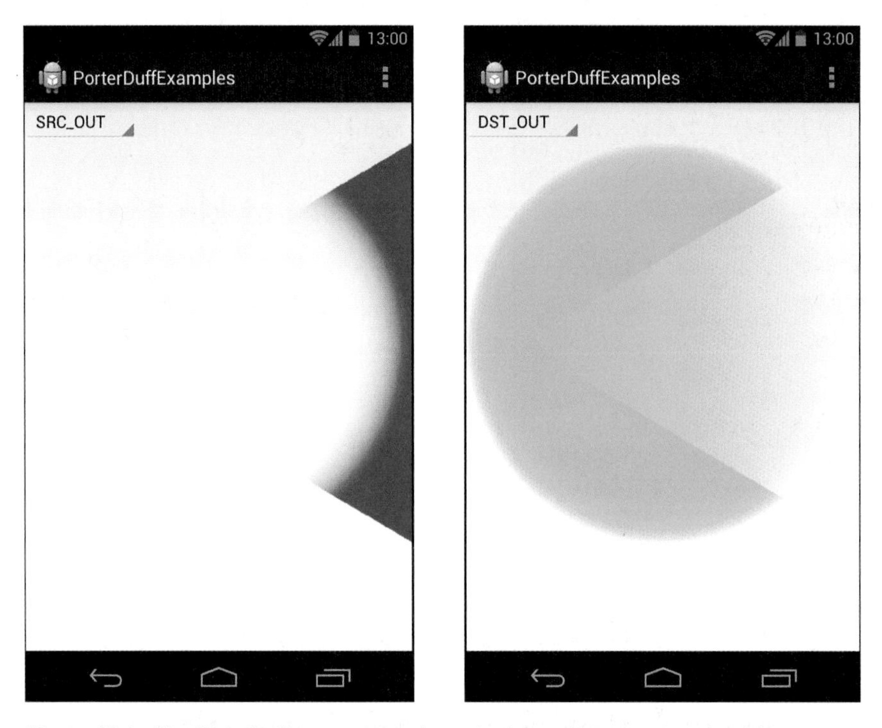

Figure 13.4 The PorterDuff `SRC_OUT` mode on the left and `DST_OUT` on the right

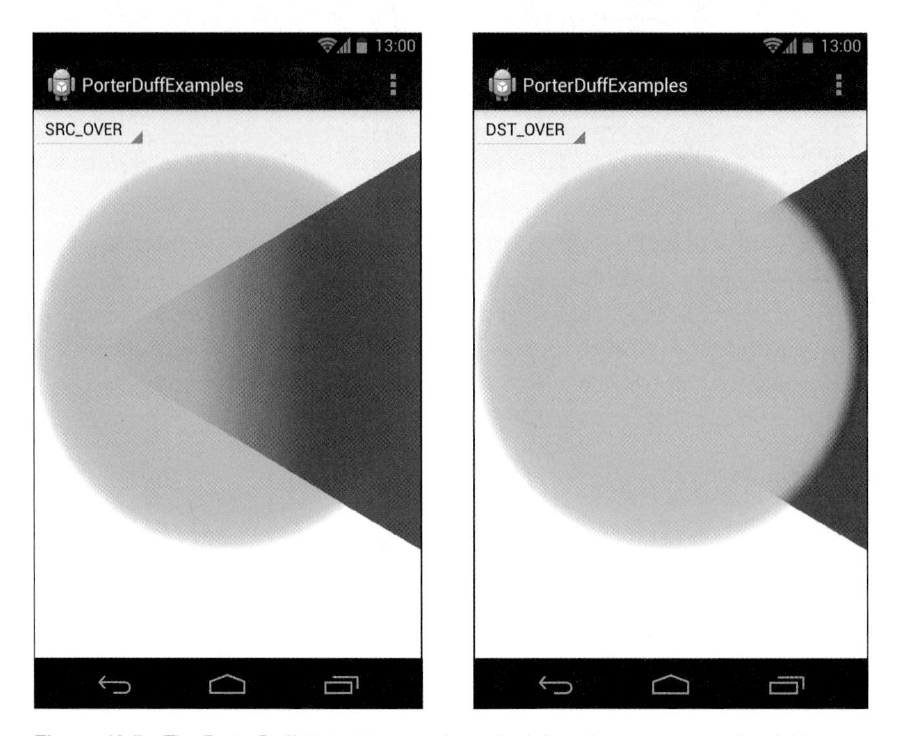

Figure 13.5 The PorterDuff `SRC_OVER` mode on the left and `DST_OVER` on the right

`SRC_ATOP` and `DST_ATOP`

Formula: [Da, Sc × Da + (1 – Sa) × Dc]

"Source atop" puts the source image on top of the destination image, but only where they overlap. It directly uses the destination's alpha channel for the resulting alpha values. The color is determined by taking the source color times the destination alpha and then adding back the result of the inverse of the source alpha multiplied by the destination color. Basically, it's putting the source on top of the destination using the destination's alpha value; then, for however transparent the source is, that amount of the destination shows through. See Figure 13.6 for an example.

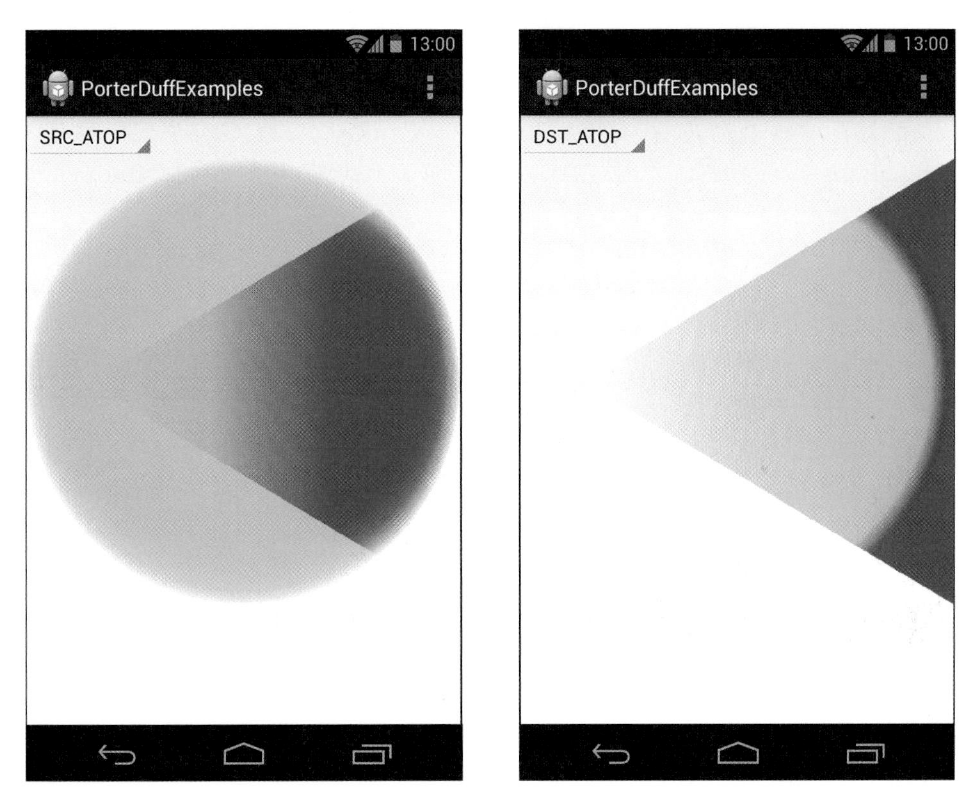

Figure 13.6 The PorterDuff `SRC_ATOP` mode on the left and `DST_ATOP` on the right

`Lighten`

Formula: [Sa + Da – Sa × Da, Sc × (1 – Da) + Dc × (1 – Sa) + max(Sc, Dc)]

The "lighten" mode combines the two images and will only brighten the areas where they overlap. The areas that are fully opaque in one image and fully transparent in the other will take the opaque portions without modification. For the alpha channel, the source and destination alphas are added together and the product of the two is subtracted from that result. To determine the color, you multiply the source color times the inverse of the destination alpha, add the destination color times the inverse of the source, and add whichever is greater, the source or the destination color. See Figure13.7 for an example.

Figure 13.7 The PorterDuff `Lighten` mode

`Darken`

Formula: [Sa + Da – Sa × Da, Sc × (1 – Da) + Dc × (1 – Sa) + min(Sc, Dc)]

The "darken" mode is extremely similar to the lighten mode. Anywhere that is opaque on one image and transparent in the other uses the opaque version without modification; however, anywhere that has some opacity in either image results in the color being darker because the final addition in the color calculation takes the darker of the two color values instead of the brighter. See Figure 13.8 for an example.

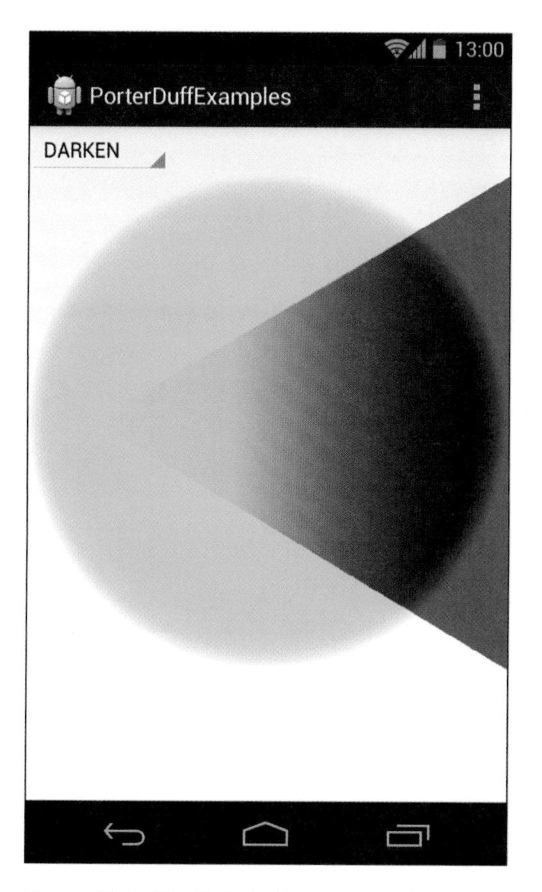

Figure 13.8 The PorterDuff `Darken` mode

`Add`

Formula: Saturate(S + D)

The "add" mode literally adds the source values to the destination values and then clamps them to the maximum value if they're too large. See Figure 13.9 for an example. The formula calls this clamping "saturate" because of the name of the Skia method, but it's just limiting the maximum value.

For instance, if the source has `.7f` for the red channel and the destination has `.6f` for the red channel, you get `1.3f`. Because that's greater than the maximum value of `1f`, the result is `1f`. Addition always brightens colors (unless you're adding a black image, in which case it does not affect the other image). Note that this `Mode` was added in API level 11 despite the fact that the documentation does not say so.

Figure 13.9 The PorterDuff `Add` mode

`Multiply`

Formula: [Sa × Da, Sc × Dc]

The "multiply" mode is one of the easiest to understand from a math perspective, but it can take a few examples before you understand the visuals. The source alpha and destination alpha are multiplied to get the resulting alpha channel, so only pixels that are fully opaque in the source and destination images will be fully opaque in the resulting image. The source color and the destination color are multiplied to get the resulting color. The name "multiply" is obviously very fitting when you look at the math. Because you're multiplying values that are never bigger than 1, you will never get a brighter color when multiplying. Multiplying pure white would just give you whatever the other color was because each channel is represented by a `1f`. That means, except in the case of white, multiplying will always give you darker colors. Anywhere that is fully transparent on either image results in transparency. See Figure 13.10 for an example.

Figure 13.10 The PorterDuff `Multiply` mode

`Screen`

Formula: [Sa + Da – Sa × Da, Sc + Dc – Sc × Dc]

The "screen" mode results in images that are very similar to the "lighten" and "add" modes. In fact, the alpha channel is calculated the exact same way for lighten and screen; the difference is that the color for the screen mode is calculated the same way as the alpha (whereas the lighten mode handles it differently). See Figure 13.11 for an example. Note that this `Mode` was added in API level 11 despite the fact that the documentation does not say so.

`Overlay`

This is the one `Mode` where the formula is not included, and that's because it is variable. If double the destination color is less than or equal to the destination alpha, one formula is used; otherwise, another formula is used. The alpha is calculated the same way as screen, though. The key difference is the way that the colors are blended. See Figure 13.12 for an example. Note that this `Mode` was added in API level 11 despite the fact that the documentation does not say so.

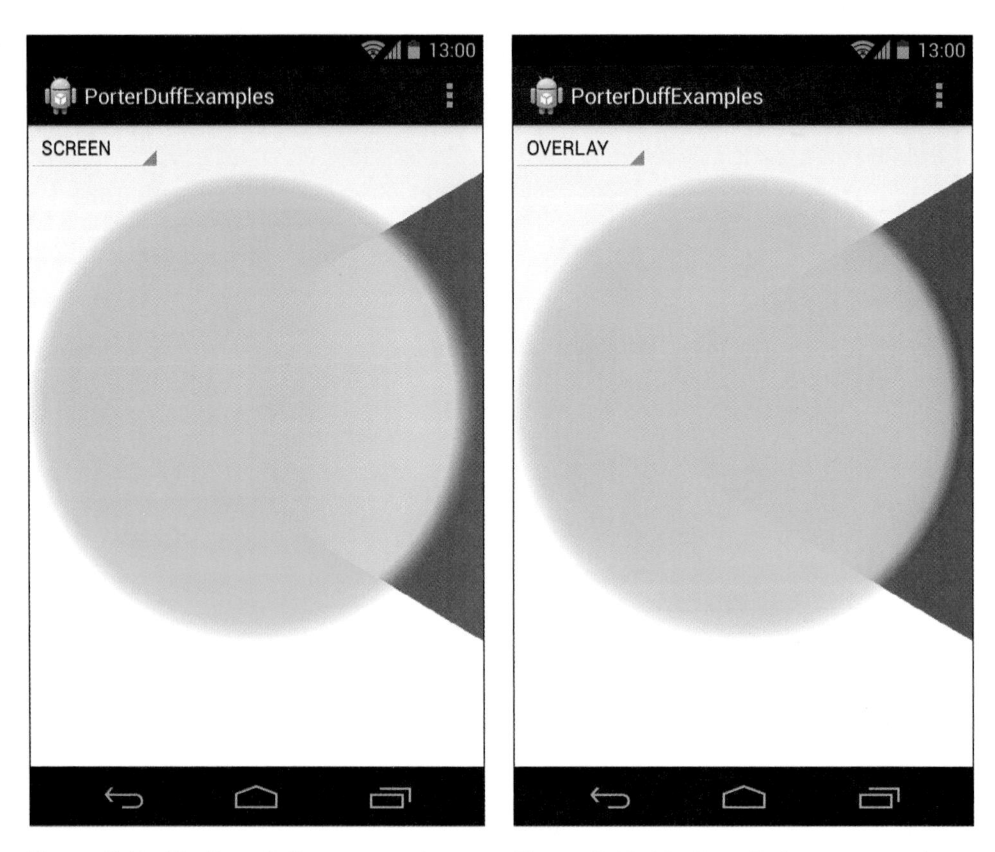

Figure 13.11 The PorterDuff `Screen` mode

Figure 13.12 The PorterDuff `Overlay` mode

`XOR`

Formula: [Sa + Da – 2 × Sa × Da, Sc × (1 – Da) + (1 – Sa) × Dc]

"Exclusive or" is another that's easier to visually understand. Anywhere that the source and destination overlap is cleared. This is done by adding the source and destination alpha channels and subtracting double the product of the source and destination alpha channels. The color is determined by multiplying the source color by the inverse of the destination's alpha, multiplying the destination color by the inverse of the source's alpha, and combining the result. See Figure 13.13 for an example.

Creating a Simple PorterDuff View

For your first use of `PorterDuff Mode`s, you're going to create a simple app like the one shown in the previous figures. This will let you easily test any of the `PorterDuff Mode`s with any images you'd like to better understand them. You can use a `Spinner` to select a specific `PorterDuff Mode` while running the app, allowing you to easily compare the differences among them.

Figure 13.13 The PorterDuff XOR mode

Create a new project (the sample one is called PorterDuffExamples) and add two images to it that you want to combine as the source and destination images. Next, create a new class called `PorterDuffView` and set `View` as its super class. Be sure check the box to implement all the constructors. To keep this view efficient, you will want to create class variables to store the `Paint` called `mPaint`, the `Bitmap` (which will be the combination of your two images) called `mBitmap`, and the `XferMode` called `mXferMode`. The `Paint` object can be immediately instantiated.

You need to add a method to allow you to set the `PorterDuff.Mode`, so create a method called `setPorterDuffMode(PorterDuff.Mode)`. It should simply set the `mXferMode` to a new `PorterDuffXferMode` that takes the `Mode` that was passed in. It also needs to null out the reference to `mBitmap` because it will need to be re-created with the new `XferMode`. At this point, your `PorterDuffView` should look like Listing 13.1.

Listing 13.1 The Initial `PorterDuffView`

```
public class PorterDuffView extends View {

    /**
     * The Paint used to draw everything
     */
    private Paint mPaint = new Paint(Paint.ANTI_ALIAS_FLAG);

    /**
     * The Bitmap containing the two images blended together
     */
    private Bitmap mBitmap;

    /**
     * The XferMode to combine the images with
     */
    private Xfermode mXferMode = new PorterDuffXfermode(
➥PorterDuff.Mode.CLEAR);

    public PorterDuffView(Context context) {
        super(context);
    }

    public PorterDuffView(Context context, AttributeSet attrs) {
        super(context, attrs);
    }

    public PorterDuffView(Context context, AttributeSet attrs, int
➥defStyle) {
        super(context, attrs, defStyle);
    }

    /**
     * Sets the new PorterDuff.Mode, removes the existing Bitmap and
     * invalidates the view
     *
     * @param mode PorterDuff.Mode to use
     */
    public void setPorterDuffMode(PorterDuff.Mode mode) {
        mXferMode = new PorterDuffXfermode(mode);
        mBitmap = null;
        invalidate();
    }
}
```

Next up, make a method called `createBitmap` that will do the heart of the work. To support a range of image sizes, you will create a `Rect` that represents the image scaled to the size of the view. To keep the example simple, it assumes the images are square, so it just takes the smaller of the width or height (called `minDimension`) and creates a `Rect` based on that (thus, if your view is 500px by 800px, the resulting `Rect` is 500px by 500px).

You will use the static `createBitmap(int, int, Config)` method of `Bitmap` to create the actual `Bitmap` (`mBitmap`) you will draw into. The two `int`s represent the width and the height (in this case, both are the `minDimension`) and a `Config` that says how many bits are used to represent the colors in the `Bitmap`. You want to pass in `Config.ARGB_8888`, which means the alpha, red, green, and blue channels each get 8 bits for 256 levels per channel. This is the highest quality configuration and is almost always the one you want to use. Using a lower quality configuration can result in visual artifacts and, depending on the images you pass in, might make the compositing harder to understand.

Create a new `Canvas`, passing in the target `Bitmap` you just made. This `Canvas` will handle the calls to draw the images into the target `Bitmap`. To get a `Bitmap` instance of one of your images, use the `BitmapFactory`'s static `decodeResource(Resources, int)` method, passing in a reference to `Resources`, which you can obtain with `getResources()`, and the identifier for your image (the example uses `R.drawable.shape1`). Use the `Canvas`'s `drawBitmap(Bitmap, Rect, Rect, Paint)` method to draw the newly loaded `Bitmap` into the target `Bitmap`. Notice that there are several methods for drawing `Bitmap`s. This one takes the `Bitmap` to draw (the one you just loaded from `Resources`), a `Rect` that represents the portion of that `Bitmap` to use for drawing, a `Rect` that represents where to draw the `Bitmap`, and the `Paint`. You can leave the first `Rect` null, which means the full image will be used. The second `Rect` will be the one you already created, and the `Paint` will be `mPaint`.

Now, use the `BitmapFactory` again to load your second image but, before drawing it, call `setXfermode(mXfermode)` on your `Paint`. This sets it up to use the transfer mode when drawing (in this case, whichever `PorterDuff.Mode` has been set in the `PorterDuffXfermode` object). Draw this second `Bitmap` to the target `Bitmap` using the same `Canvas` method you used for the previous image. Finally, remove the `Xfermode` from the `Paint` by calling `setXfermode(null)`.

When you're all done with the `createBitmap()` method, it should look like Listing 13.2.

Listing 13.2 The `createBitmap()` Method

```
/**
 * Creates mBitmap using the set XferMode
 */
private void createBitmap() {

    // Prepare the Bitmap
    final int width = getWidth();
    final int height = getHeight();
```

```
        final int minDimension = Math.min(width, height);
        final Rect rect = new Rect();
        rect.right = minDimension - 1;
        rect.bottom = rect.right;
        mBitmap = Bitmap.createBitmap(minDimension, minDimension,
➥Bitmap.Config.ARGB_8888);
        final Canvas c = new Canvas(mBitmap);

        // Create the destination Bitmap and paint it
        Bitmap b = BitmapFactory.decodeResource(getResources(),
➥R.drawable.shape1);
        c.drawBitmap(b, null, rect, mPaint);

        // Create the source Bitmap, set XferMode, and paint
        b = BitmapFactory.decodeResource(getResources(),
➥R.drawable.shape2);
        mPaint.setXfermode(mXferMode);
        c.drawBitmap(b, null, rect, mPaint);

        // Remove the XferMode
        mPaint.setXfermode(null);
    }
```

You are almost done with the custom view, but there is a little more to do. You need to override the `onDraw(Canvas)` method to actually draw your `mBitmap`. First, check if `mBitmap` is `null`. If it is, call `createBitmap()`. Now it should make sense why you remove your `mBitmap` reference when setting a new `PorterDuff.Mode` in the `setPorterDuffMode` call (to create a new `Bitmap` using the new `Xfermode`). Although you should not allocate objects in the `onDraw(Canvas)` method, it is okay to do so when the object is then retained for future draw calls. Outside of the `if` block, simply call the passed-in `Canvas`'s `drawBitmap(Bitmap, float, float, Paint)` method. Notice that this one takes two `float`s instead of two `Rect`s. These `float`s specify the left and top position in the `Canvas` to draw the `Bitmap` to. The `Bitmap` will not be scaled. You are simply saying, "Start the top-left corner of the `Bitmap` here and draw all that will fit." Because you already handled the scaling by using the `Rect` earlier, calling this method with the two `float`s is very efficient.

Now you have a view that can be given a `PorterDuff.Mode` and will draw a `Bitmap` that consists of two images composited together with that `Mode`. The only problem left is that if your view changes sizes, the `Bitmap` does not update. To fix that problem, override the `onLayout(boolean, int, int, int, int)` method. After calling through to the super method, check if the `mBitmap` is not `null` (if it's `null`, you don't need to do anything). If it's not `null`, that means you need to check to see if it is the right size. Get the width and height of the view (you can just subtract the left from the right and the top from the bottom to get the dimensions) and check whichever dimension is smaller. The smaller dimension should match the width (and height, since it is square) of the `mBitmap`. If it doesn't, then clear the reference so that it can be created the next time the view is drawn. See Listing 13.3 for the complete class code.

Listing 13.3 The Complete `PorterDuffView`

```
public class PorterDuffView extends View {

    /**
     * The Paint used to draw everything
     */
    private Paint mPaint = new Paint(Paint.ANTI_ALIAS_FLAG);

    /**
     * The Bitmap containing the two images blended together
     */
    private Bitmap mBitmap;

    /**
     * The XferMode to combine the images with
     */
    private Xfermode mXferMode = new PorterDuffXfermode(
➥PorterDuff.Mode.CLEAR);

    public PorterDuffView(Context context) {
        super(context);
    }

    public PorterDuffView(Context context, AttributeSet attrs) {
        super(context, attrs);
    }

    public PorterDuffView(Context context, AttributeSet attrs, int
➥defStyle) {
        super(context, attrs, defStyle);
    }

    /**
     * Sets the new PorterDuff.Mode, removes the existing Bitmap and
     * invalidates the view
     *
     * @param mode PorterDuff.Mode to use
     */
    public void setPorterDuffMode(PorterDuff.Mode mode) {
        mXferMode = new PorterDuffXfermode(mode);
        mBitmap = null;
        invalidate();
    }
```

```
    @Override
    public void onDraw(Canvas canvas) {
        if (mBitmap == null) {
            createBitmap();
        }
        canvas.drawBitmap(mBitmap, 0, 0, mPaint);
    }

    @Override
    protected void onLayout(boolean changed, int left, int top, int
➥right, int bottom) {
        super.onLayout(changed, left, top, right, bottom);

        // If mBitmap is set, make sure it's the right size
        if (mBitmap != null) {
            final int width = right - left;
            final int height = bottom - top;
            final int minDimension = Math.min(width, height);

            final int bitmapWidth = mBitmap.getWidth();
            if (minDimension != bitmapWidth) {
                mBitmap = null;
            }
        }
    }

    /**
     * Creates mBitmap using the set XferMode
     */
    private void createBitmap() {

        // Prepare the Bitmap
        final int width = getWidth();
        final int height = getHeight();
        final int minDimension = Math.min(width, height);
        final Rect rect = new Rect();
        rect.right = minDimension - 1;
        rect.bottom = rect.right;
        mBitmap = Bitmap.createBitmap(minDimension, minDimension,
➥Bitmap.Config.ARGB_8888);
        final Canvas c = new Canvas(mBitmap);

        // Create the destination Bitmap and paint it
        Bitmap b = BitmapFactory.decodeResource(getResources(),
➥R.drawable.shape1);
        c.drawBitmap(b, null, rect, mPaint);

        // Create the source Bitmap, set XferMode, and paint
```

```
        b = BitmapFactory.decodeResource(getResources(),
➥R.drawable.shape2);
        mPaint.setXfermode(mXferMode);
        c.drawBitmap(b, null, rect, mPaint);

        // Remove the XferMode
        mPaint.setXfermode(null);
    }
}
```

Now that you have a custom view, you need a layout to make use of the view. Edit `main_layout.xml` to simply be a vertically oriented `LinearLayout` with a `Spinner` and your custom view. The `Spinner` will be used to select the `PorterDuff.Mode` and your view will display it. The layout should look like Listing 13.4.

Listing 13.4 The Layout with Your Custom View

```
<LinearLayout xmlns:android="http://schemas.android.com/apk/res/
➥android"
    xmlns:tools="http://schemas.android.com/tools"
    android:layout_width="match_parent"
    android:layout_height="match_parent"
    android:orientation="vertical"
    tools:context=".MainActivity" >

    <Spinner
        android:id="@+id/spinner"
        android:layout_width="wrap_content"
        android:layout_height="wrap_content" />

    <com.iangclifton.auid.porterduffexamples.PorterDuffView
        android:id="@+id/porter_duff_view"
        android:layout_width="match_parent"
        android:layout_height="match_parent" />

</LinearLayout>
```

Open `MainActivity.java` and add two variables to the class: `mAdapter`, which is an `ArrayAdapter` that holds `PorterDuff.Mode enums`, and `mPorterDuffView`, which is a reference to your custom view. In `onCreate(Bundle)`, set your content view and set the reference to `mPorterDuffView`. Then get an array of all the available `PorterDuff.Mode`s by calling `PorterDuff.Mode.values()`. Create a new `ArrayAdapter`, passing in the `Context (this), android.R.layout.simple_spinner_item` (for a basic layout), and your array of `PorterDuff.Mode`s. You need to also call `setDropDownViewResource(int)`, passing in `android.R.layout.simple_spinner_dropdown_item`.

Get a reference to the `Spinner` and set the `ArrayAdapter` on it. Make your `Activity` implement `OnItemSelectedListener` so that it will be notified of changes to the `Spinner`, and call the `Spinner`'s `setOnItemSelectedListener` method, passing in the `Activity`.

You don't need to do anything in the `onNothingSelected` method, but in the `onItemSelected` method, you need to update your custom view with the newly selected `PorterDuff.Mode enum`. To get the selected `Mode`, call `getItem(int)` on your `ArrayAdapter`, passing in the position `int`. See the complete `Activity` in Listing 13.5.

Listing 13.5 The Complete `Activity` Class

```
public class MainActivity extends Activity implements
➥OnItemSelectedListener {

    private ArrayAdapter<PorterDuff.Mode> mAdapter;
    private PorterDuffView mPorterDuffView;

    @Override
    protected void onCreate(Bundle savedInstanceState) {
        super.onCreate(savedInstanceState);
        setContentView(R.layout.activity_main);

        // Get reference to the PorterDuffView
        mPorterDuffView = (PorterDuffView)
➥findViewById(R.id.porter_duff_view);

        // Create array of PorterDuff.Modes
        final PorterDuff.Mode[] porterDuffModes =
➥PorterDuff.Mode.values();
        mAdapter = new ArrayAdapter<PorterDuff.Mode>(this,
➥android.R.layout.simple_spinner_item, porterDuffModes);
        mAdapter.setDropDownViewResource(android.R.layout.
➥simple_spinner_dropdown_item);

        final Spinner spinner = (Spinner) findViewById(R.id.spinner);
        spinner.setAdapter(mAdapter);
        spinner.setOnItemSelectedListener(this);
    }

    @Override
    public boolean onCreateOptionsMenu(Menu menu) {
        // Inflate the menu; this adds items to the action bar if it
➥is present.
        getMenuInflater().inflate(R.menu.activity_main, menu);
        return true;
    }

    @Override
```

```
    public void onItemSelected(AdapterView<?> parent, View view, int
➥position, long id) {
        mPorterDuffView.setPorterDuffMode(mAdapter.getItem(position));
    }

    @Override
    public void onNothingSelected(AdapterView<?> parent) {
        // Ignored
    }
}
```

Creating Custom Drawables

Android's `Drawable` class is a great abstraction for anything that can be drawn to the screen. In some ways it is like a view, but it is much easier to understand and work with for a variety of uses. By extending `Drawable` to create custom effects, you can easily add those effects to almost any view by setting the `Drawable` as the background.

The Important Methods

Before you create your own `Drawable`, you need to know about the following methods:

- **`draw(Canvas)`**—Handles drawing to the canvas, similarly to how `onDraw(Canvas)` works for views.
- **`getBounds()`**—Returns the `Rect` within which the `Drawable` will fit.
- **`getIntrinsicHeight()`**—Returns the ideal height of the `Drawable`. For instance, a `Drawable` that is drawing a `Bitmap` might return the height of the actual image.
- **`getIntrinsicWidth()`**—Returns the ideal width for the `Drawable`.
- **`getOpacity()`**—Returns an `int` that defines whether this `Drawable` is translucent, transparent, or opaque. Each `int` is defined in `PixelFormat`.
- **`onBoundsChange(Rect)`**—Notifies your `Drawable` that its bounds changed. This is the ideal place to do any one-time dimension calculations.
- **`onLevelChange(int)`**—Notifies your `Drawable` that the level has changed. For example, a level can be used for a `Drawable` that shows the amount of battery left (where the value would be between 0 and 100, but the `Drawable` itself might only have five different appearances).
- **`onStateChange(int[])`**—Notifies your `Drawable` that its state (for example, whether it is pressed or focused) has changed.
- **`setAlpha(int)`**—Sets the alpha value from 0 (transparent) to 255 (opaque).
- **`setColorFilter(ColorFilter)`**—Sets the `ColorFilter` for the `Drawable`.

When you create a new `Drawable`, you need to implement the `draw(Canvas)`, `getOpacity()`, `setAlpha(int)`, and `setColorFilter(ColorFilter)` methods at a minimum.

Using a `Shader` for Shaping Images

In a generalized sense, a `Shader` provides the `Paint` object with pixels (colors) to draw. A simple example is a gradient such as a `LinearGradient`. When you use a `Paint` to draw a rectangle on the `Canvas`, for instance, the `Paint` gets the color for each pixel from the left to the right via the `Shader`. You will now create a `Drawable` that uses a `Shader` to round the corners of an image. This is a common design requirement, and using a custom `Drawable` that draws with a `Shader` is a clean and efficient way to accomplish this.

The code to create this custom `Drawable` is fairly minimal, so you can easily add it to an existing app, if you'd like. This example will use a new app called `CustomDrawable`. Create a class that extends `Drawable` called `RoundedBitmapDrawable`. It needs to have variables for a `Bitmap` (`mBitmap`), a `Paint` (`mPaint`), an `int` for the radius of the corners (`mRadius`), and a `RectF` for drawing the `Bitmap` (`mRectF`). The constructor should take a `Bitmap` (the image that will be rounded) and an `int` (the radius). It should call the method `setBitmap(Bitmap)`, which you will create now. The `setBitmap` method is public and takes the `Bitmap` that will be drawn. It should create a new `BitmapShader`, passing in the `Bitmap` and a `TileMode` for the X and Y axes. The `TileMode` is used if you draw outside of the `Bitmap` and do not scale it. Just pass in `TileMode.CLAMP` for both values (clamping repeats pixels at the edge of an image, for instance, and image that is 100 pixels wide that is drawn in a space that is 200 pixels wide would have its very last pixel repeated an extra 100 times to fill the extra space). Set the `Shader` on the `Paint` with the `setShader(Shader)` method and call `invalidateSelf()`. Similar to the `invalidate()` method in a view, this requests that the `Drawable` be redrawn in the future.

Override `onBoundsChange(Rect)` to create a new `RectF` to set as `mRectF`. Implement `setColorFilter(ColorFilter)` to call through to `mPaint`'s method of the same name and call `invalidateSelf()`. Implement `setAlpha(int)` to do the same (to make it more efficient, you can check if the new alpha value is different from the old one). Your `getOpacity` method should return `PixelFormat.TRANSLUCENT` because there will be varying degrees of alpha in the resulting image. You should override the `getIntrinsicHeight()` and `getIntrinsicWidth()` to return the height and width of `mBitmap`, respectively. Finally, you can implement the `draw(Canvas)` method, where you will simply call `drawRoundRect(mRectF, mRadius, mRadius, mPaint)` on the passed-in `Canvas` to do the actual drawing. The final class should look like Listing 13.6.

Listing 13.6 The Full `RoundedBitmapDrawable` Class

```
public class RoundedBitmapDrawable extends Drawable {

    private Bitmap mBitmap;
    private final Paint mPaint = new Paint(Paint.ANTI_ALIAS_FLAG);
    private int mRadius;
    private RectF mRectF;

    public RoundedBitmapDrawable(Bitmap bitmap, int radius) {
        mRadius = radius;
        setBitmap(bitmap);
    }

    @Override
    public void draw(Canvas canvas) {
        canvas.drawRoundRect(mRectF, mRadius, mRadius, mPaint);
    }

    @Override
    public int getIntrinsicHeight() {
        if (mBitmap == null) {
            return 0;
        }
        return mBitmap.getHeight();
    }

    @Override
    public int getIntrinsicWidth() {
        if (mBitmap == null) {
            return 0;
        }
        return mBitmap.getWidth();
    }

    @Override
    public int getOpacity() {
        return PixelFormat.TRANSLUCENT;
    }

    @Override
    public void setAlpha(int alpha) {
        int oldAlpha = mPaint.getAlpha();
        if (alpha != oldAlpha) {
            mPaint.setAlpha(alpha);
            invalidateSelf();
        }
    }
```

```
    public void setBitmap(Bitmap bitmap) {
        mBitmap = bitmap;
        final Shader shader = new BitmapShader(bitmap, TileMode.CLAMP,
➥TileMode.CLAMP);
        mPaint.setShader(shader);
        invalidateSelf();
    }

    @Override
    public void setColorFilter(ColorFilter cf) {
        mPaint.setColorFilter(cf);
        invalidateSelf();
    }

    @Override
    protected void onBoundsChange(Rect bounds) {
        super.onBoundsChange(bounds);
        mRectF = new RectF(bounds);
    }
}
```

Now that you have a custom `Drawable`, you need somewhere to put it. Create a simple layout with a `LinearLayout` as the root and an `ImageView` inside. You will be setting the custom `Drawable` on the `ImageView`. See Listing 13.7 for the complete layout.

Listing 13.7 A Simple Layout with the Custom View

```
<LinearLayout xmlns:android="http://schemas.android.com/apk/res/
➥android"
    xmlns:tools="http://schemas.android.com/tools"
    android:layout_width="match_parent"
    android:layout_height="match_parent"
    android:orientation="vertical"
    android:padding="10dp"
    tools:context=".MainActivity" >

    <ImageView
        android:id="@+id/image_view"
        android:layout_width="wrap_content"
        android:layout_height="wrap_content"
        android:contentDescription="@null" />

</LinearLayout>
```

In your `Activity`, the `onCreate(Bundle)` method should set the content view, then create a `Bitmap` using the `BitmapFactory` like you did earlier in the chapter. Decide on a radius (the example uses 10dp, defined in `dimens.xml`) and create the custom `Drawable`. Then you just need to find your `ImageView` and call `setImageDrawable(Drawable)`, passing in the custom `Drawable` you instantiated. See Listing 13.8 for the full `onCreate(Bundle)` method and Figure 13.14 for an example of what this can look like on a device.

Figure 13.14 The custom `Drawable` showing a rounded image

Listing 13.8 The `onCreate` Method

```
@Override
protected void onCreate(Bundle savedInstanceState) {
    super.onCreate(savedInstanceState);
    setContentView(R.layout.activity_main);

    // Create the custom Drawable
    final Resources res = getResources();
    final Bitmap b = BitmapFactory.decodeResource(res,
➥R.drawable.photo);
```

```
        final int radius = res.getDimensionPixelSize(R.dimen.radius);
        final Drawable d = new RoundedBitmapDrawable(b, radius);

        // Find the ImageView and set the Drawable
        final ImageView iv = (ImageView) findViewById(R.id.image_view);
        iv.setImageDrawable(d);
    }
```

For ways to improve the `Drawable`, take a look at the source code for `BitmapDrawable` (https://android.googlesource.com/platform/frameworks/base/+/refs/heads/master/graphics/java/android/graphics/drawable/BitmapDrawable.java). It has additional methods for setting other properties worth looking at now that you understand how to make a basic `Drawable`. Consider next how you would add support for padding or further improve the `Drawable`.

Summary

In this chapter, you learned about advanced image compositing techniques by using `PorterDuff.Mode`s. You should now understand how to create `Bitmap`s to draw into using advanced painting techniques. You should know the basic concepts behind a `Shader` as well as how to instantiate and apply them to `Paint` objects. You can bring all this knowledge together in custom `Drawable`s to make it easy to apply advanced drawing techniques to a variety of views.

This chapter marks the conclusion of the main portion of the book. Now that you have worked through all the chapters, you should understand the entire process of developing and designing an app, from creating sketches to implementing custom views. After this chapter, you will find appendixes to help you get the right assets ready for publishing your app and a reference to some commonly used Android techniques.

APPENDIX A

GOOGLE PLAY ASSETS

Google Play is the primary method for distributing Android apps, and it has the largest world-wide reach of any Android app store. Although there is no lengthy review process, you should have all of your assets ready for the store before you launch the app, even if you're doing a "soft" launch (that is, a launch with no explicit publicity). Having the right assets ensures that you reach the maximum number of users by showing them what is great about your app and by enabling it to be featured by Google Play. Note that you can also provide locale-specific assets, so you can provide graphics for each of the languages you support, including screenshots. Whenever possible, you should provide assets for every locale that the app supports.

Application Description

Although this book is focused on design and the impact of design on the user experience, not emphasizing the importance of a good app description would be a major failing. The app description not only lets you tell the users what your app is about and why they must download it now, but also gives you the opportunity to set their expectations.

Use concise, clear language that explains what your app is and what need it fulfills. Many users will only read the first portion of your description, so make sure you get the most important pieces across right away. If there are any problems with the app, be upfront about them. For instance, if the app is a prototype that demonstrates functionality but drains battery quickly, say so. If the app is intended for a specific audience, make that clear up front (for example, "This demo for Android app developers does X, Y, and Z"). If you created a weather app that only supports forecasts for one country, be explicit about that right away (and, in this specific case, consider limiting it geographically to those in that country). Setting expectations not only allows users to filter themselves (for example, "Oh, it doesn't work in my country, so I won't try it"), it makes them far less likely to leave negative feedback. By not setting the expectations right away, you run the risk of negative reviews from users who had their own expectations (for example, "Why doesn't this stupid app provide weather forecasts in my country?").

Do not make your app description sound "market-y." In other words, this is not the place to brag excessively about your app or talk about how it was downloaded a million times in the first week. Focus on what the user gets out of it. What makes it different from the competition? Is it faster, better presented, or easier to use?

If your app fulfills a new need or an uncommon one, you have to explain what that need is. For instance, you might make an app for pilots to track their flight details, automatically populating time and distance based on the device sensors. You can declare the audience immediately (for example, "This app allows pilots to..."). Because pilots know the importance of keeping maintenance and flight records, you can instead emphasize what your app does to make that record keeping easier and what records it actually keeps. If your app is a new take on an existing and common app type (for example, a new Twitter client), you have to put the emphasis on what makes your app special. You can assume that people looking at your app know what Twitter is and what they want to do with your app, so your description needs to state what makes your app different from the other Twitter apps out there.

Do not use automatic translation for your application description. It may be tempting to use Google Translate or a similar service to automatically translate your description into other languages, but you should avoid doing so. In most cases, doing so will get the gist of your app's meaning across, but it will often be riddled with minor errors or awkward phrasing that will not convey a sense of professionalism. You don't want a user's first experience to be with a grammatically flawed description; otherwise, it could be the last.

The Change Log

Whenever you update the app, update the change log. No exceptions. Many people are afraid to put anything there for fear that they risk sounding like the app was flawed; however, no app is perfect. How did the update make it better? Did you fix a crash bug? Did you fix some silly typos? Is there new content for users? This is your chance to show existing users that they are not forgotten, and it's your chance to show potential users that the app is constantly improving. Existing users want to know whether the change is worth downloading now, later, or ever. When you don't update the change log or you put something generic, such as "fixes," you're telling the users that the update isn't important.

Be specific. "Fixed rare crash on launch for Nexus 4 users" is good, but "Fixed bugs" is not. Be concise. "Added support for Hungarian" is good, but "Updated the whole app to support users who have their device set to Hungarian" is excessive. This is not the place to fully explain new features; instead, you can briefly introduce them ("Added swiping for faster navigation") and then explain them on first launch of the app, if needed.

Application Icon

The application icon for Google Play must be 512×512. Only PNG images are supported, so you should upload a 32-bit PNG that matches your default launcher icon. Whenever possible, it's ideal to create assets such as your application icon as vector graphics so that they can be scaled (and sharpened or otherwise adjusted) to match a variety of sizes.

The application icon is one of the most important parts of your app. It is often the first graphic a user sees related to your app, and it's the one users search for when launching your app. It needs to convey what your app is about in a simple but recognizable way. That means it needs to follow all the standard conventions.

A good icon...

- **Uses the majority of the space available to it.** This means the touch target is obvious and you don't have an overly thin icon. Icons that are too thin don't look touchable and they can often be lost against certain backgrounds.
- **Has a notable shape.** Android does not force all app icons into the same shape, so this is one of the best ways to make your icon stand out. Is it an analog clock? Perhaps you should consider a round icon. Is it for tracking stars in the sky? Maybe you could try a star or constellation shape. Look at the variety of shapes in the default apps. There aren't just circles and rounded rectangles but mail-shaped icons and icons that look like headphones.
- **Sticks to a simple color scheme.** Look at the apps that come on an Android device and you should notice a very common pattern among the default icons. Most of them stick to a simple but distinct color scheme. Gmail is red and white. Play Music is orange and gray.

Calendar is blue and white. Where shapes are similar, colors are different (for example, Clock is a white and gray circle, but Downloads is a gray and green circle).

- **Uses a straight-on, slightly overhead angle.** This is intended to give your icon a hint of depth without making it visually complicated. Usually adding just a few lighter pixels along the top edge of your icon is enough to accomplish this.

Take a look at both the Google Maps icon and the Google Music icon in Figure A.1. Notice the bright, playful colors and the distinct shapes. Both of these types of apps typically have very simple icons. A flat map with rounded corners is the obvious choice for a mapping application, but that's not very recognizable. By adding the bends to the icon, Google has made this icon have a hint of depth and, more importantly, made it a distinct shape. Music applications are another example where people typically do something simple such as a rounded rectangle with a music note or CD on it. Google used the unique shape of headphones to ensure the icon stands out and chose a vibrant orange color to make it more distinct. Consider how bland the icon would have been with a standard black headband instead of orange.

Figure A.1 The Google Maps and Google Music icons

Screenshots

Screenshots can be 320×480, 480×800, 480×854, 1280×720, or 1280×800. They should be 24-bit PNGs to keep the graphics crisp, but JPEGs are also acceptable. As new resolutions become more common on Android devices, support for new screenshot sizes is added, so be sure to double-check what sizes you can upload in the developer console when you are submitting your app (https://play.google.com/apps/publish/Home).

A lot of users will look at the screenshots before they've even begun to read your app description. Screenshots provide the first glimpse into what your app is really like, so they're absolutely vital to include. Google Play requires two screenshots, but you should provide more. Ideally, you should provide one screenshot for each primary section of the app. For instance, an email app could show a screenshot of the inbox, a full email, replying to an email, and any other core functionality, such as searching.

Screenshots are an excellent way to show off support for alternate form factors. If you support tablets, include a few tablet screenshots. This is often one of the first places users look to see if their tablet is supported, and seeing only phone screenshots will be perceived as an indication that tablets are not supported. Some users will even back out of an app's details in Google Play without reading the description or downloading the app to give it a try because they're using a tablet and the screenshots don't indicate support for tablets.

Do not use Google Play screenshots for promotional material. Some people make the mistake of using them to advertise for other apps, but they are meant to be specific to the app they are for and shouldn't have added text on them that doesn't reflect the user experience. Do not show screenshots of unimportant screens just to have more screenshots available. For instance, it does not make sense to include a screenshot of the settings screen for most apps (an exception being for apps that are intended for power users or focused on customizability). Settings screens generally have a lot to look at and interpret and don't reflect the primary user experience of the app. Do not include a screenshot of a splash screen. It can be tempting to include one because of the effort that often goes into designing a good splash screen, but such a screenshot does not help the user understand the app. Exclude distracting pieces from the screenshots. For instance, you should consider removing onscreen navigation from phone-sized images and removing any status bar notifications from each screenshot. Be sure to review each screenshot. It's easy to make the mistake of taking a screenshot of an app that includes user-generated content that might not be appropriate. If your screenshots are taken on a device that's customized (for example, one that has a custom style for the status bar), modify them to look like what the user will see to keep the focus on your app and not the trim.

Feature Graphic

The feature graphic must be 1024×500 (although it will be resized for use in a variety of places). Ideally, it should be a PNG, but a JPEG with minimal compression works well, too. In either case, it must be a 24-bit image (no alpha channel).

Your feature graphic is an important part of marketing your app. It's the large image that goes at the top of the Google Play web page for your app and it's scaled down to be used in the Google Play app at a variety of sizes. Many designers are very tempted to put a lot into this image because it is fairly large, but it should be clean and clear so that it can scale effectively. Consider it to be similar to a movie poster or a book cover. The goal is to entice viewers with strong visuals that emphasize the characteristics of your app.

Consider incorporating your logo or icon into the design of your feature graphic. You should always include the name of your app in a very large font because this graphic can be used to represent your app on its own. If you scale this image down to one-tenth the normal size and you cannot read the app name, your text is not big enough. Another common piece of this image is a tagline of some sort. This is a brief bit of text that gives the user some sense of what your app does, preferably in a memorable way. The tagline is especially helpful for apps that have a name that doesn't necessarily explain what they are. If your app is called "Image Cleaner" and it is an app that takes images and automatically processes them in ways to improve their appearance, your tagline might be something like "Automatically makes your images beautiful" or "Bad images in; good images out." Sometimes simplicity can be powerful, but you have to be careful to make sure you are telling enough. For instance, your tagline might be "Your images. Beautiful." That in itself might not be clear enough, but your graphic might depict a blurry image turning into a sharp one or something similar to convey the rest of the meaning. Whatever the tagline is, it needs to reflect the voice of your app (is your app playful, sophisticated, or snarky?) and give some feel for its purpose.

You should not include small text in this image. It's far too tempting to include some bullet points or even a brief intro into what your app is, but these small bits of text just become blurry, unprofessional lines once the graphic is scaled down. You should also avoid including screenshots in the feature graphic for the same reason. Once the image is scaled down, the screenshots are not useful and can detract from the message (besides, there's already a spot specifically for screenshots). Further, people are often tempted to put their screenshots into device mockups to make them look like the devices are really running the app. That can look really nice at large size, but again it's terrible at a smaller size and, perhaps worse, it becomes outdated extremely fast. Android devices change very rapidly, adjusting constantly to consumer demand, new technologies, and growing trends.

In Figure A.2, you can see the Google Maps feature graphic. It is extremely simple (not a bad thing) and clean. The distinctive map is emphasized here again, along with a simple six-word tagline. Notice the fonts are large and extremely high contrast to ensure they are readable even when the graphic is displayed much smaller. The Google Music app takes a similar approach (shown in Figure A.3). The icon is prominently displayed, as are the name and tagline.

You can see an example of a more mediocre graphic in Figure A.4 for a fictional app called PhotoProto. This fictional app allows users to take photos of wireframes that have been drawn and then create simple prototypes by identifying touchable areas that can link between different wireframes. Look at it and consider what is good and bad about it before reading on.

Figure A.2 The Google Maps feature graphic

Figure A.3 The Google Music feature graphic

Figure A.4 does a few things well. It has large text that will be easy to read at any size. It also has a vibrant background that will help it stand out. The two elements of the app, a camera and a wireframe, are both included in the graphic. The graphic could use some work though. The camera is meant to look sketched, but at smaller sizes it will look like strange line art. If a camera is included in the graphic, it should be larger. The wireframe on the right is also a bit too separated from the content on the left. Some minor tweaks could also be made to improve the graphic, such as adjusting the spacing between the word "prototypes" and the word "from." Sometimes looking at the feature graphic in context helps you see the problems you should fix. Figure A.5 shows its fictional Google Play listing on the Web, and Figure A.6 shows what it would look like if the app were featured within the Google Play app.

Figure A.4 A fictional app's feature graphic

Figure A.5 The fictional app's feature graphic displayed in Google Play for the Web

Figure A.6 The fictional app's feature graphic displayed in the Google Play app

> **tip**
>
> Although you might hope that just making an amazing app is enough to get it noticed by the world, the reality is that preparing proper Google Play assets makes a significant difference. The obvious required pieces, such as the screenshots and description, are extremely important, but now you also know how important the feature graphic is. Without it, your app will have fewer downloads and will not be featured no matter how amazing it is. If you're still looking for some help understanding what good assets look like, consider visiting Google Play (https://play.google.com/store/apps) and viewing some of the featured apps.

Promotional Graphic

The promotional graphic has to be 180×120. It should be a PNG to avoid JPEG artifacts at such a small size, but you can upload a JPEG image. There is no support for an alpha channel, so it should be a 24-bit image.

This graphic is probably the least important asset. It originally served a purpose similar to the feature graphic in the Android Market (before the rebranding to Google Play) for phones. Apps that were being promoted in the Android Market would have the promotional graphic shown at the top and in a few other places. Neither the current Google Play app for devices nor the Google Play website show the promotional graphic anywhere.

All of this does not mean that the promotional graphic has no value; it just means it has less value than some of the other assets. If you do not have the time (or want to spend the time) creating a promotional graphic, a good option is to use a resized version of your feature graphic. If you have done the feature graphic well, scaling it to the size of the promotional graphic should give you something reasonable. You may choose to remove some text or to sharpen other text to ensure it is readable, but the purpose of the two images is very similar.

Video (YouTube)

Adding a video for your application is a great way to demonstrate the app in action. You can give the user a quick view of what the app looks like and how usable it is. Video has the advantage of being able to better demonstrate the app in use and take advantage of audio, but it is a supplement (not replacement) for screenshots. Screenshots must be to-the-point, faithful depictions of the actual app experience. The video, however, is open to a full range of options. It can be as simple as a user demonstrating the app with a voiceover explaining each screen, or it can be as involved as a comedic movie short meant to entertain and delight the user.

The type of movie should be reflective of the type of app and its personality. Is your app cool, to the point, and entirely utilitarian, or is your app bright, playful, and exciting? The former would lend itself to a video that demonstrates the key features of the app, and the latter is more open to entertainment. Regardless of the type of app, be sure to keep your video short (30 seconds to three minutes).

Paper Camera (https://play.google.com/store/apps/details?id=com.dama.papercamera) is an app that allows you to take photos and videos using various effects that make the media look like pastels, sketches, and so on. Their demo video is beautiful in its ability to accurately portray the app in the real world with a simplicity that makes it understandable and accessible to all levels of users. The app itself is also a great example of how to use a fully custom UI that is still intuitive. You can see the video on YouTube at https://www.youtube.com/watch?v=_Aw6jEVnE2o.

Quick Office Pro (https://play.google.com/store/apps/details?id=com.qo.android.am3) is an office suite for your mobile device. Because the app is focused on productivity, the video reflects this with a very utilitarian demonstration, showing point by point how you can use the app and what features it has. This helps users not only see what the app can do, but they can see why they would use this app (especially useful when many of the target users would probably be thinking, "Why wouldn't I just open my laptop to work on the documents?"). Again, you can see the video on YouTube: https://www.youtube.com/watch?v=LRzszvrAiKk.

Promoting Your App

Once you have your app listed in Google Play with the assets specified in this appendix, you might consider promoting your app elsewhere. For instance, you might write to various blogs and ask them to cover your app. Be sure to include the Google Play link and a brief blurb about what the app is right away (you do want to include more details, but you are emailing people who are dealing with a significant volume of emails that are just like yours, so you have to get to the point in the first paragraph). Do not include any attachments in the email; instead, provide a link to download promotional photos, videos, and so on. Unlike for the screenshots for Google Play, you can use device mockups for the screenshots in this case (take a look at the official Device Art Generator, which allows you to just drag and drop images to put them in a device: http://developer.android.com/distribute/promote/device-art.html). Provide a point of contact for any questions. Never send the email multiple times; otherwise, your app quickly goes from being a potentially interesting new app to one that has to be spammed to be noticed. Finally, be willing to accept that your app won't be covered by everyone you email and that most of these people won't have the time to respond to you.

APPENDIX B

AMAZON APPSTORE ASSETS

Amazon has grown significantly as a distributor of Android apps. They released Amazon Appstore for the United States in early 2011 as an add-on application available for Android devices. Later in 2011, they launched the Kindle Fire, a seven-inch tablet that has reportedly sold millions of copies. In August 2012, Amazon launched their Appstore in additional countries just before releasing an update to the Kindle Fire. Although Amazon's Appstore is growing in popularity, very little information is available out there for how to prepare the assets you need for distribution via that store. This appendix details what you need and how to make your assets as effective as possible.

Overview

Amazon Appstore is in some ways similar to Google Play. Many of the required assets are the same or very similar for the two stores, but Amazon has taken a fundamentally different approach in the publication of apps. Amazon says that all developers who wish to distribute apps through their store must pay the developer program fee ($99 per year), although this fee has been waived for all developers so far. All apps submitted to Amazon's Appstore must be reviewed by Amazon to meet their quality guidelines.

Another key difference of Amazon's Appstore is that Amazon takes a much more active role in their app distribution. They will create complete app descriptions with full product pages for developers to help promote applications, but they also reserve the right to change the price of any app in their store. It's a good idea to learn as much as you can about any app store you submit to, whether it's Google Play, Amazon Appstore, or another store. More details about Amazon's mobile developer program are available online at https://developer.amazon.com/welcome.html. Amazon also has a detailed frequently asked questions (FAQ) section at https://developer.amazon.com/help/faq.html.

The Application Icon

Like Google Play, Amazon Appstore requires a high-resolution version of your application icon. It should be a 512×512px 32-bit PNG. You also need to create a 114×114px version. The larger size will be used for your app's product page on Amazon as well as in search results. The smaller version is used as the actual app icon on the device.

The same rules that apply to an icon made for Google Play apply to the icon made for Amazon Appstore. In particular, the rules laid out in Appendix A, "Google Play Assets," are very applicable. They are duplicated here intentionally:

A good icon...

- **Uses the majority of the space available to it.** This means the touch target is obvious and you don't have an overly thin icon. Icons that are too thin don't look touchable, and they can often be lost against certain backgrounds.
- **Has a notable shape.** Android does not force all app icons into the same shape, so this is one of the best ways to make your icon stand out. Is it an analog clock? Perhaps you should consider a round icon. Is it for tracking stars in the sky? Maybe you could try a star or constellation shape. Look at the variety of shapes in the default apps. There aren't just circles and rounded rectangles but mail-shaped icons and icons that look like headphones.
- **Sticks to a simple color scheme.** Look at the apps that come on an Android device and you should notice a very common pattern among the default icons. Most of them stick to a simple but distinct color scheme. Gmail is red and white. Play Music is orange and gray.

Calendar is blue and white. Where shapes are similar, colors are different (for example, Clock is a white and gray circle but Downloads is a gray and green circle).

- **Uses a straight-on, slightly overhead angle.** This is intended to give your icon a hint of depth without making it visually complicated. Usually adding just a few lighter pixels along the top edge of your icon is enough to accomplish this.

If your app is available on both Google Play and Amazon Appstore, you should use the same icon for both. Users may switch from one store to the other on a given device, so avoid creating any confusion about your app that would arise with two different icons. If your app is available for both iOS and Android, the icons do not need to be the same, but they should be similar. On iOS, your app icon is limited to a rounded square, but you should not place the same limits on it for Android.

For additional details about creating an effective icon for your app, refer to the "Application Icon" section of Appendix A. You can also see two examples in Figure A.1 of Appendix A.

Screenshots

You must have at least three screenshots for publishing on Amazon Appstore, although you should strive to have more (up to ten) whenever appropriate. These screenshots should be PNGs to avoid the lossy compression of JPEGs (although you can submit JPEG screenshots). They must be either 1024×600 or 800×480, although it's likely that additional sizes will be supported soon.

Screenshots need to be representative of your app. Include each of the major sections of your app, including, if applicable, one that shows the menu for the app. This will give users a sense of both what your app looks like and what is in it. Exclude screenshots that do not help users understand your app, such as splash screens, and screenshots that may confuse users, such as complex settings screens. Do not create artificial images to use as screenshots and do not add promotional graphics or text to the screenshots.

Many applications include user-generated content. If yours does, be sure to only include screenshots with content you have permission to display. Alternatively, you can create specific dummy content that is reasonably representative of the user experience.

Promotional Graphic

The promotional graphic for Amazon Appstore is very similar to the feature graphic required for Google Play. Both graphics must be 1024×500px and can be JPEG images or PNG images (but PNG is recommended). In both cases, the application name should be prominent in large text, and a logo or icon should be included that signifies the product. The Google Play feature graphic is shown at the top of the app's page (as shown in Figure A.5 from Appendix A), but the Amazon Appstore promotional graphic is typically the second in the series of images available for an app (see Figure B.1 for an example). Both graphics are used in other locations to help promote your app, so it's definitely in your best interest to make sure these graphics are good.

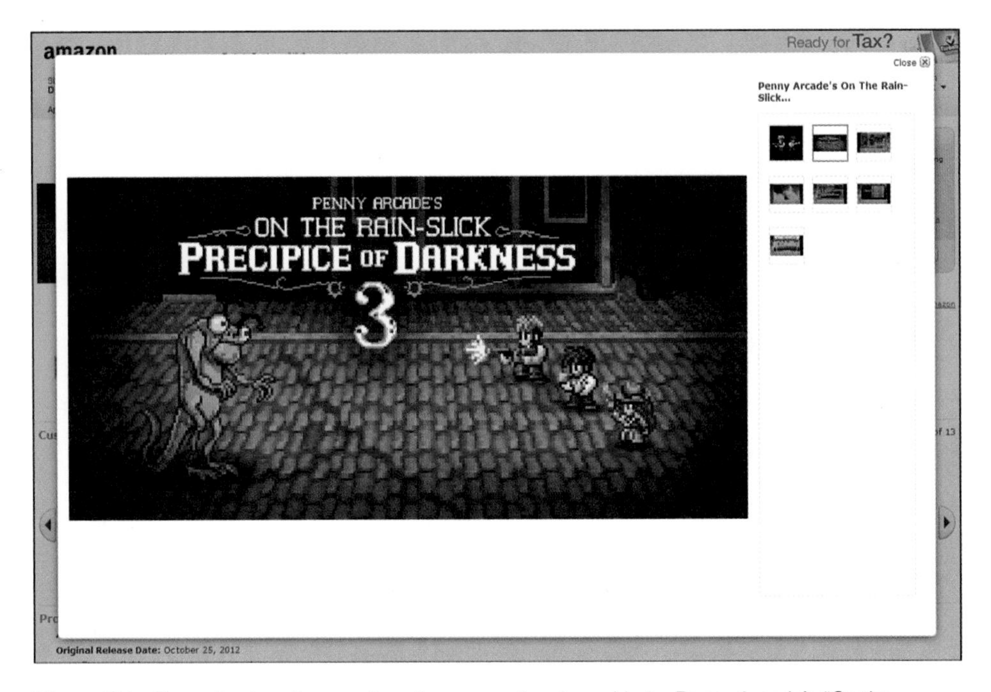

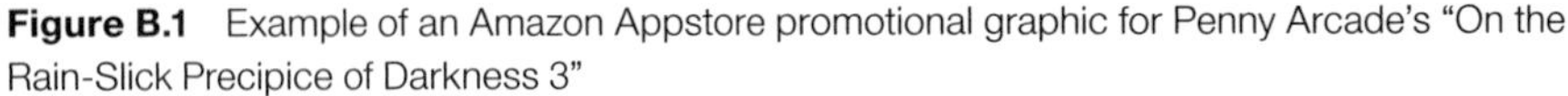

Figure B.1 Example of an Amazon Appstore promotional graphic for Penny Arcade's "On the Rain-Slick Precipice of Darkness 3"

The promotional graphic should never duplicate information that is available elsewhere on the product page, with the exception of the app name and logo. In other words, do not show the price, screenshots, application description, and so on. It is especially important that you do not include the price on the promotional graphic because Amazon may choose to promote your app at a different price. Make sure that all text is at least 50px away from the edges of the image and that all text can still be read when the image is scaled down to 300×146px.

Videos

Videos are an excellent way to demonstrate your app in actual use. You can emphasize parts of the user experience that aren't as easy to show in screenshots alone, such as simplicity of use, smoothness of the UI, and methods of interactivity. Unlike Google Play, where you're limited to a single video link, you can have up to five videos, and they should only be used for showcasing the app (do not, for instance, feature live actors talking about your app or a long introductory video).

The following are the technical requirements for any video you submit to Amazon:

- A minimum of 720px wide at 4:3 or 16:9
- A maximum of 5MB
- A minimum bitrate of 1200Kbps
- One of these supported formats: MPEG-2 or MPEG-4 (H.264 codec), WMV, Quicktime, FLV, or AVI

APPENDIX C

COMMON TASK REFERENCE

While working on Android apps, you are likely to learn certain tasks well. You will know the `Activity` and `Fragment` lifecycles without needing a reference. You will know how to execute code on a background thread. You will know how to do many tasks because you will have to do them all the time. However, some tasks you only need to do every now and then. You need to do them just often enough that you wish you could easily remember how to accomplish them, but not often enough to necessarily memorize them. Appendix C is meant to show you how to do some of these tasks without having to memorize them.

Indicating Loading in the Action Bar

There are two basic types of progress indicators: determinate and indeterminate. A determinate indicator indicates an amount of progress (for example, a bar colored to the halfway point can represent a task that's 50 percent complete) and should always be favored over indeterminate indicators when possible. One typical use case is when downloading content. Generally, the server will tell you how much content there is, so you know how much progress you've made based on the bytes downloaded so far.

An indeterminate indicator just indicates that work is going on, but it does not give a sense of progress. It is meant to tell the user the app isn't frozen; it's just busy. Most indeterminate indicators are circular and rotate while the task is being completed, but there are others, such as pulsing lights. An indeterminate indicator is the right choice for tasks you can't reasonably report the completed progress. Some complex algorithms fall under this category. This is also a good choice when it's not practical to report the progress, such as when working on several tasks at the same time and waiting on multiple resources before anything can be shown.

Android's `ProgressBar` class supports both types of indicators, but two other techniques are also useful. The first is to indicate progress along the top of the app; see Figure C.1 for an example and note the progress bar at the top of the action bar. This is particularly useful when your display primarily consists of a `WebView`, but it can be used any time you want to indicate progress with a task. Because this is indicator appears at the top of your app, it should only be used for significant loading, such as the whole screen loading. It shouldn't be used for smaller inline content (for example, if your app is displaying a news article and at the bottom it shows related articles but has to load those from the Web, that process should use an inline loading indicator instead of one at the top of the app).

To use this progress indicator, you need to request it before setting up your UI. Retrieve a reference to the `Window` object with `getWindow()` and then call `requestFeature(int)`, passing in `Window.FEATURE_PROGRESS`. To indicate progress, call your `Activity`'s `setProgress(int)` method (note that the `int` you pass in should be in the range of 0 to indicate no progress and 10000 to indicate completion and fade out the indicator). See Listing C.1 for a sample implementation of an `Activity`'s `onCreate(Bundle)` method that uses a `WebView` to load a site and indicates progress.

Listing C.1 An Example of Using a Progress Indicator for a `WebView`

```
@Override
protected void onCreate(Bundle savedInstanceState) {
    getWindow().requestFeature(Window.FEATURE_PROGRESS);
    super.onCreate(savedInstanceState);

    final Activity activity = this;
```

```
        final WebView wv = new WebView(this);
        setContentView(wv);
        wv.setWebChromeClient(new WebChromeClient() {
            @Override
            public void onProgressChanged(WebView view, int progress) {
                activity.setProgress(progress * 100);
            }
        });
        wv.loadUrl("http://www.google.com");
    }
```

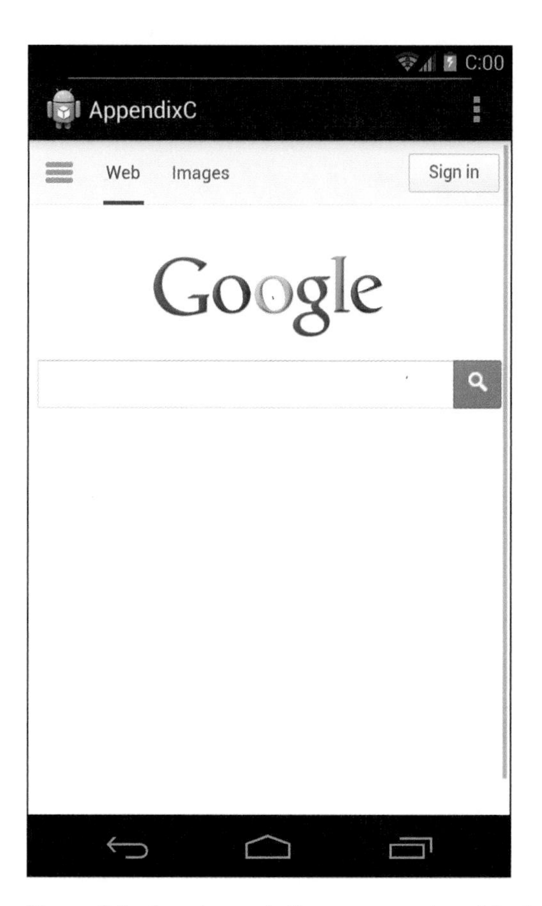

Figure C.1 App demonstrating a progress bar at the top of the action bar

The second useful technique is for indicating indeterminate progress. Android actually supports this in the same way as determinate progress—by requesting the `Window.FEATURE_INDETERMINATE_PROGRESS` feature and using the `setProgressBarIndeterminateVisibility(boolean)` method to show and hide the indicator. Unfortunately, this method rarely looks good, and you frequently want to allow users to manually refresh. A nice way of doing this is to have an action in the action bar that serves as your refresh button when content is not loading and the indeterminate indicator when content is loading.

First, you need to create an XML menu. It should include an item for refreshing, along with anything else you need. Presumably refreshing is something the user will do relatively frequently, so list it first and set the `showAsAction` property to `ifRoom`. Remember that common action bar icons, including the refresh icon, are available via the Android design site's download page (https://developer.android.com/design/downloads/index.html). See Listing C.2 for a sample XML menu.

Listing C.2 Example of an XML Menu with a Refresh Item

```
<menu xmlns:android="http://schemas.android.com/apk/res/android" >

    <item
        android:id="@+id/menu_refresh"
        android:icon="@drawable/icon_action_refresh"
        android:showAsAction="ifRoom"
        android:title="@string/refresh"/>
    <item
        android:id="@+id/menu_settings"
        android:orderInCategory="100"
        android:showAsAction="never"
        android:title="@string/menu_settings"/>

</menu>
```

Now you need a layout that's shown in place of the icon when loading is happening. You can make this look however you'd like, but a simple example is shown in Listing C.3.

Listing C.3 Simple Progress Indicator Layout for the Action Bar

```
<?xml version="1.0" encoding="utf-8"?>
<FrameLayout xmlns:android="http://schemas.android.com/apk/res/android"
    style="@android:style/Widget.ActionButton"
    android:layout_width="wrap_content"
    android:layout_height="wrap_content" >

    <ProgressBar
        style="?android:attr/indeterminateProgressStyle"
        android:layout_width="32dp"
        android:layout_height="32dp"
        android:layout_gravity="center" />

</FrameLayout>
```

With the menu and layout complete, you just need to implement the code in your `Activity` or `Fragment` to use them. First, you need to inflate the menu, adding the items specified in it, by overriding `onCreateOptionsMenu(Menu)`. Use `MenuInflater` to inflate your XML menu and then obtain a reference to your refresh item by using `Menu`'s `findItem(int)` method. At this point, your app will look like Figure C.2.

Figure C.2 The action bar showing a refresh button

Override `onOptionsItemSelected(MenuItem)` to check if the passed item is your refresh item. If it is, start refreshing your content and call `showLoadingIndicator(true)`, which you'll implement next (note that the example calls `showLoadingIndicator(true)` at the start of the `AsyncTask` because you might trigger this `AsyncTask` in other ways, which should also show an indication of loading). If it is not the refresh item, call through to the super method.

Create a method called `showLoadingIndicator(boolean)` that will be used to show the indicator (when passed `true`) and hide it to show the refresh button (when passed `false`).

If the method is passed `true`, disable the `MenuItem` and call `setActionView(int)`, passing in the resource identifier for the layout you made. By default, a `MenuItem` will generate its own layout such as the icon and/or text for that item; setting an action view gives it a specific layout to display instead of the default one, so you use that to change from a refresh icon to a loading indicator. If the method is passed `false`, you enable the `MenuItem` and call `setActionView(null)` to change back to the refresh icon. Figure C.3 shows what this looks like while loading.

Figure C.3 The refresh icon has changed to an indeterminate loading indicator

note

The `getActionView()` and `setActionView(int)` methods were added in Honeycomb (API level 11). If your app supports Android versions older than that, you should use reflection to see if this method is available. If it is not, fall back on using another method to indicate loading, such as `Activity`'s built-in support for indeterminate progress bars, explained earlier. If you're using a library to support older versions of Android, it may use a custom implementation of `MenuItem` that does support the method. In that case, you just need to make sure the layout you use for the action view uses a style that is available on the devices that are running older versions of Android.

For a full example, see Listing C.4. It uses an `AsyncTask` that just sleeps for two seconds before returning to simulate doing real work.

Listing C.4 Sample `Activity` Using an Action Bar Refresh and Loading Indicator

```
public class MainActivity extends Activity {

    private MenuItem mRefreshMenuItem;

    @Override
    protected void onCreate(Bundle savedInstanceState) {
        super.onCreate(savedInstanceState);
        setContentView(R.layout.activity_main);
    }

    @Override
    public boolean onCreateOptionsMenu(Menu menu) {
        getMenuInflater().inflate(R.menu.activity_main, menu);
        mRefreshMenuItem = menu.findItem(R.id.menu_refresh);
        return true;
    }

    @Override
    public boolean onOptionsItemSelected(MenuItem item) {
        if (item == mRefreshMenuItem) {
            new FakeTask().execute();
            return true;
        }
        return super.onOptionsItemSelected(item);
    }

    /**
     * Shows and hides the loading indicator
     *
     * @param show boolean true to show the indicator; false to hide it
     */
    public void showLoadingIndicator(boolean show) {
        if (show) {
            mRefreshMenuItem.setEnabled(false);
            mRefreshMenuItem.setActionView(R.layout.actionbar_
➥indeterminate_progress);
```

```
            } else {
                mRefreshMenuItem.setActionView(null);
                mRefreshMenuItem.setEnabled(true);
            }
        }

        /**
         * AsyncTask that fakes 2 seconds of work
         */
        private class FakeTask extends AsyncTask<Void, Void, Void> {

            @Override
            protected void onPreExecute() {
                super.onPreExecute();
                showLoadingIndicator(true);
            }

            @Override
            protected Void doInBackground(Void... params) {
                try {
                    Thread.sleep(2000);
                } catch (InterruptedException e) {
                    // If the Thread is interrupted, just return
                }
                return null;
            }

            @Override
            protected void onPostExecute(Void result) {
                super.onPostExecute(result);
                showLoadingIndicator(false);
            }

        }
    }
```

Dismissing the Software Keyboard

Generally, Android does a good job of showing and hiding the Android keyboard as needed, but there are times when you need to dismiss the software keyboard manually. Perhaps you've made your own custom view that needs to dismiss the keyboard at certain times, or maybe the user has entered enough text into an `EditText` that you're able to show results but the keyboard would otherwise obscure them. Whatever the reason, dismissing the software keyboard is actually very easy to do. You just need to get a window token (`IBinder`) from an onscreen view such as your custom view or the EditText and use the InputMethodManager's hideSoftInputFromWindow method. See Listing C.5 for a simple example.

Listing C.5 Using the InputMethodManager to Dismiss the Software Keyboard

```
InputMethodManager imm = (InputMethodManager) getSystemService(
➥Context.INPUT_METHOD_SERVICE);
imm.hideSoftInputFromWindow(editText.getWindowToken(), 0);
```

Using Full Screen Mode

Most apps should not use full screen mode. Generally users are jumping into and out of apps in seconds or minutes and are not engrossed enough in an app to warrant hiding the status bar at the top of the screen. There are a few exceptions, such as for a noncasual game (most casual games, such as Solitaire, do not have a need to take the full screen) and temporary full screen use for video playback, for example. When in doubt, ask yourself whether your app is more important than your users knowing about the important emails and other notifications that may appear.

If your Activity should always be full screen, such as for a game, then your Activity should specify a theme in the AndroidManifest.xml file. As of Android 4.0, device manufacturers are required to include the device default theme and the Holo themes as part of the compatibility test suite (any manufacturer that wants to include Google's apps such as the Play Store must ensure their devices pass the compatibility suite, which ensures platform consistency across devices). That means the easiest way to have an Activity appear full screen is to include android:theme="@android:style/Theme.DeviceDefault.NoActionBar.Fullscreen" in the activity tag of the manifest (if your app extends Holo, then replace DeviceDefault with Holo). The theme prior to Holo that was full screen was Theme.NoTitleBar.Fullscreen, so apps that support older versions of Android can use that. If you are implementing a custom theme and cannot extend those, you can specify android:windowFullscreen as true and android:windowContentOverlay as @null.

Starting with Honeycomb (API level 11), Android added support for software system buttons (that is, the back, home, and recent apps buttons could be shown on the screen). That means the concept of "full screen" has changed slightly because being truly full screen on a device with software buttons prevents the user from pressing any of those buttons. To handle that issue, View was given a method called setSystemUiVisibility(int) that allows you to hide that system navigation or to dim it. For example, if the user taps a view that is displaying a video to play it full screen, the view can call setSystemUiVisibility(View.SYSTEM_UI_FLAG_HIDE_NAVIGATION) to become full screen. For games and such, where you don't want to hide the system navigation because the user still needs it, you can instead dim the navigation (making the buttons appear like faint dots) by passing View.SYSTEM_UI_FLAG_LOW_PROFILE int instead.

Keeping the Screen On

Sometimes you need to keep the screen on while your app is in the foreground. For instance, you might be showing a video and you don't expect the user to interact with the device for a few minutes. Because the user isn't interacting with the device, it may time out and turn off the screen. Many developers mistakenly use WakeLock for this simple task. Not only does WakeLock require an extra permission, it has to be manually released to avoid excessive battery drain.

The easy way to accomplish this is to get a reference to the Window and set the FLAG_KEEP_SCREEN_ON flag. The call looks like this: getWindow().addFlags(WindowManager.LayoutParams.FLAG_KEEP_SCREEN_ON). The nice thing about using this method is that it doesn't require a special permission. It will also only be enabled while your app is in the foreground. That means you don't have to worry about your app keeping the system on even after the user has pressed the home button and moved on to something else. When you no longer need to keep the screen on, you call getWindow().clearFlags(WindowManager.LayoutParams.FLAG_KEEP_SCREEN_ON). Although this method of keeping the screen on when you need it is much better than using a WakeLock, keep in mind that the screen is typically a device's biggest battery drain, so keeping the screen on more than necessary will adversely affect battery life.

Determining the Device's Physical Screen Size

In the past, devices were broken up into broad size categories of small, normal, large, and extra large. Although the recommendation now is to use density independent pixels and the various resource qualifiers covered in Chapter 4, "Adding App Graphics and Resources," there are still times when you need to know which size "bucket" the app falls into at runtime. You do this by getting the Configuration object from Resources and checking the screenLayout field. The screenLayout contains more information about the display, such as when it's "long" and in which direction the text is laid out, so you need to use the SCREENLAYOUT_SIZE_MASK to pull out the specific int you're looking for. See Listing C.6 for an example.

Listing C.6 Determining a Device's Size at Runtime

```
switch (getResources().getConfiguration().screenLayout &
➥Configuration.SCREENLAYOUT_SIZE_MASK) {
    case Configuration.SCREENLAYOUT_SIZE_XLARGE:
        // Extra large (most 10" tablets)
```

```
            break;
        case Configuration.SCREENLAYOUT_SIZE_LARGE:
            // Large (most 7" tablets)
            break;
        case Configuration.SCREENLAYOUT_SIZE_NORMAL:
            // Normal (most phones)
            break;
        case Configuration.SCREENLAYOUT_SIZE_SMALL:
            // Small (very uncommon)
            break;
}
```

Determining the Device DPI

For the most part, you never have to directly consider converting to/from pixels and density independent pixels. When you get dimensions from `Resources`, the work is done for you. When you specify sizes in your layouts, the conversion happens automatically. However, sometimes you do need to know the device DPI, such as when implementing a custom view that handles density-specific drawing. You know that one pixel on an MDPI device is two pixels on an XHDPI device, but how do you know the density of a given device? See Listing C.7 for an example of how you can determine the density at runtime.

Listing C.7 Determining a Device's Density at Runtime

```
switch (getResources().getDisplayMetrics().densityDpi) {
    case DisplayMetrics.DENSITY_XXHIGH:
        // Display is around 480 pixels per inch
        break;
    case DisplayMetrics.DENSITY_XHIGH:
        // Display is around 320 pixels per inch
        break;
    case DisplayMetrics.DENSITY_HIGH:
        // Display is around 240 pixels per inch
        break;
    case DisplayMetrics.DENSITY_MEDIUM:
        // Display is around 160 pixels per inch
        break;
    case DisplayMetrics.DENSITY_LOW:
        // Display is around 120 pixels per inch
        break;
    case DisplayMetrics.DENSITY_TV:
        // Display is a 720p TV screen
        // Sometimes also used for 1280x720 7" tablets
        // Rarely should you ever specifically target this density
        break;
}
```

Checking for a Network Connection

The majority of apps make use of a network connection, so checking whether there is a connection or not can be very useful. If your app needs some assets on startup or fetches new data, you should check if there is a network connection to notify the user when one is not available. Being proactive gives a much better user experience than just waiting for a failed network attempt and showing an error. By actually telling the user that the device does not have a network connection (preferably in an unobtrusive inline UI element), you enable the user to possibly fix the problem (for example, if the user has accidently left the device in airplane mode or has not yet connected to an available Wi-Fi network) and you also take some of the blame off your app. Instead of your app showing failed connection errors or having unexplained missing assets everywhere, you inform the user right away that something is wrong. See Listing C.8 for an example of a static method you might want to put in a utility class (keep in mind that this just determines if there is an active network connection, not if the device is connected to the Internet).

Listing C.8 A Static Method for Determining if a Device Has a Connection

```
/**
 * Returns true if the device has a network connection
 *
 * @param context Context to access the ConnectivityManager
 * @return true if the device has a network connection
 */
public static boolean isConnectedToNetwork(Context context) {
    boolean connected = false;
    ConnectivityManager cm = (ConnectivityManager)
➥context.getSystemService(Context.CONNECTIVITY_SERVICE);
    if (cm != null) {
        NetworkInfo ni = cm.getActiveNetworkInfo();
        if (ni != null) {
            connected = ni.isConnected();
        }
    }

    return connected;
}
```

Checking if the Current Thread Is the UI Thread

You should never modify views from a background thread, but there are times when a piece of code can run on the main (UI) thread or a background thread, so it's necessary to determine whether or not it's the UI thread. Fortunately, this is really easy. The `Looper` class has a static method called `myLooper()` that returns the `Looper` for the current thread. It also has a `getMainLooper()` method that returns the `Looper` for the UI thread. If these objects are the same, your code is running on the UI thread. See Listing C.9 for an example.

Listing C.9 How to Check if the Current Thread Is the UI Thread

```
if (Looper.myLooper() == Looper.getMainLooper()) {
    // UI Thread
} else {
    // Other Thread
}
```

Custom View Attributes

Although custom view attributes were covered in the last few chapters of the book, some additional attributes are available. Unfortunately, the Android site does not currently provide a list of these, and it can be tough to interpret them when reading through the ones in the Android source.

Create an `attrs.xml` file in res/values. This file will specify which XML attributes are available for your view. For a complete example, see Listing C.10.

Listing C.10 A Sample `attrs.xml` File That Specifies Many Custom Attributes

```
<?xml version="1.0" encoding="utf-8"?>
<resources>

    <declare-styleable name="MyCustomView">

        <!-- boolean -->
        <attr name="booleanExample" format="boolean" />
        <!-- integer -->
        <attr name="integerExample" format="integer" />
        <!-- float -->
        <attr name="floatExample" format="float" />
        <!-- fraction (actually a percentage like "50%") -->
        <attr name="fractionExample" format="fraction" />
        <!-- string -->
        <attr name="stringExample" format="string" />
        <!-- color -->
        <attr name="colorExample" format="color" />
        <!-- dimension -->
        <attr name="dimensionExample" format="dimension" />
        <!-- reference -->
        <attr name="referenceExample" format="reference" />
```

```
        <!-- enum -->
        <attr name="enumExample">
            <enum name="zero_enum" value="0"/>
            <enum name="one_enum" value="1"/>
        </attr>
        <!-- flag - the user can use multiple flags -->
        <attr name="flagExample">
            <flag name="oneFlag" value="1"/>
            <flag name="twoFlag" value="2"/>
            <flag name="fourFlag" value="4"/>
        </attr>
        <!-- reference OR color -->
        <attr name="referenceOrColorExample" format="reference|color" />
        <!-- existing attribute -->
        <attr name="android:textColor" />
    </declare-styleable>

</resources>
```

To use these values, you need to specify a namespace and use that prefix before each value in your layout. You used to have to specify your package as part of the schema (for example, `xmlns:app="http://schemas.android.com/apk/res/com.iangclifton.auid.appendixc"`), but as of ADT 17, you can use `res-auto` to have this automatically handled for you (for example, `xmlns:app="http://schemas.android.com/apk/res-auto"`). This second method is recommended, but the first method is mentioned here because you will still see it in many projects. ADT is smart enough to use completion on the custom attributes when you're editing the XML layout, so you can use Ctrl+spacebar (or Cmd+spacebar) to complete custom attributes or to suggest possible values for the enum and flag types. See Listing C.11 for a simple layout that specifies each of the custom values. In this case, you don't really need the outside `RelativeLayout`; it's just there to show where to define your namespace.

Listing C.11 Simple Layout Using a Custom View with Custom Attributes

```
<RelativeLayout
    xmlns:android="http://schemas.android.com/apk/res/android"
    xmlns:app="http://schemas.android.com/apk/res-auto"
    xmlns:tools="http://schemas.android.com/tools"
    android:layout_width="match_parent"
    android:layout_height="match_parent"
    tools:context=".MainActivity" >

    <com.iangclifton.auid.appendixc.MyCustomView
        android:layout_width="match_parent"
        android:layout_height="match_parent"
        android:textColor="#FFFF0000"
```

```
        app:booleanExample="true"
        app:colorExample="#FFFF0000"
        app:dimensionExample="100dp"
        app:enumExample="one_enum"
        app:flagExample="oneFlag|fourFlag"
        app:floatExample="5.5"
        app:fractionExample="10%"
        app:integerExample="42"
        app:referenceExample="@string/app_name"
        app:referenceOrColorExample="#FF00FF00"
        app:stringExample="My String" />

</RelativeLayout>
```

Your custom view needs to use `Context`'s `obtainStyledAttributes` method to retrieve a `TypedArray` of the attributes that were specified in the XML layout. You can then get the various attributes from that `TypedArray`. Most of these are pretty simple, but a few need a little bit of explanation. The enum type does not return an actual `enum`; it just ensures that only one of the possible choices is selected. It's up to you to make use of the `int` to decide what to do. The flag type needs to use "bitwise and" operations to determine which values are set. The reference in this example isn't actually used to do anything other than print its `int`, but you can get the value the reference points to with the `Resources` object. When a value can be multiple types, and those types are different (for example, color or reference), you can use the `peekValue` method to get a `TypedValue` object and determine the type from there. See Listing C.12 for a simple custom view that reads all these attributes and then creates a string to display that shows which ones were passed. Figure C.4 shows what this view can look like on a device.

Listing C.12 A Custom View that Utilizes a Variety of Custom Attributes

```
public class MyCustomView extends View {

    // Enum values
    private final int ZERO_ENUM = 0;
    private final int ONE_ENUM = 1;

    // Flag values
    private final int ONE_FLAG = 1;
    private final int TWO_FLAG = 2;
    private final int FOUR_FLAG = 4;

    private final String mDisplayString;
    private final Paint mPaint = new Paint(Paint.ANTI_ALIAS_FLAG);
    private StaticLayout mLayout;
    private final TextPaint mTextPaint;
```

```
    public MyCustomView(Context context) {
        super(context);
        mDisplayString = "No custom attributes";
        mPaint.setColor(Color.BLACK);
        mTextPaint = new TextPaint(mPaint);
        mTextPaint.setTextSize(context.getResources().getDimension(
➥R.dimen.customViewTextSize));
    }

    public MyCustomView(Context context, AttributeSet attrs) {
        this(context, attrs, -1);
    }

    public MyCustomView(Context context, AttributeSet attrs,
➥int defStyle) {
        super(context, attrs, defStyle);

        final TypedArray customAttrs =
➥context.obtainStyledAttributes(attrs, R.styleable.MyCustomView);
        final StringBuilder sb = new StringBuilder();
        int currentAttribute;

        // boolean
        currentAttribute = R.styleable.MyCustomView_booleanExample;
        boolean booleanExample =
➥customAttrs.getBoolean(currentAttribute, false);
        sb.append("Boolean: " ).append(booleanExample).append('\n');

        // integer
        currentAttribute = R.styleable.MyCustomView_integerExample;
        int integerExample = customAttrs.getInt(currentAttribute, 0);
        sb.append("Integer: " ).append(integerExample).append('\n');

        // float
        currentAttribute = R.styleable.MyCustomView_floatExample;
        float floatExample = customAttrs.getFloat(currentAttribute,
➥0f);
        sb.append("Float: " ).append(floatExample).append('\n');

        // fraction
        currentAttribute = R.styleable.MyCustomView_fractionExample;
        float fractionExample =
➥customAttrs.getFraction(currentAttribute, 1, 1, -1);
        sb.append("Fraction: ").append(fractionExample).append('\n');

        // string
        currentAttribute = R.styleable.MyCustomView_stringExample;
        String stringExample = customAttrs.getString(currentAttribute);
        sb.append("String: ").append(stringExample).append('\n');

        // color
```

```
        currentAttribute = R.styleable.MyCustomView_colorExample;
        int colorExample = customAttrs.getColor(currentAttribute,
➥Color.BLACK);
        sb.append("Color: ")
          .append(Color.alpha(colorExample))
          .append("a, ")
          .append(Color.red(colorExample))
          .append("r, ")
          .append(Color.green(colorExample))
          .append("g, ")
          .append(Color.blue(colorExample))
          .append("b ")
          .append('\n');

        // dimension
        currentAttribute = R.styleable.MyCustomView_dimensionExample;
        float dimensionExample =
➥customAttrs.getDimension(currentAttribute, 0);
        sb.append("Dimension: ").append(dimensionExample).append('\n');

        // reference
        currentAttribute = R.styleable.MyCustomView_referenceExample;
        int referenceExample =
➥customAttrs.getResourceId(currentAttribute, 0);
        sb.append("Reference: ").append(referenceExample).append('\n');

        // enum
        currentAttribute = R.styleable.MyCustomView_enumExample;
        int enumExample =
➥customAttrs.getInt(R.styleable.MyCustomView_enumExample, -1);
        if (enumExample == ZERO_ENUM) {
            sb.append("Enum: ZERO_ENUM\n");
        } else if (enumExample == ONE_ENUM) {
            sb.append("Enum: ONE_ENUM\n");
        } else {
            sb.append("Enum not specified.\n");
        }

        // flag
        currentAttribute = R.styleable.MyCustomView_flagExample;
        int flagExample =
➥customAttrs.getInt(R.styleable.MyCustomView_flagExample, -1);
        if (flagExample == -1) {
            sb.append("Flag not specified.\n");
        } else {
            if ((flagExample & ONE_FLAG) != 0) {
                sb.append("Flag contains ONE_FLAG.\n");
            }
            if ((flagExample & TWO_FLAG) != 0) {
                sb.append("Flag contains TWO_FLAG.\n");
```

```
            }
            if ((flagExample & FOUR_FLAG) != 0) {
                sb.append("Flag contains FOUR_FLAG.\n");
            }
        }

        // reference OR color
        currentAttribute =
➥R.styleable.MyCustomView_referenceOrColorExample;
        TypedValue tv = customAttrs.peekValue(currentAttribute);
        if (tv == null) {
            sb.append("Did not contain reference or color.\n");
        } else if (tv.type == TypedValue.TYPE_REFERENCE) {
            sb.append("Contained a reference: ")
➥.append(tv.data).append('\n');
        } else {
            sb.append("Contained a color: ")
➥.append(tv.coerceToString()).append('\n');
        }

        // android:textColor
        currentAttribute = R.styleable.MyCustomView_android_textColor;
        tv = customAttrs.peekValue(currentAttribute);
        if (tv == null) {
            mPaint.setColor(Color.BLACK);
        } else {
            mPaint.setColor(tv.data);
        }

        customAttrs.recycle();
        mDisplayString = sb.toString();
        mTextPaint = new TextPaint(mPaint);
        mTextPaint.setTextSize(context.getResources().getDimension(
➥R.dimen.customViewTextSize));
    }

    @Override
    public void onDraw(Canvas canvas) {
        canvas.drawColor(Color.WHITE - mPaint.getColor());
        mLayout.draw(canvas);
    }

    @Override
    protected void onLayout(boolean changed, int left, int top, int
➥right, int bottom) {
        super.onLayout(changed, left, top, right, bottom);
        if (mLayout == null || changed) {
            mLayout = new StaticLayout(mDisplayString, mTextPaint,
➥right - left, Alignment.ALIGN_NORMAL, 1, 0, true);
```

```
            }
        }
    }
```

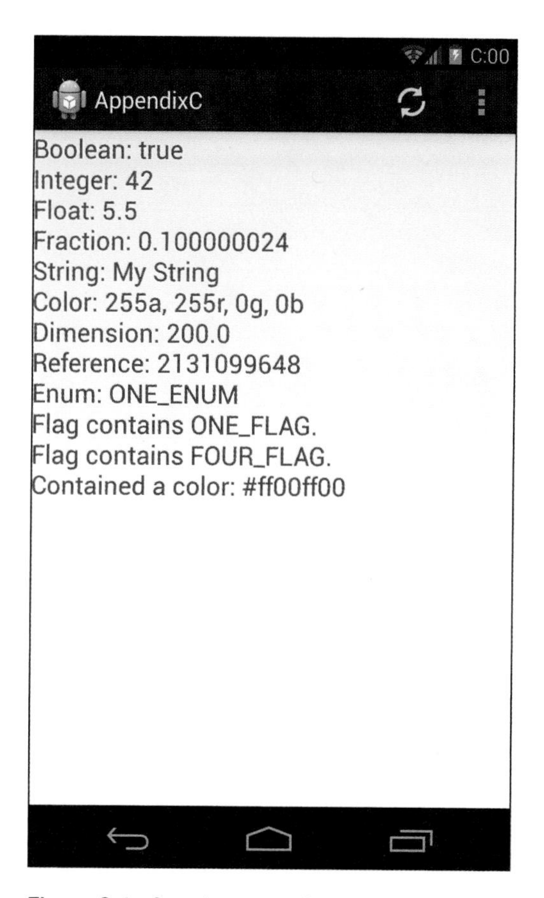

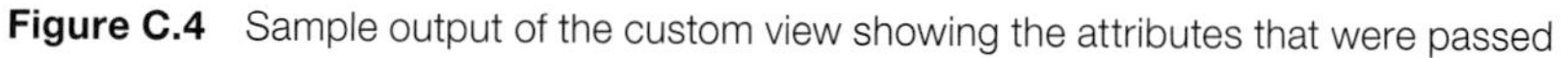
Figure C.4 Sample output of the custom view showing the attributes that were passed

> **note**
>
> Although you may have read straight through this appendix to see what it offers, it's largely intended to be a reference. There are those times when you can't quite remember things such as how to specify a custom attribute that is an enum, and trying to figure it out by racking your brain, looking at the source, or even browsing the Web can be a slow process. That's when this appendix is meant to be helpful. Hopefully you will reference it when needed, so you can focus on the important parts of your code.

INDEX

Symbols

A

B

C

D

E

F

G

H

I

J-K

L

M

N

O

P

Q-R

S

T

U

V

W

X-Y

Z

You Tube

TURNING IDEAS AND SKETCHES INTO BEAUTIFULLY DESIGNED APPS
ANDROID
User Interface Design
Ian G. CLIFTON
Safari
Books Online
FREE
Online Edition